Praise for

MY FRIEND THE MERCENARY

"James Brabazon has written a fully adrenalized book about civil war, mercenaries and the tiny margins by which fate determines the course of one's life. He is not only a beautiful writer but an incredibly brave reporter, and this book reflects both brilliantly. I was also in the Liberian civil war in 2003—on the other side—and I remember hearing that there was this crazy Brit who was running with the rebels as they advanced on the capital. Brabazon's account of an attempted coup by friends of his in Equatorial Guinea is a classic story of intrigue, greed and violence in one of the most dysfunctional countries in the world. It is a gripping story which I couldn't read fast enough." —Sebastian Junger, author of *War*

"An outstanding memoir about the power of friendship in the morally complex theatre of war. James Brabazon is a fearless reporter and a brutally honest narrator. I couldn't put this book down." —Andy McNab, author of *Bravo Two Zero*

"When you combine the virtually lawless political environment in West Africa with ruthless mercenaries, desperate rebels, shady arms dealers, greedy oil executives, soulless intelligence operatives and the lure of illegal diamonds, you have a recipe for a spellbinding adventure story. With *My Friend the Mercenary*, first-time author James Brabazon certainly cooks this mix into a fast-paced page-turner." —*The Globe and Mail*

"The first two thirds of Brabazon's extraordinary confessional, *My Friend the Mercenary*, is the story of how the professional partnership of a young, liberal British filmmaker and a hit man for apartheid South Africa developed into intimate comradeship. It was a strange and dangerous liaison, and it found itself in the heart of darkness. . . . The concluding chapters of his book present as full and convincing an account of that failed assault on Equatorial Guinea as we are likely to read." —*The Scotsman* (UK)

"Adrenalized. . . . Reads like a political thriller. Brabazon's searing narrative captures both the allure of war—the rush of danger, the deep camaraderie, the get-rich-quick mirages—and its brutal realities. It's both a seductive paean to and a harsh exposé of the mercenary ethos." —*Publishers Weekly*

"Brabazon's book is alarmingly frank. . . . It is a compelling insight into a devastated region that is the playground of rapacious warlords, Western intelligence agents and opportunistic businessmen." —*Sunday Business Post* (UK)

"Unsparing prose, a visceral shock ride into horror."
—Jonathan Kaplan

"Intensely vivid. . . . The first two-thirds of the book offer as thrilling a narrative as any war novel on the shelves, and the finale is as clear a picture of the murky world of postcolonial Africa as readers are likely to get. A haunting memoir and tribute to an extraordinary comrade-at-arms." —*Kirkus Reviews* (starred review)

MY FRIEND THE MERCENARY

James Brabazon

HARPER PERENNIAL

Published by Harper Perennial, an imprint of HarperCollins Publishers Ltd., by arrangement with Canongate Books Ltd., Edinburgh.

Originally published in Great Britain by Canongate Books Ltd: 2010
First HarperCollins Publishers Ltd hardcover edition: 2011
This Harper Perennial trade paperback edition: 2012

The names and identifying characteristics of some individuals portrayed in this book have been changed to protect their privacy and safety. The author has reconstructed certain, mainly private, conversations to the best of his recollection where it has not been possible to refer to audio, video or written records.

HarperCollins books may be purchased for educational, business, or sales promotional use through our Special Markets Department.

HarperCollins Publishers Ltd
2 Bloor Street East, 20th Floor
Toronto, Ontario, Canada
M4W 1A8

www.harpercollins.ca

Library and Archives Canada Cataloguing in Publication information
Brabazon, James
My friend the mercenary / James Brabazon.

ISBN 978-1-55468-549-3

1. Brabazon, James. 2. Du Toit, Nick. 3. Liberia—History—Civil War, 1999–2003. 4. Coups d'état—Equatorial Guinea—History—21st century. 5. Mercenary troops—Equatorial Guinea—Biography. 6. War correspondents—Africa—Biography. 7. War correspondents—Great Britain—Biography. 8. Journalists—Great Britain—Biography. I. Title.

PN5123.B72A3 2012 070.4'333092 C2011-905848-0

Printed and bound in the United States
RRD 9 8 7 6 5 4 3 2 1

For Jacob

Name me someone that's not a parasite, and I'll go out and say a prayer for him.

Bob Dylan

A Note on Pronunciation

In Afrikaans, the ‘v’ in *vok* is soft, and pronounced like an English ‘f’; the ‘g’ in *ag* is guttural, and to the English ear sounds like the German ‘ach’ in ‘achtung’; the ‘j’ in *ja* is pronounced like the ‘y’ in ‘yes’.

CONTENTS

Map of Africa xiii

Map of West Africa xv

Prologue: Black Beach 1

Part One

1. Shake Hands with the Devil 7
2. Dead Presidents 30
3. A Journey Without Maps 47
4. Spider House Rules 73
5. University of Bullet 104
6. Whisky Papa 122
7. Charnel House 140
8. The Great Escape 157

Part Two

9. A Stranger's Hand 175
10. Blood Brothers 196
11. Wanderlust 220

12. The Revolution Will Be Televised 245

13. Too Tough to Die 269

14. Arms and The Mann 289

Part Three

15. Simon Says 327

16. Lawyers, Guns and Money 358

17. Congo Mercenary 380

18. The End 395

Epilogue: Illumination Rounds 419

Acknowledgements 453

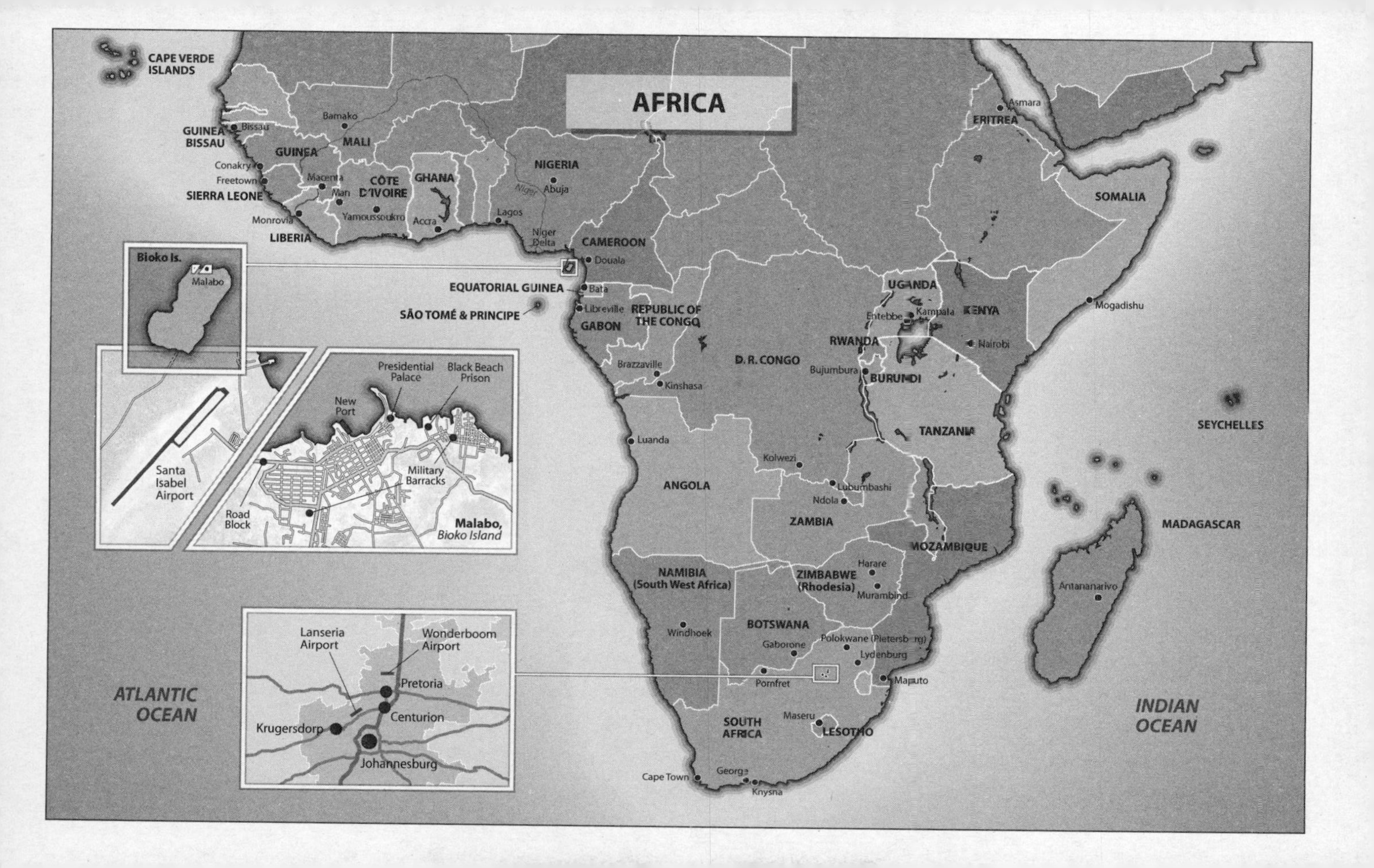
AFRICA
CAPE VERDE ISLANDS
GUINEA BISSAU
Bissau
Bamako
MALI
GUINEA
Conakry
Freetown
SIERRA LEONE
Macenta
Man
CÔTE D'IVOIRE
Yamoussoukro
GHANA
Accra
Monrovia
LIBERIA
NIGERIA
Niger
Abuja
Lagos
Niger Delta
CAMEROON
Douala
EQUATORIAL GUINEA
Bata
SÃO TOMÉ & PRINCIPE
Libreville
GABON
REPUBLIC OF THE CONGO
Brazzaville
Kinshasa
D. R. CONGO
Luanda
ANGOLA
ERITREA
Asmara
SOMALIA
Mogadishu
UGANDA
Entebbe
Kampala
RWANDA
Bujumbura
BURUNDI
Nairobi
TANZANIA
Kolwezi
Lubumbashi
Ndola
ZAMBIA
MOZAMBIQUE
Harare
ZIMBABWE (Rhodesia)
Murambind
NAMIBIA (South West Africa)
Windhoek
BOTSWANA
Gaborone
Polokwane (Pietersburg)
Lydenburg
Pomfret
Maputo
Maseru
LESOTHO
SOUTH AFRICA
Cape Town
Knysna
SEYCHELLES
MADAGASCAR
Antananarivo
INDIAN OCEAN
ATLANTIC OCEAN
Bioko Is.
Malabo
Santa Isabel Airport
Road Block
New Port
Presidential Palace
Black Beach Prison
Military Barracks
Malabo, Bioko Island
Lanseria Airport
Wonderboom Airport
Pretoria
Centurion
Krugersdorp
Johannesburg

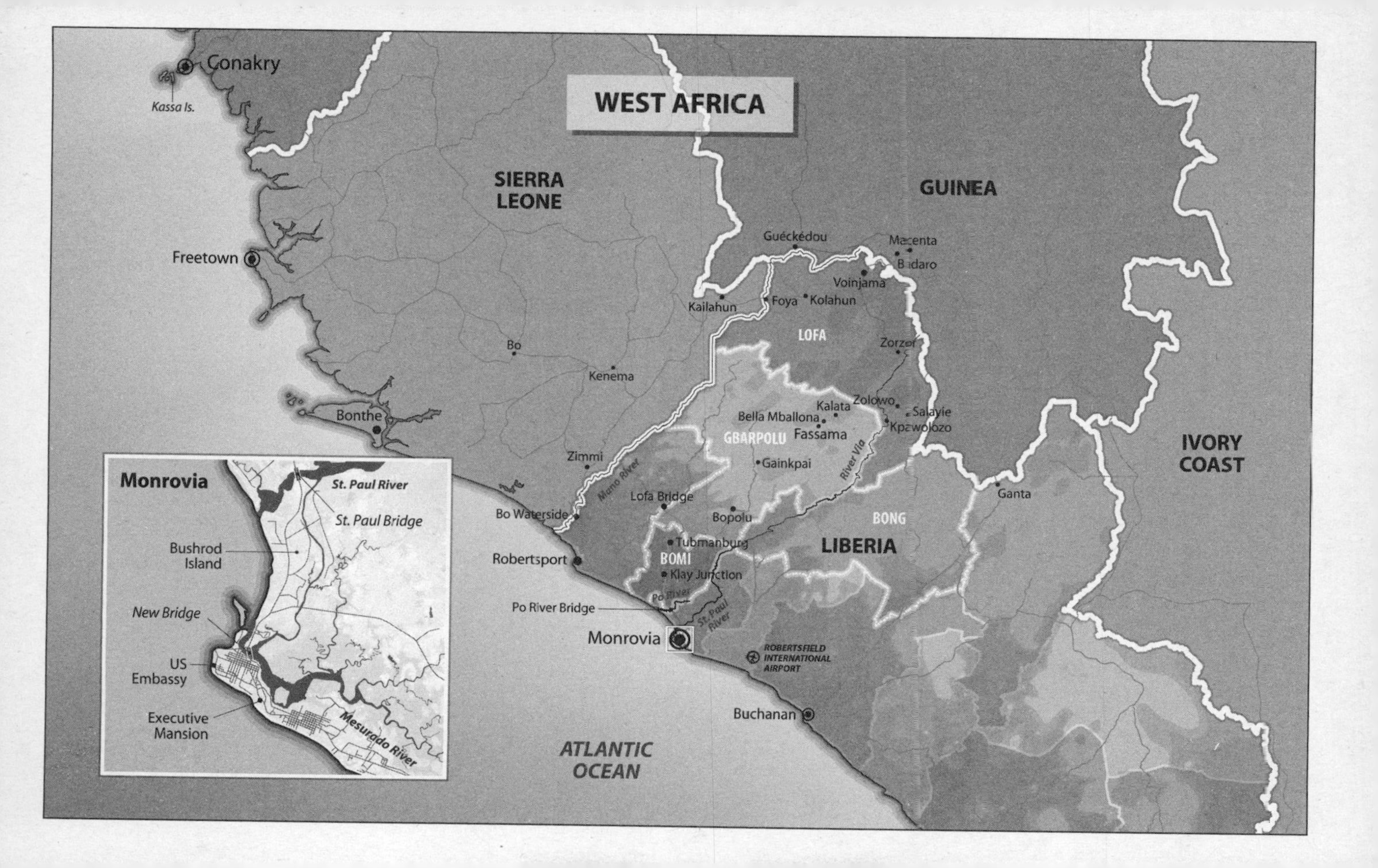
WEST AFRICA
Conakry
Kassa Is.
SIERRA LEONE
GUINEA
IVORY COAST
LIBERIA
Freetown
Bonthe
Bo
Kenema
Zimmi
Bo Waterside
Robertsport
Po River Bridge
Monrovia
Buchanan
ROBERTSFIELD INTERNATIONAL AIRPORT
ATLANTIC OCEAN
Guéckédou
Macenta
Kailahun
Foya
Kolahun
Voinjama
LOFA
Zorzor
Zolowo
Salayie
Kpawolozo
Kalata
Bella Mballona
Fassama
GBARPOLU
Gainkpai
River Via
Mano River
Lofa Bridge
Bopolu
Tubmanburg
BOMI
Klay Junction
Po River
St. Paul River
BONG
Ganta
Monrovia
St. Paul River
St. Paul Bridge
Bushrod Island
New Bridge
US Embassy
Executive Mansion
Mesurado River

PROLOGUE

BLACK BEACH

A man is hanging naked from the ceiling by a meat hook. His feet are bound, but his mouth is open – screaming a confession. He is surrounded by half a dozen soldiers in ragged uniforms whose fists are caked in his blood. Unsatisfied with his answers, they taunt him in a language he doesn't understand and slam a rifle butt into his testicles. Nine days after the arrests, the most extreme bouts of punishment have begun. The air fills with the bitter-sweet tang of roasting meat. The flames spouting from the soldiers' cigarette lighters burn the fat on the soles of his feet until it spits and crackles like a Sunday joint. It is the last thing he will feel. Opened wide by pain, his eyes take in the horror of the blood-spattered chamber he's strung up in and then his heart gives out. His yellow corpse is cut down and stretched out in front of the other prisoners.

Further down the corridor, the interrogations continue. A dim light burns, illuminating a prisoner, half a dozen soldiers and a seated government minister sweating in a smart suit, nodding approval. Next to the minister, behind the soldiers, a man holds a video camera, capturing the scene in minute, digital detail. The pictures reveal the prisoner, silent, hog-tied to a pole, suspended face down. Electrodes are clamped to his genitals, wet rags stuffed into his mouth.

Next door, his comrades lie crying, broken and bleeding, crammed tight into a separate sixty-foot cell with two hundred other prisoners. Baked under a corrugated roof by the relentless sun, they are picked out one by one for interrogation, random beatings or public humiliation. One begs to be shot. Another has his fingers broken.

In the last cell a man is screaming on the floor. His hands have been cuffed tightly behind his back. His legs have been pinned at the ankles with shackles, which have been hammered shut by the soldiers. Skin and muscle split as metal bites down to bone. Boots stamp on his feet, ripping out toenails. The prisoner's name is Nick du Toit. He is South Africa's most notorious mercenary, and one of my best friends.

Nick confessed before this torture began – in public, at gunpoint, in accurate, extensive detail, a day after he was seized. Now he no longer knows, nor cares, what he confesses to. His story shifts to fit the fantasies of his jailers, but it is a desperate, pointless game. In this ramshackle collection of wooden huts and concrete cells fenced off from the sea and the world beyond by rolls of barbed wire, Nick's tormentors are not seeking the truth: they want revenge.

Nick is dragged up from the stone floor and forced to kneel. The commander enters the cell and puts a pistol to his head. He has come to execute him, but the gun is empty. Laughing, the guards knock him unconscious with their rifle butts. The same ritual is repeated over and over again.

Nick is left to the mercy of the rats in his tiny, five-by-seven cell. His hands and feet remain chained. Like an animal, he eats scraps of food from the floor, where he must also sleep and defecate. There is no daylight: he is kept in pitch darkness, and beaten daily. And then the septicaemia sets in. Pus oozes from his open wounds – sustaining the cockroaches that feast on his sores. By the time he is dragged outside his eyes have sealed shut. The soldiers immerse his head in freezing water and then rip the scabs from his eyes.

This is how Nick begins his 34-year sentence in Black Beach prison, Africa's most notorious jail. He was arrested on 8 March 2004 along with fifteen other men as he tried to overthrow the government of Equatorial Guinea, a tiny West African country fabulously rich in oil. But there is just one person missing from the scene. What Nick doesn't see when he opens his eyes that day is me. Had all gone according to plan, I could have been lying next to him: I was supposed to film the coup.

PART ONE

1
SHAKE HANDS WITH THE DEVIL

Treading quickly on the halo of my noon shadow, I skirted the edge of the pool. I glanced at my watch. It was midday on 11 April 2002. I was exactly on time. At a table in the luxury hotel in Johannesburg two white men sat waiting. One, muscular with a ponytail, hid behind a pair of black sunglasses; the other, older and with a neat side-parting, stroked the end of his moustache, scrutinising the terrace and my arrival. I threw out my palm in a premature greeting, and they rose in unison to return it with a gruff 'Howzit?'

I'd met the ponytail in Sierra Leone the year before. A 37-year-old South African former paratrooper and one-time mercenary, Cobus Claassens had fought in the troubled West African state during the mid-nineties with a military company called Executive Outcomes, a private South African-run army which had been hired by the Sierra Leonean president to defeat rebels who threatened to overrun the capital, Freetown.

With the highly trained soldiers of EO on the ground, the rebels were quickly and comprehensively destroyed. Cobus stayed on after his contract wound up, carving out a living from the freelance security contracts that hovered like flies around the carcass of the country's diamond industry.

He was back in South Africa for a short holiday – a chance to see family and chase some business contacts. I'd met up with him a few days earlier when a chance conversation had planted an idea for a filming trip in West Africa. It was as preposterous as it was compelling: I would get access to a war in Liberia that no other journalist had filmed, and few even knew was happening. To do so I would need his help, and his man.

I stepped under the shade of the umbrella and saw them clearly.

Cobus spoke first.

'This is Nick du Toit. Nick – this is James.'

His Afrikaner accent bent itself awkwardly around English vowels. Nick, a plain, forgettable-looking man in his forties, reached over the table, and shook my hand. There was something awkward about him, as if his hands and ears were too big for his body, like a teenager waiting to grow into his skin. I wondered if this was really the soldier that Cobus had in mind. Nick's gaze was alarmingly direct, but not aggressive. He released my hand, sinking his six-foot frame back into the chair. Drinks arrived.

'Great to meet you,' I said to Nick. 'Thanks for coming along.'

I was struggling to disguise my unease. I was here to recruit a war hero to protect me while I filmed in Liberia. I thought I knew what I needed – what I had already been told I would require: a bodyguard; an experienced soldier; someone capable of defending me under fire – someone, frankly, extraordinary. Nick looked like none of these things: if anything, his white-and-blue checked shirt, freshly pressed chinos and neat row of pens in his breast pocket made him look profoundly ordinary, like an accountant or mild-mannered manager. Disappointment sagged into my shoulders.

Tilting our beer bottles inward, the three of us touched the necks lightly. The gentle double-click of glass on glass was swallowed by the rhythmic pumping of the hotel's infinity pool cascading gallons of crystal water beside us. There was no one in it. It was too hot to swim.

'Nick was a Recce, a Special Forces operator down here, in 5 Reconnaissance. He was about to be made a full colonel when he quit. He knows the type of area you're going to very well.' Here Cobus paused for effect. 'Nick was with me in Sierra Leone, actually.'

I liked Cobus, but he was a consummate hustler. I was beginning to wonder if he'd sold me a pup. Cobus was sure to take a generous commission from whatever I paid Nick to hold my hand in the jungle. Like a car salesman throwing in a full tank of petrol to sweeten the deal, he added: 'He's an experienced combat medic. Aren't you?'

'Ja,' Nick agreed, 'we were all trained to a certain standard, but the medical side became a bit of a speciality of mine. We did a lot of long-range stuff in Angola. I had to patch myself up once. We trained in civilian hospitals, too. They had all sorts of injuries, a bit more interesting than just the ones you got in the army.'

Nick looked down at the table, almost self-conscious. His voice was quiet, matter-of-fact. There was no hyperbole, apparently no bullshit.

I knew almost nothing about the 'Recces', other than what I'd learned hanging out with Cobus. South Africa's equivalent of the British SAS, they were highly trained killers and survivors who fought both conventionally and controversially in the service of the apartheid state during the bush wars and insurgencies that had torn Southern Africa apart for a quarter of a century. They were dedicated, arguably fanatical professionals – but unlike the SAS, they had not, ultimately, been under the control of a democratic government. In fact, the South African Army closely resembled everything I had been taught to despise when I was growing up: it was hard to shake the feeling that the Recces must have been more Waffen-SS than Special Air Service.

'A colonel? Have you worked with journalists before?'

I just couldn't see how Nick was going to rub along with the media, however well he might know the jungle.

Nick's gaze, set by a pair of profoundly blue eyes which reflected the turquoise pool beside us, fixed on me again. His expression was open, but unreadable. Somewhere below us, the bizarre but unmistakable toot of an elephant filtered through the hum of the city. Nick was studying me intently, like a farmer weighing up the price of a steer at auction.

'No, but from what Cobus tells me it sounds like it could be a lot of fun.'

Fun? I thought. *Is that really what people who kill other people for money think is fun?*

'A colonel?' I repeated to him.

Disbelief crept into my voice. He looked away for a moment, as if embarrassed at the mention of his former rank, and then nodded.

'It was a desk job at the end. I went private – Sierra Leone with EO and then mining in Angola. EO was quite an adventure. We ran a mobile Fire Force team; Cobus was my second-in-command.'

He must have seen my head jerk in surprise. I knew very well what Cobus's unit had got up to in Sierra Leone – and Nick had just outed himself as his commanding officer. That meant that men under Nick's command had killed a great number of rebels at close quarters, and then routed them. It was disturbing to think how much blood they'd seen shed between them. I changed the subject.

'I don't know how much you know, but Cobus thinks I need someone to hold my hand in Liberia. I'm planning a three-week trip into rebel-held territory.'

I paused and looked at him, trying to judge his reaction. His face was still impassive. I realised that I was trying to sound convincing and knowledgeable about Africa in front of two

Africans who had been fighting here while I'd still been in school. Suddenly I felt lost. I bluffed my way onwards.

'No one has any real idea what's going on there. The main thing I want to do is meet the leadership and hopefully film some fighting – to prove a war is really happening. You're very highly recommended.'

This last line was addressed to Cobus, who now seemed equally impassive. My confidence was ebbing fast. I had never attempted anything remotely like the trip I was suggesting – I didn't even know if it was feasible.

I turned back to Nick. His demeanour might have been underwhelming, but his experience was – apparently – compelling.

'Are you interested?'

A thick, conspiratorial smile spread across his face and we all shifted our chairs closer. Cobus reached and took Nick's notepad, turning over a fresh page. My gut tightened a little more. Cobus folded away his shades.

'Here's the plan.'

Wrapped up in a comfortable bubble blown out of my own hubris, by the time I met Nick I thought I knew who I was: someone who had already plumbed the depths of human suffering. In the eight years since I had left university – an ivory tower that encouraged boyhood curiosities for the scandals and scrambles of African history – I had worked mainly as a stills photographer in some of the world's worst trouble spots, or so I'd thought. I'd taken pictures in Kosovo, Afghanistan and the occupied Palestinian territories, and spent long periods of time working in Zimbabwe. I'd photographed artillery barrages at 12,000 feet in Kashmir, and taken photographs in Eritrea where corpses littered the battlefield, but I'd never seen close-quarter combat.

When I'd started taking pictures at school I'd been mesmerised by the work of Robert Capa and Don McCullin. I thought that a camera and the right attitude were all I'd need to follow in their footsteps. I was wrong. I hadn't been prepared for the competition. In London it seemed that every other person I met was a photographer and all of them were scrambling for a piece of the action. I was barely scraping a living and couldn't see how to break through to the life of a professional photographer I'd imagined for myself.

I met Cobus in Sierra Leone during my first trip to West Africa in 2001. I arrived as the violent, decade-old civil war in Sierra Leone was finally drawing to a close. With a box of film and a couple of battered cameras I found myself en route to the capital, Freetown – a 29-year-old photographer on assignment, shooting a magazine feature about the deployment of British troops. I was accompanied by Robert, an American writer who promised an interesting footnote to my story: we would be staying with a former mercenary.

After clearing customs we were bundled into a helicopter transfer to the city, and then whisked away by Land Rover at the other end. Eventually, we ended up at a pleasant bungalow on the outskirts of the capital. It was stiflingly hot. A smiling, muscle-bound South African opened the door. I stepped over the threshold into Cobus's home. I may as well have stepped through the Looking Glass.

Robert had arranged to stay with him for a fortnight. He assured me I'd be welcomed, too, but, in fact, he'd never met Cobus, either. He'd only hooked up with him through the notice-board of a private military website. In a fit of largesse, Cobus had invited 'us' to stay. He handed us a set of keys, and told us that there would be a Mercedes and driver sent along for our use in due course. If we had any problems, we just had to call.

I had no idea who Cobus was, nor, indeed, what 'problems' I might need to call him about. No one mentioned the word 'mercenary', but with his military bearing and house full of khaki equipment, he clearly had a story to tell.

I came and went from the house, finishing the magazine assignment – grateful for the car, and the meals cooked up by his housekeeper, which stretched my meagre budget. The magazine piece practically wrote itself: everyone had something to say about the war they'd narrowly survived. A double amputee described how he'd had his hands severed by rebels from the Revolutionary United Front; others spoke of soldiers in their early teens holding them down while their eyes were gouged out, and the sockets filled with molten plastic from burning carrier bags.

The RUF was infamous for its extreme atrocities. The mutilation of civilians was a favourite tactic. Their fighting units went by the names of Blood Shed Squad, Burn House Unit and Kill Man No Blood Unit – this latter group prided itself on beating people to death without a drop of blood being spilled. The Born Naked Squad stripped their victims naked before killing them. So it went on. Their military campaigns were known by a series of cruelly honest code names, too, including Operation Burn House, Operation Pay Yourself and the brutally self-explanatory Operation No Living Thing.

In my second week in the country I flew with the United Nations to the Parrot's Beak – dangerously insecure bandit territory to the east of the country. While Freetown had been effectively disarmed a few weeks earlier, and now lay under the control of the British and UN, not a single round of ammunition had been surrendered in the Parrot's Beak. As we landed, sixty or so children limped their way out of the thick undergrowth and made their way to the edge of the clearing. Held as slaves by the RUF, they had been forced into combat as child-soldiers, raped or confiscated as 'wives'.

I felt lucky to witness the moment of their freedom, but also felt a sense of shock at my own ignorance. I had no experience of the actual events that shaped these people's lives, and yet here I was, taking photos and gathering stories like a tourist collects souvenirs.

Back in Freetown, Robert left in a hurry to get to his daughter's graduation in the US, and I found myself alone with Cobus on his couch, staring at storm clouds piling up beyond the window.

'So who are you?' he asked, pouring another glass of Red Heart rum. He sounded genuinely interested, his Afrikaner accent only mildly inflected with irony. I was perplexed. After two weeks of sleeping on his couch – an occupational speciality of mine – he knew exactly who I was.

'How do you mean?'

'I mean, who *are* you?' he repeated, stretching and swallowing his vowels in turn.

It suddenly struck me that my arrival may have been more of a shock than he had let on.

'Hang on, you did know I was coming to stay, didn't you?'

He smiled and shook his head, and handed me the glass of rum.

'Oh God, I am so sorry.' Humiliated, I put the glass down. 'I thought you'd invited us both. I'm sorry, I should have asked. I'll find a hotel, it's . . .'

As I stood up and moved towards my bags, pulling my camera over my shoulder, a motorbike pulled up outside. A few seconds later the screen door slammed and a stout, slightly comic-looking man with a Mediterranean tan bustled into the room.

'Yossi, this is James. He's a journalist, a friend of mine. He's been staying with me.'

I put my hand out and said hello. Yossi looked me level in the eye, and spoke in a thick Israeli accent.

'If you take my photograph, I will kill you.'

Suddenly, Yossi didn't look so comic. I looked at Cobus, whose eyes were flashing me a smile.

'I've got a brilliant idea,' I said.

Yossi hadn't taken his eyes off me, or my camera.

'How about I don't take your photo?'

Yossi and Cobus laughed.

'Yossi and I have some business to sort out,' Cobus explained. 'James, why don't you, er, make yourself even more at home? I'll be back later.'

The screen door banged to and the motorbike coughed. I was alone. I could either take the Israeli's threat at face value, and leave – or accept Cobus's generosity and make the most of my final few days before my flight home. I fidgeted, and finished the rum.

Over the next six days, Cobus showed me his Freetown. It was a city haunted by the recently departed war, but a city, nonetheless, where you could still enjoy yourself. We went to a casino, and gambled away the last of my field budget; we drove out to an ape sanctuary, where I took the most profitable single picture of my career – a portrait of a unique albino chimpanzee called Pinky. Along the way I was introduced to the rogues' gallery of mercenaries, soldiers and businessmen that Cobus called friends.

Yossi turned out to be a sniper, who had commanded an elite undercover squad in the Israeli Defence Force. During the Lebanon war in the '80s, his unit had fired fifteen shots, and killed fourteen enemy commanders. Settling in Freetown as a businessman in 1990, Yossi started his own security company. Shortly before I left, he came and asked me a favour. Almost shy, he wondered if, possibly, I might take some photos of his children. As I snapped away, I saw him at the edge of the frame, scrutinising my lens.

Other characters popped up at house parties and in beachside bars. I met Neall Ellis, Nellis as everyone called him, on the beach with Cobus. A legendary helicopter gunship pilot, Nellis had flown for the South African Air Force before joining EO. Already a legend in the air force, he had quickly become a local hero in Freetown after almost single-handedly holding off a fresh rebel advance on the capital in 2000 when Sierra Leone had been abandoned to its fate, and most of the professional soldiers were long gone. He had flown dozens of sorties in his Russian HIND gunship until, finally, the British managed to secure the city.

Cobus and Nellis were fascinating to me. I had been brought up to revere the black liberation movements that South Africa tried to eliminate in the '70s and '80s; but they told the other side of their war, the politically incorrect accounts that were never taught in school. I felt like a priest in the company of whores. Their banter was infectious, their honesty disarming and the beer flowed into the night. Their stories of courage and friendship were all too easy to get carried away with.

At night, feeling less priestly, Cobus and I stuffed his Mercedes full of pretty girls, taking them from one bar to another as curfew approached. Then, back at his house, ensconced on his sofa with an apparently endless supply of rum and Coke, we talked about his twin obsessions of diamonds and history. I put my earlier nervousness to one side and asked him about his time with Executive Outcomes.

Cobus handed me a photograph from across the table. He stood, centre-frame, unrecognisable in combat fatigues, his face blacked with camouflage paint. A dozen or so other mercenaries clustered around him. It was impossible to tell if most of them were even white or black – so completely had their identities been obscured by the trappings of war.

'I was hired from friends amongst the senior Executive Outcomes people. I signed up in May '95. I was offered three times what I was making in the army, so I quit and became a mercenary.' Several of his friends joined up as well. 'We didn't even know which country we were being sent to fight in. They told us on the plane flying up there from South Africa that we were going to Sierra Leone, the worst place in the world.'

He smiled at the irony of having made it his home, and re-filled his glass.

For Cobus, the fight became personal. Wiping out the rebels was more than simply a job to be done for money – in the face of their legendary cruelty he felt increasingly obliged to 'cleanse' the rebels from the forest. He styled himself an Angel of Death, with justice, he believed, firmly on his side. His mobile force, commanded by Nick du Toit, went and smoked them out. On one occasion they received a report of an attack on a village, and arrived to find women with sticks thrust into their vaginas, and old men with their throats slit. Eventually the rebels were found twelve miles away, terrorising another village.

Cobus and his men fanned out through every hut and hunted them down. There were no surviving rebels; no prisoners; no mercy. Cobus's face hardened.

'At a certain point a human being becomes less of a human being, and more of an animal, and then he should just be culled and got rid of as quickly as possible so the rest of humanity can go on with their lives.'

I had no such stories to share. Cobus's uncompromising attitude to summary justice was hard to digest, too far outside my own experience to judge properly. Cobus bade me goodnight. I cleared away the cigarette ends and empty Coke bottles, and pulled a mosquito net over the couch where I'd slept for the last three weeks.

My time in Sierra Leone was up. Cobus took me to the airport by speedboat, and urged me to stay in touch. As the boat sliced through the clear blue water, I asked him if he had any regrets.

'We did something that gave some hope to these people,' he answered. 'But yes,' he said, 'yes.' The beach loomed up, and the engines idled. 'I regret not having killed more of the rebels.'

Like his stories from the nights before, his comments did not invite discussion. He set his stall out: whether you bought into it or not was irrelevant to him.

I did as Cobus asked, and stayed in touch. Eight months later, in February 2002, I'd hung up my stills cameras and taken my first steps towards a career as a television producer. I went to Zimbabwe with a Kenyan production company on behalf of the BBC – who were banned from entering the country. I knew the country well from working there as a photographer, and the job was a surprise success. Using a mixed British, South African and Zimbabwean crew, we managed to keep images and analysis flowing to the BBC producers cutting the nightly news reports that documented Robert Mugabe's descent into criminality. When the job was done, we decamped to South Africa and the company set up an office in a trendy area of Johannesburg to try and capitalise on the reputation we thought we'd earned. I flew down to George, on the Garden Route, to see Cobus, home on leave from the claustrophobia of Freetown.

Slipping a .45 into the back of his trousers ('You never know in this fokken country'), we drove out to an oyster bar in Knysna to shuck the day's catch with his wife and children. He was as candid as ever. After EO's contract had been wound up, Cobus, it transpired, had been sought after by other masters – including the United States Government.

Not long after my visit to Sierra Leone in June 2001, he'd gone to neighbouring Guinea to visit a friend who worked for US Intelligence in the region. On Kassa Island, off the coast, American Special Forces were training Guinean soldiers. Cobus had gone along for the hell of it to test-fire the US military's M4 carbine. In gun-heaven, he'd noticed that several of the 'Guinean' soldiers spoke English with thick Liberian accents – and not French, the local language.

I didn't understand why the American Army would be training Liberians.

'A new war has broken out in Liberia,' Cobus told me. 'Details are very hard to verify, but it looks like a rebel army has sprung up on the border between Guinea and Liberia. There are a lot of guys in the east, the area around Macenta, from the different factions that fought against Taylor in the old war.'

The old war, he explained, was another West African tragedy that unfolded alongside – and helped precipitate – the war he'd fought in Sierra Leone. Between 1989 and 1997 Charles Taylor and other warlords waged a vicious civil war against the Liberian Government – and between themselves. It was a war that Taylor finally won when he was elected president in 1997.

'Taylor took his revenge on the other warlords after his election, and most of their fighters fled to Guinea. In '98 the shit really hit the fan. They started fighting it out in Monrovia again and the fighters loyal to the warlord the Yanks had been supporting just fokken ran to the US embassy. Then the Americans put together a rescue mission before Taylor could massacre them.'

Cobus had been part of the rescue mission and wore a stars and stripes patch on his uniform. In the four years that had followed, Taylor's enemies had slowly re-grouped, and the president himself had become an international pariah. Accused by the United Nations of funding, arming and training the limb-hacking RUF rebels in neighbouring Sierra Leone, his regime had military and commercial sanctions slapped on it.

9/11 changed the picture. Fed up with Taylor's government, and incensed at reports that he may have allowed al-Qaeda operatives safe passage through his country, the Americans were now keen to help their old friends again. Taylor, it was decided, had to go.

'There's a long history to this,' Cobus informed me. 'In '96, the US Government had given weapons to ULIMO-J fighters – those are the same guys that they later helped in '98 – through a private contractor when it looked like Taylor was going to fuck them up. Now proper battles are being fought a hundred miles away from the largest UN deployment in history, and no one knows a fokken thing about it.'

He spat the initials of the UN, who, despite maintaining a massive peacekeeping operation in Sierra Leone, had done nothing to intervene in Liberia.

'They are incredibly fokken useless.'

His rolled 'r's hammered the point home. No one, apparently, outside Guinea and Liberia (and US Intelligence) really knew what was happening.

Our oyster shells had piled up into a grey, crenulated mountain. We climbed into his car and headed back to his house. I thought about what Cobus had told me. If I could get access to a rebel army in this unknown, unreported war it would be a genuine scoop – in fact, it could make my name as a journalist.

'This American friend of yours,' I asked, trying to sound off-hand, 'can he get me in? I mean, would it be possible to film?'

The sun was dropping towards the sea. Cobus adjusted his sunglasses as he drove.

'I'll have to ask him. I'm not exactly sure what the situation is at the moment, how much territory they control. The Americans are, you know, trying to help them with some small arms and logistics – nothing heavy, just enough to keep them going, to see if they can hit Taylor, to see if they're any good.'

We rounded the hill, and swung back on ourselves for a sweeping view of the ocean. Cobus killed the engine, and we dropped the windows. The truck filled with the scent and sound of the sea.

'I'll let you know.'

Two days later my phone rang. I stepped away from the bar I was propping up in Johannesburg, extricating myself from the din of lunchtime banter. I'd half-forgotten that I was waiting for Cobus to call me. In the cold light of day, it seemed unlikely that US Intelligence (who- or whatever that might be) were going to broker introductions between a rebel group (that may or may not exist) and a journalist. It seemed even more unlikely that the rebels would want any part of it.

'James, it looks like those jokers are going to play ball. You're in.'

'I'm what?'

'You're in. I spoke to the Yanks and told them they can trust you, that you're not interested in fucking them or anything, that you just want to get the story of the rebels out. As long as you agree not to broadcast anything about the Americans, I don't think it will be a problem.'

I couldn't believe what I was hearing. For a moment my mind went blank. What was I supposed to say? I imagined myself surrounded by gun-toting rebels in an anonymous jungle clearing and felt a rush of nervous excitement.

'You need someone who can look after you, run an evacuation. Someone to watch your back.'

I glanced back into the restaurant, and then at my feet.

'Cobus, I don't even have a budget for this. It's going to be very tight.'

Getting the Americans on board was just the beginning of the process, not the end. In order to film anything, I would need equipment, personnel – and money.

'I hear you, I hear you. Look, don't worry, we'll sort something out. All the payments will be run through me. I'll help manage it from Freetown. I'll be in Jo'burg at the end of the week. There's a guy I have in mind. Let's meet at the Westcliff Hotel on the eleventh . . .'

Nick ordered another round, and we started jotting down notes by the poolside. The plan was simple enough, or so it seemed. Cobus would man a UHF military radio in Freetown – one they had used in the army and on a different frequency range from the local sets – which had enough range to reach Monrovia, the capital of Liberia, and much further than we planned on going. Nick and Cobus would be in regular contact, with Nick relaying our daily GPS co-ordinates, so that Cobus could liaise with the Americans in case of an emergency. We would take with us a satellite phone as a back-up, bullet-proof vests, water purification equipment and essential food and supplies so that we would not be a burden on the local population.

It occurred to me that perhaps the rebels would not be keen on my bringing in a mercenary as my bodyguard. I picked my words carefully. Cobus was sanguine.

'If the Americans tell them it's okay, they'll accept it. Besides, it's in their interest to have Nick along. The last thing they want is to have to look after you if there's a problem.'

His reasoning had merit, but his almost complete reliance on the Americans concerned me.

'Nick,' I asked, 'will you be armed?'

'Yes, but not immediately. We can't take weapons in from here. Well, we could – but people might get the wrong idea, hey? I expect I'll get an AK from the rebels when we get in. I don't think it will be a problem.'

Nick looked over my shoulder as the beers arrived at the table and we lapsed into silence. A chalk-white tourist edged away from the safety of his lounger and dropped into the pool. I fanned myself with a lunch menu, and accepted what he said. I wanted him to be armed, and I wanted to know what he thought he would be armed for. As the ripples dissipated, he explained how the AK might be used.

'If there is a problem,' he continued, 'I'll make enough space for us to get clear – just that. If necessary, we can walk out.'

My mind drew a blank: walk out of where? To where? I imagined the forest I'd seen in Sierra Leone, Nick emptying his rifle into the faceless enemy, while I ran, scared, into the trees.

'I like the "we" bit,' I said. 'I haven't done anything like this before.'

The words hung between us. Cobus cut across the silence. 'Don't worry. You're going to have to take in a big crew. You can be sure that they don't know jack-shit about filming, but the more people you're in charge of, the more they're going to be impressed by you.'

Nick was smiling in agreement. I was writing furiously.

'Take big cameras, too, so you look like a proper news crew. They'll love that.'

I noted the implication that we wouldn't really be a proper news crew at all: I couldn't fault him on that. We agreed that Nick would acquire a comprehensive medical kit and procure our supplies. The production company would put together the crew, and I would draw up the necessary paperwork.

'How are we going to get there, exactly? If we go into Conakry directly . . . that's going to be bloody tricky.'

Conakry, the capital of neighbouring Guinea, where the rebels' political office was located, was one of the hardest places on earth to enter as a journalist. The airport had a special place in the International Journalists' Travel Bestiary: rapacious customs officials, unpredictable soldiers and sinister government agents made clearing immigration like running the gauntlet. Nick leaned in to hear the answer. He was as concerned as I was.

'Don't worry,' Cobus reassured us, 'I'll be there before you. I'll meet you at the airport with one of their guys.'

Apart from the reputation, or lack thereof, of its international airport, I knew next to nothing about either Guinea, or Liberia. In the days since my phone call with Cobus confirming the meeting, I'd dredged the Internet for any clues as to what might be going on. I'd turned up almost nothing.

The few reports that suggested there was renewed fighting were often sceptical. One BBC dispatch thought it possible that Liberian president Charles Taylor was fabricating attacks against his army in order to justify relaxing the international community's arms embargo against him. Indeed, in February 2001, Charles Taylor had written personally to Kofi Annan, the then United Nations Secretary General, asking for the weapons ban on his regime to be lifted owing to the threat he faced from Guinea – a request that was flatly denied.

Liberian dissident websites in America talked of a new rebel alliance against Taylor, dedicated to removing him from office and empowering the marginalised indigenous tribes. There were no photographs, few names and no verifiable facts. Apparently, no European journalists had met them, and no one had filmed them. Opaque in the extreme, they styled themselves the 'LURD' – Liberians United for Reconciliation and Democracy – apparently under the leadership of a former used-car salesman called Sekou Conneh. Conneh's position – and even existence – was questioned by many serious commentators. Only a few references to him existed in print, one of which was a bizarre press release allegedly issued by his 'press secretary' – a man clearly not over-burdened with work.

The United Nations' most recent report – a 116-page update on the 2001 Security Council Resolution that had re-imposed a stringent arms embargo and travel and diamond sanctions against Taylor's government – devoted less than one page to the LURD. Containing few hard facts about the organisation, it referred to a leader called 'Kone' and described their command structure as 'factionalised', with support from Guinea for its limited incursions declining. The report concluded that 'the activities of LURD may have peaked'.

Only two factors convinced me of LURD's actual existence: first, Cobus was adamant that the Americans were in contact with them; and second, only a genuine committee of die-hard, unsmiling insurgents could adopt such a bizarre and awkward name.

'One thing I want to discuss', I remembered, 'is filming you, Nick.'

He and Cobus looked at each other, and then back at me.

'It's inevitable that you're going to end up on camera, at the edge of a frame or in the background, at some point,' I explained. 'It's going to make my life impossible if I'm always making sure you're out of every shot. Basically, you're going to have to trust me that your face won't be in the final programme.'

Nick nodded. I, of course, had no idea what the final programme might be.

'That's fine, man. I don't see any problem with that. Just don't mention my name. You can leave me off the credits for this one.' Nick relaxed back into his chair. 'This beer is not bad, not bad at all.'

Cobus handed the small, spiral-bound notepad back to Nick, and they exchanged some words in Afrikaans. I steeled myself, convinced of my decision.

'Great. Well, we've got a deal.'

I reached over to shake Nick's hand. He took mine again, and I felt an enormous sense of relief wash away my earlier doubts.

'I'll sort out the finances with Cobus. All we need now is for the rebels to agree.'

'I'm very confident they will,' Cobus answered. 'The Americans have got a lot of leverage. One of their senior guys is apparently quite friendly with them.'

I let the subject drop, and swallowed the growing ambiguity of my position with my last mouthful of beer.

That evening I reflected on the meeting and the complicated web of interests. It was clear that, without Nick, I was powerless. Without me, Cobus had no means of getting his man in on the ground with the Americans. And without either Cobus or me, Nick had no job. I thought I had come to interview Nick – in fact, we had all interviewed each other. I had no idea why the American military wanted to facilitate my visit, and I didn't want to think about it.

I was all too aware of the potential pitfalls of working with both the Americans and the South Africans. Although there were countless matters still to resolve – not least the issue of who Nick really was, and what he had seen and done to earn his rank and reputation – I was on the brink of what might be a real scoop and had no appetite to ask awkward questions. There would be plenty of time to get to know Nick once we were in Liberia.

The following week I hooked up with the crew: a cameraman, a shaven-headed white South African called Dudley Saunders, and an irrepressible Zulu soundman by the name of Mandla Mlambo. I'd worked with Mandla in Zimbabwe earlier in the year; Dudley came on unofficial loan from the South African

Broadcasting Corporation – the SABC. He had filmed his fair share of the horrors that engulfed the country's townships at the end of apartheid: 'necklace' burnings, beatings and riots among them. None of us had travelled to Liberia before. We drank beers, and tried to imagine what might be in store for us.

I wrote two long letters to the LURD rebels ('to whom it may concern'), and faxed and emailed them to Sierra Leone care of Cobus, as planned. I asked for access to their leadership, their bases and their forward-deployed fighting forces. In return I promised objectivity, a fair hearing and the potential for mass-media exposure – but I was careful not to give any guarantee that this exposure would be entirely or even partially positive. The facts would have to speak for themselves.

Cobus took the letters to Conakry in person and saw that they were delivered, a week later and with American endorsement, into the hands of Sekou Conneh – the LURD's national chairman. Conneh replied, immediately, with an emphatic 'Yes' to Cobus through intermediaries in Conakry.

I applied for the notoriously difficult Guinean visas for the crew, and had them authorised on the spot. The production company shipped in flak jackets from Nairobi, and cut a deal with Cobus. Dudley and Mandla would be put onto three-week paid contracts. There would be no fee for me for going to Liberia. I was kept on the books with a modest retainer; the only money I might receive for going would be a share of profits after future, and as yet unimagined, sales. The BBC expressed interest, but gave neither promises, nor cash. In short, the production company was taking an enormous gamble on the trip, with cash it did not have to spare.

Nick, who lived in Pretoria, drove to Johannesburg to meet me. We bought tents, dried food, water purifiers, mosquito nets and enough medical supplies to equip a small hospital. Everything was written down and ticked off meticulously in his notebook.

It was strange to see Nick again, this time without Cobus. Tidily dressed and with a sober eye for detail, he made it feel more like I was preparing for a camping trip with my dad rather than getting ready to go to war with a soldier of fortune. As we unloaded the last of our purchases, the mobile phone in his breast pocket suddenly started playing 'Eye of the Tiger'. He fished it out and answered in Afrikaans. His voice quietened, the hard edges of the language softening in a sing-song to-and-fro. I guessed he was talking to a child.

'*Rocky*,' I said, when he'd finished talking. 'Great film.'

'Ag, it's my daughter, man. She calls me Tiger. It's like a family joke.'

We shook hands, and I left more easily in the knowledge that behind the inscrutable Special Forces persona and violent professional credentials was a young family and a reason to come home.

In my final week I travelled first to London, and then on to Glasgow for a last weekend with my girlfriend, Rachel, who I'd been seeing on and off for over a year. Our first date had been a blind date arranged through a mutual friend over the phone. I'd flown somewhat desperately on spec to Glasgow on the off-chance that she might be even half as intriguing as her text messages suggested. She met me off the plane. Half English, half Italian, she had olive skin, bright green eyes and a disarming figure: she was the kind of girlfriend that other people had. I couldn't believe my luck.

Nick and I kept in touch on a near-daily basis. His quiet enthusiasm was infectious; his planning left apparently no room for error. I only hoped that on location he would start behaving less like my dad, and more like a bodyguard. Dates were confirmed.

We would all fly in to Guinea Conakry together on the same day. Cobus would fly in first from Freetown; then Nick, Dudley and Mandla from South Africa; and then me, from London, arriving last on 29 May 2002.

I said goodbye to Rachel and acquired a satellite phone and a brick of US dollars in cash to clear the anticipated hurdles of bribery and corruption ahead. I was off to war on the nod of a rebel leader who may not exist and an American spook whom I'd never met.

Nick emailed me a final shopping list. As I scanned the list, my eye settled on the last item: 'Balls of Steel'.

2
DEAD PRESIDENTS

I stepped off the Air France flight at Conakry airport into a wall of damp heat. By the time I had managed the hundred yards between the aircraft steps and the terminal building, I was wet with sweat. Soldiers in drab olive uniforms lounged against dirty walls, white-ringed circles of sweat spreading out under their arms. They toyed with their rifles, adjusted black berets, lit cigarettes. Two of them were shouting at a young man in a frayed brown suit. I stared conspicuously at my feet. A queue formed in front of a small, wooden cabin that served as passport control. A man with a pistol in his belt pulled a woman and her child out of the line and made them stand to one side for reasons that were as obscure as they were menacing. No one spoke. A single fan creaked overhead, stirring the flies. I shuffled along and discreetly checked my British mobile for reception: nothing. My South African phone was lifeless, too. I comforted myself that Nick and Cobus would be waiting for me on the other side, and held my passport out to the woman at the head of the queue.

'Occupation?' she demanded in heavily accented French.

'Producteur,' I replied. 'Producer.'

She looked at me blankly, beads of moisture welling on her

top lip. She clearly had no idea what a producer did. That made two of us.

'Quelle est la nature de votre voyage, monsieur?' she persisted.

Good question, I thought. I plumped for business.

'Affaires.'

She scrutinised my photograph and laboriously thumbed through a dozen pages looking for my visa. I braced myself for an argument. When she found it she looked at me quickly, thumping an inky stamp down onto the pages.

'Bienvenu,' she smiled. 'Welcome.'

I was in. I picked my way carefully through the assembled passengers to the wheezing luggage carousel and waited for my bag. Looking around, I felt indescribably conspicuous. The only other white people on the plane had long since vanished. Ten feet away from me a mob of customs officials with rolled white sleeves and tight blue trousers were busy filleting the suitcases, cardboard boxes and cloth bundles that my fellow passengers were desperately trying to drag past them towards the blinding glare of the exit. All manner of re-saleable goods – including cartons of cigarettes, French liqueurs and, somewhat hopefully, a big bar of chocolate – were liberated from their rightful owners and spirited away behind the trestle table they used like a butcher's block. They were going to have a field day when they searched me.

I shouldered my rucksack, picked up the camera bag destined for Dudley and headed for the light. Amazingly, no one stopped me. I was tempted to turn around and ask them what the hell they thought they were playing at – and then I was outside again, and very much alone. Cobus and Nick were nowhere to be seen.

I waited. Soldiers strolled past me. A series of smartly dressed men of indeterminate occupation asked me for a light. I was quickly becoming the centre of attention. This did not augur well. A mixture of fear and anger ran through me. After another ten minutes, I'd had enough. I walked over to a dilapidated yellow taxi and woke the driver. At least I knew where we were staying.

'Hôtel Petit Bateau, s'il vous plaît.'

He stared at me, apparently uncomprehending.

'Monsieur?'

I pressed a folded ten-dollar bill into his hand. His eyes focused.

'Okay, ça va. On y va.'

He turned the ignition, and I clambered in.

Conakry revealed itself to be a low-rise smudge on the tip of a headland that jutted into the Bight of Benin. The Republic of Guinea is a poor country, and its capital city certainly played the part. Despite possessing perhaps up to half of the world's known aluminium ore reserves, as well as an abundance of gold, diamonds and timber, the people of Guinea were among the poorest in Africa. Labouring under the authoritarian regime of an old-fashioned 'blood and iron' dictator called Lansana Conté, they had few pleasant prospects ahead. The national motto of *Work, Justice and Solidarity* could, a plethora of reports by international human rights groups implied, more accurately have been replaced with *Corruption, Favouritism and Instability*.

At the very tip of the headland I found the hotel, isolated, clinging onto the side of a pier. If it had been possible to keep going, and I wished it had, the next landfall was Venezuela. Flanked by fishing boats and enveloped in the rank smell of low tide, it looked structurally unsound – a ramshackle collection of apparently unconnected glass panels, exposed masonry and white-painted cement pillars.

Dudley and Mandla were waiting for me in the lobby, lolling on a sofa that looked as if it had been dragged kicking and screaming out of the 1970s. Nick and Cobus had left to meet me only half an hour earlier – everyone's plane, except mine, had been delayed.

'We got all the kit in no problem. Cobus and the security chief at the airport just waved us through,' Dudley rumbled, evidently still impressed. 'Could I suggest we have a beer? I think there is precisely fuck-all else to do here.'

He'd clearly reached the same decision about Conakry as I had during the short drive in. By the time I'd checked in and joined Dudley and Mandla on the terrace, Nick and Cobus were walking towards us.

'Sorry, man, the flight was a right fuck-up. Did you get through okay?'

Nick folded himself into a chair next to me as we shook hands. A contrite Cobus settled next to him.

'No problem,' I reassured him.

It was true. It wasn't a problem, but I was nervous about what lay ahead. *Whatever happens,* I thought, exhausted from the flight and the humidity, *I'll at least have the safety of their company.*

'Good to see you,' I said, looking at them both, and then, pointing at the perspiring glasses of draught lager on the table. 'Beer?'

'That', replied Nick, 'is a very good idea.'

For the second time we clinked glasses and said cheers.

By the time I went to bed that night, we had already, between us, eaten our way through the hotel menu. *Des grandes bières pression* and *poulet frites* were the best of a poor offering. I noted that, for a thirsty man, Nick drank very little and ate without the sarcastic complaints of the rest of us.

Nick's conversation – punctuated with asides to Dudley in Afrikaans – focused on what we would need to learn from the rebels when we met their representatives the following day. Cobus reassured us that the Americans would make sure we were properly briefed the next morning. Prior to leaving for Conakry, it had been impossible to conduct any kind of meaningful risk-assessment or work out an accurate filming schedule. We had no idea what territory the rebels controlled in Liberia, or how securely it was held; consequently, we had no idea where we were going, or how we would get there.

Although troubling in many respects, this lack of clarity was also compelling. Five weeks before we'd arrived in Conakry, the UN Security Council had released a report compiled by its Panel of Experts on Liberia. Their investigators had managed neither to cross into rebel-held territory, nor to meet any LURD representatives in Liberia itself. 'Access', they concluded, 'was impossible.' It seemed that the war in Liberia had none of the trappings of modern media conflicts: no satellite TV reporters on rooftops, no pictures produced by local cameramen – nothing. In order to get it, I would have to be on the spot, personally. It promised to be more like the old-fashioned assignments undertaken by photographers like Capa or McCullin than the video-game footage of the Gulf War.

An overland crossing from either Sierra Leone, or, more likely, Guinea itself, seemed probable – especially given that the Americans claimed the rebel leader was based on the Guinea–Liberia border. Flying into Monrovia, the capital of Liberia, and then moving up-country clandestinely to meet the rebels was off the cards. The one 'fact' that Cobus thought indisputable was that there really was some kind of front line, and crossing it would be impossible, whether it was 200 yards or 200 miles from Monrovia.

Moreover, the criminal regime in Monrovia did not admire the foreign media. Two years before, a television news crew working legitimately on behalf of Channel 4 in London were arrested on charges of espionage and held for nearly four weeks. More recently, the outspoken independent newspaper editor Hassan Bility had been arrested and detained indefinitely without trial. If the government got wind of what we were up to, we would not be let off lightly. I didn't fancy our chances in front of a Liberian court martial, and neither did Nick, given that he had jointly overseen the somewhat extensive eradication of the Taylor-funded RUF in Sierra Leone seven years before.

From Guinea's Atlantic coast, where I was now getting soaked on cheap local beer, the country curved inland like a fat banana, bordering Liberia and then Ivory Coast in the east. It was over this thickly forested border, presumably under the noses of the Guinean Army, that we would most likely have to slip. And from there on, everything was unknown.

The following day US Intelligence – in the shape of two muscle-bound, square-jawed, sunglass-wearing leviathans – arrived early for breakfast. They sat at a far table on the terrace, the scene before them was picture-perfect: bright morning sunshine lit up scrubbed white tables; an inviting, deep-blue sea dazzled behind. The hotel had turned out to be an oasis of functional anonymity at the edge of the bustling, dysfunctional capital city. Nick, sporting the smart–casual chino look, was sitting with them, his ubiquitous notepad already a mass of neatly ordered ciphers. Cobus appeared with a cup of coffee and guided me in as I neared their table.

'James, this is Frank. Frank, this is James Brabazon, who we've talked about. I think you should be able to help him with this project.'

Cobus was the consummate networker.

'Hey, James, how you doing?'

Frank took my hand with a grip that suggested he could bench-press my body-weight without drawing breath.

'It'll be a pleasure to help out. This is George, from the embassy.' He nodded towards the other giant by way of introduction, and added, presumably referring to the rebels, 'He's met some of these jokers before as well.'

'So you're a journalist, then?' George wanted to know.

I smiled my *Yes; but I'm okay really* grin that anyone in the media who encounters the military learns to flash on demand. George, it turned out, was a soldier's soldier. While we exchanged pleasantries, he explained that he'd been in the middle of the Battle for Mogadishu, the notorious Black Hawk Down episode in Somalia nine years before. Oozing an avowed dislike for armed Muslims, he was looking forward to the next big scrap coming up in Iraq: hacks of any description were clearly not part of his social circle. Cobus cut across him.

'James isn't like a normal journalist, he's all right. We had some great times together in Sierra Leone. I was educating him into some of the finer points of Freetown's nightlife.'

I liked the way Cobus was selling me. He made me feel like one of their team.

'Great,' said Frank, 'not one of those fucking tree-huggers. What is it that you want to do, James? What do you want to achieve?'

As he spoke to me, he pulled a small brown envelope out of his backpack. It concealed a deck of photos. Frank knew full well what I hoped to achieve, but he wanted me to repeat my pitch. I recounted my mantra: I wanted to prove the rebels existed, see how much territory they controlled, find out what their agenda was. As I talked, Frank collaged the table with tessellated snaps of young men posing with Kalashnikovs. Frank and George peeled off their Oakleys to scrutinise the out-of-focus, over-exposed images. Nick scanned them carefully, too, picking out a shot here or there for closer attention before passing them on to me. Dressed like LA gang-bangers, most of them looked barely out of their teens – and terrifying.

It turned out that these pictures, combined with exaggerated LURD reports and radio intercepts that were difficult to translate, were about the extent of Frank's on-the-ground intelligence. Starved of accurate information about the conduct of the insurgency against President Taylor – US foreign policy was leaning towards his removal from office – Frank, in his role as a senior field officer in United States Intelligence, saw my proposed trip as a perfect platform to obtain vital information about the rebels and their war. Indeed, he had already interceded on my behalf with the exiled Liberian rebel hierarchy based in Guinea, a member of whom, I was assured, would be joining us shortly.

Frank was keen to go a little further, though, and implied that, in return for helping to facilitate access to the rebels, I might like to provide a full intelligence briefing when I got out. It seemed like a reasonable request. Frank was helping me; I would help Frank – that was only fair.

It was time for another introduction. Frank stood up and raised his palm.

'Here we go,' he whispered.

I looked up from the table of two-dimensional rebels to see a real one walking towards me. Wearing a pretty patterned shirt and designer sunglasses, and carrying a small leather briefcase, the LURD commander looked the picture of middle-aged urban sophistication.

'Hey, Joe,' boomed Frank, 'how's it going?'

Joe was going just fine.

'Ah, Frank, tings movin' nah. I' all righ' to see you in Conokry.'

His deep Liberian accent, the first I had ever heard, was immediately mesmerising. It was a voice from another era, a way of speaking English that had been brought to Liberia in the nineteenth century by freed slaves from the southern states of America. Endings of words, and other consonants, too, were dropped or swallowed in a unique Old American drawl: 'now' became *nah*, 'it' lost its 't', which Joe pronounced *ih*; 'th' became a hard *t* or *de* – not unlike the accents of my Irish cousins.

Introductions were made all round. Joe in turn introduced himself as Joe Wylie, the LURD rebels' senior military adviser. He sat next to Nick, as I launched into my sales pitch again.

'I' all righ' nah to go to de bush, you go' green ligh' to go Voinjama side,' Joe interrupted me. 'Boh befo' we go, deh certain, er, modalitie' dat we got to mak' correc'.'

Joe's conversation snaked around the twin subjects of 'modalities' and 'sensitivities' with increasingly obscure jargon. As he set out his stall, I reflected on the ease with which the rebel and the Intelligence man sat in each other's company. The relationship between Frank and Joe seemed close. Ultimately, I suspected Joe would bend to Frank's wishes, but it was equally clear that Joe wanted to run my trip.

'Joe,' I asked, in an attempt to cut through the bullshit piling up between us, 'what don't you want me to film?' The Americans seemed to like this direct approach.

The sensitivities became clearer. In return for allowing me into their territory, and to interview their leaders, I would have to agree not to disclose details of the armaments the rebels received from the American-backed government in Guinea. This condition was enthusiastically endorsed by Frank.

These weapons were being supplied in direct contravention of a UN Security Council Resolution. They weren't messing around. Frank's motivations were suspicious; Joe's downright dangerous. This realisation alone pushed me closer to Nick. I knew precious little about him but, if nothing else, he was paid to be on my side.

Coffee and croissants arrived for Joe. On the one hand, the request was reasonable – I could imagine British or American forces applying the same restrictions to reporting on the details of their supply lines in wartime – and on the other, it was, happily, unenforceable. I had no idea what actual support the Guinean Government was giving the rebels: the only way to find out was to agree to the demands of the rebels and the Americans and get in on the ground.

All this talk of 'modalities' left me feeling uneasy. Talking sense with Joe was like trying to eat soup with a fork: I could see there was another issue on the horizon, but didn't know how to get to it. I suspected I was, very slowly, being asked for a bribe. It was Nick who eventually broke the impasse. He wanted to know how we were going to get into Liberia, and when; who would come with us, and what we could expect in terms of security along the route. Joe's answer was uncharacteristically illuminating.

'We pick you u' fro' here an' carry you all de way, no problem. Everyting safe.' The flecks of grey at his temples burned white as the sun climbed above the hotel. 'As soon as we finalise de whole operation, we ca' roll. Y' know we'll mak' you mobile, an' mah boy' will protec' you. Boh y' gotta give os someting – y' gotta pay-hay.'

It was a request for cash, up front.

'Y' don' pay-hay, y' nah goin' anywhere. Dey ten-thirty de whole deal,' he clarified, looking me in the eye.

'Right, I see. So basically we're hiring the vehicles from you?'

I was trying to frame this in the most positive light I could find. That was indeed the case. Security along the route needed to be paid for, too. I looked doubtful. Guinea, after all, was one of the hardest places to navigate in Africa. I had been informed by an old Africa hand before I left London that official scrutiny, and general suspicion of foreign visitors, did not end at the airport; rather, it began there and grew exponentially the further one moved from the capital. I could expect dozens of roadblocks if I travelled by car, all manned by bored, officious soldiers who more than likely would not have been paid on time, or possibly at all.

I put this to Joe, who asked to see my passport. I fished out the battered red book from a pouch behind my back, and half-heartedly proffered it to his outstretched palm. He flicked to my visa page, and pointed out, at the top of my visa stamp, two letters scrawled in shaky Biro: 'PR'.

'Do you ha' any trou'wo a' de airpor'?' he asked.

Nick and I confirmed that no, we had not had any trouble at the airport.

'Yor visa ha' been issue' by top bra' fro' way, way, way up.'

PR stood for 'President of the Republic'. The fact that our trip had been underwritten by the top brass in the president's office was a real shock: although it made our travels possible, it also made us entirely dependent on his favour. Joe told us that the 'modalities' would be finalised when he returned the next day, with a price 'fro' de Lady', which meant nothing to me. I nodded wisely.

Again, Nick pressed him for territory the rebels controlled, but he was vague and talked only of large areas and thousands of rebel troops. We concluded he simply didn't know.

'There's one other thing, James,' Frank added. 'Taylor is flying a couple of civilian helicopters, including an Mi-17 that's giving Joe's guys a lot of trouble – observing their movements, deploying militia behind their lines, that kind of thing. The LURD got lucky and managed to shoot one down with a twelve-seven last year as it came in to land. Nick might help them out with some training, teach them how to bring this one down, too.'

Nick smiled slowly in recognition. This might have been news to him, too. I blurted out the first thing that came into my head.

'Can I film it?'

As soon as the words were out, I regretted them. It sounded like I was endorsing the plan for Nick to train the rebels. I felt sick. Journalists did not take sides. They certainly didn't help shoot down helicopters.

'I don't think that should be a problem,' Nick answered, apparently thinking on his feet. We all slid around under the canopy of the umbrella to benefit from the shifting crescent of shade. 'We'll set up a decoy and prepare a simple rocket-propelled grenade ambush along the funnel that the chopper takes in over the target.'

Despite myself, I felt a surge of excitement. Perhaps I would get to film a mercenary operation in progress – that was almost unheard of.

What was apparent was that Nick was already part of the arrangement I was brokering with the Americans and the rebels. Trusted by Cobus and Frank, he was welcomed by them both. My lot was being thrown in with Nick whether I liked it or not. The fact that I was his boss, that I was responsible for his being paid, fuelled the uneasiness. Whatever he did in Liberia, I might, professionally, end up being accountable for.

I was standing at the threshold of what promised to be an actual scoop and it was too late to turn back: contracts had been signed, airfares paid, and fees were mounting. We all shook hands.

After Joe left, Frank filled Nick in on what the rebels were armed with, while I took notes. He thought they had another seven or so 12.7s (a large-calibre machine gun), in addition to the one they'd shot the helicopter down with, and a couple of (even larger) BZT 14.5mm anti-aircraft guns. What they didn't have were light support weapons – hand-portable, belt-fed PKM machine guns to back up infantry attacks. Instead, they relied solely on rocket-propelled grenades.

'We've got that locker out near the airport here,' Frank remembered, turning to Cobus. 'It's got a couple of PKMs and a shitload of ammo. We'll try and get that to them, keep them sweet. Anything to stop them complaining.'

I stopped taking notes. The Americans were interested in arming the rebels, however lightly. What I wasn't clear about was whether this was a personal thing between Joe and Frank, or agreed policy directed against Taylor. I phrased the question carefully.

'Frank,' I asked, 'have you been working with Joe for a long time?'

'Joe and his guys are okay; they're crazy but they know the deal. Man, Joe still frickin' owes us for '98. We pulled his ass out of the embassy in Monrovia before Taylor cut his balls off.'

Frank recounted the rescue of the Liberian fighters from the US embassy four years before – the same operation that Cobus had first mentioned to me in South Africa. Frank had played a key role in the operation.

'I loved working with Cobus and those guys,' he reminisced. 'Man, it was fun.'

That night I quietly recapped on my situation under the sagging web of my mosquito net. Within twenty-four hours the strain of responsibility had ballooned into a heavy burden of uncertainty. One concession had led to another: I had promised not to implicate the Guineans, or the Americans, in a war that they both supported; I had agreed to act as a *de facto* agent for US Intelligence, and give an as-yet-undisclosed amount of (someone else's) money as 'security' payment to a rebel commander; and I had agreed to allow someone in my professional charge to help shoot down a helicopter on the basis that I could film it. I hadn't even dared to ask about the weapons locker and the shared history with the rebels, or the Americans training Liberians on the island not far from our hotel. When I started out on my career eight years before, an enthusiastic graduate with a camera and an over-developed sense of curiosity, I hadn't imagined I would end up here.

One way of looking at it was that I was already fatally compromised. The other was that I was playing a difficult game rather well. So far I had not blown it, nor acceded to any demands with anything other than a nod. I went round in circles. My gut feeling told me Nick was okay, although I could not spell it out to myself in any way that really made sense. Drinking beers with him and making fantastical plans to shoot down Government helicopters was one thing – but physically walking into war side by side was another matter altogether.

The next morning Joe pitched up with a retinue of other, equally well-dressed rebels, and then quoted me their fee: $10,000, in cash, up front. I laughed. So did Nick. I sent Dudley and Mandla upstairs to pack their bags in a show of defiance; we were leaving if the price didn't tumble. Other trouble spots were flaring up in the news. Iraq was beginning to dominate the headlines, and Indian and Pakistani forces were trading heavy fire over their borders, seemingly in preparation for war. I'd go there, I explained. Anywhere. A story in India or Iraq wouldn't be an exclusive, but it might actually earn money. Cobus weighed in, assuring Joe that I really would leave. I also reminded him that the LURD's national chairman, whoever that might actually be, had personally invited us in.

Later that afternoon, Joe returned with a revised quote: $3,500 for vehicle hire for the duration of our trip, including all security to and from Liberia and unspecified 'expenses' for Joe. He had a deal. If I'd had to pay for private car hire, it would have cost about that much – and no one was going to hire me a car to drive into rebel-held territory. I called the production company, and then handed over a wad of US dollars – 'Dead presidents', as Frank called them.

Two days later, in the dark early morning, a Guinean Army truck and a new four-by-four roared up outside the hotel. It was time to leave. Downstairs, I was greeted by an enthusiastic Joe Wylie and a Guinean driver in military uniform sporting a red beret.

'This is Bengura,' yawned Cobus. 'He is the president's personal driver.'

Nick, who had shed his chinos in favour of a pair of long black shorts and leather hiking boots, stopped supervising the loading of our bags and came over to listen. I noticed in the red glow of the truck's side-lights that his calf muscle was disfigured with a knot of scar tissue.

'You mean the LURD chairman's driver?' I was both impressed and confused.

'Yes,' said Joe, 'he is Conneh's driver.'.

It was the first time I had heard the LURD leader's name spoken.

'Yes,' added Cobus, 'and he is the Guinean president's driver. You'd better be nice to him, though; he probably drives like a cunt. The Red Berets are their fucking elite troops, God help them.'

With that Cobus and I shook hands, and then embraced. He and Nick did likewise, laughing in Afrikaans. Dudley, Mandla, Nick, Joe and I crammed ourselves into the four-by-four while Bengura, who stank of alcohol, hauled himself into the driver's seat. I lit a Marlboro, and gave him the packet. A waving Cobus receded in the wing-mirror as the new dawn smeared the windows of the hotel a ruddy pink, and we turned our faces to the east.

Eighteen hours later we arrived tired and disoriented at the walled compound of the LURD rebels' headquarters in eastern Guinea. Young men in jeans and T-shirts milled around. Joe assumed an air of authority. Older men came out to greet him and then us, smiles and laughter all round. Except for a lone Kalashnikov propped up in the corner of the wide open porch, and the indecipherable crackle of a field radio, there was no sign that this was the main operations centre of a rebel army.

Nick unloaded our bags, and then nosed his way around the squat white bungalow. Plates of rice topped with fiery chillies and stewed cassava leaf appeared from inside. We ate, and I strung a hammock between two pillars either side of the veranda, rocking myself into surreal, mosquito-pestered dreams that dripped with insecurity and tension.

Nick woke me at dawn.

'Good morning,' he greeted me as I fished my ear plugs out. 'We're off.'

We piled back into the vehicles, joined in the truck by half a dozen rebel soldiers wanting a lift back into Liberia.

We were not driving for long before Bengura swung the four-by-four off the main road and into a large Guinean Army base outside the village of Badaro.

'We goin' pay our respec' to de garrison commanner,' one of the rebels who'd hitched a ride informed us. 'My name Oscar, an' I de liaison for de Lor' an' de Guinea Army.'

I shook his hand. Like all the rebels I'd met so far, Oscar pronounced 'LURD' as *Lor'*.

Dudley was holding a smaller, mini-digital video camera, so he could more easily capture our arrival in Liberia. Joe reminded us that filming in Guinea was not allowed. Seventy-two hours after agreeing to Joe's conditions for access to the rebels, I was faced with my first dilemma. I went round the car to Dudley. Leaning over next to him, while making sure that Nick and Joe were out of earshot, I re-tied my bootlaces.

'Can you get this?' I asked.

'Sure.' And then, 'Fuck. The fucking recording lamp is on.' A bright red eye on the top of the camera blinked at us. 'I'll have to put it over my shoulder and cover it with my arm. We'll get audio at least.'

Mandla lit a cigarette. 'All right, Duds?' he smiled, winking.

We all moved in together, following Oscar along dimly lit corridors until we reached an office where we were met by the rotund, sweating camp commandant. He introduced himself as Commander Lamine. Everyone shook hands and then sat down and looked at me. I had absolutely no idea what to say. Was it essential or forbidden to say who I was, what I was doing and where we were going? I looked at Joe, who looked at Nick, who smiled and looked at the floor. I took a breath, reminded myself that, in Cobus's words, I was not a normal journalist, and then repeated my sales pitch, this time in French. Commander Lamine looked at me as if it was the most normal thing in the world to have a journalist ask him for permission to cross illegally the border he was charged with guarding in order to film an outlawed rebel group, several members of whom were sitting in the room with him.

'Bravo,' he boomed. 'We are all brothers here, unified in our fight against the same enemy. We are thankful that our friends here fought bravely to defend us against Taylor's invasion of our republic.'

Everyone stood up to shake hands with him, or be embraced. I had expected to slip into Liberia under the noses of the Guineans, possibly with their tacit consent – not to be officially back-slapped across the border.

Dudley nodded at me – he'd got the audio on tape – and we were off again. From now on I decided that I would record everything, and delay my decision on what part of my word to keep until the edit suite. For the time being Nick didn't have to know what I intended. He was, after all, my employee.

The road deteriorated into a track at the point where a lone soldier lifted a bamboo barrier to let us pass. A ragged Guinean flag fluttered over his billet. We passed into no-man's-land. Minutes later a pick-up truck laden with armed rebel fighters careered towards us, the young men shouting wild greetings, waving their guns in the air. Nick scanned the bush that encroached on our vehicle intently as a wave of excitement washed me over the border.

We had arrived in rebel-held Liberia.

3
A JOURNEY WITHOUT MAPS

After an hour of sliding over narrow jungle tracks, the headquarters of the rebel army emerged from the bush. Voinjama had once been home to around 5,000 people, but now windows gaped like blind eye sockets; doors hung on their hinges like toothless mouths. Only a few hundred civilians remained, and most were connected in some way to the fighters stationed there.

I was ushered into the office of the rebel leader – a dark room in the corner of one of the very few buildings not severely damaged by fighting, neglect or the ravages of the environment. Nick was close behind me. As my eyes grew used to the gloom of the tiny space, I picked out several men with their hands outstretched in welcome. I didn't know whom to greet first. I had never seen a picture of Conneh – in fact, until twenty-four hours previously I wasn't sure he even existed. After an awkward shuffling of feet, a large, young-looking man in a grey double-breasted suit rose up behind a desk littered with walkie-talkies and old computer hardware, and an aide introduced him.

'I presen' Lor' Forces Nationa' Chairmon, eh Excellenceh Sekou Damate Conneh, J'ior.'

'You wehcom,' Conneh said. 'Wehcom to free, free Liber'a, so feel free.'

Like a well-rehearsed door-to-door salesman, I repeated my pitch by rote. I made it clear to Conneh that the outside world's extremely limited understanding of his awkwardly named organisation – Liberians United for Reconciliation and Democracy – was uniquely defined by his enemy, and almost all of the information about the LURD in circulation was lies disseminated by President Taylor's public-relations machine. Conneh grabbed the opportunity to put his own side of the story across.

'De people o' Liber'a mo' be free,' he assured me, 'an' de Lor' Forces a' foiteen fo' deh freedon, an' fo' peace.'

Unlike Joe Wylie, whose educated American drawl was comparatively easy to understand, Conneh and his cohort were extremely difficult to decipher. It was like doing a linguistic jigsaw puzzle – in forty-degree heat, with weapons, in the dark. When they spoke to each other, I was lost. My English was equally impenetrable to them.

'Y' mo' sho' dis freedon, our freedon, to de worl'. Cha' Taylah a crimina', a *liar*. We mo' bri' 'im to josteh, to *internationa'* josteh,' His Excellency continued. 'Milli-*ahns* o' people wi' see wha' Lor' Forces foiteen fo' on de BBC. *I*, Sekou Conneh, wi' bri' Cha' Taylah dahn – *personally*!'

Conneh, who, it turned out, had been elected to the post of chairman at the age of forty-two a mere six months previously, was by no means an intellectual. I knew from Frank that the chairman was thought to have been elected as a weak compromise candidate, but I suspected that even he realised that his personal position of power would be greatly protected from the vultures vying for his job once he had been established on-camera as the head of the rebel army, inside Liberia.

His manner was listless, his English coming in fits and starts, heavy emphasis randomly sprinkled throughout his speech. The only courtesy asked of me was that I would provide him, and other senior commanders, with interview questions in advance of recording. I was assured that no harm would come to me, my crew or my possessions at the hands of the rebels.

'Yor safe *here*.'

He opened his palms in a gesture that seemed to imply that I might in fact be safe only in his office. He immediately identified Nick, whose name he pronounced *Nack*, as a '*milit'ry* man', and invited him to stay for a closed meeting with several senior commanders to discuss upcoming strategy. I hadn't realised how seriously the LURD were going to take Nick and his mysterious military credentials – he was going to be a brilliant source of intelligence. It was also clear that any idea I had of being in control of Nick was unfounded: I was going to be entirely dependent on what he chose to tell me.

Outside, I took him to one side while Dudley filmed the growing chanting crowd of armed young men gathered by the chairman's office.

'Go for it, man,' I begged him. 'You've got to get them to agree to take us to the front. If we spend two weeks here, I'm fucked. We're all fucked. We've got to see some fighting.'

Nick took a long draw from a bottle of mineral water.

'By any means necessary,' I added, trying to make sure we were on the same page.

''n Boer maak 'n plan,' he said. 'A farmer always makes a plan.'

He passed me the bottle and paused to take in the scene of a couple of dozen dancing rebels. The refrain of their song was a simple one, led by a commander with a camouflage bandana and bedecked with AK magazines.

'Tay-lah da wo-ma' . . . Se-kou da man . . .', and then, at the finale, 'Monkay com' dahn! No mo' Monkay!'

'Taylah de Monkay,' the commander enlightened us, 'eatin' all de fru' at de tap o' de tree!'

Cheering followed, and then it started over again. Most of the rebels were in their late teens or early twenties, with a few younger children mingling with them. The older men wore a mishmash of different military outfits – mostly the dull olive green of Guinean uniforms, the darker tiger stripes of the Liberian armed forces or the universally familiar camouflage of British army surplus. The majority, though, dressed in homage to LA gangster-chic: heads were covered in bandanas; ripped jeans adorned with thick belts fastened by oversized buckles hung from skinny waists, and a collection of beads, amulets and bracelets hung from every neck. To a man they wore plastic flip-flops, which they called slippers. Many went topless, their sharply defined abdominal muscles criss-crossed with bandoliers of spare AK magazines, adorned with small Chinese hand grenades; all were drenched in sweat from the dance.

Nick shook his head, and pronounced judgement in Afrikaans. 'Vok.'

And with that, he ducked back into Conneh's office.

Dudley, Mandla and I stayed outside, introducing ourselves to the young fighters, who shook hands by clicking their middle fingers together after the main clasp. Everyone was polite, interested and armed. AK-47s were ubiquitous, with RPGs – rocket-propelled grenade launchers – scattered among them here and there. All weapons were handled with alarming nonchalance.

There was no sign of Nick for an hour, so we busied ourselves with filming the locals. Conversations jolted backwards and forwards, always involving a constant re-positioning of one's self away from the sharp end of an AK. My eyes were drawn to their safety catches, to see if they were set to safe (rare) or fully automatic (usual). Most discussions were shrouded in the earthy tang of cannabis smoke and uttered in half-pronounced Liberian idiom. Their reasons for fighting – or at least for joining LURD – were straightforward. Some of the older troops had fought against Taylor in the previous war and felt cheated by the ceasefire; others wanted to avenge the deaths of brothers, mothers, friends. Many were just bored. Most were hungry.

We weren't being threatened in any way – quite the opposite – but the situation was profoundly threatening. They looked like caricatures of soldiers; cartoon killers. Many confessed to spilling the blood of their own countrymen, and claimed they would do so again. Not having Nick next to me felt uncomfortable, and I peered at the HQ for signs of life – but he was locked in conference with the commanders.

When he emerged, two hours later, Nick brought us up to speed on the briefing. He announced that Conneh insisted that almost half of Liberia was now under rebel control. That was a revelation. Their furthest position south was in Bomi Hills, in a town called Tubmanburg – a day's walk from the capital Monrovia. Elsewhere there was serious fighting in the towns of Foya and Gbarnga. In Foya – only forty miles away on the Sierra Leone border – the Government was said to be using RUF mercenaries to brutal effect. Although the Sierra Leonean troops were all but surrounded, the LURD were unable to oust them: regular food and ammunition drops from Taylor's helicopter sustained them in the face of daily attacks. The thought of a well-armed detachment of the most notorious fighters in West African history breaking out of their cage and heading to the rebel HQ filled me with dread. It was one thing to ask to go to, and film, some fighting to prove the capability and intent of the rebels, quite another to hear that the enemy was two days' march away. I peered into the bush, as I had done in Sierra Leone a year before, searching for the same enemy.

Over the next three days I interviewed Conneh, who insisted his forces had the capacity to oust Taylor within a month; Joe

Wylie, resplendent in crisply ironed US military fatigues and a white T-shirt; Brigadier General Deku, the senior field commander who had led the chanting; and a plethora of other fighters, administrators, politicos, fantasists, civilians and stoned liggers. Everyone was confident of success.

Nick and I shared a room in a building across from the HQ – me in a hammock, him on a rotting mattress. At night we took anti-malaria tablets with a slug from a whisky bottle.

I remained apprehensive of him, and of being alone in his company. Although I had convinced myself to trust him out of necessity, I knew almost nothing about him, or his motives. He spent as much time with Conneh as he did with me, and when we were together – even though he was optimistic about the film – he said very little. When I could, I stayed close to Dudley and Mandla, who camped out in a room across the hall, and together we picked over the bones of the information we were harvesting.

It transpired that the LURD had been fighting the Liberian Government since late 1999, expressly and specifically, they claimed (tirelessly and repeatedly), to remove President Charles Taylor from power. 'When Taylah go,' almost every rebel had told me, 'we wi' lay dahn our weapon'.' No Taylor, no war: simple ideology, simple objective, simple cause. But from what the rebels were saying, the complicated truth was that the wars in Sierra Leone, Guinea and Liberia were the same war. Liberia was the rock thrown into the regional mill-pond, whose ripples drowned a generation of young men educated in violence.

The elections that ended the first civil war in 1997 and made Charles Taylor president were designed to make one government and one national army out of all the warring factions. Two of the strongest factions, ULIMO-K and ULIMO-J, felt excluded from this process of incorporation. Fearing assassination, they fled, re-grouped, reunited with some of their old comrades-in-arms and re-named themselves LURD. Membership was extended to anyone with a grudge against Taylor.

The LURD went from strength to strength. The president of Guinea used the Liberian rebels as firepower in 2000 to fend off an invasion of his own country by Taylor. Conneh was elected chairman: his wife was the Guinean president's spiritual adviser – 'the Lady' that Joe Wylie referred to at our meetings in Conakry. Under her influence the Guinean Army began covert support for the LURD, supplying them with arms and ammunition – and the advance towards Monrovia had begun.

I sat smoking my way through my dwindling supply of duty-free cigarettes, perched on the balustrade of our poured-concrete veranda. Mandla and Dudley lounged in their own sweat, struggling to digest the latest gift of boiled rice and stewed leaves. In the oppressive heat of the afternoon, despondency was taking hold. I had achieved what no other journalist had done so far – I had met the LURD, interviewed many of their senior leaders on tape, and crossed into rebel-held territory. So what? It didn't even begin to approach what a TV commissioning editor would want to see in a final programme. Warfare – so-called 'bang-bang' – on tape, at close quarters, was the only way to rescue the project: it would prove whether the rebels had the capacity to oust Taylor.

After three days of treading in ever-decreasing circles, salvation appeared in the form of the national chairman and his entourage lumbering towards our lodgings.

'Tomorro' y' wi' go to our territory in Bomi,' Conneh announced, looking at no one in particular. 'General Deku wi' carry y' all de way dahn t' Tocmanbur'. Tell de BBC we bringin' *dahn* Taylah!'

I would be allowed absolute freedom to film on the journey to Tubmanburg in Bomi Hills, and was given a typed, signed *laissez-passer* that guaranteed my freedom of movement and security throughout Conneh's sphere of influence.

The crisp letterhead was adorned with Liberia's Lone Star flag and a cartoon handshake superimposed on the national map. The logo was completed by what were supposed to be the rays of the sun, but looked like an air-burst artillery shell. Signed by Conneh, it was rounded off with a blue ink-stamp that read 'LURD'S FORCES'.

We were off the next day. It was official.

My excitement was short-lived. Deku, thirty-year old Brigadier General Musa Donso, the former ULIMO-K deputy chief of staff, whom I'd interviewed the day before, wandered over to talk to us. He looked wild, sweat clinging to his braids and fuzzy moustache. It was almost impossible to make out anything he said – the endings of his words were cut short, his accent confused further by an excited, emphatic delivery.

'Mah man, da plai' fa' o', hmm!' he confided. 'I' wi' take two week to go com' back 'ere. Boh we readeh, an' we are prepare' to move, no'-stap.'

Fourteen days to get to Bomi Hills and the town of Tubmanburg and back would take me right to the limit of our schedule. Deku explained the difficulties ahead, and why we too must be 'ready and prepared'. We would have to walk long stretches, and cross a wide river, so we could take only the bare minimum of kit – and only that which, in an emergency, we could carry ourselves. In the morning we would drive through Guinea to the Liberian town of Zorzor, before continuing to our jungle jump-off point. Nick – whom Deku also called 'Nack' – took the news with a smile.

'Strip everything out,' he advised. 'Take only what you need to film with, one set of clothes to walk in and one dry set to sleep in. I'll pack everything else.'

Dudley decided to leave the big Beta camera behind – it weighed a ton, and was not working properly in 90 per cent humidity. Instead we would rely on the smaller professional mini-digital video camera he'd discreetly used to record the meeting with the Guinean Army.

'What', I asked, as Nick bundled up our flak jackets, food and most of our clothes into the bags we would leave behind, 'shall I do with my balls of steel?'

'Wear them round your throat,' he suggested, 'then they won't rust when we cross the river.'

The next morning, just after dawn, I stuffed my one permitted bag into a pick-up truck, and wedged myself into the cab. Nick and the others were in the vehicle in front. It was no use – no matter how I twisted my legs, my knees were jammed tight against metal. The young guys around me smiled and tried to make space, but the front of the truck was just too packed with people. I retrieved the bag, walked to the other vehicle, and got in. I felt calmer. Joe Wylie turned up and complained that I had taken his seat. It was like being on a dysfunctional school trip. Conneh, cast now in the role of headmaster, told Joe that he should stop complaining and get in the other vehicle. I was beginning to like him.

We set off back towards Guinea in high spirits. Going to Tubmanburg was great news for me for other reasons: Taylor was using his helicopter in Foya, which was in the opposite direction. Our new schedule would hopefully remove the possibility of shooting it down. We arrived in Macenta for fuel and spares in good time. Weapons were kept out of view of the locals. Joe's truck was nowhere to be seen. An hour passed, and then we heard it careering through the gateway of the compound.

The windscreen had caved in completely, and the door panels cut into jagged tears. The driver's door opened, and blood spilled onto the concrete below: a man lurched out, his clothes, hands and face wet and red. The tailgate snapped down, more blood ran onto the floor. Joe staggered to one side, and sat down, deep in shock. As Dudley filmed, the story coalesced around us. A young rebel sitting behind the driver had accidentally pulled the pin on his hand grenade. He turned towards the window to throw it clear but it blew up in his hands, cutting him in half. His torso and legs had been dumped by the road. Pieces of intestine stuck to the grey faux-leather seats. The driver, now writhing on the floor by my feet, had his right arm and shoulder shredded with shrapnel. Nick bent over him, surgical gloves on, methodically tending to the wounds. Incredibly, no one else had been killed. Joe somehow managed to escape unscathed, his neat uniform spattered with dark spots of blood.

I watched Nick coat the man in iodine, and helped out with the other, lighter injuries. When he was done, Nick straightened up and washed the blood off his hands.

'Vok, he's lucky. Most likely he'll be okay. One of the kids was playing with a grenade.' He shook his head and looked at me, his disbelief turning to a smile. 'You're fokken lucky, too. You would have been sitting next to him.'

Joe took himself back to Conakry as we continued that night to Zorzor. The war was not 'out there', as I had been fooling myself: it was everywhere, all the time. I stared out into the black river of the road ahead. Nick's background remained an enigma, but his medical skills as sold by Cobus were not. The driver probably owed him his life.

Dawn in Zorzor broke with the scraping of rice pots and the excited banter of the newly arrived rebels. The rebel commander in charge was Prince Seo, the LURD's chief of staff. A former ULIMO-J fighter, he had been given the second-to-top job in order to promote unity among the former factions that made up the LURD. Most of the fighters and commanders were ULIMO-K Muslims from the Mandingo tribe. Seo was a Christian, from the Krahn tribe. His appointment was a sop to the Krahns, whose troops were desperately needed on the front.

Seo presided over a wasteland. A group of children kicked a jagged fragment of skull along the main street. The buildings were in a state of collapse. The few remaining civilians scavenged in the ruins of their houses for food, cutting wild plants. Even to my untrained eye, their babies displayed clear signs of severe malnutrition.

Seo also presided over an enormous arms cache. While the chief of staff was occupied in the radio room, Deku showed me the weapons, and allowed Dudley to film as they were distributed to his men for our journey to the front line. One locker was piled high with new AKM assault rifles, still packed in their factory grease and sealed in plastic bags. Tens of thousands of rounds of ammunition were stacked up in green plastic packets; rocket-propelled grenades, fuses and bombs, also fresh from the factory, lined the walls. All of it came from Guinea.

Nick was offered his choice of weapons. Turning them over in his hands, working the bolt in the breech and inspecting the working parts, he settled on an AK that was an older Russian model – more robust and with a better trigger, he said, than the newer Chinese-made ones. A folding stock meant it would be lighter to walk with. He removed and pocketed the cleaning kit from the stock of another rifle. He snapped a brown magazine into place, picked up another four loaded magazines for back-up and slipped a cut green plastic bag with a couple of hundred rounds in it into his haversack: that made about 350 bullets in all. He saw me eying the shiny brass cartridges tipped with small copper points.

'I'll get some more in the next town,' he said.

Deku prised open the lid of one large green box, to reveal an unexpected cargo.

'Missah,' he grinned, 'fo' Taylah helico'ter.'

Inside the box, two Strela SAM-7s – guided surface-to-air missiles – nestled with the battery packs and instructions required for use. They were serious hardware. In the right hands they were capable of bringing down a commercial airliner. The LURD had captured them from Taylor's forces when they had fought alongside Guinean troops in 2000, he explained. Even Nick was impressed. Although he hadn't mentioned anything more to do with shooting down the helicopter, he now had the tools to do it should we come back this way.

Nick dropped the safety catch on his AK by two notches, and snapped back the bolt with a *click-clack* familiar from just about every war movie I'd ever seen. Very slowly he put the rifle to his shoulder, and squeezed the trigger twice. With flat, ear-splitting blasts he sent the copper-tipped bullets into the soft earth ten feet in front of him.

He re-loaded the clip twice, so that a live round was chambered in the breech, on top of a full magazine – a maximum thirty-one rounds – and then we walked back to Seo's house, where we'd spent the last two nights. I was relieved that Nick was armed, even if the sight of him, unshaven, tearing up the dust in his long black shorts and T-shirt had looked more Mid-West Gun Club than elite Special Forces – but this was just part one.

The next morning Nick emerged from our room transformed. Gone were the shorts and polo shirt. In their place he wore full battle dress: British Army camouflage trousers, a light khaki South African Defence Force short-sleeved shirt and his old Reconnaissance Regiment webbing – stuffed with AK magazines, water, a small medical kit and his GPS. Wrapped in a plastic bag, poking out of his breast pocket, his notepad and pens were about all that I recognised of his former sartorial self. His

AK hung down in his hand, like an extension of his arm. I was in awe: a little boy surprised to find his Action Man had come to life.

We jumped into the vehicles and drove south. As we arrived in the village of Zolowo, an edgy LURD rebel fired an RPG into the forest. The deafening *bang . . . whoosh . . . crunch* of the launch and explosion caught me off-guard. I was trying to take this in my stride, to hide my nerves, though I didn't understand why they were firing at trees.

'Because the Government soldiers are scared of the bang,' Nick told me, 'and no one knows where they are.'

It was a bloody big bang. It scared me. So did the idea that the enemy was out *there*, somewhere.

Dudley and Mandla, meanwhile, seemed unfazed, their constant banter insulating them from the uncertainty that gripped us from one hour to the next. Dudley was especially pleased at having a captive audience to film. While Nick paced out the perimeter, we got to work filming a rag tag bunch of civilians: women who tended to listless babies and men who told stories of the jobs they once had, aspirations that got lost in the war. These people were scared as much by the nagging hunger pains in their stomachs as by the boom of the grenade launcher. Their situation was not unique.

There was no running water, no electricity, no healthcare, no separation of powers and no accountability by anyone to anyone. I could not see one house that did not bear the scars of war, and spoke to no one who was not desperate for something. The civilians gave graphic accounts of the brutality and rapine of Government soldiers; at the same time the rebels were requisitioning food from a population that had not planted a rice crop in three years. Others murmured that they were forced to haul ammunition hundreds of miles against their will. 'A kin' o' slavery', one rebel commander admitted.

The hamlet of Zolowo clung to the edge of the Liberian forest like a child tugging at the skirts of a distracted mother. We were about to step into a belt of equatorial jungle that had once stretched all the way from the Rift Valley to the shores of the Atlantic. Steam rose in dense clouds from the forest floor in the half-light of the pre-dawn chill. The civilians I had interviewed and who I'd assumed were refugees were, in fact, our porters, the 'slaves' forced to carry the LURD's ammunition to the front line. They lined up to be handed small, 100g bags of salt – a valuable and scarce commodity during the war. It was their payment for the long walk ahead. Dressed in ragged shirts and torn trousers, and shod in flip-flops, they loaded AK bullets, a mortar, rice, a goat and a small generator – amongst a hoard of other essentials – onto their heads and backs. They also carried my bags. I accepted it, and was cautioned to offer no payment except in cigarettes. I was learning to be a spectator, to mix what I knew was right with what I knew had to be done.

One group of rebels went up ahead, followed by porters, then us, followed by a group of women carrying children and bundles of cooking pots, and then a rear-guard of more fighters. Nick walked behind me, our footsteps crunching into the forest floor just out of step, so that his footfall came to me like an echo. He cradled his rifle across his chest, and as I looked over my shoulder he smiled and said simply, 'It's a nice morning for a walk, Mr Brabazon.'

The porters disappeared silently into the trees ahead of us. Like a grand expedition in the vein of Greene or Stanley, the scene had a timeless quality, as if the last hundred years had never happened. Only the occasional glint of gun-metal gave away the fact that we were on the threshold of a very modern war.

The forest took me in with no resistance. Wet leaves stroked me into an exotic land of deep shadows and animal calls; everywhere was impenetrable green; everywhere life stirred, just out of reach. Rank and earthy, the ground breathed a perfume of mulch and decay that grew stronger as the canopy leaned in over our heads. Gradually I forgot that Zolowo had been attacked two days before, and stopped looking for enemy soldiers. I put one foot down, and then the other.

After an hour, I became light-headed, drenched with free-flowing sweat. There was precious little sugar or salt in our diet. My muscles began to cramp. My knees were jolted painfully by the endless tree roots – some waist-high – that snaked into the woods like gnarled arteries feeding the dark tree trunks all around us. After only two hours, I was disturbed by hunger; tiredness had become exaggerated to something like collapse. It was impossible to march to any sort of rhythm. I waded through streams, my boots soaked and heavy, and climbed gullies slippery as glass. The rebels offered constant encouragement. 'Take time,' they would caution, if they saw me stumble, and then 'Sorry' (pronounced *sarry*) if I fell or cursed. If anything, they seemed embarrassed that it was such a long way to walk: this was not how guests were supposed to be treated.

Then it rained, and the rebels stopped while thick chutes of water cascaded down through the dense, oily green canopy. I sat down heavily on a swollen tree root, and peered cautiously into the dark undergrowth. I remembered we were near the war and shuffled closer to Nick. I handed him my water bottle, which he filled under a water spout falling from the trees and then handed back to me. I took a long drink. After half an hour the rain eased almost imperceptibly, and we walked again, as if marching in a boiling shower. The path had become a running stream, and my toes sprouted blisters.

Nick cleared his throat as we splashed along.

'You don't have children, do you?'

'No, man. I've got a girlfriend, Rachel. She's eight years younger than me.'

I wondered when I was going to see her again. *You really need to call her*, I told myself. She was on vacation from university, where she was studying English.

'I'm a very lucky boy,' I said, remembering how pretty she was.

'Are you going to get married?' Nick laughed.

I thought there was no reason not to one day.

'But, to be honest, I'm not exactly the best proposition right now. Look at me – I'm a disgrace!'

I was caked in mud, peppered by mosquito bites, and I itched furiously from the sweat running down my thighs. Swinging my legs over yet more deadfall, I asked after his family. He began to talk.

'I've got three kids, two boys, Nico and Jacques, from my first marriage. Nico's the eldest, just getting ready for technical college. Marzaan is my youngest – the one who calls me 'Tiger'. She's nine. When I got re-married I got a whole new family – a whole new life. I never thought I'd get married again, and then there I was, saying "I do" and getting two new daughters, my wife's children, into the deal. They're a bit older.'

Nick wanted to chat. So did I. His son, Nico, was a source of concern. First of all he'd wanted to join the army, but was now threatening to give up his college course for a dead-end job and a little cash so he could do as he pleased. Nick wanted stability for him, prospects. The new army was no good, all the fighting was done, a long time in the past.

'It's tough for young white guys in South Africa now. They've got this black empowerment to struggle with. No one wants to give them jobs, so they go abroad. We're dying out, man. It's finished for us, Africa is finished for us. When I joined up, I just went and did it.' He confessed, 'My old man was not very happy – he wanted me to go to work on our grape farm, but I wanted some excitement like all young guys. Of course, I thought I knew best.'

'Did he forgive you?'

'Ja, I think he was secretly quite proud. We had a general that lived on the neighbouring farm, and I think he told my dad about the Recces, what we were doing. It was a secret outfit then. Our bases were sealed, completely closed to civilians. Not even other soldiers were allowed onto them. When I came home on leave he'd bought me half a bottle of Red Heart rum, because he knew we drank that in the Recces. It was a huge deal for him to spend money on alcohol; he was very strict like that. So, ja, it turned out okay, but there's no real future for white people in the army now. It takes years to get promoted. It's all reserved for the new black guys, so most of the white people have left.'

Nico didn't want to go abroad. He was lost, and so was Nick as he tried to reason out how best to be a good father in a different world from the one he'd grown up in. When he joined the South African Defence Force in 1975, Southern Africa was about to go up in flames. Vast swathes of the continent, as well as his native South Africa, laboured under white-minority governments: South West Africa, Angola, Mozambique, Rhodesia, Western Sahara and Djibouti all denied black Africans equal political or human rights. Within months of joining up, Nick was at the spearhead of the South African Army's invasion of Angola, and his country's vigorous intervention in the political life of the continent. By the time he resigned his commission twenty-one years later, by then aged thirty-eight, the political domination of Africa he had been raised to accept as his white birth right had all but vanished. With it had gone his marriage and any certainty for the future.

He'd left his first wife and his sons as his career in Special Forces became ever more demanding. He was deployed to Rhodesia and then later fought in Angola, Mozambique and South West Africa. I wondered what her side of the story would be like: Nick, the absent father? Nick, the secretive Special Forces operator, never saying where he'd been, or knowing how long he'd be home for?

Nick had little to say about her, and nothing but praise for the dedication and fortitude of his new wife. He re-married while he was still in the Recces. Eleven years on, he still spoke like a man who couldn't believe his luck.

'She is a real woman, you know, very strong-willed. She doesn't take any kak, man. It's like having a *beautiful* sergeant-major at home.'

His voice changed when he mentioned his daughter, at whose gentleness and unconditional love he was amazed. From behind me his tender monologue – soliloquy, perhaps – drifted over my shoulders and into the trees until finally the pair of us lapsed back into silence.

I heard the River Via before I saw it – a deep, bass rumble that lifted at times to sound like the rushing of wind through trees. Its expanse was breathtaking – all the more so because we had to wade or climb across on improvised deadfall bridges. Too fast for boats, the swirling eddies of the current snatched anything that dipped into them. Suddenly, the enormity of the task facing the rebels revealed itself. Every soldier from the northern bases; every round of ammunition fired at the front; every pot used to cook on had to cross this river.

I took my boots and socks off, and somewhat hopefully rolled up my trouser legs. My bare feet slipped on the glass-like trunks of submerged branches, and were quickly cut on the blanket of sharp stones that littered the river bed. Almost immediately I was up to my waist in fast, angry water. Everyone linked arms where they could, but within minutes we were in disarray. One man lost his footing halfway across, and two cases of mortar bombs slipped to the bottom, leaving the rebels with only five shells.

A pallet of ammunition followed, as more men stumbled and cursed, and then one of our bags with medicine in it vanished as a porter went up to his neck in a deep trench. I suddenly felt weak in the face of the river, the jungle. I looked down into the ripples and held my hand out to Nick.

'Can you help me, please?' I asked. 'I can't do this by myself.'

Nick threw his arm out immediately. I fixed on the far bank, and picked my way along, his hand locked around mine. We waded to the bank and climbed out as Dudley, dripping, filmed us.

On the far bank we bumped into a group of LURD rebels returning from the front line. Lawrence Geedra, a lieutenant with shrapnel wounds in his legs, sat up on his stretcher and took a cigarette from me. His unit of thirty-seven men had been ambushed at Lofa Bridge, near to where we were heading. Seven had been killed, and four wounded. In the preceding week there had been another two ambushes, and six injured. The war was hotting up. A plume of blue-grey smoke twisted up from Geedra's lips. The stretcher-bearers shouldered their loads and then staggered into the lethal river, back the way we'd just come.

As we marched on, hacking our way through the bush towards the village of Kpawolozo, I felt an overwhelming urge to turn back and follow the injured men. I was walking the wrong way. I should have been following the wounded out, not re-tracing footsteps that had led to their demise.

I tried to distract myself with happier thoughts – nights out with Rachel and delicious meals in clean, cool restaurants. Eventually, I daydreamed of childhood. The soft Irish lilt of my paternal grandfather, Martin, comforted me in whispers and half-remembered phrases. He was an inspiration to me. He'd passed away two years ago. Sixty years before I set foot in the forest, he hacked his way out of Burmese jungle, retreating in the wake of the Imperial Japanese Army's victorious push through South East Asia. With few war stories of my own to recount, I told

Nick instead how my grandfather took his men across the great Irrawaddy River, with terrible losses. Comrades died as they marched, friends stepping over friends' bodies. Consumed with thirst, they drank fetid ditch water and sucked rusty liquid from the radiators of abandoned vehicles, knowing it would poison them. Military discipline dissolved. Their commanding officer was shot by his own men. Disease, exhaustion and injury crippled them all – many for life. Nick grunted politely to let me know he was listening.

'I mean, it makes you think – this could be even worse,' I suggested, slipping on the slimy tendrils of a half-buried tree root. 'He survived for weeks on end on nothing but his wits, pursued by the entire Japanese Army.'

'They were tough old guys, that generation. They fought a proper war. I wonder what they'd make of our friends here?' A rebel with spiky dreads and a radio with dying batteries playing wonky reggae jogged past us in flip-flops. 'They can move, though, that's for sure.'

My grandfather imparted his hard-won wisdom to the wide-eyed boy who sat, enthralled, at his feet. For hours I would listen to him, and to my mother's father, Don, as they talked modestly about their wars and their heroic though unsung adventures – in Asia and fighting the Germans in the deserts of Africa.

As I explained to Nick, it was from Martin – a professional soldier from one of Ireland's most respected families – that I first heard the word 'mercenary'. On three occasions he had wanted to fight as a professional soldier: in Spain in 1936; in the Congo in the early 1960s; and again in 1968, by then aged fifty-four, in Biafra. On each occasion his ambition was thwarted, respectively, by the lure of the East and the British Army, the demands of a young family and, finally, age and ill health.

The mercenary life ran deep in my family. Much to Nick's amusement, my grandfather's aspirations were certainly not without precedent – soldiering for foreign armies was in my family's blood. 'Brabazon' is the English version of a Frankish clan name that means, simply, 'mercenary'. By the Middle Ages, my surname became a generic word for a European soldier of fortune. It was with hundreds of our mercenary clansmen, led by my many-times great-grandfather Jacques The Mercenary, at his side that William of Normandy defeated Harold near Hastings.

By the time my grandfather set foot on the quayside at Liverpool in the Great Depression a thousand years later, dozens of family fortunes had been made and lost. Martin arrived with the clothes he stood up in, and an old violin. Boarding houses in the nation that had once been subjugated by his mercenary clansmen greeted him with signs that read: *No Blacks, No Dogs, No Irish*.

Exile was a family preoccupation. Another ancestor – Arthur Dillon – commanded an Irish Jacobite regiment in France. In what came to be known as 'The Flight of the Wild Geese', fourteen thousand Catholic troops fled *en masse* from Ireland to France at the end of the Williamite War in 1691. The Irish regiment bearing the Dillon name – which served in Spain, Italy and Germany, and fought on the American side at the Siege of Savannah during the American Revolution – helped to define the notion of the romantic mercenary in popular consciousness. When Irish mercenary officer 'Mad' Mike Hoare – whom my grandfather admired for being 'a wild card' – launched his most high-profile operation in the Congo in 1964, he named his unit 'The Wild Geese'.

In the early 1980s, when I was still a boy, the African mercenary action thriller of the same name was shown on television. I watched it as an exciting homage to my own family's bloody history and convinced myself that it elevated the mercenary to contemporary moral crusader. One crucial fact escaped me: mercenaries were not volunteers. If there was one episode of my childhood that distilled my ambition for adventure into a moment of clarity, it was Richard Harris running for his life along a runway, pursued by a bloodthirsty African militia.

Although it was clear from looking into the histories of mercenaries in the Congo that 'liberating the people' was often a thinly veiled excuse for military campaigns characterised more by murder and theft than by any humanitarian considerations, Hoare's real Wild Geese did at least save the lives of hundreds of civilians trapped by ruthless Simba rebels. And what Martin had sought – by wanting to sign up to fight in Spain or Africa – was to volunteer for causes that he *had* believed in passionately, not to find employment as a professional killer. The rise of fascism in Spain, and the wholesale targeting of civilians by the Nigerian Federal Army in Biafra, appalled his sense of what was just and righteous. A hugely experienced soldier, he believed he could make a difference, and regretted into old age that he had been too ill to fight.

Now I was cutting my own path with a real live mercenary, though what Martin would have thought of my bodyguard I wasn't sure. He had always professed a deep-seated hatred of apartheid and of the mentality that spawned it. There had as yet been no moment to ask Nick about his tenure as a professional soldier, but his past, or my perception of it, hung in the air between us. As an adult, my only actual experience of mercenaries had been in Sierra Leone with Cobus, where the little I knew about the victory of Executive Outcomes over Revolutionary United Front rebels made me appreciate how beneficial unleashing soldiers of fortune had been for an undefended civilian population. Cobus had spoken frankly about the dark side of his war, too. Of the few RUF fighters taken alive, several were tortured for information. That hadn't seemed to unduly disturb the residents of Freetown, though. Painted on the rear bumpers of taxis in the capital had been the legend: *In God We Trust, but EO is our Saviour.*

By the time I'd arrived in Sierra Leone in 2001, the country was in the shaky grip of the world's largest deployment by the UN: 18,000 troops had been deployed for around $1 billion a year. Militarily they had achieved no more, and often much less, than EO had done six years earlier. The mercenaries had been willing to do what the UN had not – pick sides, take casualties and use lethal pre-emptive force. Indeed, the much-maligned Blue Helmets were only able to deploy effectively *at all* after the British Army aggressively secured Freetown, mimicking in many respects what EO had done before them.

I felt buoyed to have told Nick something of my antecedents, and happy that what I had to say about conflict seemed to be of genuine interest to him. I was happy, too, that I was finally living the life of my grandfathers, whom I admired so much. I stepped onwards with a growing sense of pride in my own endeavour; but the line between the stories of my childhood and the reality of the civil war I was here to report started to blur. The rebels around me played the parts of the soldiers my grandfathers had served with; their war struck me as a struggle for liberation against an unjust, ignoble regime. I was using the dreams of my childhood in the same way I had when I was growing up: as an escape route – then from the disturbing legacy of my parents' marriage, and now as a respite from the violence I imagined was over the horizon.

That night I slept outside with the others, our bellies still empty after the meagre bowl of rice Deku had served us. The walk had drained me more than anything I had ever done and I was beckoned into a restless kaleidoscope of dreams, each one complete with a grand moral purpose – the young Great European Adventurer saving a troubled African country from itself.

More unconscious than asleep, I came to fitfully in the dead of night to witness a weird scene played out in the firelight. A group of young rebels, their identities hidden in silhouette, took turns to sodomise one of the porters in front of the fire. There was no noise, just a deep murmur of voices and the spit and crackle of burning greenwood. Then I slipped back into troubling dreams.

The next morning the march continued through villages and settlements freshly burned, some completely razed. What walls still stood bore the names of the rebels and Government troops who last occupied them: first we picked our way through the remnants of the rebel Wild Dog Battalion HQ, and then those of the Last Battalion, who had been reportedly slaughtered shortly before our arrival. The few civilians who remained greeted us warmly, breaking with us bitter kola nuts, which were eaten in traditional welcome. I scoured the bushes (in vain except for scraps of torn clothes) for the mortal remains of the Government's defenders – but it seemed that the jungle consumed the casualties with frightening speed and purpose. The villagers believed the souls of the dead lingered in the trees. It was not so much the Kingdom of Heaven as the Forest of the Damned.

As the day rolled on, the trees thinned and the canopy broke above us. Now we walked under a naked, burning sun. My knees started to buckle; Dudley was limping; Mandla, stoic and uncomplaining throughout the march, had shed most of the skin on his feet as giant blisters welled up and sloughed off into his shoes. Nick ploughed on, silent. Our walk had taken us more than a hundred miles towards the coast. As we reached the village of Fassama, we passed the wrecks of logging machines. Like dinosaur skeletons, the rusting remains of great Caterpillar half-tracks sprawled by the side of rotting mountains of timber – yet more evidence of Liberia's descent into economic catastrophe.

We were told to rest, and wait for the diesel (coming from Bopolu, a town further south) that would take us and two of the

LURD's very few vehicles onwards to Tubmanburg, and the front line. The porters, exhausted and half-starved, vanished into the village.

For two days we played cards, smoked and let Nick nurse our injuries. Nick coated Mandla's open sores with iodine, a small boy who hung around our thatched mud hut wafted the flies away with a switch of palm frond in return for food and clean water.

Eventually it became clear there was no diesel, nor would there be any.

After forty-eight hours, Deku announced that our departure would happen 'maybe soon'. Even the other rebels looked downhearted by this prognosis. Dudley shaved his head for want of something to do. I paced the floor with a growing sense of despondency. We still had no film.

Apart from their failing health, Dudley and Mandla posed another problem: they were only on the books for another week and it would take them that long to get back to Conakry, if they were lucky. Endless satellite phone calls were made to the production company in Kenya, and to South Africa. It had been our working understanding that, if push came to shove, their contracts could be extended. But this was apparently no longer the case. Dudley was due back at work at the South African Broadcasting Corporation, and nothing short of his resignation could have kept him in Liberia. I pleaded in vain for another week.

'It's just not possible, James,' our man at the SABC told me. 'Dudley would lose his job.'

'But I thought . . .'

My final protest petered out. What had I thought? That they would 'make a plan', as I'd been promised? The project was slipping through my fingers. I had been foolish not to see this coming from the outset.

Dudley became downhearted. He wanted more than anything to see the project to its conclusion. Yet he and Mandla appeared seriously injured by the walk, and it seemed to me that buried underneath their dissatisfaction at having to return home there was also a pervasive sense of relief. I didn't blame them, but I felt betrayed nonetheless, and nervous about the conversation I would have to have with the rebels.

In the end, perhaps sensing my agitation at the prospect, Nick volunteered to broach the subject with Deku. He stressed his own continued commitment to get to Tubmanburg, as Conneh – the LURD's national chairman – had promised we would. Deku agreed to appoint an escort team for them. A detachment of fighters would turn around and march Dudley and Mandla all the way back to Zolowo. I couldn't leave until I'd found a way to rescue the project. Nick, of course, would stay with me.

Dudley and Mandla packed their bags and readied themselves for the long walk back. Dudley gave me the professional Canon mini-digital video camera, twenty tapes, three batteries and a charger. This, with the addition of my satellite phone and charger, a tiny amateur Handycam, a pocket stills camera and a small tape player with a built-in screen, was the extent of my equipment. I stared at them like an illiterate gazing at the pages of a novel. I had no idea what to do with any of it, but there was no time for a lesson now. We embraced, and Nick bade them farewell in Afrikaans. Then Dudley remembered something. From out of his bag he pulled a small booklet.

'Here's the instruction manual for the camera,' he said as he handed over the smudged white bible. 'Good luck.'

4
SPIDER HOUSE RULES

'You're who? With what rebels? Where are you calling from?'

An incredulous BBC producer took the call. An hour later a BBC World Service presenter called me back to do a pre-recorded interview. Before we started, he wanted to get a couple of things clear.

'Can you talk freely? I mean, do you have a gun to your head?' He sounded genuinely concerned. 'Are the rebels forcing you to make this call?'

The satellite phone crackled. I assured him I was able to talk unhindered. There were, however, two things I did not want to discuss, for the sake of my own personal security.

'I can't talk about how I got into Liberia. I need to protect that route so I can get out again. The other thing is Guinea. I don't want to talk about Guinea at all. The rebels are very sensitive about it, about their relationship with Guinea. They've asked me specifically not to discuss it, and my security depends on agreeing to that for now.'

The presenter told me quickly that I could explain that myself, and began the interview.

'So how did you get into Liberia? How did you meet up with the rebels?' the presenter asked.

I flushed with anger and embarrassment at my own naïvety. I repeated there were some things I couldn't discuss for my own safety. Second question: 'President Taylor has alleged that the rebels he claims are attacking his government are backed by neighbouring Guinea. Have you seen any evidence of that? Where are they getting their weapons from?'

I was livid, but picked my way carefully. I had seen caches of brand-new weapons near the Guinea border, but had not seen any weapons physically cross the frontier. I repeated that the LURD claimed only to use weapons captured from Taylor: all that was true.

Eventually, the interview began to take a more benign course. What were the rebels' aims? Did they have the support of the local population? Did they intend to attack the capital?

When it was over, I hung up and felt immediately apprehensive. I realised I'd been shaking. Dudley and Mandla would not yet be out of the woods, and one slip could be enough to inflame the rebels. I was finally doing my job as a journalist. That would have consequences – I just could not imagine what they might be.

As the sun dipped beneath the tree line encircling the village, Nick and I switched on the radio and sat in silence with Deku and a couple of other fighters, listening to the broadcast. Distractions of any sort were hard enough to come by in Liberia. The radio was a particularly good one. At five o'clock every evening, without fail, the entire village tuned in to the Africa Service of the BBC World Service on a collection of tiny, almost-broken shortwave radios. It was a ritual I had observed wherever we'd stayed with the rebels. The *Focus on Africa* programme was the rebels' link to the outside world, and the main conduit by which they gleaned information about Charles Taylor's government.

As soon as my interview had aired, Conneh called me. He was full of congratulations. Deku offered me one of his precious

Ronson cigarettes (a rough local smoke that made Marlboro Reds taste like menthol lights) and shook my hand with joy.

'Jay, you' real journalis'! On BBC! Taylah wi' be cryin'!'

I had proved to the outside world that the rebels existed, that they were armed, and serious: suddenly, they were famous. Over the next hour or so, practically every rebel soldier in Fassama came and shook my hand and shouted my name – which they all pronounced *Jay*, almost completely swallowing the 'm' and dropping the 's' – as I sat and smoked on the doorstep to our hut. The next day I discovered I was famous, too. One of Charles Taylor's cronies gave a counter-interview, dismissing me as a rebel propagandist who had illegally entered the country to help their terrorist agenda. The rebels went wild. I was one of them. They celebrated a re-run of my initial interview with bursts of gunfire; village elders presented me with a carton of 200 cigarettes – worth a king's ransom in barter – in thanks for my 'effor''.

Nick was fascinated by the effect that the radio had on the LURD.

'Boetie,' he approved, 'that is fokken lekker.'

The radio had been transformed into a weapon, my weapon. Nick liked that, and so did I.

It didn't look like we were leaving Fassama any time soon, so Nick and I made home as best we could. We didn't have much to work with, though. We were shacked up in a stereotypical African rondel meant for an entire extended family – fifteen feet in diameter, with rough whitewashed walls and a thick rush thatch supported by gnarled hardwood beams. It felt cramped with just the two of us. There was one bed, which Nick insisted I have, and a simple wooden table and two chairs just right for playing cards. The thatch roof was a nesting ground for half a dozen spiders the span of my hand, who clung from cloud-like webs supporting thousands upon thousands of tiny eight-legged progeny. I dreaded the day when they would descend the walls and consume us.

'I knew this guy in the army. He got bitten,' Nick warned me. 'It was a strange wound and we couldn't figure out what the hell it was. There was this little circle of red dots, and the skin in the middle just wouldn't heal. One day, when we thought it was looking better, it just collapsed into a hole in his thigh, completely rotten. He nearly lost his leg. That's a fokken spider bite for you. Better leave them alone.'

In addition to the spiders, our hut was home to an iridescent blue emperor scorpion as large as a langoustine. It made a nest under the front step, and fraternised with the bunch of young rebels who hung around our stoop. They let it climb up their arms, and posed for photos with it. They found another one, smaller and black, and tried to make them fight. Sensibly, the two scorpions refused.

Night times were not much fun: I lay prone and damp in my sleeping bag, straining to hear the dry scuttle of the spiders and scorpions that wormed their way into my dreams. I got into the habit of banging my boots out every morning, and never putting my fingers anywhere that I couldn't see was free of venom.

Supplies ran low. We'd been on the road for two weeks. We drank the last tea I'd brought from home, stirred in the last sugar cube and opened the last tin of sardines. What little we had, we gave to the women who cooked for us. Our rice ration fell, and our stew arrived with either no meat, or worse, rotten meat.

Six days after we had arrived in Fassama, Deku took his AK off into the forest. He returned in the afternoon with a huge smile and an Abyssinian hornbill under his arm that he'd practically blown to bits. Its long, blood-soaked, gloss-black feathers had collected red dust kicked up from the village paths; its bulbous red throat-pouch sagged onto its breast. They can live up to forty years – when they don't meet rebel soldiers – a far longer life expectancy than the fighters that would now devour it. The meat, which was divided equally between me, Nick and the commanders, tasted like spicy lamb. Both mouthfuls were delicious. It was the last meat I would eat for two months.

Later that day, Nick, his patience tested by interminable games of gin rummy, organised some target practice. We fired his AK into a strip of corrugated zinc that we fished out of the ruins of a house on the edge of the village. I stuck on a piece of paper torn from my notebook as a target. At fifty yards, I managed to group my shots into a circle the size of a saucer. Nick, meanwhile, put most of the rounds through the same expanding hole. None of the rebels could hit the paper; most missed the four-by-three sheet of zinc entirely. In between shots, Nick explained how the rifle worked; how to hold it safely; work the bolt; move the safety catch; extend the stock. It felt heavy in my hands, deafening in my ears. Its simple function – to kill as efficiently as possible – may have been grotesque, but the power of it, and the rejection of compromise it promised, were undeniably seductive.

We returned the Kalashnikov to the hut to clean the barrel. As we ambled through the heat of the afternoon, Nick commented that I hadn't been a bad shot, that my weapons-handling was safe. He was impressed, and I felt absurdly proud.

'There's only so much you can do with these sights,' he said, pointing at the AK's open iron sights, set to their general combat position of 200 yards.

I nodded, but felt obliged to admit my weapons-handling hadn't always been so good.

As we reached the hut, I told Nick that I was well known in the South London comprehensive school I attended for my fascination with war. Aged fifteen, to my dread horror, I was given a semi-automatic pistol by a menacing gang of older boys. They wanted to know how it worked.

'I ejected the empty magazine very carefully,' I recounted. 'It sounds ridiculous, but I'd read how to do it in a book my grandfather gave me for Christmas. I pulled back the top slide, to clear the breech, and cocked it.' I mimicked the hand-action of loading a pistol as I had done a thousand times in my childhood games. 'And then – I still can't believe I did this – with the barrel pointing right into this group of kids, I pulled the fucking trigger. *Click*. They all laughed, but it was loaded.'

Nick gave me a sideways glance.

'Seriously. I pulled back the slide again, and a cartridge jumped out. It must have been stuck in the breech.'

I'd given the pistol back in silence. Perhaps they thought I'd done it on purpose. I wasn't certain it was a live round, but none of them ever bothered me again.

Back inside the hut Nick showed me how to field strip the AK. My hands fumbled with the unfamiliar parts. Before long I reeked of gun oil. I did it again, and again. It was fun. When I set my mind to something, I have a tendency towards perfection – an obsession that drove other people – Rachel for one – to distraction. Once I'd sussed it out, I tried with my eyes closed.

'How come you know the AK so well?' I asked, as proud of my efforts as any DIY enthusiast. 'I thought you used R4s and R5s in the South African Army?'

'Well, that's what we were issued with. They were good rifles, modified Israeli Galils which we made ourselves. But the guys we were fighting all used AKs, and we couldn't carry enough ammo on long-range patrols – so we started using AKs, too, and using ammo captured from them. It was much easier.'

Introducing me to the workings of the rifle proved an excellent way to take my mind off the heat and boredom of the village. And then it dawned on me. Nick was putting me through this drill because he thought I might need to know for real. In the event that we were overrun, or left to fend for ourselves, I would be expected to fight. At what point exactly, I wondered aloud, would things have got so bad that he'd like me to start shooting people?

'When your life depends on it.' It was an obvious answer to a question he clearly thought redundant. 'But you won't have to. Like I said, I'll make enough space for us to get clear.'

Nick's frankness encouraged me to ask another question that had been troubling me: if we were captured, would we be arrested or would we be executed?

'You should be okay,' Nick tried to comfort me, 'as long as the guys who take you don't get too excited. Once the Government have you, there'd probably be a show trial or something, like they planned with that other crew, and then you'd be released.'

He didn't stress the 'you', but the inference was clear: they might not shoot a journalist, but a captured mercenary could expect to be shown little mercy.

Evening settled on the hut; thin wisps of wood smoke curled up under the door and through the window, infusing our den with earthy incense. Our earlier conversation had been weighing on me.

'Nick?' He looked up at me from yet another hand of rummy. 'Were you ever taken prisoner?'

'No, I'd be dead. They didn't take prisoners.' He paused. I looked at him, expecting more. 'I had a very narrow escape once, though . . . in Angola.' He rearranged the cards in his hands as he spoke. 'I jumped in with my guys from Namibia. We used to HALO in from twenty-four thousand feet, so we'd land without them hearing the engines. The 'chute opens at about a thousand feet. No one knows you're coming. The target was a camp where they were training . . .'

'Was that SWAPO?' I interrupted.

'Ja. Actually, they weren't all that bad as fighters.' He put his cards on the table. 'We thought we had the drop on them by this kraal. It was evening, almost dark. You could just make out the outlines of the huts on the far side. One of my guys stayed outside, and two of us went in the kraal to surprise them. Vok, it was a trap. They were hiding in the bushes around us. The guy next to me went down straight away. He was hit hard. I jumped the thorns around the kraal and they shot me through the calf as I was running. The other guy was killed as well.'

'How close were they, how near when they fired at you?'

'Ag, about ten yards.' My jaw dropped. How could anyone survive that? Nick carried on, oblivious. 'I just kept running. Luckily, the bullet went straight through the muscle. I ran all night. Eventually, I climbed up the tallest tree I could find and waited for a chopper to come and get me. The pilot found me the next morning. Vok, there were too many branches above me to get close enough so he sat the Puma on top of the tree and crushed all the loose foliage at the top. Then he brought it in next to me. I jumped and the crew chief grabbed me. That's why I never wear a flak vest. You can't run with them, and so far no one has shot me in the chest.'

Later, I fell asleep to an imaginary gun battle, re-playing the scene as my imagination directed it, of Nick escaping as a hail of machine-gun fire erupted around him. It was time to accept that I was a little jealous of my bodyguard and his life at war.

In the morning – the third Sunday in June – I filmed a church service in the village, and was then asked to address the congregation. The pastor whispered that the people in the town were keen to know who we were, and what our 'mission' was. Liberians were punctilious about extending every courtesy to their guests, even potentially unwanted ones whom they had to feed, and I felt obliged to explain myself. The congregation was Pentecostal and enthusiastic, their singing and good humour weirdly at odds with the apocalypse that consumed the country outside. I gave a simple account of myself – emphasising that I wasn't a soldier – and told them I was here to tell their story. Everyone clapped. Someone said 'Amen!' I thanked the gathering of women and elderly men – dressed in their finest, or only, clothes – for their hospitality. They sang hymns, and I filmed some more. Then Conneh's press secretary gave them a lecture on the righteousness of the rebels' cause. No one clapped.

Outside, I shot a detachment of soldiers drilling, singing songs, preparing to move out to fight on the front at Gbarnga. I began timidly, Nick's advice about not straying too far from the hut uppermost in my mind: it was calm, boring even, in the village – but the enemy, as I couldn't help but think of them, could be squatting in the bush, watching every step we took. As I became more accustomed to using Dudley's camera, I slowly came to see the rebels for what they were. It was easy to dismiss them as a disorganised rabble, but in reality they had a strong sense of self-identity. The songs they sang, the catechisms they chanted, bound them tightly as a single fighting force. They took orders from a drill instructor – indeed, the mere fact that they were drilling *at all* was unexpected.

The fighters ignored me and let me move around them, taking whatever pictures I liked. Many of the rebels had been with us since Voinjama, or Zorzor, and they were getting used to me wandering around.

Feeling pleased with myself, I moved on to the village square, where I saw a man – a rebel fighter – being stripped naked and held down over a table. Other fighters gathered round and began to beat him savagely with canes and a hide whip. He was shouting, and I could see his muscles straining as he tried to lever himself clear of the table. I raised the camera and turned over a few seconds of tape before stopping. My gut instinct told me not to film. They looked over at me and said nothing, before resuming the beating. I left them to their bloody business and went back to the hut, shaken. The national chairman's guarantees notwithstanding, God only knew what they would do if they decided they'd had enough of me.

I found Nick back at the rondel, writing in his notebook.

'They're giving someone a hell of a hiding out there. They've got this guy pinned down over a table in the square.'

Nick looked up.

'I didn't film it,' I added quickly. 'It was quite intense. I didn't want to piss them off.'

I'd seen fist fights in London, but this looked more like torture. The guy didn't stand a chance.

'Ja, they have their own rules. African people is quite violent, sometimes. Deku was saying to me that the elders here have been complaining about the young guys stealing food. Maybe it's a punishment for them. They need the support of the people here or they're finished.'

I hadn't thought of it like that. He was right. The rebels could coerce and commandeer only so much. At a basic level, they had to have the support of the people they claimed to be fighting for.

'Best to stay out of their way. Keep around the hut,' he advised, 'especially when they get excited.'

I was finding it harder to distinguish 'good' from 'practical'. Liberia was a world away from the cocktail terrace where I'd first met Nick, and further still from life at home in Britain. The people I was now deeply embedded with were frightening and sinister. I'd always baulked at the idea that 'African people' were anything other than individuals, even though most of the Africans I'd met were either at war, or in a state of oppression. In Eritrea I'd taken photographs along the front line with Ethiopia as the tiny nation squared up to the massive losses inflicted by a devastating trench-based war; in Zimbabwe I'd spent weeks with opposition supporters, running the gauntlet of Government attacks and intimidation. Despite the fact that Sierra Leone had been on the road to recovery when I arrived at the end of the war, I'd photographed countless numbers of people terrified that the rebels may yet come back and hunt them down.

Liberia was different, though. There was no front line marked with barbed wire, no righteous opposition movement and absolutely no prospect of a peace agreement. I had no idea what 'ordinary life' in Liberia might look like, and there was no one to ally with except Nick.

Worse, I reflected that my sympathies towards the man being whipped had been tempered by my eagerness to film the event. Only later did I wonder what might have happened to him, and consider the justice of summary physical punishment. West Africa pulled like iron on the needle of my moral compass. I was struggling to keep it pointing true.

Over the two days that followed we made forays into the neighbouring villages – me with the camera, Nick with his rifle. The threat of attack was ever present. I had imagined that we were travelling to a front line, but in truth we were ourselves the front line. Every time the little bubble of our group – me, Nick and the rebels – percolated through the jungle, we risked confrontation with Government troops similarly on the move. This may have been the rebels' controlled area, but the forest was criss-crossed with dozens, hundreds, of bush paths and hunters' tracks, and it was impossible to guard them all, stop infiltration. We stayed only as long as it took to film.

I found the locals to be a curiously naïve bunch – urban, even – despite being isolated in the middle of the bush with no infrastructure to support them. I asked one old man, marooned by severe arthritis on an island of shade under a tree, what creatures lived in the forest. 'Tigah,' came his surprising reply. 'Dey very dangeros,' he added, unnecessarily. The rebels agreed.

'And what about the rivers?' I wanted to know. 'Are they dangerous, too? I mean, do they have dangerous creatures in them, like poisonous snakes?'

'Mos' de snek in de bush 'ere poisonos. One bweh, dey wi' kill you. An' alligator' plenteh in de swam'. Dey wi' ea' you raw.'

Nick smiled at me. Tigers and alligators do not live in the wild in Africa. The locals confessed to never leaving the paths in the jungle, and made obscure references, perhaps harking back to the slave trade, to 'white devils' that lived among the trees and snatched children.

In the village of Garbi – a collection of dusty straw huts clustered around a beaten-earth square – I interviewed Tetema Howard, a 48-year-old mother of ten, as she threshed the last of her rice with bare feet on a rush mat. She spelled out her predicament as she rolled the chaff and grains beneath her heels. She was living on the remains of a harvest gathered more than two years ago; her eldest daughter fled when Fassama was attacked six months before; she was the sole provider for her family, and had no land of her own. Seemingly oblivious to the stinging midday heat, her husband, ill, lay unstirring in the hut behind her. She told me, bluntly, that she was hungry. What, I asked, would she do when this rice ran out? She remained silent for a long time, her eyes searching my face for an answer. Eventually, she looked at the ground and murmured, in an almost inaudible whisper, 'I lea' mah ow' way Go'.' *It's in the hands of God.*

God Himself seemed strangely absent. There was no medicine, no clinic to go to, no one to turn to for help except us. Nick gave out quinine tablets for malaria, strapped up long-broken limbs and distributed the last of his precious boiled sweets to the children that tugged at our sleeves as I practised how to film. Many of the younger ones had not seen white people before and stared at us amazed, before plucking up the courage to touch us, or, more commonly, hide in terror. I smiled a lot, and a little of the romance of Great European Explorer returned – something to cling onto, absurdly, in the face of the rebels' increasing amorality.

All the time Nick scrutinised the bush around us, took GPS readings of paths and villages, and stayed carefully out of camera shot. In the evenings I played the pictures back on the mini-VCR, and decided I was just good enough, professionally speaking, to shoot the film I was here to make. We were starting to carve a routine for ourselves. Every morning, at ten to nine, Nick and I sat glued to the morning's classic serial: Robert Graves's memoir of the Great War, *Goodbye to All That*. Not only was it a cracking yarn about hope in the face of overwhelming odds, it reminded us that, however bad our life seemed in the Spider Hut, it was luxury compared to the privations of the trenches.

I was surprised to find that Nick had a very different view of the First World War from my own. Whereas the horror of that conflict had been drilled into me at school, it did not figure highly in the collective historical consciousness of Afrikaners. Instead of the mud of Flanders, for Nick and his countrymen the twentieth century was christened by the blood of the Second Boer War.

'Those guys', he opined, 'really knew how to fight. You could really learn something from them.'

He propped his AK against the wall, and sat naked to the waist on his sleeping bag, swatting mozzies, chatting the day away. There was nowhere to go. Enthralled by the account given by Graves, Nick first questioned my attitude to the First World War, and then we turned our attention to the Second Boer War – what he called 'the English War'.

Between 1899 and 1902, a ragtag collection of sharp-shooting Afrikaner farmers (or *Boers*, in Dutch) and local black Africans took on the might of the British Army, and at first won convincingly. Arguably the world's first modern war – a total war – the fighting saw two new forms of tactics crystallise. As the British retaliated, concentration camps were built to house Afrikaner civilians, tens of thousands of whom died of malnutrition and disease; crops and farms were burned in an unrelenting scorched earth campaign that deliberately targeted the families of the Boer fighters; and prisoners of war were exiled by the thousands. The battles left the free Boer Republics of the Transvaal and Orange Free State crushed. Hitler and his generals would study the tactics of the British in South Africa closely, and employ them with even more murderous enthusiasm a generation later.

On the Afrikaner side the soldiers of the Boer Republics pioneered, then perfected, a new form of combat in response to the overwhelming force they met from a regular army: it was to them that Nick traced his military heritage. Each Boer community had formed its own irregular unit known as a Commando. Because these men shot animals either to eat, or in self-defence, they knew how to make every shot count: for the khaki-clad farmers, it was a lot easier sniping British soldiers than it was hunting antelope. After the Republics were occupied, the Boers fought a devastating guerrilla war. They targeted water treatment plants, railways, bridges – practically any aspect of the infrastructure vital to the British occupation they could disrupt or destroy. Hundreds of British troops were killed, or humiliated by capture at the hands of irregular fighters. The poor farmers of the bushveld had transformed themselves into the first modern guerrilla army. In his gun cabinet at home, Nick told me with pride, he still kept his grandfather's old Mauser rifle – the iconic weapon of the Boer Commandos.

As Nick saw it, the resentment the British campaign engendered in the Afrikaners lit the fuse of Boer vengeance. It led to the foundation of the Afrikaner Broederbond: a secret, exclusively white, male Protestant organisation dedicated to the advancement of Afrikaner interests. Its philosophy was born out of the deep conviction that the Afrikaner people had been planted in South Africa by God Himself, destined to survive as a separate 'volk' with its own calling. The traditional, deeply held religious convictions of the Calvinist Afrikaners gave their struggle an aspect of Christian predestination that led to a quest to free the whole of South Africa from the English-speaking British and secure its future in the hands of Afrikaans-speaking whites. The consequences that would have for the country's black and mixed-race inhabitants were immaterial.

The original drive for independence from the British that had in part prompted the Boer Great Trek into the interior from the 1830s had joined to it a new impetus for total independence under a Nationalist government. Together they formed a kind of Christian Nationalism that dominated South Africa until 1994. When Nick was growing up in the '50s and '60s, apartheid wasn't just a unique political idea, it was a religious certainty.

Finding ourselves united despite a century of mistrust and resentment was not inevitable: Afrikaner opinion of the English at times echoes stereotypical British attitudes towards the Germans. It felt like ancient history, but my great-grandmother, who helped raise me, had been twelve years old when the Boers surrendered. She never forgave them for unsettling Queen Victoria's last months on the throne. Nick laughed.

'I served with a lot of English guys from Rhodesia in the Recces,' he told me. 'They were good, they knew the terrain we were fighting very well and all the tricks the terrorists would use.'

'Did they have to learn Afrikaans?'

The language was perplexing, though its guttural intensity seemed somehow fitting for barking orders.

'Yes, but we had to learn English, too. That's how I learned to talk it properly. The army would switch between English and Afrikaans on the parade ground: we'd do one month on, one month off. What we spoke to each other was mainly Afrikaans, though. You could use any language with your friends.' Our breakfast had arrived late: rice in water with a sprinkling of dried milk powder that the rebels hopefully called 'ride pudding'. It was a cruel disappointment. As we sat at the card table licking the plates clean, I wondered if Nick had a lot of foreign troops in his unit. It was a history that I knew almost nothing about.

'In Special Forces it was a bit different. My regiment, 5 Recce, was reorganised in 1980 with a lot of Rhodesian SAS. We had Angolans, and some guys from Mozambique, too. There were a few Portuguese officers – most of them came over in '75 from Angola. There was this one guy who was really great, from the Portuguese Hunters, but he must have been in his late forties. He was on my selection course. He did everything great, but he just couldn't do the last run. Vok, if you didn't cross the line at six o'clock, you were out. We dragged him the last bit, and pushed him over a wall. He just made it. By that time we were all nearly dead on our feet.'

I asked him if he had any black troops in the Recces. His eyebrows shot up. Maybe he worked out then how little I really knew about his world.

'Most of those foreign guys were black,' he said, 'with only a few whites.'

I was shocked: I had imagined that the apartheid state's shock troops would have been composed uniquely of blond-haired, blue-eyed Afrikaner boys.

Our conversation was posing a lot of questions, most of which I did not know how to ask.

'No, man. We had apartheid, but in Special Forces, we were far ahead of the rest of the country in terms of race relations, and equal pay and what-not. I had black South Africans in my Commando, too. At the end there were quite a number in the junior ranks. When you're fighting like we did, you have to know the guy behind you is watching your back whether he's black or you're white or whatever. At first, though, there were hardly any of us, anyway. When I passed selection my group took the total number of Recce operators in the whole army up to twenty-four. We had a totally different life from outside. We were relying on each other in battle. You couldn't have any of that political shit getting in the way. You had to trust them. Some of them were good fighters, especially the Angolans.'

We sat as still as possible as the day heated up, me with a cigarette constantly at my lips, Nick lying prone on his mattress unpicking the threads of his life, which took him from a smallholding to the battlefields of Southern Africa. Nick grew up a farmer's son in Lydenburg, to the east of Pretoria, and imbibed a sense of national identity that was as casual and unthinking as drinking water or breathing air.

'I spoke Afrikaans, only Afrikaans.'

When he talked about his mother tongue, his accent seemed to pitch and swell with his rendition. 'A's became harder, 'r's rolled out of recognition, 'u's sounded almost French.

'Then I started to go with my dad to the market to help him sell the things we had on the farm. At first I was completely fokken lost because there were people there who only spoke English, the people who were buying. I learned a bit, and I got quite good at it, and helped my dad, who didn't understand a word.'

As he grew up, the fact that the races were separated (and non-whites oppressed) under the system of apartheid was a given fact, and criticism of it remote and unthinkable – not because it was beyond criticism, but because there was nothing to compare it with. The Government strictly controlled the media: no Afrikaans newspapers criticised or even questioned the system of apartheid until well into the 1980s; there were no independent radio stations; and no television whatsoever until 1975 – the year that Nick joined the army.

'You see, it was like this,' he went on, in an effort to explain. 'We had some trouble with these black kids who belonged to the guys who worked on the farm. They'd been stealing small stuff, and I managed to get hold of one. My dad and I didn't have a clue what to do with them, so we took the boy to his father. He thanked us and said he'd deal with it. Vok! He put him in a grain sack and suspended him from a beam in the barn. Every time he walked past he gave him a right moering with his belt. And he was a big guy.'

I looked over at him in the sweltering hut. He still looked impressed at the memory.

'They just did their own thing. They were good people but, *man*, they were tough. Our lives were just . . .' He searched for the word in English. '. . . *different*. We didn't have any problems back then.'

Nick's words hung between us. It was as if he was pining for a simpler time, an illusion unburdened by the weight of history.

Our conversation petered out into the lethargy of another hot afternoon. I sat and smoked. Nick became withdrawn; I wondered if he regretted talking with me about the army, about his life. By that evening, he'd hardly uttered another word. I feared I'd offended him in some way, and kept my head down. Absorbed in turn by the camera manual and a private game of patience, I'd not paid attention to his comings and goings. I lit our Charles Taylor lamp at dusk (a rudimentary palm-oil lamp, so called because the villagers said the president had left them with no power and no other lights; you couldn't even buy a candle) and peered at him hunched on the floor between the jumping shadows thrown up by the dirty orange flame. His eyes looked sallow, his face waxy in the flickering light.

'You okay?'

'I've got dysentery. Quite bad cramps. Ja, it's a bit . . .'

He tailed off. I stood up and gathered up my sleeping bag.

'Here, have my bed. It'll be much more comfortable for you.'

He didn't protest, and I knew at once he must be in pain.

'Ja, thanks. I'll be okay in the morning.' He looked unconvinced. We both knew that was a lie. 'Vok!'

He got up abruptly and staggered out of the doorway into the humid twilight. Our latrine was on the edge of the village about fifty yards away.

That night he ate nothing, and ducked in and out of the hut a dozen times. I looked with new eyes at the rancid stew we'd been given. Suddenly it seemed the most potent threat to our survival. It was time for antibiotics.

'Do we have any Flagyl, you know, metroni, er, what's-its-name?'

'The metronidazole and the cipro went in the river.'

Nick was impassive. We had no tablets to treat him with, and no rehydration salts to drink, either. I poured him a cup of purified water from the gravity-feed filter he'd carefully set up when we arrived. A few minutes after draining it, he was out the door, mumbling in Afrikaans.

If the order to move came in the morning, we were in trouble. For days I'd been desperate to leave; now I craved time for Nick to recover.

The next day saw Nick slide further into the fog of his illness. His temperature jumped, the cramps worsened. All conversation stopped. I gave him water as often as he'd take it. He sipped at the cup distractedly. There was neither salt nor sugar with which to improvise an electrolyte solution. At regular intervals he convulsed in agony.

'When you, er, *go*, man, er . . . what's it like?'

At first we had lived alongside each other almost gingerly – always respectful of each other's space and privacy. Now all bets were off. I wanted to know what his excrement looked like, to help gauge how ill he really was – but it was hard to ask outright.

'It's just fokken water. And pus and blood.'

There was not much more to say. I sat and played cards. Deku came to see how Nick was, and looked concerned. He looked up to Nick as an 'ol' sol'iah' and was shocked to see him prone on my bed, for once unsmiling.

'Sarry,' he offered, dumbfounded, and asked the women who cooked for us to put extra hot peppers into our food to help 'kill de bug'. Later that evening he reappeared with a boiling cup of herbal infusion. Nick drank it. I guessed we both thought the same: it couldn't do much more damage. He dozed off in between shivers and lurching for the latrine.

By the third day, Nick was unspeaking and unmoving. I called the production company and explained the situation. They suggested getting a doctor to phone me for advice, but Nick *was* a paramedic. The truth was there was nothing to be done.

'Good luck,' came the sign-off.

I hung up, and sat on the scorpion step outside the hut and smoked. I tried to keep calm. I could keep giving Nick water to drink, but he would need a drip if this didn't lift immediately. I'd seen it done dozens of times in Zimbabwe when I'd lived for a short time in a bush hospital out in the boonies. We had the right needles, tubes and saline in our kit to do it; but mess it up, and I could kill him. If air got into the giving set, it could trigger a massive heart attack. I walked back into the hut, and peered at Nick in the sweaty gloom. His face was set like a mask, his body completely still.

'Nick?'

Nothing. I put my hand on his shoulder, and rocked him gently. His body felt heavy and unyielding. His eyes didn't flicker, the lids hardly closed. I shook him harder. Everything became very quiet, all the background rattle and hum of the village draining from the bubble of stillness emanating from around his bed. I spoke his name again, louder, and put my hand on his forehead.

He was cold, waxy; a fine layer of cool moisture clung to my hand. I was convinced he was dead.

My first thought was this: *how will I get his body home?* Thereafter, my mind raced with logistical conundrums. I didn't even know whom to call. I had no idea what his wife's number was. I felt nothing. The situation was overwhelming; it paralysed any emotion. I stepped back, and took in the scene – his body facing away from me, curled up in the foetal position on my mattress. It burned into my memory, a disturbing photographic negative.

For the first time since leaving London, I was entirely alone. I was by myself in the middle of a malarial swamp surrounded by mad Africans in a country governed by a psychopathic president. The only way out was a week's walk through dense forest, and swimming a river that would be even higher than when we first crossed. I had the physical reserves for neither. Anyway, that would only get me to the border. Home was another world away. Outside the window, the evening collected sounds of cooking and women laughing.

I swore into my hands. Nick was dead. What had begun as an adventure was ending in tragedy – farce, almost. Weird thoughts flooded in – a boat trip as a child with my grandparents in Arundel; Nick's old Mauser rifle unclaimed in Pretoria; my car parked at home in Canterbury. And then I remembered with a jolt what a doctor had told me in Zimbabwe, that it can be very hard to tell if people were actually dead or not, even for a trained medical professional.

I leaned in over him and looked at the open V of his shirt. I concentrated hard on his chest. At first I saw only a blur of hair and pale skin. I thought about the drip, the saline, and dismissed it again. I wiped the sweat out of my eyes, and then saw an almost imperceptible movement in Nick's chest. I thought it was my own body that was shaking, rocking my vision. I squinted at his thorax, and lips, and then back to his sternum. He was definitely breathing. I exhaled hard and slumped on the floor, resting my back against the metal frame of the bed. On cue, Nick straightened his legs and groaned in his sleep. It was probably another cramp. *Nice one, Tiger*, I thought, *keep kicking*.

I sat up that night and watched him. He hardly moved. At dawn the palm-oil lamp guttered out and his fever broke.

The next day he was walking again, and managed to spoon a thin pepper soup between his cracked lips. His recovery was startlingly swift, and we began to dissect his ailment in gory detail. He seemed to take illness for granted in the way that someone does who has endured worse, and knows he'll recover.

'Has this ever happened before?'

'Ja, but I haven't had it that bad since 1985 in Zimbabwe. We were on this undercover raid, and I was completely gevok. It hit me like a hammer out of nowhere.'

'Zimbabwe? Whereabouts? I loved it there. I was in Harare, and also in Murambinda, out in the sticks in Buhera.'

'Harare, and the bush. We were planning to hit some terrs there; they had a base in Zim, which they used for attacks over the border in South Africa. The war was quite active then.'

By 'terrs', he explained, he meant 'terrorists' – ANC activists commonly referred to by most of the people I'd grown up with as freedom fighters, or guerrillas, in black liberation movements. By 'war', I knew he meant South Africa's mounting onslaught against her neighbours, which sought to destabilise their governments and eliminate these so-called terrs. I was still too relieved by his recovery to be shocked, but the revelation was clear: Nick really hadn't been a regular soldier. He was a very specially trained operator. In some people's eyes the raids like the attacks on Zimbabwe would make him an assassin, a murderer even – or at least an accessory to murder. This, he told me in between diminishing stomach cramps, was what his unit, 5 Recce, was best at, in fact specifically designed for: unconventional, counter-revolutionary warfare. That was one of the reasons why it contained so many black troops.

'I was one of the founder members of 5 Recce,' he said with transparent pride. 'Eventually, we divided into three Commandos and a Small Teams section. I started off in One Commando – which was dedicated to pseudo-operations. When I became too well known for that, in '78, I moved to Five-Two as the second-in-command – they were more conventionally operational, with a lot of those Portuguese and Angolan guys mixed in. Eventually, I ended up as the commander of Five-Three, which was an offensive unit mainly made up of Rhodesians. They were good guys.'

Pseudo-operations became regarded as among the most controversial carried out by the South African Army. The tactics had been learned from Rhodesian Selous Scouts after being pioneered by the British in Kenya during the Mau Mau uprising. Special Forces operators, posing as enemy fighters, lured members of the armed resistance into death traps. In Rhodesia, local white pseudo-operators were said to have attacked black *and* white civilians to spread fear and turmoil – portraying the liberation movement as bloodthirsty murderers in a bid to manufacture justifications for even more draconian military crack-downs. Always careful to maintain that he personally had been a conventional soldier fighting an unconventional war, the real implications of Nick's past remained hard to grasp.

His men searched buildings suspected of being terrorist bases, shot whoever was inside, gathered evidence and then blew them up. He spoke about it matter-of-factly, and – despite the terrible history it recounted – occasionally with humour. It was on a similar raid that Nellis (the gunship pilot I had met in Sierra Leone), having picked up a bunch of Recces fresh from a Commando raid in Zimbabwe, landed his helicopter unexpectedly before crossing the border back to safety. To the amazement of his passengers, Nellis got out of the cockpit and urinated copiously. 'I just 'ad to 'ave a piss on Bob's Zimbabwe, eh?' he'd cackled on the beach at Freetown. Nick smiled, but didn't comment. I'd noticed he'd never named anyone when talking about his army days.

As careful as we were to respect each other's privacy, and personal space, we had not questioned each other's beliefs about anything more complicated than our daily survival. Nick's illness, and these revelations, collapsed that space into a vacuum. Now I knew what Nick might look like in death, and that he had (definitely) killed people while he was in the service of the South African Government. This last point seemed obvious in retrospect – but it was one thing to assume it, another to be told it for certain. I'd known, of course, that at some point I would have to confront Nick's past, however ugly it was, and try to come to terms with it. Despite our earlier chats, I'd been putting it off. My upbringing was clear about it. The apartheid government of the 1970s and '80s, and those who supported it, were treated by my family, friends and school teachers with the same moral disapprobation as the Nazis. Zimbabwean independence, celebrated in 1980, was my first political memory.

'Apartheid served a purpose,' he said, simply. 'It put us ahead of the other African countries.'

I was disarmed by Nick's honesty. I had expected him to hide it, like a dirty secret, or at least make excuses. Instead, he seemed proud chatting about it, apparently without any idea of the symbolism his career had for an outsider like me. Killing 'terrs' had been his profession, and in his eyes it was a noble, necessary enterprise. There was no easy way out of this conversation. I tried a different tack.

'Do you believe in God?' I asked later that evening, trying to fathom the depths of his cultural beliefs. 'I mean, were your family religious?'

'Ja, very. But, ag, you know . . . Who knows? There's definitely someone up there. But I'm not ready to fokken meet Him just yet.'

I laughed as he went on to say that he had no truck with the idea of apartheid being somehow sanctioned by God Himself. He'd seen enough people blown to bits to know that they were all the same on the inside.

It was a testament to human individuality that Nick, the product of a small, conservative, white settler farming community, was not a rabid racist. In fact, he never used racist language; he never appeared to judge people by their colour alone; and I'd never heard him use the word 'kaffir' (or 'nigger', its rough English equivalent).

I wasn't looking for reasons to excuse Nick of anything – but I thought I wanted to understand him. We were going to be together for a long time – for weeks, at least. But in that hut, in the glow of the lantern, as Nick came back to life and I struggled with my own physical and mental exhaustion, I gave up trying to judge him. Seeing Nick prone and helpless had helped to fade my earlier awe of my own GI Joe; in its place familiarity bred not contempt, but respect. Nick was who he was, and nothing would change that, certainly not my political misgivings. He had a right to his past; he'd fought for it, whatever I may think of it.

Over the following day Nick's cramps dissipated, and colour came back to his cheeks. He pulled his camouflage trousers on, and returned from a short visit to Deku with another two AK magazines and a few small boxes of ammunition. He was better.

Twenty-four hours later, on 23 June 2002 – the day Nick and I were originally supposed to have finished filming, and be settling into a flight back to Johannesburg – I sat shivering on the floor. I drew the sleeping bag around my shoulders as my teeth chattered out a tattoo in the muggy heat of the mid-morning. By the evening, my body had ejected everything in my stomach.

'This isn't going to be a lot of fun, is it?' I stammered.

Nick nodded in careful agreement, helping me back onto my old mattress. We traded places. He made himself a nest out of his sleeping bag on the floor beside me.

'Ja, it's the fokken cramps that does it. Take these.'

He rummaged through our surviving medical bag, and handed me tablets to ease the spasms we both knew were coming. That night I staggered to and from the latrine, while rebel guards barked out warnings.

When the cramp finally arrived it hit me like a chainsaw in the guts. By the morning, my anus was oozing blood and mucus. I sipped from the cup that Nick held out to me, and drifted in and out of sleep.

In the darkness of the following night, the guards shouted more vigorously as I left the room. One chambered a round in his rifle.

'It's me – James,' I hissed into an infinity of shadows. *Fucking shoot me*, I thought, *anything to end this*.

By the small hours, I could no longer walk. Monsoon rains lashed the thatch and walls of our abode. I crawled to the door of the hut and let my backside hang out over the step, my body balled up in a soaking knot of skinny limbs and aching muscles, serenaded by hundreds of frogs belching in the dark. I was, literally, shitting on my own doorstep. Nick closed the door behind me as I crawled back in.

After dawn broke, I drank water, and immediately cramps rolled up and down me like a tide of razor blades washing through my intestines. Without any of the strength acquired by Nick from his military training, my body surrendered. Nick picked me up, hauling my arm across his shoulder, and drag-walked me to the ruins of a house a hundred yards away. He held me up by the wrists as I squatted over a pit and purged myself until I thought I would pass out.

All day he ferried me to the house and back, helping me to undress, explaining to the rebels what was wrong. 'Sarry' they would say in unison, and offer me cups of unfiltered well water. It seemed ridiculous that only hours before, I'd been contemplating Nick's political rectitude. Once a man has held you up while you take a crap, little else matters between you. Either you are mates, or you are not.

Later that day Nick came back to the hut with a small, smartly dressed Liberian man. He held out his hand. In it was a twist of paper containing a dozen Flagyl antibiotic tablets. I had never been so grateful for anything, ever.

'This man is a kind of doctor,' said Nick.

'Oh, yeah-o. I di' mah trenin' lon' time ago. An' nah, dese day' . . .' He trailed off. 'I tink dis wi' mak' y' bedder.'

I offered him a packet of cigarettes in thanks, which he politely declined. After he'd left, Nick filled me in. Deku had been very concerned that I would not pull through like Nick had, and they had sent out men to go to a village where a local doctor was treating wounded rebels. They had all but run out of everything – Nick and Deku had acted just in time. I had been given what were probably the only antibiotics for fifty miles.

My fever broke. I woke from profound sleep the next morning to the sweetest noise I could have asked for: the growl of a Toyota diesel engine. Nick and Deku flooded the hut with light as they swung the door open. The rebels had ambushed and commandeered a United Nations ambulance some days previously. Now loaded with fuel, RPGs and AK ammunition, it would drive us to the front line as soon as I was strong enough.

Slowly I recovered. Finally, I was strong enough to venture out to film the ambulance being loaded with more weapons. The warmth of happiness lifted my mood. We were going to make it after all. I grabbed my satellite phone, extended the aerial and moved around, waiting for the reception signal to lock steady. I was jubilant – I couldn't wait to let my colleagues in Kenya know not only that Nick was better, but that we were finally heading to the front.

'From here we're driving to Bopolu, about a hundred clicks south, and then on to Tubmanburg. We should be there in a couple of days, depending on the rain. Deku says there's been some heavy fighting there, but the rebels are doing well.' I paused. 'Well, who knows how they're doing, but I think they're holding out, otherwise we wouldn't be going there.'

I expected to be congratulated. The line went quiet. And then the owner of the company broke the news. The Liberian film had dried up their cash flow. The business had been running on the assumption that, if they needed to, they could liquidate other assets to keep the money coming in. That was now impossible. All the fees up to that point would be paid, but no more. Cobus had been let go, the office in Johannesburg would be ditched. Liberia was a financial vortex for them. With no prospect of a return on their investment, and still no TV commission forthcoming, it was time to pull the plug.

'If you can pull it out of the bag, great.' The boss's voice rumbled on. 'We'll still pay your retainer, but there is no more money for Nick. You'll either have to go on alone, or cut a deal with him yourself.'

I felt winded, but thanked him for his candour and cut the call while there was still some battery power left. I stood in silence, looking at the patterns I'd kicked in the dust as I'd pleaded for more money. How do you tell a heavily armed mercenary that he's, well, *fired* – and that there's no money to pay him another single day, not even if it takes another month to get home?

'Nick?'

He was cleaning his AK, ready for our departure in the morning. He looked up, saw the anxiety in my face, and clicked the safety on.

'It's a fuck-up. The company has gone bust,' I blurted. 'There's no more cash. The only hope is if I finish the film, but they can't pay any more day-fees from now on – not for me or you.'

I sat down on the stool opposite him, stilled with apprehension. Heat was seeping into the day; it was almost too hot to sit outside.

'What do you want to do? I've got some dollars they think I've spent, and there's the kit . . . I mean . . . I think the game's up.'

He cut me off before I embarrassed us both.

'This is like rowing the fokken Atlantic. We're halfway there. Let's carry on. You need to film some action.'

'It'd be hard enough to get out now,' I countered, giving him one last get-out, 'but if we go forward, it could take us ages.'

I trailed off. It was our Cortez moment, and we both knew it. A long silence unfolded between us before he shifted his weight, and burned our boats.

'Forget the money, James.'

I looked at him, incredulous.

'Really,' he smiled, 'it will be okay.'

I waited for a caveat. None came. What I thought would be the hardest conversation to have, had been the easiest. Nick was no longer my employee. He was my friend.

As dawn filtered through the tree tops the next morning, we left Fassama and our hut. We'd been in Liberia for three weeks; two of them in the Spider House. It was a relief to be on the move again, even if we were heading to the front line at Tubmanburg. The ambulance and another rebel pick-up truck, now re-fuelled, sped past the skeletons of the logging station and down the beaten-earth road used to haul logs to Gainkpai and Bopolu, with their hazard lights flashing. Each vehicle was crammed full to bursting with rebels, fuel and ammo (and the goat from Voinjama). Our Land Cruiser alone had more than thirty rebels packed on board. Those who couldn't find a seat walked. We bumped over ditches and swerved around dead branches littering the road. We drove for hours until the sun dipped in the sky and the town of Bopolu emerged from the bush.

We were to stop here overnight. I took the opportunity to film Seeya Sheriff, known as Cobra – the LURD's deputy chief of staff. It was a bizarre interview. Cobra either didn't want to play politics, or didn't know how. Through his almost inaudible drawl, I fathomed that the national chairman's idea of establishing an interim civilian government in the wake of Taylor's defeat was not quite what Cobra had in mind.

'Deh wi' be no election,' he told me in a hoarse whisper. 'We establish military junta. I wan' 'ear nattin' abou' election. Our only mishan eh to destroy Taylah.'

That night we stretched out on a proper mattress with laundered sheets in a spider-free room. The windows even had curtains. The beige tiled floor and whitewashed walls reminded me of the youth hostels I'd stayed in as a child, hitchhiking with my father.

At daybreak we were off again. I put my bag into the ambulance and jumped up into the passenger seat. Nick shook his head.

'Cobra says it is too dangerous. The road from here to Tubmanburg is really not safe. If we hit an ambush, they'll try and take out the vehicles with RPGs and then open up with small arms, AKs. You don't want to be anywhere near them.' He must have seen the begging look in my eyes. 'We really have to walk. Ja, it's fokken dangerous in that thing.'

He jerked his head towards the Toyota packed with explosives and fuel. Buckling up his Recce webbing, and slinging his AK across his chest, Nick set out with me and Deku and around a hundred other fighters into the bush.

For hours we were drenched by the monsoon rains. Huge, curled palm fronds channelled the downpour into gushing spouts. When we rested under the blast-mangled zinc roofs of abandoned houses, the rain drummed out a persistent rhythm, drowning all other sound, thoughts. We stood mute, exhausted, peering into the green and grey world beyond the road.

As the rain eased, we marched on. And then, three or four hours into the trek, a volley of shots went high up into the air above our heads from somewhere in front. One rebel fired over the empty jungle in reply. Deku jumped on him.

'Don' sta', don' sta'!'

No one fired. Nick moved to my side, AK in his hands, stock extended.

'Ja, nice and slowly. Let's just keep moving. If there are any more shots, try and stay low.'

Tiredness, pain and adrenaline washed through my body. I was sleepwalking my way to the front line.

Eventually, with the light failing and a nine-hour walk behind us, the Monrovia Highway hauled us into Tubmanburg. As the rain came down in lightning-lit sheets, the town's besieged population of hungry civilians and rebel fighters poured into the streets. Young men in cut-down jeans and soaked bandanas chanted victory songs. Everyone was shaking hands; local fighters embraced the newcomers; ammunition passed from hand to hand. The entire town was engulfed by rebels in riotous good humour, singing in the rain. Under the awning of a shuttered shop, I looked out across a bright patchwork of umbrellas as volleys of AK rounds went up to the clouds over the front line. I was laughing. Nick beamed at me. We had made it.

5
UNIVERSITY OF BULLET

By the time we arrived in Tubmanburg, the LURD had been in control for nearly two months. Nestled in the Bomi Hills, the dilapidated old mining town a mere thirty-five miles north of Monrovia consisted of maybe 200 houses huddled around a rare strip of metalled road that led to the capital. All of these forlorn concrete dwellings – thinly covered by scraps of rusting corrugated zinc – had been damaged by the ebb and flow of conflict around them. Many had been raked with machine-gun fire, or partially destroyed by what Nick said were armour-piercing RPGs. At least two-thirds of the town lay deserted. Most of the civilians preferred near-starvation in the relative security of the surrounding, malaria-infested jungle to the urban shooting gallery they once called home.

As he showed us to our billet, Deku recounted with relish how his men had defeated Taylor here, pitching up out of the forest and strolling into town.

'Y' cudda seen 'em ronnin!' he hollered as we neared a cluster of dwellings a couple of hundred yards off the main road. 'Dey nah stron' enough fo' our forces.'

The local Government garrison fled in disbelief. Hardly a shot had been fired. After the LURD victory, though, quite a few shots had been fired by both sides. In the seven weeks since the town's capture, Deku admitted that the occupying rebels had seen almost daily combat with Government militia.

Our quarters were in a white, two-storey house. Stone steps guarded by a delicate metal banister led up to a broad balcony. It reminded me of my mother's house in Canterbury, with added bullet holes. In the evening gloom, I could make out with relief the comforts of a sofa and an easy chair on the balcony. Our bedroom – a good ten-foot square and furnished with one double bed, a wardrobe, two dressing tables and actual curtains – was luxury compared to the privations of the Spider House. To my delight and astonishment there was an en suite bathroom with tiled concrete bathing trough – and an intact ceramic toilet bowl. It was the most imposing house I'd seen in town, but there were no clues to the identity or whereabouts of the former occupants. With the exception of these few sticks of furniture, it had been completely gutted.

'Lekker.'

Nick liked it. He stripped off his battle dress and pig-skin army boots, flopped on the bed and wrinkled his nose as he was enveloped in a cloud of dust.

I unpacked my clothes and grandly hung them in the wardrobe. One spare pair of trousers, two shirts and two pairs of pants and socks were all I had. My wash bag consisted of one toothbrush, one thin bar of soap and a skinny tube of toothpaste. On Nick's advice, I'd ditched my heavy, waterlogged leather hiking boots – which had helped wreck my knees – in favour of a pair of lightweight trainers. All the equipment I needed to film with was stuffed into the pockets of a dirty beige photographer's waistcoat. Nick was in the same boat. We had walked into the war in the clothes we stood up in.

By the time I'd rigged my mosquito net over my half of the bed (Nick found the nets claustrophobic and slept without one), it was dark. I stretched out next to him, finally taking the weight off my knees. He was, without doubt, the strangest bedfellow I'd ever had.

'Y' comin' see som' rea' *ac*-shan,' Deku promised excitedly, sticking his head around the door. 'Everyting alrigh'?'

He peered at us through the gloom, like a boarding school matron checking on her boys. I nodded.

'Trus' me. Dey try, boh dey can' mak' i'. We readeh, an' we prepare'!'

Satisfied with our condition, he ducked out to fetch a palm-oil lamp and candle stubs, and check the whereabouts of the portable generator that my camera and telephone batteries relied on. His voice trailed off, barking orders to the fighters sent to guard us as he headed for the stone steps that tumbled down to the commanders' wives quarters. Nick got up to test the military radio we had borrowed from Cobus. It didn't work. If the satellite phone failed, we would be entirely cut off.

Over dinner that night we were introduced to the local commanders. They had *noms de guerre* as comic as they were lethal: Dragon Master, Bush Dog, Jungle Root and Nasty Duke all held court in this decrepit fiefdom. Despite their unorthodoxy, the rebels displayed a surprising degree of organisation and discipline. I'd seen that the commanders expected, and received, salutes; orders were followed; rank obeyed and respected. The younger fighters exuded an unsettling nervous energy.

Plates of rice and spicy stewed cassava leaf appeared. Dragon Master (a 27-year-old brigadier general whose real name was Sekou Kamara, and who, with Deku, jointly outranked everyone else in town) chatted at length about the rebels' command structure. Gone was the reticence of the Big Men in Zorzor and Voinjama. Dragon Master and Deku were able to give a frank and surprising account of their army's capabilities.

'Lor' Forces ge' two brigade'. De foi' brigade divahdeh in two battaliahn', an' each battaliahn ge' abou' tree or fou' companie',' Deku reckoned, 'an' each companie ge' abou' fifty man. De secon' brigade de same, boh dey ge' eigh' battaliahn'.'

'We also ge' two battaliahn' o' Special Forces, an' each o' dem ge' two companie' o' fifty man,' Dragon Master continued. His red beret and smart fatigues were rendered orange in the dirty lamplight, making him look like a cartoon devil. 'I de commanner de Executive Manshan securidy force uni' an' also de strike force commando. Special Forces take order direc' fro' de nationa' chairmon.'

Nick and I both jotted down notes, trying to unscramble their accents. I suspected Frank in Conakry would give his eye teeth for this information. Tubmanburg was part of 'Cobra Movement'.

'De area where we are nah, da' de Jongle Lion base,' continued Dragon Master. Seo's troops in Zorzor were the 'Voltage Movement', and Foya was the 'University of Bullet'.

'Everywhere i' Liber'a i' de University o' Bulleh.'

One of the older commanders laughed, slapping his AK. We all laughed and then Deku did what any self-respecting Liberian battle-front commander would do when considering an imminent onslaught by the enemy: he lit a joint.

In Voinjama, Joe Wylie had given the official number of LURD fighters at 14,000, which was ridiculous. On the basis of the figures that Deku and Dragon Master were touting, it was reasonable to assume that LURD's total number of men-at-arms was likely around 2,500 men, with an unknown number of porters and assistants. That such a tiny army could control a third of Liberia spoke volumes about the vulnerability of President Taylor's regime.

As if to underline the unreliability of any statistics in Liberia, Dragon Master guessed the rebels' strength in the town was now at about 1,000. Given that he also thought that everyone within a mile radius had spilled onto the streets to celebrate our arrival (or, more accurately, as I now realised, the arrival of the ammunition in the ambulance), I revised that down to around 500 – still about a fifth of their entire army. In amongst them, I'd seen at least fifty fighters on the wrong side of puberty.

The commanders left an hour later in high spirits after Deku ran out of grass. I'd been tempted to ask for a drag, but I was already light-headed from the heat and lack of food. Besides, I didn't want Nick to see me get high. It would have been like skinning up in front of my dad.

'What do you reckon their Special Forces are like?' I asked later that night, as Nick and I lay side by side on the double bed.

'There's a bit of confusion, I think,' he replied, too tired to laugh. 'They seem to think that if you give someone a special task to do, that makes them Special. They have no training.'

We lay in silence, and then he continued.

'Deku and, ah, fokken, er, what's his name? Dragon Master? They seem to think you'll see some fighting here.' He paused again. 'It's a straight walk from here to Monrovia. The president is not going to like that much.' Nick managed to chuckle to himself.

I wanted more than anything to get into the war, to see it at first hand, to understand it, and to film it. I was motivated by simple curiosity, too. The 'war' had become a personality about whom we spoke, but never really saw: the absent A-list star supporting thousands of extras in an unfinished, unfathomable production. I lay awkwardly beside Nick. It was always hard saying goodnight, announcing as it did, albeit politely, *I'm too knackered to want to talk to you any more*.

'Ja, well . . . Sleep well.'

Nick shifted his weight onto his side, and we drifted off together.

In the morning we were collected from our room and taken across town for an excursion by an excited cluster of rebels. As we walked through waterlogged streets, and then tall wet grass, the remaining townsfolk viewed us with a mixture of amusement and incomprehension. Children caught our eye and vanished behind bullet-drilled doors; a wrinkled old woman shook her stick at us, croaking incomprehensibly in tribal language.

'I wonder what they make of us?' I asked.

'They probably think we're mercenaries,' Nick postulated, 'though neither of us is getting paid so far.'

A sickly smell hung in the air, like the tang of a forgotten steak at the back of a refrigerator. It wasn't long before we found the source. A corpse straddled our path. He was stripped naked, lying on his back. Dark congealed blood on his left shoulder showed where he'd been opened up by a bullet. The boy had been twenty, or younger, and was handsome. He looked serene. A few paces on another man lay dead, his cheek prised open, the back of his skull missing. A deceptively small hole had been bored neatly into his chest by a high-velocity rifle round. He wore jeans; a bloodstained T-shirt lay knotted up in the grass nearby. He was not serene, but angry. They both stank. Like an obscene chef wheeling out the day's specials trolley to expectant customers, the war had served me up an intriguing, indigestible entrée. I wanted something to lighten the mood and the sadness in front of me.

'He would have been okay,' I broke the silence, 'if only he hadn't lost his head.'

My words evaporated into the putrid air. Nick said nothing, and took in the scene quietly, examining the corpses, considering the area. He was impassive. The rebels looked at me. I understood why they had brought me here. This was evidence of their power.

I started to film. The mangled face of the second body leaped into the viewfinder. It wasn't like looking at it with air and space around it; now all I could see was torn flesh and broken bone. The lens was supposed to be a filter – I'd heard that said so many times, and accepted it as true. It was, but it did not lessen the impact: it distilled and magnified it. I lowered the camera, and then the rebels smiled, and promised me plenty more in the days to come.

'We wi' ki' all o' dem,' one fighter assured me.

I had seen dead bodies before, but this was the first time I had seen people whose deaths spoke intimately about my own situation: they had been killed in the centre of town as we had marched towards it the day before. We had heard the shots. Now all I could do was take refuge in forced humour.

Later that day, as the weather closed in, threatening a storm, I called a senior BBC producer from under the citrus tree in our courtyard. I hoped he might be interested in our film. The bodies were good news, of sorts.

'I heard shots, but, ah, I've seen no combat yet. It's getting closer, though. The war's near. We're definitely onto something here. I've seen casualties.'

I was being grilled on what I had on tape.

'Well, that's bad news for you but great news for us, James! It sounds like you're getting the film,' came the cheerful reply, 'but we really need the bang-bang. Let me know when you get some. Right now it's, er, well, we still can't pledge anything up front.'

I hung up and went on the balcony to write up my notes. It was an uncomfortable truth: in order to get paid, I needed to see combat. At least I now knew what was expected of me.

Mid-morning the following day, little pops and whistles jumped above the usual soundtrack of life in town. Nick and I had ambled over to what remained of the local market to film stallholders. Despite the previous fighting, the centre of town was bustling with skittish children and large women selling cracking corn, old torch batteries and fat, edible snails. I cocked my ear towards the south end of town. It sounded as if the rebels were firing in the air again. Then two explosions boomed in the distance, their flat resonance rumbling down the street towards us. *No – it's a battle*. The rebels were being shot at. I froze as Nick scanned the road ahead. Within seconds the street was empty of everyone except fighters; rice had been spilled on the floor, shoes lost in the rush to flee for cover. A chill ran through me. This was it – and I had no idea what to do.

A score of fighters abandoned their radios and tore off noisily in their flip-flops towards the gunfire. I fumbled with my camera, replacing the battery, trying to clean the lens but smearing sweat across the glass instead. Nick took the AK off his shoulder, and we ran with the fighters.

'By the time we get there, the contact will be over.'

Nick knew how far away the bangs were. I didn't, and I didn't want to believe him, either. I wanted to see, to film, a fight. Even Nick's language was exhilarating: a 'contact' was his way, the army's way, of describing a shoot-out.

Up ahead of us, about fifty yards down the stony path, a rebel soldier jumped to his feet from the wooden seat he'd been perched on, yelling support for the others passing him. We ran towards him as he cocked his rocket-propelled grenade launcher. As he stood up, the four-foot wooden bazooka tube slipped between his hands, and dropped hard on the floor. The jolt detonated the charge. The primed grenade sitting in the end of the launcher roared up to the sky in a blaze of flame and an ear-splitting bang. The soldier disappeared in a cloud of smoke and swirling debris, and then fell backwards. The grenade exploded above us, scattering shards of burning metal into the zinc roofs of the houses about us. When I looked back at the ground again, I saw that the back-blast – the powerful exhaust emitted from the bottom of the tube when the grenade was launched – had sucked up the shale from the path and turned it into shrapnel. His legs had been blown off.

Nick and another man dragged him into a house, and laid him on a rickety wooden table. The other man was a medic, and took bandages and white gloves out of his pockets. Nick helped put an intravenous line in the rebel's arm. There was nothing I could do to help. I filmed. Here was real evidence of the war. Sinew and shredded flesh clung to his thigh bone. One leg was pared down to a skeletal strip of calcium and gristle. His genitals had been obliterated.

After a minute of struggling to frame and expose black people in a dark room with a bright white door opening behind them, while not getting Nick on camera, I gave up and just watched. The fighter rolled from side to side, his mouth gasped in air, but there was no screaming. Nick shook his head and I went outside. I struggled to light a cigarette. My hands were shaking. The contact was over, the rebels jubilant at repelling the attack. Nick emerged.

'Is he dead?'

I took a long draw on the pungent smoke. My nerves settled a little.

'Ja, very soon. In a few minutes he must be. There's nothing to be done.'

I struggled to absorb what I had witnessed. The unfilmed images sloshed around my mind, swimming at the edge of my consciousness. I had seen a few seconds of war, and it was vile, pointless and deeply unsettling.

As we walked back to town, I reflected on the complexity of filming the moment, too. I had struggled with the camera even though we were in no immediate danger. What would I do if I was being shot at?

It wasn't only a question of technical competence. With no commission to fulfil, no editorial brief to work to, I had no idea what to film. With a very limited supply of tape and fuel for the generator, I had to make big decisions about when to switch on and film. When I did, it had to count.

I decided to switch on shortly afterwards for Lee Watson. Born in 1922, Lee had been a resident of Bomi Hills all his eighty years. I found him in the midst of the congregation at the town's

Catholic church. In a dusty hall to one side of the market place, Lee and his fellow worshippers had come together for their daily prayers a hundred yards away from where the young fighter had just fallen. Lee's rosary and smart blue jacket were at marked odds with the fantastic uniforms of the rebels. Deep lines on his face framed the eyes of a generation that had seen Liberia emerge triumphant from its dark age of colonial exploitation, and then watched it disintegrate into butchery.

As I walked into the church, no one stirred. It was only when I cleared my throat and said hello that anyone asked who I was, or what I wanted. Almost all of them were blind.

Lee sat in front of my lens and gave me his history, the history of his people and the history of their wars.

When Lee was a child, a kind of slavery was still legal, and widely practised, in Liberia until 1936. People from tribes like his were forced to work against their will by the descendants of the original freed slaves from America who settled the country a hundred years before he was born. They governed until 1980. For the rebels (who were predominantly Mandingos), President Taylor represented the re-birth of this colonial hegemony: they said they wanted to remove him in favour of a government of Liberia's indigenous tribes. In his lifetime, Lee had seen Bomi Hills re-christened Bomi Holes, as enough iron ore was extracted to make Liberia the third-largest exporter in the world. And now, after twenty-two years of upheaval, he sat in the ruins of the Liberian dream, surviving on a handful of rice a day. Partially sighted, he helped his fellow parishioners get to and from church.

'We have not laugh',' he said, when he had finished, 'we have never smile', boh we are always cryin'. Tears ronnin' down!'

And as he said it, tears spilled down his cheeks into his grey-flecked goatee.

Back at the house, Deku dropped in to ask a favour. I'd been standing on the balcony watching children playing football with the rebels, as women scoured aluminium cooking pots in the shade of the citrus tree. I resented the intrusion.

Could I call the BBC and tell them that the LURD had captured Klay Junction – a strategic crossroads on the way to Monrovia – that morning?

'Have you?' I asked, forcing a smile, handing him a cigarette.

'No,' he admitted. And then, after a pause, 'Boh we soon ged i'.'

My heart sank. Deku was asking me to broadcast propaganda for the LURD. I had wondered when this would happen – but I hadn't expected it to be so direct. Nick's face broke out into a grin. This was going to be tricky.

'You see, the thing is, Deku,' I began cautiously, 'what makes my reports so useful for you is that I can prove they are true. If I say that Klay is in LURD hands, and it's not, and the BBC happens to have their guy in Monrovia visit Klay at the time, then no one will believe anything I say, ever again.'

Deku hunched his shoulders, and listened intently.

'This is very powerful,' I said, nodding at the shortwave radio in his hand, 'but you have to use it carefully. Any time you want me to call them about something I can see with my own eyes, or anything you or the national chairman want to tell them, just let me know. That's what I'm here for.'

Privately, I accepted that my reporting on the radio was almost useless. At any given time I could see about a mile of the war – the view from the exact spot on which I stood. Martians could have landed over the next hill, and I would have been none the wiser.

Deku nodded and reluctantly accepted my argument. He lit a joint and ambled off back into town.

I was relieved Deku had backed down without an argument. Nick looked disturbed, though. The real significance of Deku's request had passed me by. Nick laid it out for me.

'Klay is in Government hands – but we've always been led to believe the LURD occupied it. That means they – we – are, in fact, almost cut off. There were only two routes in from the north, one down the main road from Bopolu, the other a bush track too narrow for a vehicle. If they cut the back road, we are really fokken trapped.'

It wasn't funny, but he rolled the 'r' on *really* so hard I laughed.

'So what do we do?'

'Let me ask them about another route out, maybe to the coast. Let's hope they put some ambushes out and stop them coming into town.'

I dreamed that night of maps and battles with blind men, of old Lee Watson and the slaves who became free to enslave, and were in turn brutalised. Lee Watson's story made Conrad's *Heart of Darkness* look like a cheap romance. I didn't dream of the dying rebel, though; nor the Government corpses. I struggled to bring their faces into focus. Their identities were already a blur.

Breakfast the next morning was nothing short of a miracle. One of the commanders' wives had cooked us banana bread, which we devoured like men possessed. In addition, Deku's 'small-sol'iah' had brought us a present: three pineapples. Nick was already shucking the skin of the ripest one with his Gerber before the boy-soldier could put the others down. Running through our ever-shaggier beards, the juice of the heavy fruit was the most perfect thing I had ever tasted. I had eaten no sugar for two weeks, eaten almost exclusively rice and cassava leaf for nearly a month. It seemed impossible that the day could improve. And then one of the younger commanders, a captain whose name is lost in the smudged margins of my diary, popped his head above our parapet.

'My man Jay, y' tink y' wan' to com' wi' os to lay ambush?'

In the pouring rain, Nick and I squatted with the captain by the side of a concrete shack on the edge of the Monrovia Highway. The battle plan was impossible to follow – orders were incomprehensible. They seemed to be waiting for an attack.

'Let them go first,' advised Nick. 'We can come out if they're winning.'

Standing next to me, half a dozen teenagers with guns wiped the rain out of their eyes. One was no more than twelve. Without warning, the rebels on the other side of the road opened fire. It was impossible to tell at whom. They ran. Then our guys ran, and Nick and I – abandoning our plan in unison – ran with them towards the unseen enemy. I panned and zoomed, jumped the camera about, trying to focus on rebels firing into the tree line.

'It's all outgoing,' Nick shouted above the din. 'You're okay.'

With my eye to the viewfinder, I didn't spot the decomposing body of a Government soldier the LURD had laid across the road as a juju scarecrow. A piece of rib bone stuck to my trainers, putrid flesh clung to my laces. My foot had gone straight through him.

'Fucking hell! Tell me where I'm going!' I bellowed at Nick. 'I can't see shit when I'm filming.'

I kept running, fiddling with the zoom, while my brain screamed *You've got guts on your shoe!*

The attack petered out. I had shooting on tape, but no exchange of fire. The enemy, if there'd been one, used perverse tactics: for three days in a row they'd charged into town down the main road, taken casualties, and then retreated with nothing to show for the injuries they'd sustained.

I wiped my shoe in the sodden grass. It smelled like the bodies on the pathway two days before: heady and sick-making.

Back on the balcony, I re-played the tape on the clam-shell VCR. Two dozen rebels, and Nick, gathered around. If the radio had won over the commanders, this won over everyone else. I'd made them the stars of their own mini-TV show. With almost no idea what I should be filming, I'd just gone with the flow of the action. It was raw, shaky, and it just about worked. I felt proud of myself. Laughing, shouting, back-slapping – the kids with guns wanted to watch again, and again. Deku came up to see what the fuss was about.

'We gonna sho' y' so' *rea'* military *ac*-shan,' he promised, grinning. 'Ju' wai'.'

Later that afternoon, once the rebels had disappeared, Nick and I tried to relax. We sat there like old housemates killing time before the pubs opened. The things he'd told me about his army days were intriguing, and I wanted to know more about his career as a hired gun.

'How do you feel about being called a mercenary?' I asked.

The words were out before I knew I would speak them. He looked at me quizzically.

'Cobus doesn't seem to mind. Actually, I think he's quite proud of it,' I clarified, quickly.

Nick had taken his boots off and rolled his trouser legs up, the better to examine his mosquito bites. With his open sandy shirt and pale legs, he looked like he'd been transported from Blackpool beach.

'Really it's just a technical term to describe people who conduct unofficial operations, but it's become a swear-word. I prefer "professional soldier". Ag, do you know any soldiers who don't get paid to fight? Even these guys . . .' He jerked his head towards the din of the rebels' chatter in the square below. '. . . *specially* these guys are in it for what they think will be a big pay-day when Taylor goes. The guys from Executive Outcomes were really proud of what they did. They didn't see it as a bad thing. It was just like being in the regular army, but fighting for a different government. We were invited there by the official, recognised president. All right, it was a military junta, but we oversaw the transition to democratic elections. I don't think of that as mercenary work. It's security work, like I'm doing now.'

What about shooting down helicopters? I wondered to myself. *In what sense is that 'security work', exactly?*

'Anyway,' he continued, 'I developed my main business in armaments.'

'What, you sell weapons?'

This was news to me.

'Ja, I've got this company with Paul, my business partner, called MTS – Military Technical Solutions. We started off with mainly parts for aeroplanes, but we also broker deals for arms and ammo.'

Matter-of-fact and very open, Nick seemed happy to chat about his trade. I was fascinated to learn how it worked. Everything I thought I knew about arms dealing derived from James Bond films and Frederick Forsyth novels.

'Ja,' Nick agreed, surprisingly, 'you get those characters, but I try and steer clear of them. I get a lot of ammo from Uganda. One of my contacts drives a truck up to the front line where the Government is fighting – or supposed to be fighting – the rebels, and buys AKs and ammunition from their commanders. The commanders then tell the Government that they've been in heavy fighting and ask to get a re-supply. The soldiers don't say anything, because they don't want to fight.'

It was a self-fulfilling business prophecy: when journalists reported that the war was escalating, the president justified spending more cash on more guns, some of which he bought from countries like Britain, brokered by men like Nick. It was, at best, a decidedly amoral way to make a living.

'And what happens to the Ugandan ammo?'

'It gets shipped to Madagascar and then gets passed on. It ends up everywhere.'

He looked out across the roofs of the town.

Here, I thought, but I held my tongue.

'I've got a contact in Monrovia who is busy with Taylor brokering deals with Libya,' Nick continued. 'I need to talk to him in the next few days. He says there's a big shipment coming into Robertsfield airport on an Ilyushin.'

'Taylor is importing cargo planes full of weapons from Libya?'

I wondered whom Nick had been talking to on the satellite phone. I'd assumed it had been his wife – but Nick had been gathering intelligence of his own.

'Ja, it seems that way.'

I tried to calculate what Nick might really be up to.

'Does Frank know about this?'

'No, this guy is a friend of mine from the old days. He worked in South African Intelligence; he might still do. He's a very useful source of info. The Americans have got their own interests.'

I swallowed hard, and thought about how to frame my next question. Putting together the jigsaw puzzle of Nick's army career made me very uneasy.

'The arms dealing . . .' I said. 'Did that begin after EO? Actually, when did you join EO?'

At this exact moment, Deku clambered up the steps and joined us on the balcony. Nick nodded in greeting and settled back into the sofa, re-lacing his boots.

'I came out of the army in '94—'

Deku cut across him.

'My ma', wou' y' li' to make a repor' abou' dis?' He was smiling, clutching a blue A4 notepad. 'Y' can see dis wi' you' own eye' *now*.'

What I saw were numbered lists of names of Government troops, neatly written in Biro, accompanied by the serial numbers of the Kalashnikovs they'd been issued. The most recent entry was that day: 3 July 2002. Under the heading 'Names of Soldiers Who Went on Attack', there were thirty-one names, led by Brigadier General William Kamara. Deku's men had just killed him in an ambush, and found this, his battle diary. It was an extraordinary document: it showed, conclusively, that the Government had been attacking Tubmanburg, a key strategic position, with fewer than forty men. Furthermore, the troops were not regular soldiers but press-ganged militia sent into battle with a few RPGs and little ammunition, and who were paid in 'gin' and 'grass'.

A letter tumbled out of the notepad, addressed to the now-dead 'Commander in Charge Bomi County (frontline)'. Dated two days earlier, it ordered the now deceased brigadier general to attack Tubmanburg relentlessly. 'Serious military action will be taken against all the commanders', the letter promised, 'if the order is not effectively implemented.' After the threats, the order ended on a happy note. 'Military greetings from your Chief of Staff and take good care of your men, may God bless your operations.' It was signed Christopher Yambo, Chief of Staff, Army Division.

A hastily written note had been drafted in reply the next day. Kamara had been pulverised by a LURD grenade before he'd had the chance to send it. It said: 'Dear Sir, We were thirty-nine and five have escape, we are only thirty-four man power on the ground.' Underneath were listed the names of the five deserters.

The LURD were fighting scared civilians. Even Deku looked sad. He said he wanted to kill Taylor's men, not just anyone.

I considered the documents for a few hours. Nick, Deku and I discussed their veracity and pondered their implication. Then I called the World Service to record an interview for the next Africa Service news bulletin.

Later that evening, Nick called his contact in Monrovia. I heard him chatting in Afrikaans from the balcony as the light faded. To my surprise, Nick beckoned me down, handing me the phone.

'His name is Piet. Ja, it's fokken interesting.'

Piet, who turned out to be a 'military adviser' to Taylor, had heard the broadcast go out. So had Taylor. He claimed the president had become enraged. It made Piet laugh to think that Nick, his old buddy, was on the 'wrong' side.

I asked about the cargo plane from Libya that was due to re-supply Taylor. Yes, it was expected any day. I struggled to find the funny side of pissing off a psychotic head of state with a planeload of weapons and the men to use them – who was sleeping barely thirty-five miles away down a straight, all-but-undefended main road. On balance, Nick agreed I was right to feel a little apprehensive.

That night I went to bed wearing an eye mask and ear plugs in an attempt to drown out the chatter of the rebels' radios. I stripped down to my last almost-clean shirt and took a small, blue Valium tablet with my nightly malaria pill. I had been prescribed them years previously as a muscle relaxant after damaging my neck in a whiplash injury. I'd hung onto them in case my shoulder went into spasm again, but now I took the drug secretly and for a different reason: to launch me into sleep above the cloud of menacing images that had gathered above my pillow.

6
WHISKY PAPA

'We're under attack.' Tearing the ear plugs out, the room is filled with the *thump-thump-thump* of incoming RPGs. Still in the half-light, the room seems suddenly tiny. Nick is dressed, AK at the ready. Inside my head a voice is screaming *GET YOUR BOOTS ON!* I scramble about getting dressed, loading pockets with tape, spare batteries. As the grenade bursts thin out, sharp reports echo off the buildings in town. Over the top of them crackles a percussion of pops, which rise and fall in waves. I head for the bathroom, shaking the emptiness of Valium sleep from my sluggish limbs.

'Be quick,' Nick warns, 'and get your head down.'

Stray bullets are being sucked up by the zinc and timbers on our roof.

'We need to get outside.'

I abandon my attempt to urinate, and tear down the stairs, Nick behind me. We stand, and listen. The firing is coming from behind our house, not from the main road.

'They must have ambushed the back road. Stay here for a minute.'

I walk in a tight circle, fiddling with the camera. Rebels run past. Dragon Master strolls behind them, shouting into a field radio. Nick chambers a round into his AK, and we follow, leaving the courtyard and jogging into the narrow lanes that feed out to the bush at the edge of town. It is instinctive: I do the same; dogs running in a pack.

Filming as I run, heart pounding, my vision narrows. I see the ground in front of me in minute detail – the way a stream breaks around a reed, or stones throw soft shadows in the morning gloom – and hear gunfire and grenades, but no talking. It is as if everyone has been struck mute. And then suddenly we are out in the open. I crouch, and the grass in front of my face twitches. It is a beautiful, iridescent green and smells rich and comforting. The morning is cool, the sky steel-grey, and all around, the grass sways and twitches. Then I see more than the grass. We are being strafed by gunfire. The green blades and reeds that shimmer six inches from my nose are ripped through by rifle bullets.

I run back, then forward; stop; crouch, and then run back again.

'Fucking hell, they're coming straight through the bush.'

'Keep moving. Faster. Keep moving. You've got to move.'

Nick is behind me, hand on my shoulder, urging me on. I can't believe that I am running in battle. All the anticipation, the self-doubt, the angst, disappears. The war is now fact. *Don't think*, I tell myself, *just run*.

We're taking heavy fire, from both sides. Rebels to my right are firing back through us.

'Vok, we're going to get killed by our own guys here,' Nick shouts, casting round for cover.

'Cease firing!' I scream, running, filming. 'Fucking cease fire!'

After a hundred yards flat-out, I dive for cover. Behind the wall of a house I check my camera, force my fingers to adjust dials and settings, and then peer uphill towards the last house on the edge of town that the Government troops are using as cover.

Whooping war cries erupt from the young fighters sheltering around me. A rebel strokes his Mohican, then, changing his magazine, steps back into the line of fire.

More rebels follow. So do I, still unthinking, Nick close behind. I film as I run, framing their rifles balanced above their heads, slant-ways, gangster-style; spent cartridges spew out, burning hot. Government rounds cut up the dust in front of them, us, as we near the house on the hill. RPG traces zoom out into the trees, arcing over town. I hold the camera low now, still rolling, and sprint for cover again.

The attack is over in forty-five minutes. The Government forces retreat. One rebel blasts the bushes in a final act of frustration, and then the gunfire stops.

'I love the smell of cordite in the morning,' Nick smiles.

Then we laugh, and exhale hard.

Relaxed and confident in our survival, we walk back to town along a small, overgrown path. Nick is close, just behind me. I film as we walk; a dozen rebels in front of me, trudging through lush grass. *They could be ten feet away, and you'd never know it*, I think, settling into the walk. The rebels sling their weapons over their shoulders. Camera still up to my eye, I pan to the right, across the dense foliage by the road, and then back up ahead. As I stabilise the shot a Government soldier stands up thirty yards in front and empties his AK at us, at me.

The first round skims my camera microphone, an inch to the right of my face; I feel the second snap past my left ear. I throw myself into the long grass, the air fizzing with lead. The rebels reply with everything they have in incensed, hysterical retaliation. The air buzzes like a swarm of manic, screeching bees. I look up to see Nick snap his safety catch down and level his rifle into the bushes right by the side of the road.

'Stay low!' he roars, sensing my hesitant movement.

'I can't see, I can't see. Nick? You're my eyes, so tell me.'

A volley of rifle fire shreds the bright green leaves in an arc around us.

'Okay, mind this side. Stay on the left side.'

I get up, and follow him. He walks in a half-crouch, the stock of his rifle at his shoulder, muzzle aiming ahead. Rebels empty their magazines, blind, into the perfect cover of the undergrowth. I stand up, filming, and we inch forward, expecting more fire from the front, sides.

It was over. No one shot at us. It had lasted five minutes. I was exhausted, but euphoric. I had done it. It had taken a week since arriving at the front line; but the heat and sweat and illness and fear and confusion all finally made sense. I had filmed combat.

Back at our house I re-played the tapes. On the mini-VCR, I saw smoke spurt from the barrels of the rebels' rifles, and bullets lick up the dust around me: modern war, instant re-play. Now, from the comfort of my balcony, I realised how close it had been.

Nick sat and methodically, lovingly, cleaned his AK. After I'd cranked the generator, and hooked up the satellite phone and camera batteries, I returned to the pictures and appraised the shots. Sharp, in the centre of the frame, slightly under-exposed – the pictures were okay, but I was worried about the sound recording. After re-running the Tubmanburg TV show for the rebels, I buried myself in the instruction manual, trying to fathom the enigma of audio.

'You can really see what's going on, hey?'

Nick was a fan of the video, too.

'Yeah, but I can't work out how to split the mic between tracks, the left and right channel.'

I looked up at him. He was engrossed in the video himself, still kitted out in his full Reconnaissance Regiment battle dress.

'It's good, man. You've got it. We're getting the film. This is fokken good.'

Later that evening, as the air cooled and storm clouds piled up on the horizon, Deku appeared with our food, and ate with us. In addition to scorching-hot chilli rice, we were given a large bowl of plantain, fried in palm oil: a taste of childhood. After my parents had separated, my mother and I lived in what, with the misery of perspective, now seems like poverty. She kept her wedding ring for the sole reason that she could pawn it, at the end of the week, to buy food. For a treat we would go to Brixton market and buy plantains – which she called Special Bananas – sun-blackened under faraway skies. Deku listened awkwardly. Nick made a disparaging remark about absent fathers, and then snorted at himself. Deku thought that it was harder to be poor in a rich country than in a bankrupt one. I disagreed.

'When was the last time you called your mother?' Nick piped up. His thoughtfulness surprised me. It had been over a month since I'd spoken to her.

'Y' ca' tell her Cha' Taylah tink y' a big man,' Deku laughed, as I slipped the satellite phone out of the shoulder bag. 'We hear on de walkie-talkie da' de Go'ernmen' forces ha' bee' order' nah to le' y' escape. Dey really wan' you! Yor code i' "Whisky Papa" – Whi' People.'

Taylor was playing his own game in Tubmanburg. It was called 'wipe out the rebels and grab the white guys'. Far from being obscure, the rules were in fact very simple: there were none. The attacks that day had not been from reluctant militia, but Navy Division troops brought in under the command of Roland Duoh, one of Taylor's most trusted senior commanders. Deku estimated their strength at 500, a tenfold increase on the last attack.

'You sound like Mickey Mouse!' Mum thought the way the satellite phone distorted my voice was hilarious. 'I'm so glad you've called. How are you?'

I remembered at once why I had not been in touch. Before I left I had made a vow to myself that I would tell her only the truth about this trip. I owed her that. She'd helped me with the early stages of my research, and had an idea of the environment I was heading into – or at least so we had both thought.

'Well . . .'

I tried to think of words that would describe and not terrify. How *could* I describe watching that man have his legs shredded without making it obvious that I was in the firing line, too? Nothing came to mind.

'We've done a lot of walking, well over a hundred miles I think. You wouldn't believe the rain – it's hard to stand up in it sometimes, it's so heavy . . .'

We were on safe ground with the weather.

'Nan's having a time of it with the garden. She had Grandad lumping stones all day last weekend. She points, he digs. The grass has gone a bit brown, but the flower-beds are great. Oh, and the ducks are back!'

The dim, claustrophobic courtyard in Tubmanburg opened up into the magical vista from my grandparents' garden, with its flower-fringed panorama of the English Channel.

'I'm getting the film, but I'm being very careful. Nick is looking after me.'

'Well, you make sure that he does. You'll have a few tales to tell after this one, Jamo. I'm really glad it's going so well.'

We said goodnight with no mention of Taylor's vendetta; I stood in silence, listening to the humming insects and the faraway groan of thunder. Only then did it dawn on me that she would have been listening to the World Service all along.

I'd thought it might be upsetting to call home, but the connection back to something familiar was simply comforting. I tried to keep hold of the feeling and dialled Rachel's number in Glasgow, but cut the call. It didn't matter where she was. There would be only lies of convenience to tell. There was nothing to say that was true or kind, and I could not bring myself to frame my relationship with her with the brutal language of this war.

I climbed back up to the balcony and looked at Nick and Deku. Nick was sketching a line map from his GPS readings around town; Deku was rolling another spliff, ranting about Taylor.

'All right, fellas? I might turn in for the night.'

'Ja, see you in there.'

I nodded goodnight to them and overheard Nick's conversation with Deku as I vanished into the darkness.

'Ja, man, could you get your guys to move some of the bodies out into the forest tomorrow? You can really smell them from up here.'

I lay down on my bed, boots on, and waited for sleep.

At six o'clock the following morning I was woken by RPGs destroying the house across the road. Thick, fat *boom*s rocked the whole town. Already dressed, I grabbed the bag with my shot tapes, satellite phone and notebooks, and followed Nick out the door.

Downstairs it was a different scene from the first attack. Dozens of civilians gathered in the courtyard below us. Bullets tore lumps out of our balcony.

I squatted on my haunches behind the wall of the house opposite ours, and lit a cigarette. The crackle of incoming fire had become a melody of short, flat snaps. Two rebels sauntered up to me, looked around the corner of the house, and then raised their Kalashnikovs, firing on full auto into the town centre.

'Don' be scare',' said one, 'we protec' you.'

One of them was wearing a bright green shower cap stretched over his bald pate. Spent shells tumbled out of his rifle like a jet of hot brassy water. It was deafening. My ears distorted my own voice like a broken radio.

'Why are you wearing a shower cap?' I bellowed.

I was genuinely interested. Even by the LURD's bizarre sartorial choices, this set a new standard. It was like I'd been teleported onto the set of a *Carry On* film.

'Becau' i' rainin',' he explained.

Fifty yards away Government soldiers wearing the bright yellow T-shirts of the Navy Division were sprinting towards us, shooting. I ran.

Nick was ten feet away, trying to get sense out of a flustered rebel captain.

'Nick, fuck, they are really fucking close. We need to go right now . . . now, now, now!'

We ran together, while Shower Cap pinned down the Government soldiers. I turned around once to film the fleeing civilians and then didn't look back. We made it to the far end of the main road and waited. A rebel crouched and fired an RPG into a shack twenty yards from him.

Moments later a Government soldier, who had just been taken prisoner, was dragged up the road. He had been stripped to his underwear; hands bound, bleeding, dirty and confused. Deku began railing wildly at him as stray bullets slapped into the buildings around us. I stood and filmed steadily as the commanders argued about what to do with him, following the to and fro of their shrill patois through the viewfinder. The prisoner looked at me, the camera, eyes prised wide open with fear. I thought I saw the flicker of a smile too – perhaps at the thought that my camera, this filmed evidence, would save him. And that is what I thought, too, that I would save him, that being here, being witness to his capture, would protect him. I kept filming.

His body was beautiful: every muscle seemed sculpted out of black, sweat-polished marble.

And then all hell broke loose. As Deku ranted, a dead LURD fighter was borne down the road towards us, carried by four comrades, his lifeless arms splayed out cruciform, his yellow Nike sports top stained bright red. I framed the bloody corpse on the floor, and then, as I lifted the camera, Deku, enraged, forced the Government soldier onto his knees by the side of the road and fired repeatedly at point-blank range into his back. The prisoner's skin split, and his lungs were blown out of his chest.

I went to him, filming, as Deku strode past purposely, heading back to the front line – his metal dog-tags glinting as they swung in front of the red *Brooklyn* logo on his T-shirt. I watched as the man rasped his last desperate breaths in the dirt, his face dehumanised by pain, his eyes searching mine. I turned to a rebel standing beside me, and heard myself say, 'He's still alive.'

The rebel flashed a look of deep concern.

'Oh,' he asked, 'I mu' shoo' 'im?'

I turned back to the death. I knew then that I could not unlearn what I had seen. Education in war is a one-way street. Then I walked away and sat on a bench nearby with Nick, who had been watching my back, and lit my last Marlboro. There was nothing to be said.

I told myself it was necessary to film the rebels' atrocities in order to present a truthful image of their war. I also reminded myself of a black-and-white photo-essay I'd seen in my twenties of an execution in South Africa. Racist AWB paramilitaries had been shot dead in public by a black policeman. What stuck in my mind more than the photos themselves was the reaction of the photographers present. Those who missed the decisive moment were jealous of their colleagues who had captured death on film. Their words stuck with me. 'An execution is a once-in-a-lifetime thing,' one had said, 'even if you are covering violence and war.'

I wondered if the man Deku had shot – who couldn't have long seen the back of his teenage years – would be missed by anyone, whether there would be a grieving mother counting the days, a wife somewhere holding a photograph, not knowing. Of all the most intimate moments of his life, I, a stranger, had shared the last and most intense of all.

We edged our way back to the fighting through a maze of back alleys. Finally, the firing stopped and we broke out into the main street again. Bobbing out of view down the hill, the chanting yellow T-shirts beat their retreat. Four rebels had been confirmed killed, five seriously injured. Everyone was out of ammunition. Dragon Master confirmed there were only 200 bullets left in the main arms cache – Nick had more than that in his webbing – and almost no RPG bombs. Had the Government attack continued for another fifteen minutes, we would have been overrun. No one else, except Nick, seemed to realise how precarious our situation had become.

Trekking back to the balcony, we discussed our options.

'If they completely run out of ammo, we're going to have to take the gap,' Nick concluded. 'It's better that we take our chances alone than be caught up in a slaughter here – but it's a last resort.'

'Absolutely,' I agreed. 'Let's go see if we've made the news.'

A couple of hours later Nick tuned in to the BBC's *Focus on Africa* programme with Deku and the other commanders, while I bandaged my aching knees. We sat in astonished silence. Taylor had visited Klay Junction that very day, and now pledged to re-take Tubmanburg personally within seventy-two hours. My radio reports had brought hell down onto the rebels; my actions were now directly affecting the prosecution of the war. On the one hand, my reporting was helping them to correct Taylor's propaganda; on the other, it was inciting him to wipe them out.

That evening, exhausted porters arrived from Fassama with more bullets, RPG bombs and fuel. We were saved. I called the senior BBC producer, feeling not unlike an office worker calling home to the wife with an account of an unusual day in the office. I told him the good news. We had what he wanted.

'That's great.' He sounded genuinely impressed. I breathed another sigh of relief and my spirits lifted. Violence was a valuable commodity. 'Maybe we can get Rageh Omaar up to the Guinea border to do a series of stand-ups. We can use your combat footage as wrapping. It will be great for you.'

There was no Plan B, no other offer – nor would there be. Battle-worn, profoundly exhausted, I somehow kept my temper. I wasn't surviving these battles to make someone else look good. I decided then and there to keep this conflict just between Nick and myself, until such time as I could show my work on my own terms. This would remain my own private war.

Life with the rebels became increasingly complex. It was difficult to reconcile the polite and strangely courteous men and women, who shared out the last of their precious rice, with the brutality of soldiers at war. Deku offered me a local cigarette, from his last packet. I plucked it from the hands of a murderer as we joked about the lives – and Marlboros – we had left behind at home.

'My man Jay, be carefu' wi' yor jew',' he advised me, referring to Rachel as my 'jewel', 'becau', my man, if y' stay fa' fro' her too lon', all kinda ba', ba' ting ca' happen!'

Deku's past remained obscure. Despite having slain some mother's son in the dirt that afternoon, he had a child himself, a boy, who was growing up with Deku's estranged wife in Guinea. When he spoke of him, his eyes lit up, and he smiled. Whatever depravities he inflicted on others, Deku remained infuriatingly engaging.

I thought of the line Martin Sheen's character, Captain Willard, had spoken in the film *Apocalypse Now*. 'Accusing someone of murder in a place like this', he said, 'is like handing out speeding tickets at the Indy 500.' In Liberia, it felt like there was only me to point the finger, but the guilty were the ones keeping me alive. I cast around desperately for moral guidance. Walking through the jungle towards the front line, I had clung to the voice of my grandfather, Martin, the professional soldier, who had told me that it was only in war that men were allowed to love each other unquestioningly and unconditionally. It was that love, he told me, that allowed him to both survive and participate in the slaughter. Now, all but surrounded by the Government army, another voice came to me.

My maternal grandfather, Don, one of war's eminently sensible survivors, had adopted an entirely different approach to killing people: he was not guided by a sense of adventure, but by duty. He fought because he was asked to by his country, and saw the bloody business of combat as a job to be done for a greater good. While Martin played his folk violin and filled my head with *Boy's Own* tales of derring-do, Don got down to the serious business of bringing me up with my mum, and making sure I finished my homework on time. Of the few wartime stories he imparted, one in particular resonated with me now: surrounded, and down to his last few rounds of ammunition, it was the South African troops of whom he spoke most highly. There was no love lost between the English and the Afrikaners, but after eight months under siege, together they sprang out of the trap of Tobruk. I shared his stories with Nick, who looked shocked, and then laughed.

'My uncle was at Tobruk. Perhaps they even knew each other!' It was a wild thought.

I told Nick about my grandfather's war in the desert, and how, while out scavenging for parts from knocked-out German half-tracks, he had, quite literally, bumped into Field Marshal Erwin Rommel, himself on a recce in no-man's-land with only his driver for protection. They had saluted one another under the searing sun and driven off in different directions. What impressed Nick more than meeting Rommel, though, was the fact that my grandfather had immersed himself in my upbringing.

'Ja, it's tough on my little one, being away so much,' Nick said, remembering his daughter in Pretoria. 'She is a real Daddy's girl. She won't leave me alone when I come home. She's pretty, too – she did some of that modelling for children's clothes. I wasn't too happy about that. I stood next to the guy taking the pictures the whole time.'

I tried to consider what Don would make of this war. Alive and strong, he would be waiting for me when I came home, full of understated enquiry, and, I hoped, respect. Deep down, I knew that part of what had driven me to come to Liberia came from a desire to make him proud of me.

As the evening drew to a close, Dragon Master politely asked if he could beg a favour: could I help him make a call from my satellite phone?

'Yeah, sure. It's charged up. Who do you want to speak to?'

I was happy to help him out – they asked for very little, and fed us without question or resentment.

'I go' to koll de Lady in Conokry,' he said. 'She go' to ge' de logistic'. We' go' so' men dem readeh boh we don' know when de nex' delivery comin'.'

The significance of his reply sank in.

'You mean ammunition? You want to arrange an ammunition delivery?'

'Yeah, das righ'.'

I walked back under the tree with him, and dialled the number he gave me, scribbled on the back page of his tatty notebook. He took the phone, smiling, and chatted away unintelligibly. I took a moment to consider my position. I was now helping the rebels re-supply their army with illegal *matériel* from the Guinean Government. It wasn't up there with shooting down helicopters, but it was close. I felt like I was breaking one of the sacred rubrics of journalism: *Thou Shalt Not Take Sides*. I was almost behaving like a mercenary.

For the next four days Tubmanburg was attacked persistently. Every morning, at six-thirty sharp, and then again in the afternoon or evening, 300 or so of Taylor's crack fighters rushed our perimeter.

Rebel radios crackled with eavesdropped information. Taylor's helicopter, out of reach of rebel grenade launchers, ferried Revolutionary United Front mercenaries in from Foya. The odds mounted, but Deku's men hung on. Ammunition re-supplies arrived in dribs and drabs – but a huge shipment of 40,000 rounds, expected daily from Fassama, failed to materialise. We clung to the thought of it, the tiny brass tubes and green bombs the only long-term means of the LURD's – our – survival.

In between the lethal exchanges in town, Nick and I sat on our balcony, endlessly re-hashing escape plans, staring wistfully at the map and the ambush-ridden road to Robertsport – gateway to the Atlantic and shortcut home. We talked about tactics, and defeat, and, prompted by the memory of the execution of the absurd AWB men, I took the opportunity to ask Nick about leaving the army in 1994.

'Those so-called new Boer commandos – did you think they might actually be able to set up a separate Afrikaner state?'

'No,' he sighed, 'those extreme guys were idiots. They couldn't change anything. No, the army offered me to stay, but it was changing. The new MK commanders were useless. None of them took proper training. Lots of white guys left – though many of the blacks stayed on because it was the only way they could earn money. Anyone who was a professional, who took pride in their work, resented the new way things were being done.'

The 'MK guys' were Umkhonto we Sizwe, or *Spear of the Nation* – ANC guerrillas who'd fought against the apartheid state from 1961 to 1990.

'Some of them trained up okay, but the commanders didn't have a clue. Besides, the war was over. My second wife and I bought a shop in Atlanta, outside of Pretoria, and tried to make a go of it. I was keen to get all that army stuff behind me. I think she'd had enough of it by then.'

He stood up and disappeared into the room, emerging a minute later with two fresh beakers of water for us, drawn from our purified reserve.

'Man, that place was cursed! We used the money I got from the army to buy this general trading store, selling mostly to blacks. But vok! It was in the centre of a fokken snake pit. I have never seen so many snakes. We were completely surrounded by them.' His voice rose with excitement at the memory. 'It didn't matter how many you killed, there'd be another dozen in the morning. My wife went crazy. The store was a disaster; we had to close it. We sold up, and the EO job came along in '95.'

I couldn't decide if being surrounded by in-exterminable snakes was a more fitting allegory for his struggle to fit in with the New South Africa, or our present predicament in Siege City.

'Weren't you, I mean the army, tempted to fight in '94? Was there any desire to hold out against the ANC?'

It seemed incredible to me that, after nearly twenty years of war, Nick and his comrades had just walked away from everything they'd fought for with a shrug of the shoulders, and accepted that that was the way it would be.

'It was already over in '88. The politicians saw the way it was going, and did a deal, much earlier than people think.'

He shifted his weight and crossed his ankles in front of him, draining the water.

'There was a lot of young guys killed in Angola in '87 and '88 for nothing. We felt betrayed, but it was always like that, it's always been like that everywhere. You get the guys who is fighting, and the big men who make deals and sell them out.'

He thought for a moment, wiping the sweat out of his eyes.

'Ag, this had to happen. It was the only thing we could do. You just can't fight all the people. There was just too many of them. That's no way to live. So far this new government isn't doing too bad. The economy is okay. Part of the settlement was that they had to ditch all the Communist economic stuff. In that way, we had a victory. I think most of the people sees now that Communism would have been the fokken end.'

I'd forgotten, perhaps never really known, that the ANC were card-carrying Marxists. Once Nick warmed to the theme, it was hard to stop him. Fighting had been his life: he lived and breathed it still.

'In '87 and '88 we were fighting massive battles in Angola. We were fighting the Angolan Government, who were Marxists, and Cubans and Russians who were Communists. We'd been at war with them since independence in '75. Most of the guys who joined up or were conscripted were there to protect South Africa from that. It wasn't just a racial thing. There was no proper apartheid in Three-Two, or the Recces, and most of the guys weren't thinking about that. You know, then the Government did a deal with them, the Communists. That pissed a lot of people off. Some people say that the Russians threatened to escalate the whole thing. The Chinese, too.'

For Nick, the Cold War had been a hot one. While the West talked about fighting the Evil Empire, and finessed diplomatic moves against Moscow, Nick and his Recces were getting down and dirty actually killing Reds, whatever their colour. The South African Government supported almost anyone with an anti-Communist agenda. Psychopathic Renamo guerrilas in Mozambique – created there by Rhodesia to fight the newly independent Marxist government – were, Nick explained, covertly armed and trained in the 1980s by 5 Recce. Nearly a million people died from war or starvation; many times that were displaced from their homes. The apartheid regime also helped create, and then fought alongside, tyrants like Jonas Savimbi and his rebel UNITA army in Angola. I asked what the war in Angola had been like at the end. Had he seen any of the Cuban troops he'd said were sent by Castro to fight alongside the Angolan army? It turned out he'd fought in the battles that were a prelude to a series of massive pitched confrontations between the South Africans, Cubans, Russians and opposing Angolan armies. His Recce missions helped lay the foundations for what, at that time, was the largest battle ever fought in sub-Saharan Africa.

'You didn't see them too much unless they were dead, but ja, there was this one Cuban soldier. I found him between two tanks we'd knocked out. I turned around and saw him aiming at me from a few yards away – very close. His magazine was empty. He threw down his rifle and smiled at me.'

'What did you do?'

I tried to imagine the panic of hand-to-hand combat fought on that scale. What I had seen in Liberia so far provided a clue, but not an answer. Nick looked perplexed.

'I shot him.'

In 1987 I was fifteen years old. I doodled pro-ANC slogans on my satchel. I knew nothing. My only way forward with Nick was to judge him on what he did now and not what he said about the past: he was honest, he had stood by me and he did what soldiers do: kill. While I had been defacing my school bag, Nick had been fighting a war: not, as I'd assumed, a war unquestioningly and only in the defence of apartheid, but one, he believed, of national survival.

And that was precisely the point: I had never physically fought for anything – right or wrong. Nick had, and his past followed him like a shadow. More than anything, Nick was, just like my grandfathers, a man defined by his choices, dignified by the courage of his convictions irrespective of their correctness. For that, he was someone to follow, to trust instinctively, and to look up to. In this University of Bullets, he was my tutor.

7
CHARNEL HOUSE

Tubmanburg was burning. We'd edged our way towards the front line on our bellies. Fat machine-gun rounds droned overhead, gouging lumps of masonry from what remained of the buildings at the south end of town. Chattering incessantly, the rebels' Kalashnikovs continued the conversation, tearing up the sticky black tar of the road ahead. Nick spotted a wide alley to our right where the forest spilled onto the streets and we ran dodging between the houses to a wall on the left, where a group of commanders were assessing the battle. Just ahead of them, a line of rebel soldiers kneeled in the grass.

And then, without warning, as I was trying to catch my breath, Government troops stood up thirty yards away and engaged us openly. We flattened against the wall – me trying to film, Nick squinting into the bush, his AK swinging level.

'We have to go – now,' he said.

I shrugged his advice away. Crawling across town had taken nearly two hours. I couldn't face turning back without pictures.

'Two minutes!' I pleaded.

'No, man, now. These guys can't hold them. Now!'

I carried on filming. A rebel soldier crumpled in the bushes. We were completely exposed.

'Two minutes, okay?' I demanded.

Deku joined us, dressed in shorts and a forage cap, and echoed Nick's request, urging me back. Where had he come from? I was almost delirious with adrenaline.

'Our bom' fini', we nee' mo'.'

He looked adamant. I could barely hear him. Nick was next to me, shouting.

'They've run out of RPGs. They won't fight without them. We have to go back *now*.'

Nick was insistent. I kneeled down. All I wanted was to film the machine gun opening up. I zoomed down onto the ejection port to capture the spent brass oozing out. But then Nick's hand was on my wrist, pulling me across the street. He dragged me sideways, down, across to the house on our right, hauling me clear as our previous position exploded in a dirty fountain of broken earth. Our party had taken a direct hit; all of them had been injured. I steadied myself and stared across the road at the bloody remains of a soldier we'd been standing with.

Deafened by the blast, and transfixed by the thought of what might have been, I stood rooted to the spot as Nick mouthed commands at me. We were still in the firing line. A rifle bullet flew between our faces, punching a hole in the wall beside us. I stumbled, and Nick grabbed me.

'That was close!'

Nick was actually smiling. It was incredible. Nothing seemed to piss him off.

He pulled me to safety again. More machine-gun fire, the searing lead licking up the dust about our heels, harried us down the street. Then we were on the tarmac, and the battle was behind us.

I had become so absorbed with filming, and was so frustrated with myself for not capturing the contact on tape, that it wasn't until we were back at the house that it dawned on me how narrowly we had both survived. Nick had saved my life, twice.

On the balcony, I filled my notebook with times and details, facts and figures. With painstaking accuracy I recorded the start and finish times of contacts, as if by creating order on the page I could somehow order or influence or make sense of the chaos around me. My knees were too painful for me to concentrate properly, so I stopped to re-bandage them, strapping them tight. My body was not holding up well. My teeth now hurt too much to brush, and the skin on my thighs itched almost constantly – what from (a parasite?), I had no idea. We had run out of soap; I was filthy and my left ear had started to throb. I raised my hand unconsciously to the side of my face every few minutes.

'Is it the gunfire, James?' Nick enquired.

'I don't think so. It's actually in my ear, not my head. Why?'

'Ag, it's just I have this ringing in my ears, from the artillery.'

'Artillery?'

'Yes, from the army. We had these big G5 cannon in Angola, really good. They saved us a few times – but they weren't so hot on hearing-protection and stuff in those days. I have this, er, tinnitus. It can get really irritating.'

It was untreatable. In extreme cases, it could cause madness. I wondered if protecting journalists for no pay was an early symptom.

'How is it now?'

'It's there. It's better in the fighting; all the noise buries it. When the shooting stops, it gets quite loud, especially at night.'

We lapsed into silence.

The rebels were very low on RPGs, and Nick was right – they would not fight without them. Supply from Guinea did not seem to be a problem; getting anything over the River Via from Voinjama or Zorzor was. For us, it was doubly problematic: with

On my maternal grandfather's knee when I was two years old – photographed in Streatham, South London, 1974 – the year before Nick joined the Recces. Don fought across North Africa and into Italy in WWII with Montgomery's famed Desert Rats, but rarely talked about it. © James Brabazon.

With my grandfather Martin Brabazon – fierce jungle fighter, skilled boxer and accomplished musician; photographed in his council flat in London in 1996. It was from his lips that I first heard the word 'mercenary'. © James Brabazon.

On assignment in Kosovo, August 1998. Photographing the battle between Serbs and Kosovars in the Drenica Valley was my first commissioned foreign assignment, and my first professional experience of war. © James Brabazon

(above) Nick fires his AK during target practice in Fassama, Liberia, early June 2002. At fifty yards he put most of his shots through the same bullet hole.

(above) Frank, my contact in US Intelligence, on military operations in West Africa in the 1990s.

(left) Cobus Claassens photographed before a night ambush in Kono, Sierra Leone, while fighting for Executive Outcomes in the mid-1990s. Several of the men who fought with him went on to work on behalf of the U.S. military in West Africa – and were recruited for the Equatorial Guinea operation. © Cobus Claassens

As well as providing LURD rebels deep cover for their military operations, the Upper Guinea forest is home to half of the mammal species known to the African continent. Under President Charles Taylor, log production increased by more than 1,300 per cent. Some of the cash proceeds were illegally used to buy weapons. © Tim Hetherington

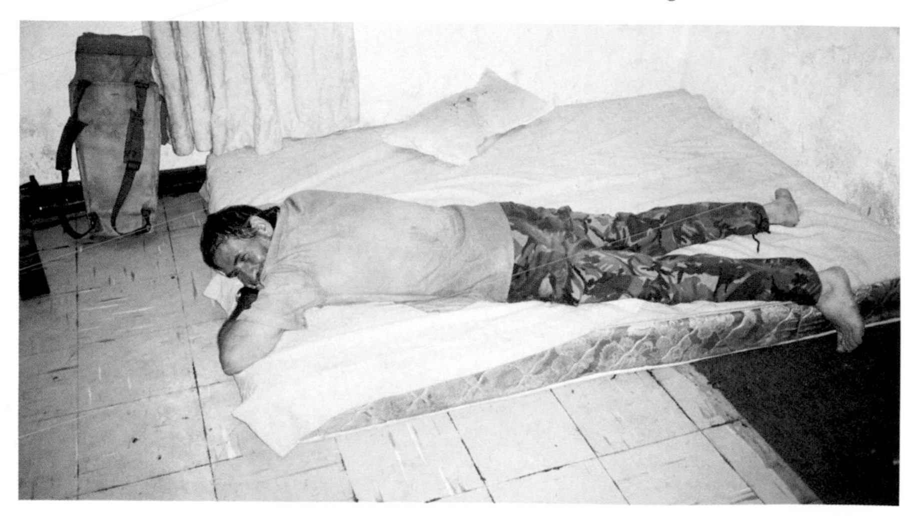

An exhausted Nick on the retreat from Tubmanburg, after walking for three days straight. Bopolu, 21 July 2002. © James Brabazon

Walking on the road south towards Tubmanburg, June 2002. Ambushes were common and it was too dangerous to travel in the vehicles. Nick's AK rests on the bonnet behind me while he takes the picture. © James Brabazon

Members of General Deku's LURD Special Forces unit pose for a photograph outside of Fassama, June 2002. Most of the people in this picture are now dead or missing. Deku is pictured centre left, holding a walkie-talkie. © James Brabazon

General Deku (seated, centre) – real name Musa Donso – interrogates a Government soldier captured in heavy fighting earlier that day outside of Tubmanburg in mid-July 2002. The prisoner was jailed briefly and then shot at dawn. © James Brabazon

Nick helping me to cross the mighty River Via – a natural barrier that prevented the rebel army from properly re-supplying its front-line troops outside of Monrovia in mid-2002.

General Deku explains military preparations for the move south from Voinjama in June 2002 to his commanders in a film still from *Liberia: A Journey Without Maps*.

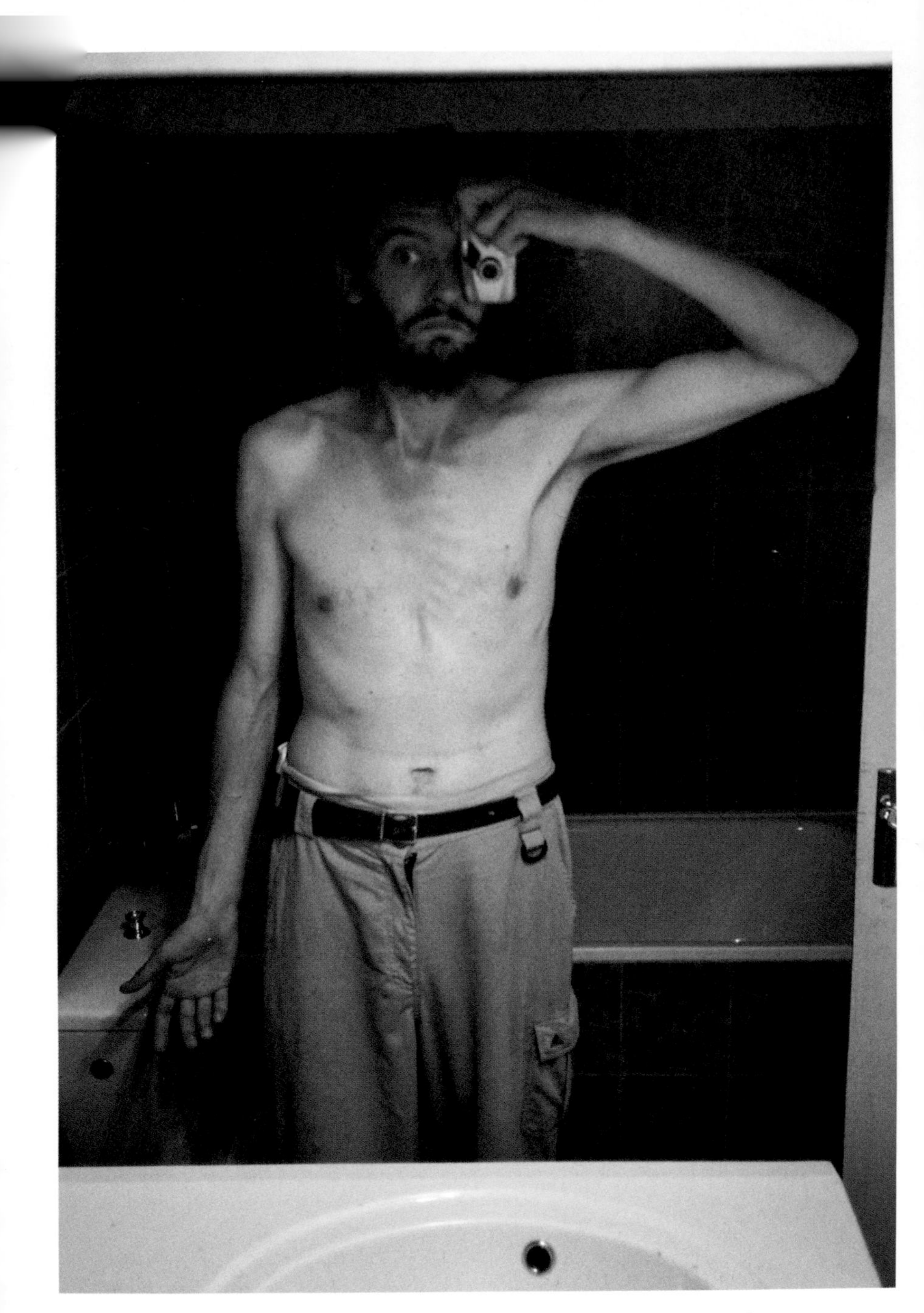

Self-portrait in my bathroom mirror in the Petit Bateau hotel, Conakry, Guinea, 3:30 pm, 29 July 2002 – at the end of the first trip into rebel-held Liberia.

Nick and I taking a break in Tubmanburg, 8 July 2002. Minutes beforehand General Deku had executed a prisoner in front of us. House-to-house fighting carried on at the end of the street. © James Brabazon

His Excellency Sekou Damate Conneh, Junior; National Chairman, Liberians United for Reconciliation and Democracy (LURD). © Tim Hetherington

Nick – in custom Recce webbing – looks out for cameraman Dudley Saunders filming civilians in the LURD rebel firebase of Zolowo the evening before the walk south to Fassama, 8 June 2002. © James Brabazon

Nick rests on an island midway across the River Via to dispense medical supplies to a wounded rebel commander, June 2002. Nick's medical expertise was employed on a near-daily basis and saved many lives. © James Brabazon

the river now swollen with the rains, the route out, as well as the route in, was likely impassable.

'I've been thinking,' Nick piped up, as if waking from a daydream. 'What these guys need is self-sufficiency. They rely on Guinea for everything, and then in the rainy season they're screwed because Taylor's supply lines are so much shorter. The civilians in their areas can't plant crops, and the rebels don't have any food or work to give them. They need to generate their own money.'

He was right, but how on earth could they generate income in this wasteland?

'You're right. This place is fucked. There isn't even any fruit left in the forest, people are so hungry,' I said.

'Ja,' Nick grinned, 'but it's what's in the ground that's interesting. The next position to us, at Lofa Bridge, has got quite a lot of diamonds.' The word flashed between us. 'They need to hold Lofa because otherwise Tubmanburg will fall, but they are so busy with fighting that there's no chance to make it pay.'

No one had mentioned diamonds before, but it was true, they were here. Although reserves were minuscule in comparison with Sierra Leone, Liberia nonetheless had enough deposits to be of interest to big mining corporations, and, it seemed, mercenaries.

As we talked, it became apparent that Nick's knowledge was extensive. He had been a senior commander in a private army charged with re-capturing the vast diamond fields only a short hop over the border with Sierra Leone from where we sat now.

'Deku says Sekou has been very much against it, the diamonds. There was some trouble a year ago when one commander was killed over some stones. He was ambushed by his own men. Now they have the death penalty if anyone mines the stones for themselves.'

It was becoming clearer that Nick and Deku, and probably the other commanders, had not just been talking about the war.

'Okay, but it still doesn't solve the supply issue. If there are diamonds, Taylor will want the area back as soon as possible – and even if the LURD can mine the stones and sell them, it's still going to be practically impossible to hold their ground there.'

That argument was good for the war *per se*, not just the diamonds. While the rebels were only supplied overland from the north, the war was all but unwinnable.

'Ja, that's why I'm going to try and get them a helicopter.'

I hadn't seen that coming.

'Is that possible?' I asked sceptically.

'I think so. If the stones are good enough, then they could either buy one outright or rent flight time from an operator based in Freetown or Guinea. They could use it to get the stones out – which is safer and solves the ambush problem – and drop troops and logistics right on the front.'

I sat in amazement.

'And', he continued, 'if you came back to do more filming, you wouldn't have to fokken walk in!'

Nick expanded the plan. He would speak to Sekou Conneh when we got back to Voinjama and 'make him a proposal'. He would need shovels, sieves, small water pumps, rice and basic foodstuffs to get the operation going: hardly any capital outlay for an extraordinary potential return. He told stories with child-like enthusiasm about lucky strikes in Angola; about men made millionaires by a single stone; about the freedom and adventure that came from mining. It was hard work, it was dangerous work, and it was absolutely, unquestionably illegal. In terms of international law, the words 'diamond' and 'opium' were almost interchangeable.

His motivation was simple. No one was paying him for this gruelling slog in Liberia. He needed to make it pay, somehow. But if mining here was going to work, what Nick needed, to make his plan come good, was a partner: someone he could trust, someone who knew the terrain, someone who was respected by the rebels. Nick, it turned out, needed me.

'Have a think about it. We could get very rich, and it's a chance to do something for the ordinary people here. I mean, they have *nothing*.'

I said nothing. There was nothing to say. What he was proposing was wild, adventurous and unthinkable.

Our silence was broken by shouting from below the balcony. A couple of rebels had come to tell us the good news: they had taken a prisoner that morning and they wanted us to witness the interrogation.

Thick-set and listless, the prisoner lay on the poured-concrete floor outside the town jail – a robust two-cell lock-up a hundred yards up the lane from our billet. He was already naked. Torn and bloodstained white underpants were all that remained of his clothing.

I looked at Nick, and said, 'He's fucked.'

On the walk down, he'd told me straight: if the prisoner is naked, he's a dead man. Nick nodded and went in ahead of me. A dreadful feeling of suspense settled as I started filming.

'We capture 'im livin',' one of the rebels explained. Most of their banter was in dialect; at times it was hard to be sure if they were speaking in English or Mandingo.

Their prisoner was an older man, well into his thirties, his light skin reddened from rolling in dust. I could see a gash by the side of the man's right knee; and, as his torso twisted around, unable to support its own weight, I saw a larger hole in the base of his back. I guessed that he'd been shot in the leg, and that the round had exited from behind.

He was encircled by the pink, red and green flip-flops of his captors, their AK barrels pointing down. Most were young, in their teens or early twenties, decked out with magazine bandoliers, bush hats and black vests. One younger kid wore a garish turquoise-and-pink striped shell-suit top with yellow shorts; another sported a blue football shirt.

'He wa' capture' on the main roa', on de fron' lahn,' a fighter in a mauve beanie hat shouted at me. Tempers were becoming excited; the younger guys crowded round, ordering other rebels to get out.

'How did you capture him?' I asked the beanie hat, from behind the camera.

'Becau' de fi'powah wa' too heavy fo' 'im!'

No sooner had he spoken than his friends ripped his hat off, laughing, exposing short braids that glistened with sweat. They were making him look good for the camera.

I wanted to know what regiment the prisoner was from. Some thought the Navy Division.

'No, he i' RUF fro' Sierra L'one,' one of the younger guys explained.

The prisoner was possibly one of the mercenaries that the radio intercepts indicated Taylor had flown in from the Sierra Leone border to help the Navy Division attack Tubmanburg.

The rebel unsheathed his bayonet as he spoke and cut open the charm that had been tied around the prisoner's neck. It was filled with dry grass and herbs.

'Dis i' traditiona' me'icine, African me'icine, to protec' fro' bulleh'.'

Two other rebels held him up and poured water into the RUF man's mouth. Their prisoner was conscious, talking, at the end of what I imagined had been a lengthy interrogation. He held his arms up, waving them, as if he were dancing.

'A-wooh! A-wooh!' chanted the rebels.

I stepped back, holding the camera steady. The rebels took it in turns to shout at the prisoner, mocking him for being captured. A woman came and looked on as a burning cigarette end was forced into his mouth, between his lips, and extinguished on his tongue.

'Cot i' ou',' said the woman.

One of the teenagers pointed at the moaning prisoner and started saying something to me about his 'power'. Wrapped in thick patois, the words were lost on me. Next to him, an older fighter who spoke clearer English translated.

'He say he wan' take de heart ou' an' ea' i'.'

'Yeah,' concurred the teenager, 'i' wi' hep me to kill.'

An AK bayonet was passed from hand to hand and sharpened on the stone steps of the jail house. Then it was passed back again, and they sliced off the prisoner's ear with three swift strokes, and stuffed it into his mouth. His head rolled, his eyes flickered. He was still alive. They dragged him to the road by his feet. His skull thumped heavily up the steps. Singing and chanting, they carried him through town. Everyone came out to look: women wrapped in colourful, striped batiks; children holding ragged soft toys; old men in ruined suits. After a couple of hundred yards, they cut the other ear off. Now they dragged, and no longer carried, him.

'Jay!' called the teenager. 'Jay, I wan' to ea' heart, I wan' ea' de man heart. I'm a wickeh boy, I'm a rebel.'

'I' ca' hep to make yor protec'shan stron' when y' ea' yor enemy, when y' ea' deh heart, as a warriah,' clarified another rebel in a black T-shirt.

'I origina' Sonny Boy,' a voice chirped up to my left. It belonged to a rebel no more than fifteen years old, likely much younger. 'I eatin' de heart in peppah sou'. Yes! I' wi' mak' my protec'shan *hu*'!'

Finally, they stopped and mocked their captive one last time before driving a bayonet into his chest just below his sternum. In all likelihood, that was what killed him, there in front of me, on film. I hoped so, because what came next was so inhumane, so abhorrent, that it was hard to trust my eyes. If I had not filmed it,

I would have come to doubt this happened, could have happened, at all.

As red and yellow intestines bubbled out of the slit in his stomach, the rebels severed his penis and testicles.

'Y' ma pusseh!' shouted the rebels. And then they butchered him.

I filmed it diligently: wide shots; cutaways of small details – the bloody knife, the man's feet; and the close-up, messy business of gutting a human being. I protected myself, my mind – or so I thought – by collecting the individual details of murder frame by frame.

Cutting up a man with an AK bayonet is not a simple task. A rock was used as a mallet to help smash the blade through the rib cage so that the prized organs could be reached more easily. As the stone came down, it made a wet *thock, thock, thock* sound, as the blows echoed in the partially opened chest cavity. The cadaver rocked to and fro with the exertion. When the organs came out they did so with a slurping pop, or a stretched-out squelch. The smell of blood was heady, and clung to the roof of my mouth in a metallic glaze.

Finally, the teenager held the heart aloft.

'I'm a totally wickeh boy,' he proclaimed.

'We a' de lion o' de jongle,' the others sang.

I zoomed in for a close-up and re-focused to find myself filming deep into the gaping chest. I panned away feeling like a voyeur, a thief, as if such intimate shots were part of the violation. But the corpse was compelling. There seemed no good reason not to film anything now. If I could have saved him, I would have; but he was already naked. He was already naked. *He was already naked*, I told myself, as the tape sped through my camera.

'We a' de Kamajor fro' Kenema,' another fighter announced, a kidney in his hand. 'I' mak' good foo' fo' os.'

'You're from Sierra Leone?' I asked.

'Yessah.'

The civil war in Sierra Leone had supposedly ended a year before, and yet here were both sides of that conflict – the previously Western-backed Kamajor civil militia and the Taylor-backed RUF fighting to the death on a daily basis. They sang and gyrated around the desecrated body, and then whooped and hollered back into town, setting out the chopped-up sweetbreads on a mocked-up market stall. Then they carried their bullion back to their billets, to be mixed with hot chillies and stewed cassava leaf, and served with handfuls of starchy white rice.

It was extremely hard to find common ground with cannibals. They had masked their crime with the language of anthropology – a tradition and legacy of ritual and magic that saw warriors in West Africa's forests consume their enemies to assume their prowess in battle. That much I knew was true from talking to Cobus in Freetown; but if that could justify the torture and murder of a prisoner of war – albeit one who likely shared similar beliefs – then anyone could justify anything. Moral relativism in war, it seemed, was the first step on the short road to genocide.

Nick had stood guard over me at a respectful distance while I filmed. He said nothing, did not interfere; he gave neither opinion nor advice. When it was over, he said, simply, 'Ag, they did that for the camera.'

I was polite, but almost angry. I disagreed vehemently. I hadn't been complicit in this brutal killing, I told him, suddenly unsure of myself.

As we walked back to our balcony, I explained that they were all from Sierra Leone, a detail that had passed him by. In fact, these were the same troops he was fighting with and against in Executive Outcomes. Then he understood. Theatrical flourishes in its execution notwithstanding, it had been absolutely genuine.

For my part, I could not honestly say exactly why I had filmed, only that it had happened, and I had been there. I was in Liberia to film; so I had filmed. To stop, to turn the camera off in the middle of this killing, would have been a bolder statement than not to have filmed at all – and could have put us both at risk. My security depended upon their respect, and their acceptance. What happened with the footage was for later discussion.

Perhaps there was another reason, too. You could watch a hundred hours of television news, and never see a death in war: fighting was re-packaged as politics; death sanitised; horror neutered before the ad-break. Shock, disgust, revulsion – these did not draw in audiences, could not sell the nine o'clock news: no one showed the visceral truth of war, especially not an uncivil war in West Africa. I was convinced of my duty to depict the reality of the fighting. There I was, up to my elbows in blood and shit, thinking: *James, you have finally found something you are good at.* And the consequences of employing that skill were something I would have to live with.

The butchering reminded me of something Cobus had said to me in Freetown, while venting against the RUF. 'In my mind, you draw a line,' he'd said. 'At a certain point a human being becomes less of a human being, and more of an animal, and then he should just be culled and got rid of as quickly as possible so the rest of humanity can go on with their lives. There should just be total annihilation for animals like that.'

I remembered the quote by heart, it had seemed so shocking. At the time I had thought it racist bile – no one was irredeemable; no one should be denied a trial to account for their crimes. Now I wasn't so sure. Perhaps ruthlessly wiping out rebels, government armies – whoever – was a sensible route for guiding West Africa back to normality after all.

I said as much to Nick. How was it possible to see the men around us as anything but bloodthirsty savages?

'In Sierra Leone, some of the local guys under my command started to cut the heads off the rebels they captured,' Nick recounted. 'I stopped that immediately. Once you do that – taking heads – you become as bad as the people you're fighting against.'

On this day, of all days, Nick seemed to me the epitome of the professional soldier; his calmness made him seem measured and wise, so much so that I failed to notice that he hadn't answered my question. The irony of asking one of apartheid's shock troops for moral guidance, though, was not lost on me. I was a long way from scribbling black power graffiti on my text books at school. Propping his AK against the balustrade and unlacing his boots, Nick explained how the RUF had launched their offensive from Liberia in 1991, led by Sankoh – a disaffected army corporal.

'At first the rebels said they wanted to stop the corruption in the government – which was really bad, even by African standards. But as soon as they got their hands on the guns, they went crazy. It was unbelievable.'

Community leaders who opposed them were decapitated, their children forced to rape their mothers, the villagers kidnapped and forced to dig for diamonds.

Nick reminded me of the history that I had learned while staying with Cobus in Freetown a year before. As more territory fell to the rebels, and more atrocities were committed, the international community looked on – unwilling to commit the troops or resources necessary to halt the RUF's advance. Bloodied by losses in Somalia and Rwanda, and the humiliation of having their peacekeepers used as human shields by the Bosnian Serbs, the United Nations did nothing. The Nigerians sent a small force to guard key installations, and ended up participating in a debauch of violence and looting themselves. The Libyans, meanwhile, had trained the rebel commanders near Tripoli, and Charles Taylor, the Liberian president who was rattling his sabre at us further up the road, was alleged to have been busy providing cash, weapons and yet more training in return for the blood diamonds mined illegally by rebel slave-labour. 'Sierra Leone', Taylor said in an interview with the BBC, 'will taste the bitterness of war.' In desperation, Valentine Strasser, then the incumbent in Sierra Leone's presidential palace, brokered a deal with EO in March 1995. In the face of absolute abandonment by the international community, Nick's mercenaries had been the only people willing to help – for a price.

The company had been founded in 1989 by agents from the South African CCB, the Civil Cooperation Bureau – a sinister counter-insurgency agency that specialised in murder, assassinations and dirty tricks. So secretive was the CCB that its existence was only officially admitted in 1990. These men, I fancied, were not regular soldiers like Nick, but were instead apartheid's willing executioners. Nick himself believed that ultimately the CCB had been designed to form the nucleus of a white resistance organisation to fight black-majority rule in the way that the apartheid government had faced an ongoing armed struggle from the ANC and MK. In the end, most of the CCB's agents had gone to jail, gone to ground – or found lucrative employment in the commercial sector.

Executive Outcomes was originally conceived as a front-organisation for South Africa's increasingly isolated regime – an apparently legitimate commercial company that, like many others, was set up as part of a sanctions-busting operation in the late '80s and early '90s. EO was then transformed in 1993 by a consortium of English entrepreneurs, including a rich businessman called Tony Buckingham and a wealthy ex-SAS officer called Simon Mann.

These men needed a South African-registered company – and experienced military personnel – to realise their wider ambition to create a modern, corporate military machine for hire anywhere in the world. They injected funding, business acumen and legitimacy. Led by experienced South African Special Forces operators, EO morphed from an underground Afrikaner cell into the world's largest private army. Complete with its own airline, hundreds of employees and multi-million-dollar contracts, it operated some of the longest supply lines in modern military history – at times from Pretoria to Sierra Leone, Cabinda and New Guinea in the Pacific. They claimed to deal only with bona fide governments: no coups, no assassinations and no support to rebel groups. And they got rich.

Strasser – Sierra Leone's 'legitimate' leader – had himself taken power with a military junta in a coup three years previously. At the tender age of twenty-five, he was the world's youngest head of state. As the RUF marched on Freetown, he feared he may also be one of the shortest-lived. He invited EO into the country for a fee of $31 million a year, to be remunerated out of diamond revenues (of which nearly $19 million would never be paid). Having previously fought very effectively against UNITA rebels in Angola, EO's foot-soldiers and commanders were confident of success.

Nick picked up the story.

'From about May in '95, around two hundred South Africans were sent out there – the rebels were right on the edge of Freetown. Ja, we was equipped only with light weapons, but we had a couple of armoured personnel carriers and one attack helicopter, which was very handy. The original guys who went there secured Freetown in six weeks.'

Nick arrived in Sierra Leone shortly after. Within eighteen months they had comprehensively destroyed the RUF's 3,000 to 4,000-strong rebel army. By the time EO's contract was cancelled under pressure from the international community, the RUF held no significant territory in Sierra Leone at all.

'The guys just did it with these,' he said, nodding to his rifle. 'They picked on the nearest RUF concentration to Freetown and attacked it. From there, we just carried on that way. We had the same weapons as these guys, the rebels here, but ours were better-maintained, and we knew how to use them.'

It wasn't simply the case that the rebels were a disorganised rabble who couldn't fight their way out of a paper bag: the soldiers that EO deployed were extraordinarily efficient and battle-hardened from two decades of war in Southern Africa. They learned from early mistakes. On one occasion, Cobus's entire squad was almost wiped out.

'Ja, before I got there, he was ambushed once by the rebels. The RUF lined both sides of the road, spaced at intervals, and let them have it with everything they had at once. The first vehicle lost a track when the driver turned too quickly, then the other driver stalled when they were hit by a grenade – a direct hit on the turret. The blast knocked out Henri the gunner's eye.'

After the fighting of the last week in Liberia, I could imagine it only too well: blood everywhere; unbearable noise; the screams of the injured.

'Ag, Henri was trapped in the turret and just carried on firing. He went through hundreds of rounds of ammunition, while Cobus led his troops round the back. He managed to counter-attack just as Henri ran out of ammo.'

As if ushered on by the darkness, rain began to lash the zinc roof of our house, sending the hidden frogs outside into paroxysms of excitement.

'It was fokken close enough, though,' Nick added.

The troops he spoke of in EO were an eclectic bunch – of whom around 90 per cent were black, not white, Africans. Many of them were, in fact, Angolans who had fought in the South African Army's 32 'Buffalo' Battalion – South Africa's Foreign Legion. Recruited to fight for South Africa against their newly independent, Marxist, government, these soldiers became among the most feared troops in the apartheid state's army. Led by white officers and supported by Special Forces commandos – including

Nick, on dozens of operations – they specialised in daring long-range attacks against their fellow-countrymen. Unloved by the new democratic government in Pretoria, their controversial unit was disbanded. All but unemployable in the New South Africa, dozens of them joined Executive Outcomes.

After the disaster of opening the general store in the Snake Pit, the lure of an adventure with the guys he'd fought alongside with for so long was irresistible. Nick went in as one of the three overall commanders of EO's ground operations. As a top dog of war, the company's stunning victory in the face of overwhelming odds was partly his own.

As well as finding a respite from the new South Africa, Nick found diamonds. Part of EO's mandate was to head straight to Kono and open the diamond field there so that Strasser's government could generate revenue and pay their bills to EO. I knew from Cobus that other rebel bases had been passed over in the stampede to get to Kono – a fact that did not sit well with many of the hired soldiers. Nick was more relaxed. He was there to orchestrate the fighting; the diamond deals were for others to arrange. No diamonds, no pay. It was that simple.

As Nick dissected the tactics of his mercenary war, like some dark bedtime story, ominous explosions erupted into the evening air beyond the horizon, muffled by the falling rain. Worryingly, they came from the Bopolu road, behind us. Initial booms were followed by the crackle of small arms just audible over the hissing downpour and the whoosh of RPGs. There was little doubt: the long-awaited re-supply of ammunition from Fassama must have been ambushed. Not only were we surrounded, but we had no means to repel the next assault.

Nick and I discussed our options. We were bored and terrified by the inevitability of the daily attacks on the town. It was time to take control. We sent the pekin who brought us our rice to fetch Deku and Dragon Master. They arrived quickly, wet from the rains, in sullen mood.

'Deku,' I began, cautiously, 'I would like you to think about doing something for us.' They looked at me quizzically. 'We would like you to send out an ambush party tonight, on the Monrovia Highway. The Government troops attack us every day from the same direction. If we can hit them before they reach the town, they'll turn back.'

Dragon Master and Deku considered it. It was unorthodox; no one liked fighting in the rain. Fighting at night was usually out of the question. Nick pressed the point home. In the morning we would be attacked, and we had three choices: evacuate now; be wiped out in a last stand with no ammo; or use what little supplies we still had to cut them off before they got here.

Deku agreed. Over our battered map, Nick laid out the basic structure of the ambush, and within an hour a platoon of men snaked off into the howling storm.

In the time it had taken to conclude the short conversation, I had crossed another line. I wanted to survive, at any cost. I had taken my chances in battle for days on end, but I wasn't prepared to be killed by the stupidity of incompetent rebel tacticians. I was making my own luck – and drawing up my own moral code for war reporting at the same time. If that meant participating, so be it.

8
THE GREAT ESCAPE

Before dawn broke, the distant rumble of explosions told us the ambush had begun. Nick and I sat in the dark, and waited for the sodden men to return to camp. They all did. No rebels were injured; no Government troops were confirmed killed. With them they brought 10,000 rounds of captured ammunition and thirty-five AKs.

I leaned on the balcony and breathed a long sigh of relief into the weak morning light. The odds had been tipped slightly in our favour.

'De bulleh' too plenteh to carry,' the dripping captain in charge of the operation informed me, breathless with pride at his daring raid. 'We burn i' by de roa' si' so dey can' use i' on os.'

A thick smile spread across his face. Nick's relief turned to anger: 10,000 rounds was a lot of ammunition; but 20,000 rounds could have been decisive. They could have hidden the valuable extra ammunition and gone back for it later. Instead, they had burned it.

At least the Government army had been prevented from reaching town. It gave us the space to try and find out what had really happened to the big shipment from Fassama, and then plan accordingly. There was still no sign, nor word, of the expected delivery – and we feared the worst.

Emboldened by what he saw as the success of the morning's ambush, Deku sent a hundred LURD fighters out from Cobra Battalion to attack the Government forces at Klay Junction immediately. They returned surprisingly quickly with another 7,500 rounds of ammunition and sixty-five captured AKs. Still wrapped up and in their factory grease, the new rifles looked like overgrown sardines freshly prised from a gigantic tin. I peeled back the plastic packaging to examine them. Deku was euphoric about the seizure; Nick was interested, as always, in all sorts of weapons; together they missed the true significance of the haul: Taylor was breaking the United Nations and regional ECOWAS arms embargo levied against him. The rifles were stamped, as usual, with their date of manufacture – in this case 2002 – engraved above the magazine port, next to the serial and model numbers. The rebels had not just captured weapons, they had gathered evidence. Nick traded in his Kalashnikov for one of the new haul. Although they were of inferior manufacture to the one he'd been using until then, it was the only way we could guarantee holding onto one long enough to deliver it to the Americans in Conakry.

'Eastern European,' he said, turning the deep black metalwork over in his hands, completely absorbed by the novelty of it.

I photographed the rifles, the serial numbers and dates of manufacture and called the BBC – who said they could not broadcast the find.

'That's a serious allegation,' the producer informed me, presumably in case I thought accusing state leaders of breaking international law was trivial. 'We'd need to see evidence of that.'

'I'm holding it in my hand,' I said, gesticulating to Nick – who was almost hugging the rifle with excitement – to bring it over. 'I can read you the serial number for you to run.'

The producer stood his ground. It seemed that breathless, chaotic details about the rebels' war were fine, but committing an act of journalism was clearly a bridge too far. I hung up in frustration, and then laughed at myself. If I could still find it within me to get cross with them for not seeing the big picture, then at least I was still focused on the story. That was what mattered most. I had crossed the line in many respects, but I was still, somewhere down there, a journalist – not a propagandist, nor a would-be diamond dealer, and certainly not a soldier.

No sooner had I hung up than the first walking wounded from the ambushed ammunition re-supply – that had apparently been hit the evening before – began to limp into town. It had taken them all night to reach Tubmanburg as they staggered along the road from Bopolu. In fact, the muffled explosions that we had heard in the rain hadn't been an ambush at all. Dragon Master held his head in his hands as he told me the story he'd pieced together from the survivors. Packed with ammunition, mortar bombs and rocket-propelled grenades, the looted ambulance (the same one that had accompanied us to Tubmanburg eighteen days before) was also carrying another precious commodity: petrol. Riding shotgun on the roof, a rebel guard had flicked away his cigarette butt only for it to be sucked into the ambulance through an open window. The entire cargo had gone up like a fuel bomb. There had been uncounted casualties.

Dragon Master was unable to look me in the eye. Deku shook his head and confessed that an even larger consignment of ammunition had been diverted to other troops in Gbarnga, who were loyal to LURD chief of staff, Prince Seo. Deku claimed that Seo wanted the victory for himself, and was deliberately thwarting the men in Bomi Hills.

It was then we knew it was over. Retreat was certain.

'Let's go and help them,' Nick said, disappearing into our room to fetch the medical bag and a handful of burn dressings.

* * *

Unable to capitalise on their two raids, the rebels fell back to what they knew best: waiting. Only one day passed – enough time to continue treating the wounded from the ambulance disaster – until the attack began. Re-supplied and reinvigorated, the Government army came at us with sustained, unprecedented force.

Every new day that passed in Tubmanburg posed the same question: why continue filming? An irrational feeling of self-justification spurred me on. The only reason I was there was to film. If I wasn't filming, what *was* I doing? The alternative was unthinkable. Watching – and not shooting – the war felt uncomfortably like being a tourist.

What was perhaps harder to understand was why Nick continued enthusiastically to plunge into combat with me. Unpaid, and with nothing more to gain from helping me steal snap-shots of the increasingly lethal battles, his motivation remained mysterious. We never discussed it. If I wanted to film, he assessed the situation, and dived in with me. He never refused and he never complained.

Over the next few days more prisoners were captured, interrogated and executed. I tried to save one man – a machine gunner who had been captured but not tortured. It would, I tried to convince the commanders, send a signal to the Government troops that if they surrendered to you, they would not be harmed. It was an idea supported by Dragon Master. The prisoner was led off to an old police cell while Deku considered the proposition. The next morning, Deku walked him out into the forest after dawn, and shot him.

I felt defeated. The only time they'd done as I asked was when I'd suggested attacking the enemy. Hungry and disorientated, battle fatigue began to settle in. I stopped taking notes. I realised that I was scared of losing my mind. In bed at night I felt as if I was falling in the darkness. My left ear throbbed intermittently; dense, inexplicable scabs had risen on my legs and scrotum; my head itched uncontrollably. Nick's health was failing, too, though he remained the quiet professional, uncomplaining if increasingly thin and pale.

Twenty-four hours later, with a sense of grim inevitability, disappointment and relief, Deku announced that Tubmanburg had to be evacuated. Almost all of their ammunition had been used up – what remained was enough to fight a planned and ordered retreat.

'Sarry,' he said, looking crestfallen at the news he brought as we stood on our balcony.

'Ja, it's time to go,' Nick replied.

I didn't know what to say to Deku.

'It's okay,' I tried to reassure him, 'you'll get to Monrovia after the rains.'

And then to Nick, as I turned to get my stuff: 'I'm good to go.'

I took one last look around our bedroom, and then rejoined Nick on the balcony. I had come to Liberia for a three-week filming trip and had ended up spending twenty-one days in Tubmanburg alone, almost all of them under fire. Below us, Deku marshalled his soldiers and dished out the precious remaining bullets. All the rebels who left were allowed one full magazine. The rest were given to the fighters who had 'volunteered' to stay. We walked down to greet him. He pledged to make a stand in the centre of town long enough for us to get clear.

'Y' see me in Bopolu,' he promised. 'I'm a jongle warriah, so I move fas'.'

We shook hands and he turned his back on us, marching off to meet the inevitable attack.

'Deku,' I called after him. He stopped and looked back. 'Are you ready?' I shouted, smiling.

'Yeah!' he laughed in reply. 'An' we prepare'!'

* * *

At 11 a.m., on 19 July, Nick and I walked out of town ahead of Deku and the LURD main force, accompanied by around 400 civilians. I had packed my camera away, and given the bag to a porter. I felt liberated.

'After you, Mr Brabazon,' Nick smiled, ushering me ahead as we turned our backs on the old mining town.

In an orderly file, we marched through slag heaps of iron tailings from disused mines, and I saw for the first time the lush, green bush to the north of the town. It was only as we left, as this vista opened up, that I suddenly realised how claustrophobic Tubmanburg had been. For the first time in three weeks, I could see further than the end of the street. It was a beautiful sensation.

My relief at leaving, though, was smothered by the increasingly brutal throbbing in my ear. As we trudged into the long grass, and as the rhythm of my feet hitting the ground gathered momentum, the pain became severe. Each footfall jarred my ear canal like a swingeing blow to the head. I stopped suddenly and vomited against a tree. Nick gave me our last painkiller, and then, from his webbing, produced a miracle: penicillin.

'That should set you right,' he promised. 'I was saving them for an emergency.'

As I swallowed two massive 1,000mg caplets with a gulp from his water bottle, I clenched my jaw and marched. I prayed the antibiotics would kill the infection before the infection finished me. I felt dead on my feet, and the walk hadn't even begun.

Taylor's army had left us one route out – a narrow hunters' trail barely six inches wide, snaking off into the forest behind the old mine works. Battered by near-constant rains, the terrain was sodden. We passed through one last village, whose dilapidated houses hardly kept the encroaching jungle at bay. Deserted, it reeked of putrid flesh. We marched in silence, and out of the shadow of a decrepit hut thatched with torn raffia hobbled a child covered with infected burns. Her limbs were swollen with gangrene. She stood and watched us pass her. The stench was unbreathable. No one stopped. No one spoke. We carried on in silence and left her there to die.

When I had walked into the jungle six weeks earlier, the war had come out to meet me, worsening by degree: the wounded men, those first fallen fighters whose corpses I had made light of. Now, as we walked out of the war, I felt like a ghost of that traveller: pity, compassion, empathy – these luxuries were gone; in their place grew determination, and disgust.

'I always prefer', Nick said, as we sloshed our way between the flooded tree trunks, 'never to take the same road twice. It's good that we're going back a different way. We'll get to see more of the country.'

I was back on the hiking trip from hell with my dad.

After seven hours of marching, the distant boom of RPGs signalled the attack on Tubmanburg. Their faint rumble belied its severity. The LURD rear-guard would now try and catch up with us.

There was no rest that evening. The fear was that the Navy Division would follow them – and us. As night fell, we moved deeper into the forest, walking at first in the gloom of twilight, and then in the pitch black. I could see absolutely nothing – not my hand in front of my face, not the path: nothing at all. Unseen roots tripped me up; tree trunks loomed up like icebergs in the dense black sea of the forest. I held the hand of the woman who walked in front; Nick clutched the back of my shirt. Torches were forbidden. Occasionally, the moon would break through the monsoon clouds and flit through the leaves high above. All it showed us was the thin silver ribbon of the sandy path snaking north.

Day broke and we walked still. By mid-morning sounds of fighting – an RPG blast every few minutes, a volley of shots in between times – flared up in the distance. At times it grew closer, and then ebbed away, lost in the trees. We were being hunted.

'Best to keep moving,' said Nick. 'Just keep moving. Those Government guys are not well disciplined. They'll probably give up or get bored of marching.'

March we did. Sixty hours after leaving Tubmanburg, with one night-time rest in a jungle village, we arrived in Bopolu. The penicillin had begun to work, but my knees were so weak I could walk only by leaning heavily on a stick. One fighter, a stout, tough guy called Abe, carried my six-foot-four frame on his back for a five-mile stretch, my feet dragging on the floor. I lay my head on his shoulder like I had done on my father's back when I was a child.

When Abe and Nick and I emerged from the bush into town, the elders laughed at us as he helped me down, and called me Moses as I leaned on my staff and shook the sweat out of my beard. Our entourage dispersed through town, looking for shelter for the night. I sat and smoked a cigarette in the town square, while Nick checked his GPS. I looked up to see the familiar lumbering gait of Deku running towards me.

'Mah man, I tol' y' I wou' see y' here.'

He took a cigarette off me and recounted the evacuation of Tubmanburg: there were no casualties; all rebel heavy weapons were abandoned; it was a decisive victory for Taylor. It had taken the Navy Division a mere thirty-five minutes to occupy the town that Deku's men had controlled for twenty-three weeks. Now we were only a day ahead of the Government army. A detachment of fighters would remain in Bopolu – Deku himself had forged ahead of the troops coming from Tubmanburg along a disused shortcut. I asked him when he thought the LURD would be able to attack Tubmanburg again.

'Ou' plennification i' to move ba' to Tocmanbur' an' make shu' we control i', becau' das ou' military targe'.' He paused, perhaps in recognition of how unlikely that now seemed. 'Fro' he',' he concluded, 'we bea' i' all de way ba' to Guinea.'

All the way to Guinea could be more than 200 miles – which, through dense jungle, would feel like twice that. It was a daunting prospect. I didn't know if I was up to it. To take my mind off the task ahead, I called my mother with the news that I was on my way home.

'That's great, darling,' she said when I told her, her voice full of the contentment of a woman who did not know her son had seen so much death. 'Listen, I've got some important news for you,' she continued.

My gut tightened at the prospect of some bad news, but it was just an invite to a wedding in Dublin I had failed to reply to. It made me laugh, to remember what was important, and what was not.

'Will you be home in time?'

I had no idea – but asked her to book me a flight and a hotel, anyway. It was something to hold onto, something normal and nice to look forward to. She was making small talk to keep me on the line.

'It won't be long now, Mum. Promise,' I interrupted her, but then the connection went dead.

In the morning more fighters joined us with more ammunition, and at dawn we were walking again. My knees were now tightly strapped, and my ear was greatly improved, but I was depressed about the journey ahead. Promises of finally seeing the war up close had sustained me through the long slog down; but the road out was just an unpleasant necessity to be completed as quickly, and painlessly, as possible.

'No one knows who controls the roads,' Nick said, sensing my frustration as we stepped off into the bush, 'so it is best we stick to these little paths.'

We walked for five days, stealing snatches of sleep in wrecked houses that rose up like wounded giants in villages that had otherwise been almost completely razed. Two days after leaving Bopolu, we heard explosions and small-arms chatter that signalled the Government's arrival in the town. We had put an extra day between us and the Navy Division. I could imagine what had delayed them: the civilian population would be paying a severe penalty for hosting the rebels, even if they had done so unwillingly.

Our food supplies were almost non-existent. We ate what fruit we could find on the trees, and Nick used his rifle to shoot down bunches of green coconuts, which he shared with all the rebels. The juice ran through my beard. It was the first time I'd drunk anything but water for a month. Occasionally, a rebel would throw a grenade into a stream and scoop out the blasted fish.

There was no one living to be seen in the jungle, but on the path a corpse blocked our way. Turned green with decay, his black skin had swollen and cracked; from a deep slash in his stomach, his intestine spilled over his sides and out onto the forest floor. We held our noses and stepped around him.

We walked through Fassama, past the front door to the Spider House, which seemed like a memory from a waking dream. I thought about the interminable games of cards Nick and I had played, my panic at his 'death' – and how absolutely unprepared I had been for what had followed. Then we headed out into the forest again, along a path untrodden by us. Nightfall on that fifth evening saw Nick and me hunkered down in the ruins of a mud-walled building. A strong, refreshing wind rushed through the burned timbers and trampled gardens of the village: a monsoon downpour was on its way. We found a tiny strip of dry ground to sleep on, in between piles of rubble. Nick strung a groundsheet over it as protection from the rain.

'Home sweet home,' he said, standing back to admire his handiwork.

We ducked inside. Opening above us, the sky emptied gallons of water onto the rebel camp. I rooted around in my bag and felt for the familiar shape of the items I was looking for. A wave of excitement crept up on me.

'Ag, I think we have run out of food. Maybe they've got a little rice left.'

Nick was ravenous; we were marching on empty.

'Well,' I announced, feeling like a kid on Christmas Day, 'this should set you right.'

From my bag I produced a tin of Heinz baked beans and a half-full quarter-bottle of Johnnie Walker.

'I was saving them for an emergency.'

'Now that is fokken great news, man!'

His face lit up in the torch beam. We took it in turns to eat the beans, cold from the tin, in secret. Then we each took a long pull on the magic bottle.

'Ah!' said Nick. He licked his lips and drew the back of his hand across his mouth, before wiping the bottle as a courtesy to me. 'That's like mother's milk.'

We finished it up, and I carefully swallowed my last Valium – ashamed that Nick might see me.

'I can't believe you were keeping that whisky all the time. You are a dark horse, Mr Brabazon,' he whispered in amazement.

I drifted off to sleep, drunk and high, crammed with Nick into a space no bigger than a coffin.

Daybreak revealed the swollen mass of the River Via, tumbling through the forest a short walk from the edge of the village. Spanning its fierce current was an improvised rope-bridge that hung, in tatters, between enormous trees on the banks.

'Now you know why I never joined the circus,' I quipped to Nick, trying not to focus on the eddies and swirls below.

'Ja, but we don't exactly have all day. I think Mr Taylor's men would still like to have a chat with you.'

I took his point and shuffled faster, eyes fixed on the far bank, white knuckles clenching the frayed guide ropes. No one fell. I watched from the far side as women with bundles on their heads and a toddler on each hip crossed over twice as fast as I had managed, unencumbered.

We trudged on, our column of refugees and fighters now stretching for nearly two kilometres. To the right of the narrow defile we struck out on, the trees thinned to reveal an open patch of grass about the size of a football pitch, populated by a lone hut.

'That would make a great place for an ambush,' I called out to Nick, behind me.

'Ja, it's perfect, hey?'

My steps rose and fell for another five minutes, and then a burst of gunfire sent me flat on my face. From behind us the rebels tried to flee from the AK rounds tearing up the afternoon air, but the path was blocked by frightened civilians. We crouched, and listened as two *thuds* preceded a lull and then a halt in the firing.

'Hand grenades,' said Nick. 'Ours, I hope.'

No more shots rang out. It was unclear if the Government troops had got around us, or if we'd run into another roving unit and re-created our own front line by chance. We walked on, and I realised how blasé I'd become since leaving Tubmanburg. I thought leaving the town had meant leaving the war. It hadn't.

Emerging at Zolowo, the track joined the wider road we'd walked down fifty days before. Salayie was in chaos. We were greeted by a horde of teenagers with Kalashnikovs and green bottles of homemade hooch in their hands. The local population was nowhere to be seen. Drunk, stoned, the fighters were running riot. All their commanders were either dead or had deserted. Heads wrapped in bright bandanas, spliffs hanging from their mouths, they made the once-picturesque village look like the set of some *Mad Max*-type movie.

'This is fokken bad. It's completely broken down here. Keep moving and try not to look anyone in the eye,' Nick cautioned.

We walked right through them. Very young fighters were openly disrespectful to Dragon Master and Deku, dancing in front of them, waving their guns around. The flimsy veneer of tribal unity that held the LURD together was cracking under the stress of the retreat. I saw Nick re-adjust his own rifle, cradling it against his chest. Any last vestiges of hope or respect I had for the LURD departed. Not only were the lunatics running the asylum, they were armed to the teeth and all under the age of fifteen.

As we marched onwards, my energy came in waves. When I thought I couldn't go on, a surge of power would grip my legs and I'd pace ahead, convinced again that I could make it after all. Nick was in the same boat. Marvellously, our energy ebbed and flowed at odds with each other, so when I was flagging, he spurred me on; when Nick slowed up, I teased him about being an old man, and he quickened his pace to keep up.

'Just think,' I said to him, as we puffed our way to the hump of a hill whose sides were moulded from red clay slippery as glass, 'every step we take is a step closer to fried chicken at the Petit Bateau. We are walking towards chicken.'

'And beer,' he added.

Despite our banter, Nick constantly had his eye on what might be on the horizon.

'Stay back,' he warned, 'let them get ahead.'

I was walking at the point of the front group. We waited together as the front unit pressed on and opened up a hundred yards between us.

'Ja, okay. Let's go.'

Nick was tired now, too. We were nearing our limit: it was well past midday and we'd been on the move without a real break since dawn. As we rounded the crest of the hill, we found a village spread out either side of the road. Running like a muddy red ribbon through a strip of open, green ground, the road ran past a dozen wooden huts built on the edge of the forest – and was flanked by two deep drainage ditches. A lone bench sat in the middle of what I took to be a sort of village green. I fixed my eye on it, and marched to it for a rest. Nick was in step behind me.

I saw the smoke before I heard the noise. From the window of one of the huts a thin blue-grey cloud struggled into the thick, humid air. Then our ears were filled for a brief moment with the sickening crackle of incoming rounds and then, a split second later, a cacophony of machine-gun rounds zooming past. I flung myself headlong into the ditch. Nick dived the other way. We'd been separated. A curtain of lead flew over my back. Up ahead, the LURD advance party had begun to reply. A volley of RPGs went off, followed by another, and another. Instead of diminishing, the shooting intensified. Joining the machine gun were bursts of AK fire and the blasts of hand grenades. Behind me a young woman and skinny older man were cowering in my ditch. Incredibly, the man was my porter; he had my bag. Smiling weakly as I wriggled up to him, he unstrapped my rucksack and then stared at me uncomprehending as I began to assemble my camera.

'I have to get this,' I heard myself repeating, 'I have to get this.'

The rebels had other ideas.

'Mah man, stop da' ting you doin'. Le' go! Le' go! Le' go!'

A commander whom I didn't recognise was crouched in the ditch with us. The very idea that I was trying to film was absurd to him. This was about survival, nothing else. He was right. I suddenly felt foolish, as if I'd learned nothing. I closed my bag, and he took it from me. I looked at the woman, and we held hands and stood up together to face the storm.

I braced myself for impact, and leaned forward, my left arm up over my head as if trying to keep dry in a squall. I could feel the bullets, see them: dirt flying up, the shot-riddled clay road; the air now thick with smoke. Seven or eight rebels lined the road ahead, launching grenade after grenade into the tree line. The noise filled my head entirely, blotting out all thought and feeling. Then Nick was there, and he grabbed me, and the three of us ran, holding hands; the commander charged ahead, my bag over his shoulder, his AK leaping and spewing spent cartridges across us. And we tumbled into the shade and cover of the trees, and lay on our backs, amazed and alive. All I could see were clouds and leaves.

'Sorry, man.'

I sat up and addressed the unknown commander, but he just shrugged and ran deeper into the forest. I turned to Nick.

'He was pissed off that I was trying to film. Fair enough, really.'

Nick didn't say anything. We picked ourselves up and began to run at a trot into the forest, following the civilians. The sound of gunfire and the screams of the injured harried us towards Zorzor until eventually the firing stopped, and the Government troops melted back into trees. Several people had been hit in the crossfire, but no one had died.

Zorzor had been only an hour's walk away. Taylor's men were close to a major LURD headquarters – which was practically undefended. If the Government took Zorzor, it would make it almost impossible for the rebels to re-supply their troops in the east. We sat on the stoop of an abandoned house and drank the rainwater cascading from the zinc roof.

'I can't go on.' Nick's voice was quiet, but even. 'I can't go any further.'

He was matter-of-fact. He took his boots off and sat back in an old wooden chair, drained. I was so exhausted that I wasn't sure I could carry on either. I suspected he was just trying to make me feel better. It seemed very unlikely that we were going anywhere anyway. Then, after an hour, Dragon Master stood up and shouldered his AK.

'Le' go! No car.'

We stared at him in disbelief, and then Nick silently re-laced his boots and I strapped up my knees.

'Ja, that is not really a surprise. It looks like we are walking the entire way.' Nick managed to smile at me. 'Not bad for an old guy.'

His beard was full now, and very white, making him look like a Father Christmas in camouflage. We put our feet to the road, and pressed on, turning off down a bush path and back into the unforgiving undergrowth of equatorial jungle. We walked more slowly now. Nick handed his AK to a small boy, employing his own pekin.

'This chicken', Nick mumbled, 'is going to be the best fokken chicken I have ever eaten.'

Then we stopped talking, and squelched northwest, daydreaming our separate fantasies of home.

Hours later – I no longer knew how many – we fell out of the fetid soup of the jungle and emerged at a clearing flanked by a brick bunker and a handful of young men in tatty green uniforms. The rebels greeted them enthusiastically: their faded yellow-and-green insignia heralded our escape. They were Guinean soldiers. After nine days of marching two hundred miles through the rain-soaked guts of the Liberian forest, we had crossed the border.

PART TWO

9
A STRANGER'S HAND

I woke up in my old bedroom in my mother's house to the sound of wood pigeons cooing in the boughs of the oak tree outside. I reached up and pulled the curtains apart, squinting as the warm light of an August morning filled the tiny room. All I could see were clouds and leaves. Downstairs Champion Jack Dupree growled on the record player. Bacon and toast were working their magic together in the kitchen – the scent of home creeping under the door to greet me. Mum tapped out a familiar Morse code with her teaspoon on her coffee mug, and cleared her throat – her way of calling to me without shouting through the house.

What was she going to make of me, her emaciated son with a shaggy beard, who crept home in the early morning the day before and slept for nearly twenty-four hours?

I wandered downstairs, into the familiar sanctuary of the dining room, kissed her on the cheek, and sat down at the dining table, which looked out over the garden. She went to speak, and then checked herself and disappeared back to the kitchen. A minute later she was plying me with an enormous bacon sandwich and a mug of steaming tea.

'You were ready for that,' she noted, taking away the empty plate a minute later. 'It hardly touched the sides.'

'Was I? Ready for it, I mean?' I said awkwardly.

I didn't feel ready for anything. She smiled and looked at me in a way that only mothers look at their own children: an inquisitor, assessing me like I'd had a bad day at school. I sat there barefoot in my favourite old green towelling dressing gown. It felt like I had surfaced from weeks under pressure into her small, quiet detached house in Canterbury. There was a lot to say – too much, perhaps – and neither of us knew where to start.

'I might have another round, if that's okay?'

She got up and smiled again, and went to cut more bread. Our cat sauntered in, sniffing the air like a sommelier nosing ripe claret. Beyond the double glazing, the heat of a perfect summer's day percolated through the leaves of the trees overhanging the lawn. The cat climbed up onto the windowsill next to me and we stared out at the garden together. She'd always been terrified of the world outside the back door. I knew how she felt.

After marching past the bedraggled border post, Nick and I had kept walking into Guinea with the rebels until we came to a small town where we found a LURD contingent waiting for us. Before we were bundled into a beaten-up white pick-up truck, Nick and I improvised a meal from the roadside market: we split open a fresh baguette (the first bread we'd eaten in two months), soaked it with condensed milk and layered it with sardines. Grinning at each other as we wolfed it down, we were too hungry to notice whether it tasted good, bad, or of anything at all. We toasted each other with bottles of orange Fanta – and set off for Macenta on a sugar high.

We rolled into the LURD compound that evening, through the high metal gates that had last opened to see us off into the war. Back then Macenta had seemed strange and foreign – a tiny town lost in the eastern forest region, cut off from normal life and filled with rebels, refugees, and all manner of people bustling through streets lined with traders and soldiers. Now it seemed normal: this was what West African towns were supposed to look like when they weren't blasted to bits by high explosive and raked by gunfire.

National Chairman Sekou Conneh was waiting for us in the forecourt where I'd watched Nick patch up the driver wounded by the freak grenade blast two months earlier. He had the kit bags that we'd left behind in Voinjama. Nothing had been stolen. Voinjama was in safe hands, he assured us, but it was unclear just how much territory the rebels expected to lose, or when they hoped to regain it.

'Taylah can' *mak' i'*,' was Conneh's only line, an emphatic statement that he clung to despite the fact that we had been chased all the way to the border. Zorzor must have been overrun behind us, or at least surrounded.

We ate a hasty and heavily salted rice meal that made our mouths burn, and then joined Conneh and Bengura, the Guinean president's almost-sober driver, for the overnight ride back to Conakry. As Bengura loaded the Jeep in the dimly lit compound, Nick and I faced Deku and Dragon Master. Somehow, it wasn't enough just to say goodbye. I wanted to leave something behind, something physical that would stay with them, with the war. The impartial journalist had got left behind somewhere on the march north.

To Dragon Master I gave my rucksack, the contents now emptied into our other bags; that much was straightforward – he'd been making admiring remarks about it for weeks. Deku was trickier. I had no idea what he wanted, only that he would definitely want something. He stood awkwardly, like a child waiting for a gift from a department store Santa. In the end I handed over my folding knife, which I had left behind in our bags in Voinjama. The absurdity of giving a war criminal a small weapon like this was inescapable; he opened and closed the blade and beamed at me in the dirty puddle of lamplight that illuminated our farewell. Whoever they were, whatever they had done – or allowed to happen – they had also helped keep me alive and filming, and I felt sad to be saying goodbye.

In Conakry, Nick and I headed straight for the terrace restaurant where we had first met Frank and Joe. The staff meandered with their usual determined sloth, their bored faces broken only by their shock at our eccentric demands. At ten o'clock in the morning we ordered four roast chickens and four large beers.

'Les autres, ils viennent tout de suite?' our perplexed waitress wanted to know.

I explained that no one else would be joining us, and then, after a tantalising half-hour wait spent staring at the kitchen door, Nick and I gorged ourselves on the soft flesh and crispy skin of the best meal of our lives. We ate every morsel, stripped every bone, drank every drop. Surrounded by our mountain of bags – we hadn't even checked in – I lit a Marlboro Red and collapsed back into my chair, blowing a plume of blue smoke up to the heavens. A cool breeze fanned us from the Atlantic. *You've done it*, I thought, *you've fucking done it*.

'I'll tell you what, Mr Brabazon,' Nick said, finishing his last mouthful of beer. 'That was great. I just hope we don't have to walk that far again to make the next meal taste as good.'

'Just you wait,' I said, 'you'll be back here before you know it. This one is going to run and run.'

We dragged our bags to our rooms. It was going to be the first day of privacy, the first night I'd slept apart from Nick in more than two months. As Nick disappeared down the corridor, I stepped into the room, peeled off the second skin of my filthy shirt and socks, and pushed open the ill-fitting bathroom door. Under the weak glow of a single bare bulb, I saw, for the first time since leaving the hotel in June, my own reflection. I was emaciated. My skin sagged and clung to my chest – pallid, and pitted with sores and insect bites. My ribs and collar bones were sharply defined; my muscles had atrophied. My face, covered with a wild, dirty black beard, was nearly hidden: all I could see of it were my confused, sunken eyes staring back from behind the glass.

I fished the small stills camera out of my trouser pocket, and pointed it at my reflection. I shrugged, and took a picture, and then another. I put the camera down, and thought *Remember this. You'll never look like this again.* I ran a tepid bath and washed the mud and blood from between my toes, and prepared myself to see Cobus's US Intelligence contact, Colonel Frank. Any earlier misgivings I'd had about debriefing him dissolved. If he wanted details, he could have them. The war wasn't over; and neither, I suspected, was my relationship with US Intelligence. While I had the chance, I wanted to make sure they were firmly behind the film project.

Once I was cleaned up, Nick and I took a taxi into town and found Frank, who was having a beer after lunch with half a dozen balls of uniformed muscle from the Green Berets. Clean-shaven, and in their early twenties, they'd recently arrived from Fort Bragg in North Carolina and were desperate to see the footage I had shot. I hooked up my mini-VCR to the TV in their billet, and rolled on a Tubmanburg fire-fight. After thirty minutes, everyone got the point.

'Man,' said one of the younger guys in a pressed shirt and aftershave, 'I sure hope we get some of that. We're all just ready to go.'

In Conakry to train the Guinean Special Forces, they were in fact, also on standby to help abduct two al-Qaeda operatives suspected of helping President Taylor launder illegally mined blood diamonds. I saw Nick's eyes flicker at the D-word. Since outlining his initial plan, the sparkling syllables had never been far from his lips. Now, though, he was silent.

I ran Frank through the basics of the rebels' situation, struggling to articulate what I had seen. It was hard to begin to explain a war whose outcome was dependent upon a carelessly discarded cigarette butt, though Frank seemed to understand what I was getting at. I dumped some clips onto VHS for him, and Nick handed over the captured AK. It was nothing if not an anti-climax: I'd been expecting a James Bond-esque debrief; what I got was a beer and a quick chat.

Frank concluded, 'If these guys are seriously going to take on Taylor, they're going to need to sort their supply lines out. The Guineans will keep them going with just enough ammunition, but it's not really in their interest for the rebels to win too quickly, or even at all. I don't think anyone sees these guys actually in power.'

We all laughed – after the mayhem of the Tubmanburg firefight on TV, the idea of a LURD government suddenly seemed absurd.

'But the president here is going to do whatever it takes to protect this eastern region from another invasion.'

It was certainly straightforward, working with Frank. He was almost certainly right, too. Nick and I stood up to leave.

'Don't forget to send me a copy of the finished film,' was Frank's parting shot, 'and stay in touch.'

His tone was quiet, and it felt as if he meant it, as if he was accepting me into his club. He shook hands vigorously with Nick, who was clearly a life-member.

Back in the taxi that returned us to the hotel, Nick turned to me after taking in the view of the city's ramshackle streets that sped past the open window.

'They spend too long in the gym, and not enough time in the field. All that muscle, it doesn't mean anything.'

I folded my arms around my wasted biceps, and agreed.

Two months and two days after we'd arrived in Conakry, it was time to go. A Guinean Army four-by-four took us to the airport. We bypassed all checks and controls and were delivered straight to the VIP lounge of the airport. In a successful bid to protect us from any last-minute assault by rapacious customs officers, I slipped $100 bills into the hands of the men who ushered us through to the air-conditioned lounge. Within half an hour I'd bought off the entirety of Conakry airport's security staff.

My Air France flight was called shortly afterwards, and here my memory fails. I can recall the minutiae of the battles we survived, whole sections of the jungle route we tramped – but from the moment Nick and I stood up to say goodbye, my mind is perfectly blank. I cannot remember if I hugged or shook hands with the man who saved my life; I cannot remember a single parting word. I remember nothing at all of coming home until I woke up to the sounds of summer in Kent.

Mum came back into the dining room carrying hot toast and undisguised concern for her son.

'I've made you an appointment to see the GP for next week – it's the soonest they could fit you in.'

My mother stood awkwardly by the kitchen door, wondering if she'd done the right thing.

'That's great, thanks. I better get myself checked out. I'm off to London tomorrow – to record a *From Our Own Correspondent* for the BBC. I'll be back for dinner. I'm going to take it easy today, though.'

I needed to decompress, to surface in peace, to let the images and memories of the last few weeks settle before I tried to make sense of them. Mum was thrilled that I was going to be on the radio; she looked proud and surprised at the same time, which lifted the frown she'd been wearing all morning. Like the rebels, the radio made it real for her.

'What would you like tonight? I might make a stew.'

She didn't need to add 'to fatten you up' – that much was inescapable. August heat notwithstanding, I needed all the calories I could get.

'That would be great, anything at all except rice. Please, no rice, probably ever again.'

All bones and tangled hair, I stood up and hugged her, and realised I had hardly touched anyone for more than two months.

'I'm afraid it's nothing terribly exotic, Mr Brabazon.' Taking his eye away from the giant magnifying glass that hovered above my hand, the doctor fixed me with a straight gaze. 'You have a bad case of scabies. Here, have a look.'

I peered down, but couldn't see the tiny mites he said were crawling in the open scabs that peppered my fingers.

'We'll get you some cream for that. It will burn – not very comfortable I'm afraid, especially down there.'

He gave a nod to my crotch. Before I'd slipped my shirt and trousers back on, the amiable professional had also told me I was, without doubt, malnourished. I was suffering severe muscle wastage and likely permanent damage to my knees. According to Nick's GPS, we had clocked up 292 miles on foot.

'You've been through – your body's been through – a traumatic episode. It's going to take you time to recover.'

We looked at each other across the side of his desk, strewn with happy family photos and notepaper headed with pharmaceutical company logos. I wondered how many GPs in Britain saw people just back from a war.

I lingered in my seat. I wasn't ready to go.

'In the week I've been home I've been feeling a bit rough,' I mumbled. 'I mean, I'm worried that the trip is going to affect me, you know, in other ways. It's nothing specific, but it was pretty . . . *extreme*. I wonder if maybe I need to see a medical professional or something? I'm a bit disoriented.'

'How *do* you feel?'

The doctor drummed the tips of his fingers on the barrel of a ballpoint pen. It was a question that had been nagging me since I'd witnessed the prisoner being butchered in Tubmanburg. Although I was not plagued by nightmares, or any tangible feeling of despair, I felt fragile, as if I was at times struggling to cling onto myself. I realised I was staring at my feet, and had not answered. I looked at him again, and shrugged.

He put down his Biro, and pushed my notes to one side and waited as I tried to gather my thoughts. I tried to slow down the revolving images of trees and blasts and bodies and faces that spun through my head when I thought about the trip. For some reason, the image that always stuck behind my eyes was of the green, gutted corpse straddling the jungle path on the way home. The memory of its dark, rotten intestines was so vivid I could, I swore, still smell them. I wanted to tell the doctor the truth, but perhaps half-truths were best here.

'It's hard to say. It's – well, it's not easy . . . I mean the last two months – what happened, it doesn't exactly make for polite conversation. There isn't anyone I can really go into it with.' *Except for Nick*, I thought. 'Actually, it was pretty fucking awful. I feel lost. Yeah, that's a good way to describe it. I think I'm a bit lost.'

After rummaging around on his desk without replying, and then thumbing through two boxes of loose files on the floor, the doctor wrote out a name and number on a slip of paper, which he passed to me with my prescription: The Priory, Ticehurst House.

'They're worth investigating. I don't think you do need to see a medical professional, but a session with one of their counsellors may be of help to you.' Smiling, he tucked the pen into his shirt pocket, just like Nick did. 'They specialise in trauma counselling of all sorts – for soldiers and the media, as well as people who've been in accidents, that kind of thing.'

He shuffled my notes away, and we stood to face each other.

'It's entirely confidential.'

I walked uphill along the familiar road that had carried me between home and sixth-form college years before and folded the square of paper into my wallet. *Confidential? Here we go*, I thought. 'Confidential' implied shame, something to hide. Was the fact that I didn't know how I felt in itself somehow shameful? If I couldn't even describe how I felt, it seemed impossible that I would be able to make a coherent film about what I'd seen. I hadn't been just an observer, either. It was dawning on me that I had been a witness, and witnessing meant something; the idea of it seemed to confer responsibility. I just didn't know to whom or for what.

It had turned into a surprisingly hot day in Canterbury. House martins dipped and dived in the clear Kent sky, but I was too wrapped up in myself to enjoy it. In the week I'd been back I tried and failed to place a newspaper article about the war in any of the London papers: they didn't know who I was, or that there was a war going on in Liberia. Apart from the five-minute piece for Kate Adie, no one seemed particularly interested. Even the investigator on the United Nations Security Council's Panel of Experts on Liberia – who specialised in illegal weapons – seemed uninterested in my material, and behaved as if he thought he was doing me a favour by talking to me at all. I'd hung up bewildered, unprepared for this degree of isolation.

I got home from my doctor's appointment, sat at the desk under the stairs, and apprehensively dialled the international code for South Africa.

'Mr Brabazon, I presume?'

It was the first time I'd heard Nick's voice since we'd gone our separate ways in Conakry. It took me straight to the balcony in Tubmanburg.

'Hi, man, how's it going? I'm still fucked, you know. How're you doing?'

'Ja, not so bad. I've been sleeping for a week, man. Marzaan agreed that I looked like Father Christmas with that beard, so it had to go. You?'

'Nah, I kept mine. It's like a little bit of Liberia right under my nose. Smells like it, too. Have you heard from the chairman?'

'Ja, he's still in Conakry, but he wants to move back to the other place next week. He says everything is going well, he's getting some guys ready for that other thing we talked about.'

Nick's voice was crystal clear, though our conversation was deliberately cryptic. Right from our first meeting in Johannesburg, he'd urged caution on the phone.

'The place near where the main base is – where those guys from next door were busy – and the town next to that are giving them a lot of trouble. Once they can get them under control, they can think about a counter-attack.'

In other words, Voinjama was safe and Sekou Conneh planned to return there, but Foya (where Taylor was using RUF mercenaries from Sierra Leone) and the nearby town of Kolahun were in Government hands. From there they would be able to ambush LURD rebel supply lines, making any significant push south again impossible unless those Government troops were properly contained or destroyed.

Nick thought that these two towns, hard up against the Sierra Leone border, were now the main focus of the war. In Tubmanburg,

Dragon Master had told me that Guinean soldiers serving as part of the UN contingent in Sierra Leone had left caches of ammunition for the rebels near to the border with Liberia. Dragon Master himself had been in charge of liaising with them, and collecting it. Given that UN peacekeeping operations there were ultimately paid for partly by British taxpayers, I could be certain that at least some of the money I paid the Inland Revenue was, one way or another, helping to keep the LURD in business. Nick, though, was interested in more direct means of financing them: 'that other thing' was his diamond-mining proposal. Conneh had approved it, at least in principle. Now both Conneh and Nick were desperate to get their hands on a helicopter.

'I'm off to a wedding in Ireland in the next couple of days,' I told him, trying to swing the conversation around to something legal. 'I should have some news about selling the film when I get back.'

That was code for *I should have some news about paying you*. He let it pass.

'Ja, well, good luck and stay out of trouble. Stay well.'

'You too, man.'

The line clicked, dead.

No matter how hard I stared, it just didn't look like me. Wild beard, dark eyes and bony body: the mirror in the bathroom of the Dublin hotel was as unforgiving as the one in Conakry. I had just watched Tara, a close friend from university, marry her American boyfriend in a wonderful, bohemian ceremony on an ancient Celtic mound just outside of Dublin. Tall, beautiful and achingly glamorous, Tara was someone I'd once harboured an impossible fantasy about marrying myself. On the way there I had imagined stopping the ceremony and proclaiming my undying love, like the hero of a feel-good romantic comedy. In the event, I'd folded my arms and stood at the back, scabies scabs itching furiously.

No one recognised me. Not my friends, not her family, whom I'd known for years – no one. When I introduced myself their eyes popped open like cartoon characters'. Afterwards, buried deep in the excited hubbub of the reception, I'd found myself standing in the bar of the hotel, trying – and failing – to catch the eye of people I'd shared another life with. I'd felt suddenly as if I was under pressure again, diving down to the trays of champagne and canapés, perfectly submerged. And then it felt as if something broke inside me – like my airline had been cut. The sounds of the wedding reception – the clink of champagne glasses, the babble of happy conversation – receded until all I was left with was the silent image of the gutted corpse on the trail home.

I broke for the door and gulped in a warm lungful of Dublin air. An English hen party staggered past; taxis and cars and tourists and lovers ambled and faltered and sped along. It was night time by the River Liffy – that was all. I was above ground, still. I'd watched the lights on the water and, feeling calmer at last, walked the short distance to my hotel room to try to find myself in the mirror. *James,* I said, as if speaking to a stranger, *you'll be okay*. I washed, rubbed more ointment into my broken skin, and swallowed the little blue Valium pills from the supply my doctor had prescribed years before.

I'd thought I had made a good job of being normal at the wedding. But the truth was that any attempt to confess the horrors of the trip were met with embarrassed silence or apparently genuine concern for my mental welfare. Sitting next to me at dinner, an actor whose films I admired told me, very gently – after a brief resumé of my journey from the front line to the wedding – that I 'should see someone'.

A week later I did just that, and drove to The Priory, near Tunbridge Wells. I couldn't imagine who it was that I would talk to once I got there – no doubt a bored professional carer who had never been to war, a do-gooder who'd never heard a shot fired in anger, never mind seen a man's heart ripped out of his chest. Nonetheless, I went with an open mind of sorts.

I had read about the psychological effects that combat had on soldiers after battle. In one study of American troops in the Second World War, it was shown that, of those men who experienced thirty-five days of uninterrupted combat, 98 per cent then went on to manifest varying degrees of psychiatric disturbance. In Liberia I had been exposed to combat, or the immediate threat of it, for thirty days straight. On the face of it, it seemed reasonable to be concerned about my mental health.

Steven was a stout, pleasant man in his mid-forties. His open face invited confidence, and his simple English, uncluttered with jargon or medical phrases, was easy to understand. Before we began, he explained PTSD – Post Traumatic Stress Disorder. It was not, he emphasised, a psychosomatic illness generated by an overactive imagination, but a physical ailment as real as fracturing a leg. Chemical changes in the brain caused by the release of adrenaline could possibly have specific behavioural outcomes that were – to continue the analogy – as physical as limping on that broken leg.

'You wouldn't be ashamed of a broken leg,' he rightly said, 'and there is nothing to be ashamed of if it turns out there is something like that inside, that we can't see, but is just as real.'

As well as vivid multi-sensory flashbacks, the onset of PTSD could be detected by a hyper-vigilant mindset that was always on the lookout for danger (and unable to relax as a result); and also by what he called 'avoidance' – patterns of behaviour, including alcohol and drug use, that strove to avoid the people, places or other triggers that could unleash memories of traumatic events.

One point he stressed above all others. It was believed that PTSD was triggered by a single event that either threatened my life, or made me feel (even if misguidedly) that my life was in danger.

'Perhaps we could begin by you telling me where you've been, what kind of work you were doing in Africa.'

And so, in that featureless room, with only water to drink and a Biro for my fingers to play with (smoking was forbidden) I began to recount the war. Steven asked many questions, prompted many answers and clarifications, but there was one question he never asked, and that was *Why?* These were the questions I had feared most: *Why didn't you stop filming? Why didn't you try to help?* I had feared I would be judged: but this man was a conduit who turned the tap on and guided the flow of recollections and fears and regrets that spilled out of my mouth and helped to make sense of them.

'And when they removed the man's heart, what did that sound like? What noise did it make?'

And then:

'What did you think when you realised the prisoner had been shot?'

And again:

'When you saw the body on the path, what did it smell like?'

I answered his questions, and then I said to him, 'You know, I never cried. Never once. Through all of that, it was as if their deaths were alien, so hard to understand, it was impossible to be upset about them. It was just happening, I was just there. And you know, that makes me feel like a monster, like a fucking monster. That's not fucking normal, man. It's not fucking normal to see that and not cry, to see kids dying of gangrene or burns, and to keep filming. I don't feel fucking normal. It's the absolute opposite of normal and it really hurts – it really hurts inside.'

And then the tears came and I thought they would not stop.

I left with red eyes, blowing snot into an over-used tissue, and somehow managed to drive to a quiet bed-and-breakfast in Dorset. I felt empty, physically drained, as if I'd been sick over and over. I looked at myself in the mirror again, and suddenly I wanted rid of my beard. I cut and shaved it until I found myself underneath.

Steven had thought I was suffering from acute stress reaction – PTSR. It was hard to disagree. I had certainly been under stress, and I was undeniably having a reaction. Another worry insinuated its way into my head, too. I began to wonder if this was the first step on a road to someone eventually telling me I was going mad. Steven said it would take up to six weeks to see if I was able to process my emotions about the events in Liberia, and full-blown Post Traumatic Stress Disorder could take up to six months to manifest.

What did happen in the next six weeks knocked me completely off-balance. The BBC producer with whom I'd been talking from Liberia turned down the footage. BBC News and Channel 4 News likewise rejected it. I had stood with bated breath in an edit suite buried in a basement in the Channel 4 News building in Gray's Inn Road. The director of the production company in Kenya had flown over to help cement a television sale. I watched the producer spool through a couple of my tapes from Tubmanburg, only to tell me that this kind of material had all been seen before, and that it was of limited interest because there was no British angle.

'Well,' I'd countered, holding onto the coat-tails of my temper, 'there are no blonde, British nurses held captive there, but these are the only pictures of an entirely unreported war. It has massive implications for the security of the whole region, including our deployment in Sierra Leone.'

She was unmoved, and I left the boss of the production company to chat it through with her. On the same day the American broadcaster ABC said no, despite a strong US dimension to the story. A couple of days later Channel 4's international current affairs department, which commissions the series *Dispatches*, also turned down the material, as would the BBC's programme *Correspondent* a few days later.

What I had been entirely ignorant of was that having the footage itself – however great I thought it – was only a part of the equation of getting a television sale. These types of programmes were part of well-established series, or 'strands' as TV people call them, which follow set patterns and use familiar reporters according to tried and tested formulae. One-off documentary commissions for an unknown like me were rare, to the point of impossible. The lack of a news sale perplexed me, though. If this wasn't good enough for them, what possibly could be? The thought that all that marching, malnourishment and violence could have been for nothing was hard to swallow.

I emailed Nick, and spoke to him frequently, trying always to sound upbeat and positive. I clung onto his friendship and understanding, and tried to cherish the achievement of surviving the trip as a thing in itself. I left the negotiations to the production company and, when it became clear that we were not going to get a sale in London, I flew to Glasgow in search of solace.

Rachel was home from university, ensconced in her parents' stone town house. Before I'd left for Liberia I'd felt the gap in age and experience between us – she was twenty-two, me thirty – but she was fun and sexy and ridiculously clever, and never let me take myself too seriously.

As soon as I saw her, I felt happy. It wasn't possible to fake that. I breathed out a sigh of relief as she smiled and wrapped her arms around me at the airport. We sat in the taxi and her bright green eyes lit on my face. I wondered what she could see, what was there that I had missed in the mirror. Not much, I suspected, just something different from the boys her age at university. Perhaps she even loved me. She tucked a thick tress of dark hair behind her ear and leaned over to kiss me. Something flickered inside.

I caught the taxi driver's eye in the mirror and pulled away, smiling.

In Glasgow, though, as in London, my mind didn't feel completely my own. Even walking down the street, hand in hand, was at times like being in a virtual shooting gallery. Intrusive thoughts flooded into my head without warning – transforming the pavement into an imagined battleground, pedestrians into casualties. I would buy a newspaper and find myself imagining what the old woman who served me would look like if a bullet opened up her forehead. I shook hands with people and wondered how I'd react if their legs were blown off at that moment; or what a machine gunner would do to the tourists in George Square. I could blink the images away, will the thoughts into obscurity – but they would return, sometimes within minutes. The brutality of what I conjured unnerved me. I told no one.

'Are you all right, darling?'

She was wrapped up in a short, blue silk Chinese-print dressing gown. We were sitting on her sofa.

'Yeah, I'm fine. It's just I'm a bit out of sorts. You know, it's weird coming home. It was such a long trip, so much longer than it was supposed to be, it's just hard getting my head around being back here.' I felt her weight shift against me. 'But it's good, I mean it's great. It's great to be here, with you, it's just . . . I don't know, I don't know how to put this, really. I saw a lot of bad things. People being killed . . . worse than that . . .'

I could hear her breathing.

'It's just hard to have left it all behind, to have been there so recently, and then get on a plane and as if by magic, I'm here.'

She sat up straight and looked at me. Her hair was a mess, her face suddenly much younger.

'But *we're* okay, aren't we? You still want to be with me?'

I smiled at her and tried to look reassuring, which ended up more like a grimace, and made her laugh. I wasn't sure I could continue a conversation about what it had really been like – it seemed somehow wrong to talk about killing when we were alone, and trying to be happy.

'Why didn't you call me when you were away?' She gave a theatrically exasperated grunt. 'I nearly split up with you so many times. Everyone knew you were away, and weren't calling me. It was awful.'

I had been too busy chasing my own demons to see it clearly until then: it had been hard for her, too. She was young and beautiful and gentle, and she wanted to have fun. She hadn't signed up for this a year ago; it was unreasonable to expect her to want to now.

'I'm sorry. I . . . It was a very unusual place to be.'

I put my hand to her face. Touching her smooth cheek made me uncomfortably aware of my skinny ribs and cracked skin.

'Let's not talk about it any more,' she said.

I closed my eyes and saw the gutted green man, hovering in semi-darkness at the edge of my mind. *Please*, I begged him under my breath as Rachel covered my face with her hair, *would you just fuck off and leave me alone*.

I left after four days, all kisses and smiles and promises. There had been tears and arguments in cinemas and restaurants, but we were still lovers. I told her nothing of the battles that I fought in the street, in our bed, in my head. The fact that she accepted me as she found me, or at least appeared to, was all that mattered. At times she made me feel almost normal, which was as much as I could have hoped for from anyone.

Back home there was still one person I was desperate to see. From London I drove down to the south coast of England, where the North Downs offer up a bird's-eye view of the Channel.

'Your mum isn't half glad you're back. She was a bit worried about you.'

My grandfather's handsome face seemed like it hadn't changed since I was a child. His high cheekbones and swept-back hair lent him a film-star quality, even when he was in tatty gardening clothes.

'Bit lively, was it?'

I had to laugh at that.

'Yeah, it was. Pretty lively – most of the time.'

'Probably a bit different to what I was doing in the desert. The jungle plays havoc with everything. I expect your other grandad could have told you about that – he probably did, actually.'

There was not much love lost between my parents' parents – but the two men had at least respected each other as soldiers.

Mum and Nan had left the room. We stood talking while a tray was loaded with cakes and coffee in the kitchen.

'That reminds me,' he continued, 'up in the loft there are some papers, a diary I wrote in Egypt, in Tobruk. You might like to see it one day. There are some old photos, too, from Palestine and Libya.'

'Were you allowed to do that?'

It was the first time he'd ever mentioned a diary. I knew immediately that 'one day' meant 'after I'm dead', otherwise he'd have been showing me already.

'No,' he laughed, 'but I was careful with it.'

'It was quite messy,' I told him. 'A lot of civilians got hurt. You can imagine it – no one has a bloody clue what they're doing. Nick and I were practically running the show at one point, trying to get out. They couldn't even set an ambush.'

'You would have liked the desert,' he said, softly. 'It was straightforward. There were no civilians, no one except us and them. You could fire artillery all day long and know you were hitting either sand dunes or Germans. Of course,' he chuckled, 'there *was* the Afrika Korps. They could muck you about all right.'

I smiled at him. He'd had his left index finger crushed being 'mucked about' by them in Tobruk.

'Sometimes I wish I could have done more, anything, actually. There were so many kids.'

I wanted to tell him about the girl with gangrene, but I couldn't speak the words.

'Where do you begin?' I asked instead. 'We didn't even have any antibiotics.'

'Neither did we!' he replied.

I looked at him, and smiled. He had told me almost nothing about his war, but sixty years later it was as crisp to him as the day they'd sailed for Cairo. I wanted to talk, to open up and tell him how lost I was; but more than that I wanted him to see I was all right – that I had been to war, and survived. Neither of us spoke for a moment.

'Yes,' he repeated, after the pause. 'You would have enjoyed my war.'

We faced each other. Then, nodding to the window, he concluded: 'Joy's done a smashing job with the roses this year. What do you make of this lot? Jolly hard work, I might add, shifting all that bloomin' earth about.'

We walked out into the garden and admired the September roses. There were no bloody images, no traces of the jungle. My trip was over. The war was finally lifting.

10
BLOOD BROTHERS

The following week I had a message from Robert, the American writer with whom I'd gone to Sierra Leone the year before. We'd stayed in touch and I'd let him know by email about my ongoing friendship with Cobus and the trip to Liberia. I called him back, curious to know what he was up to. He was now the star of his own television show – one episode of which (in Chechnya) had just fallen through.

He got straight to the point. He had called to ask if I could take him to rebel-held Liberia instead. Adrenaline surged through me. Go back?

The room was very quiet. *Go back*. Nick and I had discussed the possibility of a return trip in Conakry, but I hadn't imagined that it would be only a matter of weeks before I was contemplating it again. I had barely recovered, I hadn't sold the original film – but I was broke. I wanted a career in television; now I was being offered one and the responsibility that went with it. I took a deep breath.

'Sure,' I said, cautiously.

Calls would need to be made, paperwork got in order – and bribes paid. The line hummed as I grabbed a pen and paper. I felt nervous and excited.

'The rebels don't control much more than the area immediately around their HQ, but you can use my archive from the trip I've just done to liven it up.'

The rains were over, and a new offensive planned. It could take two or even three months to get back in.

'When do you want to go?'

His answer stopped me dead.

'Immediately.'

In true Liberian style, 'immediately' took four weeks.

Getting Nick on board was the easy part. I called him as soon as I'd put the phone down with Robert.

'That's great news, man,' was his instant reaction. Apart from the straightforward offer of work, I suspected he wanted to get back to Liberia to discuss the diamond business with the rebels – and I would be paying him to go. Working with me was actually about to earn him some money. After we'd wrapped up our call, I dialled the LURD national chairman's number in Conakry.

'Sekou? It's James . . .' The line was ominously silent. 'I've got some people who'd like to meet you, who'd like to come to Voinjama. They're good people. It's for a television programme.'

Finally, the line exploded with his strangely emphasised English.

'Jay, whe' you comin' back here? I' bee' lon' time nah,' he shouted.

But what he wanted to know, more than anything else, was whether Nick would be joining me.

Next I called Robert's New York director, Jonathan Stack, who would be overseeing the project, to work out the details: we'd go in for a couple of weeks, Jonathan included; introduce Robert to the rebels; do some interviews, and get some fighting on tape. What we didn't film then, we'd fill in with the hours of fire-fights I'd already shot.

It felt strange that only weeks previously I had never shot any film for television and now I was hiring myself out as a producer and cameraman to an Oscar-nominated director. No one seemed to question my credentials. I asked Jonathan what credit I would get. I didn't want to risk my life again simply to make someone else look good.

'The writer's the star – but you'll get your moment on camera, too,' Jonathan reassured me. 'You'll definitely get some face time. Don't worry.'

I insisted on other controls. It was agreed that sensitive information about the role of Guinea would not be broadcast until I agreed. There was one other condition: Nick's position on the project was non-negotiable.

Jonathan sounded delighted at the prospect of being accompanied by a Special Forces chaperone.

'You know, to be honest, I'm not in great shape.' There was a pause while he considered the implications of that statement, and then: 'And I had some work done on my leg recently . . . so, you know, the idea of walking for a hundred miles . . . well, that's not really a *good* idea.'

His manner was nervous, urgent and almost comic. He professed a long-standing interest in Africa – telling me that many of his films were about the lives of African-Americans. I began to explain about the conditions I'd faced with Nick, the fighting, the lack of food.

'Wow, okay,' he cut across me. 'Tell me – you know, cut to the chase – what's the worst thing that could happen?'

'You could be killed in an ambush. If we're in combat, if we film combat, you have a high chance of being seriously injured.'

'Okay, well, that wouldn't be good. And this guy Nick,' Jonathan wanted to know, 'will he help us avoid getting killed or maimed?'

'Yes.'

And that was the simple truth. I explained that Nick's being there had made the difference between life and death for me. He would be armed, and was a highly trained medic.

'Okay, he's hired!' I could hear Jonathan's sigh of relief across the Atlantic. 'Hey, anyway, I come from a Jewish background, so, you know, I grew up with weird tribal dynamics.'

That Jonathan was more than a little anxious was no bad thing. His ironic humour and acute sense of self preservation were ideal attributes for working in Liberia – no matter how hard he might be limping on that wounded knee. Humility was a good tool for survival.

I broke the news to Mum that evening.

'I'm going back, it's definite. As soon as the visas are ready I'll fly from here down to Jo'burg to hook up with Nick. He's coming with me.'

'Oh, Jamo.' Disappointment flickered in her eyes. 'You've hardly recovered, you're still . . .'

She was right, of course. 'Hardly recovered' was quite an understatement. I was still dogged by violent images on a daily basis, and the scabies sores that had spread across my body were only just going into remission.

The conversations only got harder. Rachel's tone was both indignant and dignified when I spoke to her that evening.

'James, am I ever going to spend any bloody time with you?'

It seemed like a fair question. She was more disappointed in me than angry. I didn't blame her. I was about the least appealing prospect of a boyfriend imaginable.

'I'm sorry' was all I could manage by way of explanation. I promised her that when I came home we would go away together. I would make it up to her, somehow.

The truth was I wanted the war, and another adventure with Nick, more than I wanted a safe life at home – more than I wanted her.

A week later, after I had first flown to South Africa to finalise, at last, the first sale of my original material with a local current affairs series called *Special Assignment*, and hook up with Nick, I landed back in Conakry. A few days later Nick and I drove out to the airport to meet Robert and Jonathan. Robert was as I remembered him: tall and angular, with a greying, bushy handlebar moustache. He'd brought along a mountain of camping kit, cameras and 'adventure gadgets' ranging from flashy folding knives and alcohol hand-sterilising gel, to sophisticated tiny cameras and a portable music player – complete with noise-cancelling headphones. Jonathan, meanwhile, had not been exaggerating about his physical condition. They stood out a mile from their fellow passengers heading for the arrivals building.

'Is it always this hot?' Jonathan asked.

Ten paces off the aircraft and he was drenched, as I had been when I first arrived.

'Good to meet you, too,' I replied, 'and yes, it is. I'm afraid today is quite mild. It gets worse.'

Somewhere on the other side of the apron the whine of a propeller engine sputtering into life filled the air.

'And who are these guys?' Robert wanted to know, tilting his head towards the Guinean soldiers who had accompanied us onto the runway.

'Red Berets. They're the presidential guard. Nice people to do business with, and friends with the rebels. Basically, they're the only reason we're not all under arrest. All our visas are endorsed by the president himself. I'll explain back at the hotel.'

I introduced Nick to the Americans. Jonathan practically hugged him.

'Man, it's great to meet you. Thanks for coming to get us.'

'You know Cobus from Executive Outcomes?' Robert wanted to know.

'Ja,' Nick confirmed, looking at me. 'He put me and Mr Brabazon in touch.'

Nick smiled at no one in particular.

'It's been non-stop fun ever since, eh?' I reminded him, guiding my party towards the VIP entrance.

Four months before I'd nosed my way through the airport in fear of arrest or deportation: now I had my own retinue of local hard men to open doors for me. Before long we were all heading to the familiar embrace of the Petit Bateau hotel.

En route I explained that while Nick and I had waited in Conakry, the rebels had tried to hit me up for increasingly large sums of money. In the end we'd settled on $1,500, only this time I had handed the money to a LURD spokesman called Hanson Williams, who'd then taken me straight to Aicha Conneh herself – the LURD national chairman's wife, and the president of Guinea's spiritual adviser.

Wrapped up in a bright kaftan and ruffled headdress, she'd cut a powerful, engaging figure. Ensconced behind a desk in a cramped back room of the LURD rebel headquarters in Conakry, she took my money from Hanson and counted out the Benjamins in front of us. We exchanged pleasantries in French, and shook hands. I was the first European journalist, possibly the only journalist, to have met her. I explained to the Americans that in the car back to the hotel, the almost-sober presidential driver, Bengura, had confided to me in French.

'Madam is very powerful,' he'd said. 'If she wants you to disappear, you will not be found. Even if you are a government minister.'

I'd slipped him a packet of Marlboro and thanked him for his counsel.

Nick, meanwhile, had been doing business directly with the chairman, Sekou. We'd arrived at an unspoken understanding: I would not join his diamond venture, nor discuss it with anyone else. In fact, I would turn a blind eye to it. My rationale was simple – no Nick, no access. Besides, he had helped me way beyond what anyone could have expected and so I would ask very few questions about his deal with the rebels.

The following night, once they'd begun to shake their jetlag, we all headed out to the bars of Conakry. Jonathan was adamant that he wanted to experience the local music scene, see what this part of the world was like when it wasn't consumed by a war. He had a point. It had never occurred to either Nick or me to venture out much in Conakry: it was a transit point in which to lie low; somewhere to recover from the jungle; a place of secret meetings and double-dealings.

'This is a very different sort of front line we're going to now,' Nick explained to Jonathan as we bumped our way along the dimly lit and deeply rutted streets of the capital city. 'Tonight I suspect you are going to meet the Night Fighters.'

I had no idea what Nick was talking about, but nodded sagely anyway, taking in the dark city that parted around the windscreen. I'd asked the taxi driver to take us 'somewhere interesting, with music'. He'd taken one look at us – a Boer soldier, a pale, skinny Brit, a Jewish film director and an elaborately moustachioed gadget freak – and driven us into the heart of Conakry's red light district, or at least a part of town that looked enticingly sleazy. Clearly these four men could be united only in one quest: that for beer and brasses.

A single bare light bulb hung over the door of the club like a dubious Pole Star, luring us onto the rocks of moral shipwreck. We stepped inside to be greeted, immediately, by dozens (and dozens) of barely dressed, beautiful young women. They fell upon our affluent American friends in a web of elegant arms and a burst of flashing smiles. Jonathan's face wore a resigned expression of martyrdom.

Nick was untouched. Surrounded by some kind of unfathomable Afrikaner aura, he threaded his way through a sea of slinky, sweaty black dresses and ordered a beer from the overworked barman without so much as having to deflect a single grope or lunge. Meanwhile, I was busy fending off an advance of thigh-stroking party girls. Perhaps ten or more women had dived at me as I stepped further into the club, pulling me this way and that.

It was an overwhelming atmosphere. There was something deeply sexy about the women and the music and the whole surreal scene. As the heat and sweat and perfume hit me, it was suddenly easy to believe that, in here, normal rules might not apply.

'Are they *all* prostitutes?' I bellowed over the thumping bassline.

Nick laughed at that. I sounded more awestruck than inquisitive.

'No, man. I don't think they're all pros, as such. It's just a bit of extra income for them. You are a walking wallet. There's vok-all else for them to do. These people is just fokken poor. In Sierra Leone we used to call them the Night Fighters. They are very cunning and set very good ambushes.' Nick leaned in again. 'And just in case you're thinking of getting a bit friendly, Mr B, remember that there is no antibiotic for that adventure.'

The four of us re-grouped at the bar. Chatting and drinking and wondering out loud what the trip ahead was going to bring us. Even though they'd watched my tapes, for Robert and Jonathan it was a trip into the unknown; for me and Nick, it would be like returning to our own, familiar hell. Would there be fighting? Where was the Government army? Would the rebels protect us? The Americans plied us with questions. Robert guessed it, rightly, to be an extreme version of what we'd seen together in Sierra

Leone the year before. For Jonathan, meanwhile, Liberia was an unfathomable repository of fear, and an amazing opportunity. We propped up the bar into the small hours, losing ourselves in the drinks and the small talk and camaraderie of the club, pretending to forget for an hour or two about what awaited us over the border.

'Da man die.' Sekou Conneh, the LURD rebels' national chairman, spread his hands out and looked from me to Nick and back again. He was sitting, sweating, on the veranda of his headquarters in Voinjama, where I'd first met him with Nick four months before.

'How?' I asked.

I'd been back inside rebel-held Liberia for less than five hours and things were rapidly disintegrating.

'Cholera?'

He pronounced it *clorah*, and offered it apparently more as a suggestion, or a denial, than a statement of fact. Nick and I stared at him. He stared back, and then looked to Jonathan and Robert for some sort of approval.

'I' wa' las' week, or, er, I tink i' wa' two week' ago he die fro' clorah.'

It was difficult to know what to think. The intrigue and uncertainty of war had returned in an instant.

'That's a great shame. He was a mad fighter,' I said, speaking to Sekou's shoes. 'He really looked after us.'

Then I changed the subject, and the chairman never mentioned Deku again.

We were all to be billeted in the same building that we'd slept in on the original trip, which relaxed me – the fewer unknowns the better at this stage, I reasoned. I shared a room with Robert, Nick with Jonathan. While we strung up hammocks, Nick went back in to see Sekou alone.

'What's he up to?' Robert asked, as he unpacked his anti-bacterial hand wash and T-shirts with his company logo on. 'Sneaky intel?'

'Yeah, something like that. He's hoping we can get some sort of idea about what's going on. Everyone seems pretty subdued. That shit about Deku is worrying.'

'Who was he, again? The crazy motherfucker who liked shooting prisoners but loved his wife and kids?'

'Yup, that'd be him. Tough bastard. I've never heard of anyone dying of cholera here. It's bullshit. I just don't know what order of bullshit.'

As Robert unpacked, I thought about the first trip to Liberia and Deku running towards me in Tubmanburg, dripping with sweat, shaking his AK in the air. 'Ehn y' saw me? Ehn y' saw me? I tol' y' no monkay ca' try i' any day!' he'd shouted, triumphantly. However it had happened, it wasn't surprising that he was dead. After what I'd seen in Tubmanburg, it would have been more remarkable if *any* of those rebels were still alive. What was harder to understand was that, in the relative safety of the rebel HQ, I felt sad that he was gone. I hadn't expected that. It was more than wanting the comfort of a familiar Liberian face to welcome me back into the war. I felt a genuine sense of grief at his passing. A murderer and a criminal without doubt, he had also been – albeit in Nick's shadow – a part of the miracle of my earlier survival. I owed him a debt for that, which could now never be repaid.

Nick returned an hour later with news.

'Ja, well.' Nick pulled up and straddled a white plastic chair. 'It's not great. The only territory they can hundred-per cent confirm they control is here.'

'Fuck, what about the east – Zorzor or Gbarnga?' I asked.

Nick shrugged.

'This is it. Sekou hasn't been back here since we all left together two months ago, which has pissed off the senior commanders. He says they're preparing a counter-attack, but most of their men are in Guinea. They've got the same numbers, but there's been a problem with the supply of weapons and logistics.'

Voinjama was barely over the border. In a couple of months the LURD had gone from controlling up to half of the country to being confined to a tiny, fetid toe-hold in the northwest corner. Conneh also claimed that the LURD were holding secret talks with presidents Kabbah and Wade of Sierra Leone and Senegal – but were refusing direct communication with Taylor, the legitimacy of whose government they still did not recognise.

Nick's gloomy assessment continued. 'Sekou says the LURD HQ in Macenta was looted by Guinean troops. The rebel commanders had a lot of things stolen, and all their houses were raided. It might have been a local problem. Sekou seems to think it's resolved now.'

Jonathan asked the only question now really worth worrying about.

'So where's the nearest fighting?'

'There's fighting in Foya and Kolahun. They lost both of them, but they're pushing now to get them back. The fighting is most likely quite heavy, like what we saw in Tubmanburg, James. Taylor is using those RUF guys and re-supplying them by helicopter. Most of the rebels' best fighters is down there. If they don't control that area, they can't move any supplies south.'

'Do you reckon they'll let us film that?' Robert asked.

'I don't know. Sekou says they can't let us go yet because they don't have any fighters to send with us. Voinjama is quite lightly defended.'

It was a familiar state of play. We waited; we ate rice and what Nick called 'slop' – bitter cassava leaves stewed like spinach, loaded with chillies. We filmed interviews with the local commanders and fighters; we sat and sweated, unmoving, at midday; we shot tape of new recruits being drilled and trained; and, when we'd filmed every possible angle of Voinjama and interviewed each other, we sat and read novels on our veranda, and waited some more.

I was, at least, gaining valuable understanding of the rebels' situation. Their position *was* disastrous. There were now dozens of child-soldiers in the headquarters camp, many under the age of ten, who were barely taller than their Kalashnikovs. They styled themselves the Small Boys Unit – in direct parody of President Taylor's squad of the same name in the previous war.

Robert approached one of them, a young boy wearing scraps of outsized camouflage clothing and toting a rusty AK.

'And what', he asked, 'is your war name?'

'Poo-poo Splattah,' he replied, intently serious.

'Why do they call you that?' Robert persisted, bravely.

One of the other boys answered for him, as peels of laughter rang out into the oppressive October afternoon.

'Becau' he scarey when men sta' shootin'.'

I knew what the butchery was like at the front, and what it would be like for children who were so young and so scared that all they could do was scream and shit themselves. Abused, neglected and fundamentally betrayed by the adults who claimed to protect him, he probably had only days to live.

I was, at one level, sad for the rebels' cause, too. I wanted the LURD to succeed because Taylor was arguably one of the worst presidents of the modern era – and anything to get rid of him, however imperfect, must surely have been best for the Liberian people. I also wanted them to succeed because I knew them well, because their failure before had nearly cost me my life.

Divisions within their army were growing. Fexon Jackity, the LURD's director-of-staff and acting chief of staff, had been appointed to take over from Prince Seo after the rout I'd witnessed in July. A carefully spoken man, he seemed almost too intellectual to be a fighter in this obscure war. He treated us with courtesy and respect – always striving to reassure us that Voinjama could not fall – but helping the media was clearly not high on his agenda.

'What happened to Seo, anyway?'

I wanted to know what fate had befallen the old chief of staff. Jackity adjusted his black beret and hooked a thumb under his rifle's sling.

'He wi' be retire',' he answered, directly. 'A lettah ha' bee' writte' informin' him o' dis decishan.'

Apparently, Seo was being given more time to spend with his family in Conakry, in circumstances that sounded not unlike house arrest. Conneh was also alleged to be unhappy with Seo for briefly imprisoning two local journalists in Macenta. It was a useful reminder, if one were needed, that while we were under their protection, we had no guaranteed rights at all.

'Yeah, that figures,' I replied, trying to strike up some friendly off-camera banter. 'What's the law and order situation like here, generally? Are you managing to set up the civilian structures the chairman was talking about last time?'

'Yeah, boh Lor' Forces de autority 'ere, a' dey been keepin' everyting undah contro'. We ge' speshal uni' da seein' to dat.'

The foundation of this special unit turned out to be a deeply alarming development.

'We alreadeh ha' one execushan. People know who Lor' is.'

A group of LURD fighters, led by a LURD 'colonel', were now taking it upon themselves to cleanse their own ranks – as well as the local population – of any undesirable elements. Effectively a death squad, they had put at least one civilian in front of a firing squad – but on what grounds it was unclear.

'And what about Deku? The chairman says he—'

Jackity cut me off mid-sentence.

'Him ow' men den kill 'im. Maybe i' wa' stray bulleh' or bom' boh he die righ' deh.' He looked at me, as if challenging me to ask more, and then added, 'I' wa' acciden'.'

Deku had been killed by his own man. The questions were over. I went and found Nick – resplendent in a Hawaiian shirt, sitting by our billet – and relayed the contents of my chat with the new military leader.

'Death squad? No, that is bad; that is kak, man. You can't cut your own tail off; you will bleed to death. I don't know how much Sekou has to do with it.' He picked his rifle up. 'I think they can turn around and get back to Tubmanburg, but they have to sort this shit out first – otherwise they're fucking up their people as bad as Taylor.'

The paranoia and uncertainty of being back in Liberia was doing little for my mental state. Although the violent thoughts and images that had been bothering me had evaporated within a few days of crossing the border, physically I had regressed to the state I'd been in at the end of the trip to Tubmanburg. I was feeling increasingly uninspired by the Americans' project, and bored with all the waiting around. The only thing that interested me – unearthing scraps of intel aside – was filming combat.

One night the rebels fired mortars in response to what they thought was an assault. Robert and Jonathan ran around and filmed what they could in the dark, but I slept through it. Certain we were not going to be attacked, I had abandoned my Tubmanburg sleeping protocol, and cocooned myself with ear plugs and Valium. There were no incoming rounds, and Nick left me to sleep. Perhaps he could see that I was exhausted.

By day, Nick hardly touched his AK. Instead he sat on the veranda jotting down notes and disappearing for secretive one-to-ones with Sekou. I read the fact that he had ditched his camouflage and webbing in favour of a variety of increasingly absurd T-shirts as further evidence that we weren't going to see any bang-bang. I also suspected that Nick wasn't that keen on the rebels exposing the Americans to battle, either.

I confronted first Sekou and then Jackity, directly, and demanded to see action, like a junkie begging a fix from his dealer. No one said no, but no one was saying yes, either. The answers varied from day to day. Sometimes there were no men for an escort team; then it might be possible in a fortnight; and finally we needed to wait for more ammunition. In the end I got Nick to plead our case personally. I had more or less promised Jonathan and Robert that we would be able to film fighting. Being here, and not getting shot at, was like failing to get laid in the proverbial brothel.

Embarrassed by my determination, the acting chief of staff explained to Nick that he was deeply concerned for the safety of Jonathan and Robert – and the inevitable tidal wave of bad publicity that would follow in the wake of their injury or death; or, as Nick summed it up:

'He had no objection to me or you getting killed, but he wants to make sure that our American friends enjoy their holiday.'

As it turned out, the war came to us.

Six days after we'd arrived, our afternoon reading was interrupted by the *crack-boom* of first one, then several RPGs going off in town. The reverberating echo bounced off the walls of the houses around us until it was impossible to tell what direction the firing was coming from. Then, over the rooftops towards the Kolahun road drifted the sickening crackle of incoming small-arms fire. Any fear quickly dissolved as we started to run. *Great*, I thought, *let's go*. Nick, in T-shirt and shorts, was jogging along next to me, AK cupped in his right hand. Jackity stood at the junction near our billet, waving his arms around as if he was directing traffic, in a pair of bright red trousers, a white T-shirt and purple flip-flops. An RPG was slung over his shoulder.

'Don' worry, mah man, I wi' pu' everyting undah contro',' he tried to reassure us.

As we ran to film the gun-battle, we were pursued by a gaggle of child-soldiers – and Jonathan, who lumbered behind us, face beetroot from the exertion and heat and the pain of running on his injured leg. But he kept up with us, and threw himself into the moment. Robert was nowhere to be seen. There was no time to go back for him – the attack sounded like it was fading fast.

'We're going to have to run to catch this one. Vok. They're already retreating.'

Nick was right. By the time we reached the battleground, the shooting was all but over. As the battle petered out, and we stopped to catch our breath, I took in the aftermath of the contact.

A Government soldier captured by the rebels was lying by the side of the road. Young fighters swarmed around him. I pushed my way into the crowd, which parted to show me their handiwork. The man had been partly stripped; his torso was covered in blood. I looked at Nick, who was close by, studying the road ahead. As the crowd ebbed and then wrapped around me, I saw what was happening. It was as if my eyes were adjusting to a sudden spell of darkness – I strained to add up the pieces of what was in front of me into a coherent picture.

The man had been beheaded; the serrated edge of a rifle bayonet had just worked its way through his wind pipe. I squatted on my haunches and focused quickly, carefully composing the head into the golden section of the frame while the failing afternoon sun caught the sinews of the executioner's arm. It is hard work cutting off a head with a blunt knife and he was sweating from the effort. The rebel audience grinned with approval, the boy-soldiers engrossed by the murder. Rifles were raised in triumph, the familiar rebel chants bleated over and over.

As the camera rolled, I felt calm, and shuffled closer to get a cleaner shot. Unlike in Tubmanburg, when I had filmed the butchery in the centre of town, there was no internal dialogue. It was just happening. I was just there. I was just filming. Only one clear thought lifted above the mental silence. Deep inside, a part of me was pleased that this man had been killed at that precise moment, so that I could film it. This was the 'epic Liberian journey' I had promised to Jonathan and Robert. This shot alone proved it.

As I panned the lens across the gathered crowd, Nick slipped the safety catch off his AK, and Jonathan stood blanched white, uncomprehending. As the rebels held up the severed head for its close-up, Robert appeared next to us and did a piece to camera next to the murdered man, describing the rebels' 'trophy'. After the final take, the oppressive humidity of the day exploded into a torrential tropical downpour. We sprinted across a small field and sheltered from it in the doorway of a burned-out school house, tightly huddled together with a group of boy-soldiers, who shied away from the fat raindrops as if they were bullets. I looked down to see that the decapitated head was squashed against my thigh. A piece of bright red electrical wire had been threaded through the ears, transforming it into an obscene handbag. Out in the field, which I supposed was a football pitch, another severed head – hacked off another prisoner further up the road – sat upright on an old school chair, lashed by the summer rain.

In the hours that followed we sat together on the oblong of veranda outside our billet, reading, chatting and smoking. The rebels had put the severed heads on spikes by the main road as a warning to the Government army. I thought about what we were doing, the film we were making. In many respects the trip had been a failure: as we were unable to move outside of Voinjama, it was impossible to capture the scale of the conflict and the wider impact it had on Liberia. Until that morning, we didn't have a film, and there had been no realistic prospect of getting the material we needed to make one. But I knew now that the pictures of the beheading would insulate me from criticism: we had the war on film. That made me happy. Working in Liberia was like being in an abusive relationship: when she hit me, it felt like a kiss.

Nick had remained tight-lipped about his past in front of the Americans. And then, out of the blue – almost, it seemed, out of boredom – he announced to all of us that he'd been working on plans for a mercenary contract in the east of the Democratic Republic of Congo. I lit a cigarette, and listened carefully.

'It's quite a simple plan,' Nick enthused, almost chuckling with relish. 'I'm looking at getting some weapons and a few advisers to a rebel group in eastern Congo. The idea is to start a fight with the Rwandans who have occupied that part of the country – which has got a lot of diamond fields in it. The United Nations has also got that area under control.'

I drew hard on the cigarette and tried to get Nick's attention – this was not a conversation to have with people we hardly knew. He carried on, regardless.

'We're hoping that the Congolese Army will use it as an excuse to re-occupy the area, and get the diamond fields back.'

The operation would create a diversion for Nick to bring out a stash of already mined diamonds – the proceeds of which would be shared between himself, Joseph Kabila, the US-backed president of the Congo, and an 'agent' who had contacted Nick about the plan in the first place. Then Nick dropped the punch.

'Ja, if it goes ahead, all of you can come along and film it.'

Nick, it seemed, was in the grip of diamond fever. Not only was I annoyed that he'd discussed it in front of the Americans, but I was also alarmed at how seriously Nick was taking a plan which was, on the face of it, highly likely to fail. I got up and paced around in disbelief, as the rain tumbled down beyond our veranda. Perhaps he saw the shock in my face, perhaps recounting the plan had simply been Nick's solution to another interminable evening in Liberia – but, whatever the reason, he never mentioned it again while we were in Voinjama.

I slept fitfully that night, disturbed more by our surprise conversation than by the earlier execution. I also slept dressed for combat – the rebels were clinging on by the narrowest of margins, and we were defended mainly by children.

Two days later the rebels finally agreed to let us film some shooting – on the understanding that if they did, we'd pack up shortly afterwards and move back to Conakry. The rebels were beginning to tire of the Americans' presence, and wanted to concentrate on putting a new offensive together. That morning, 17 October, the rebel battalion headquarters at Kolahun fell to the Government army – a calamity described by Jackity as 'not a major setback'. Taylor's men were now based a mere twelve miles from Voinjama. It was time to go.

A precious case of ammunition was prised open and given to a hand-picked group of men, who obligingly put on a display they called a 'fire and manoeuvre' exercise – which, to the untrained eye, looked like a bunch of men running around in circles with automatic weapons, firing them wildly into the undergrowth. However strange the spectacle, the pictures made good entertainment.

I set up a final shot of Robert watching the live rounds going off, which could be used as a dramatic backdrop for placing him in the context of the war. And then, true to our word, the next day, ten days after we arrived in Liberia, we left Voinjama and settled in for a gruelling twenty-two-hour drive back to Conakry. A day later, after checking into the Petit Bateau hotel, the Americans left us.

'Well, that was real. Thanks for a great trip.'

Tired, deeply affected and personally inspired by his experience with the rebels, Jonathan shook hands with us and set off for the plane, with Robert loping in front of him. They couldn't wait to get back to their families.

Back on the terrace at the Petit Bateau, Nick and I picked up where we left off in Tubmanburg. I was curious to know how he had ended up in the arms business – a story he hadn't finished.

'When I came out of EO in '96, I went to Angola as a concession manager for Namco on one of the diamond fields. I began to learn about diamonds there. It was supposed to be a short contract, but I stayed for a few months. I got to know the business quite well. After that I went to Mozambique with Coin Security for a year at one of their mines.'

Nick waved his hand at the waitresses skulking by the kitchen door, and held up two fingers, hopefully, for beers.

'So, basically, you'd moved from being a professional soldier into the mining industry?'

'Not really. That was just the work that was around if you had my background. It's the same today. Then, when I was back in SA, I met up with an old friend of mine, Paul Haynes. That changed my direction a bit.'

Haynes, it transpired, was an army pilot who flew clandestine missions for both the Recces and the CCB, the civilian dirty-tricks department that specialised in assassinations and black operations. Retaining close links to the South African Intelligence service (despite the new era and new government voted into power in 1994) he'd set up a company called Military Technical Services – MTS – and asked Nick to join him as a business partner.

'That must have been at the end of '98, beginning of '99. Paul was already busy with aviation and small-arms contracts. I concentrated mainly on the weapons side. It worked out very well for me. It's his company, really, but I can come and do jobs like this as well. He's a good friend. Not everyone is so lucky to have a partner like him.'

The beers clunked down onto the table. I lit a cigarette.

'So what about this bloody Congo job, then? What *is* all that about?'

'Ja, well, actually it's quite possible. The guy that contacted me represents a group of fighters more from the central part of the country, but he's also involved in the Katanga region and knows the rebels in the east.'

Katanga, Nick explained, is the Congo's massive southern province, fabulously rich in minerals and diamonds, and the source of the uranium that powered the atomic bombs dropped on Japan at the end of the Second World War. It had been a magnet for mercenaries since the 1960s. From the outset of the Congo's independence from Belgium, Katanga had striven, with hired guns for an army, to become a very rich, independent nation.

'The rebel stronghold in eastern Congo is a mountain – almost impenetrable. The only real way in would be to jump in, a low-release drop like we used to do in Mozambique.' He looked at my face, which had frozen mid-mouthful. 'I could teach you. It's not hard to do. It's just trying to find somewhere to land with no trees to break your fall that's tricky.'

'Right,' I replied, unsure if I was being set up for a punchline in an elaborate joke. 'How exactly would we do it?'

I could see myself plummeting through the darkness, camera in hand, jittery rebels lit by landing flares in the jungle clearing below.

'The ammunition would most probably be supplied by the Russians—'

'The Russian Government?' I interrupted.

'No, a private dealer with links to the old former Soviet republics. The weapons would be dropped in on pallets and we'd go in with them, at night. We'd jump at about five hundred feet.'

'Five *hundred*?'

I'd never done a parachute jump before. Even so, five hundred feet seemed very, very low.

'Ja, sometimes we used to jump at three hundred – static line – but that's really the limit. In Rhodesia I used to stand with the dispatcher at the door of the Dakota. You could just about see the DZ below. Sometimes there would be incoming tracer fire from the terrorists on the ground – but when he said jump, vok, you had to jump, right into the bullets. Makes you think what it must have been like for those guys at Arnhem. Looking back, it's amazing more people weren't killed. The Rhodesians had a few serious injuries – in the end they said vok that, we're not jumping like that any more, but we never really had a problem with it.'

I wasn't sure if this was supposed to make me feel better about throwing myself out of a cargo plane cruising at just five hundred feet or reinforce the dangers – either way, I felt apprehensive at the prospect.

'And if we jump in, how are we going to get out?'

I couldn't believe I was asking genuine logistical questions about an operation that involved throwing myself out of an aeroplane.

'Probably we'd have to walk. And we are quite good at that.'

The 'plan' was as sketchy as it was improbable, but it was intriguing, too, despite (or possibly owing to) the lack of any coherent detail. What did emerge clearly, and for the first time, was that Nick was not just the pragmatist I knew him to be. Alongside his practical expertise in the field ran another, perhaps even deeper vein of adventurous wishful thinking. As well as the financial reward, he seemed to want to do the Congo job for the sheer hell of it.

I wasn't ready to commit to his scheme, not least because the logistics of it terrified me. Apart from the extreme undesirability of a parachute jump followed by intense combat and a long hike through the jungle, I struggled with another problem, too: how to go about filming an illegal operation with integrity and professional probity that would not also provide the evidence to land Nick in jail?

'We'd just have to do it in such a way as you can film it without revealing some things, like the source of the weapons,' he said.

It was a fair point. He'd seen me agree to this with US Intelligence, and there was no reason for me to treat him any differently. If nothing else, working in the Congo would, he assured me, be an extraordinary adventure.

'You know,' I said, 'an adventurer was exactly what I'd wanted to be – from as early as I can remember. When I was growing up, all my role models were the soldiers in my family. My mum was broke, but I didn't mind because I had hours to myself to make up war games, like I was the last man surviving from my grandfather's unit in Burma, that kind of thing. Kids' stuff.'

'Ja,' said Nick, 'and then one day it fokken happens for real.'

I wasn't answering his question about joining him in the Congo, but I wanted to keep the door open while I figured it out for myself. I told him that, as I grew up, I wondered what life might be like away from the familiar and predictable routines of Britain. When I was nine years old, my father got a loan from the bank and took me hitchhiking in Ireland. We slept on the floors of youth hostels, and were fed by strangers.

'I was given my first bottle of Guinness by my Irish grandfather's ancient first cousin,' I told Nick. 'He wouldn't hear of me not drinking with him and Dad, so I sipped it by this open peat fire, feeling like a real man – and then fell fast asleep.'

In the days that followed, my father and I scrambled up mountains in Connemara that felt like they were on top of the world. Our holiday opened a window onto a real world that trumped all the games I could play at home by myself.

I had no idea what I wanted 'to do', I explained, but as I grew up, a thirst for travel gripped me completely. By the age of sixteen, I was hitchhiking by myself. Aged eighteen, in the year before I went up to Cambridge, I was inspired by the books written by the war hero and travel writer Patrick Leigh Fermor, and set off in his footsteps to Istanbul.

'When I was travelling, I started taking pictures. I had no idea what I was doing – but when I look back at that time, you know, that was really the beginning of my career. I wasn't exactly planning on the dizzy heights of the Petit Bateau, mind you.'

Nick laughed. I told him that Fermor – with whom I stayed in Greece en route to Turkey – had urged me to visit Fitzroy Maclean, the author of *Eastern Approaches*. Thought to be Ian Fleming's inspiration for James Bond, Maclean had been in the Western Desert at the same time as my grandfather. Fermor told me he thought I had a promising future in international relations.

'You know you said that your dad wanted you to work on the grape farm? My family were pretty much the same – they wanted me to do something respectable, or at least secure, like become a teacher or a civil servant.'

Nick nodded, and washed down a mouthful of roasted peanuts.

'They want the best for you,' he said, 'and you can never see their point of view – until you have your own children. Then it all makes sense, and you get even more cautious than your parents were.'

But Fermor's tales of undercover derring-do with partisans fighting the Germans had watered a seed that had already been planted by my family's own history of wartime adventures. I had wanted to go to war; and now, with Nick, I was being offered any number of options. The question, I realised, was how far I dared pursue them.

11
WANDERLUST

My ears filled with gunfire. Deku strode past me, determined, shaking the sweat from his braids. My camera found the dying man and pulled his bullet-riddled torso into centre-frame. I zoomed in to his face, his eyes.

'Would you like a cup of coffee?'

I pressed pause on the tape deck. Hannes, my video editor at the SABC's *Special Assignment* programme, was standing at the door of the edit suite, peering over my shoulder. It was midnight, and we were almost alone in the huge SABC building in Johannesburg. We'd been cutting the film of the first Liberia trip for a week. The process was exhausting.

'This doesn't get any nicer, does it?' he said, nodding at the screen.

'No, it doesn't.' I looked back at the man's death mask. 'I need a smoke. A coffee would be great, thanks, man. That's really kind.'

Hannes reappeared a few minutes later with a thin white plastic cup of boiling-hot instant coffee. We taped an empty over the smoke alarm, and lit cigarettes. Happy but tired, his kind, open face blinked at me through the miasma of hazy blue smoke.

'We'll finish it tonight,' he said. 'Once we've got this pre-title sequence tidied up, we're there. You can do the graphics and sub-titles tomorrow. I've typed up all the time codes – I'll just need to drop them in. It's a bit fiddly, but then we're really done.'

By the time midnight had arrived on that November evening, I'd learned there was a lot more to making films than getting combat on tape. Originally I believed I was making the film in Liberia – but in truth it was constructed in the edit suite. It was a painstaking process, with quite a lot of swearing in Afrikaans from Hannes and much head shaking and muttered 'if only I'd known's' from me. Eventually, we'd ended up with a thirty-minute film that I decided somewhat pretentiously to call *Liberia: A Journey Without Maps* – in homage to the writer Graham Greene's travel book about Liberia written in 1936.

A couple of days later, on 12 November 2002, the film was broadcast. A group of us – producers, and journalists from the SABC – sat around in a friend's house with cold beers and watched it go out. I could hardly breathe. When it ended there was a small round of applause, and everyone looked at me, but I was lost for words. Ten weeks of filming and twenty-two hours of tape had been crunched into a thirty-minute-and-sixteen-second film. That was the reality that everyone saw, would now always see. Any mistakes, misrepresentations, miscalculations, were now permanent 'facts'. My memories had become public property.

The only person missing from this extended party was Nick. He was already back in Liberia, negotiating a helicopter-and-diamond deal with Sekou Conneh, the LURD's national chairman. I had no way of reaching him. In the seventeen days since we'd returned from the trip with the Americans, we hadn't seen each other at all.

In the week that followed the broadcast, I was curious to hear other reactions. So with Nick himself out of range, I called his friend Piet in Monrovia, who told me that Taylor had seen the film. At first Taylor had gone apoplectic, railing against me and the fact that the film had caused upwards of a dozen international trading and investment companies to cancel their plans in Liberia with immediate effect. Then he had his own edited version of the film made (removing any mention of the president being a war criminal, and of his troops raping young girls) and made sure as many people as possible in Monrovia saw it. *Look*, it screamed, *the rebels are psychopathic killers! Only I, Charles Taylor, can protect you!* That it would be used as propaganda *by* Taylor, I hadn't foreseen. Once the film was out there, it really was uncontrollable.

Nick and I had spoken on the phone, though, just before he'd headed to the front-line area of Kolahun that Jackity had denied to Robert and Jonathan three weeks before.

'Good luck, mate. Really, be careful. I won't be there to look after you this time,' I told him, 'and it's a long way to come and rescue you.'

I didn't know if I could have gone back myself, so soon. His determination – or perhaps desperation – was impressive.

'Ja, well, I must try and behave myself. If I don't see you before, we'll have a big braai at my house next year. The family are very curious to meet this mysterious Englishman.'

We finished the call, and that was it. He was gone. I plotted his route in my head and tried not to think about the traps that might lie in wait for him.

In Johannesburg, I learned to be careful about how I described my friendship with him. Nick did not want his involvement in our Liberia project to be credited, on account of his new business venture with the rebels. What was more, the young, ethnically diverse crowd of South Africans that I worked and socialised with were not – it transpired – straightforwardly sympathetic towards apartheid-era Special Forces operators. At first I talked fairly openly about Nick's role in the film, and the fact that I hired him as my bodyguard, sometimes commenting on his past in Special Forces. Then one white colleague declared that he was 'glad that cunts like that could finally find something useful to do'.

What the fuck would you know about it? I thought. *How many people have you seen blown to bits?* As if that somehow explained or excused anything. In fact, he knew a lot more about it than me, and had seen more than his fair share of the horrors of war.

'You didn't experience apartheid,' he continued, 'which is why you can forgive its henchmen their history when it suits you. James, I had cunts like Nick trying to kill me. I used to fear for my life from these sorts of people. People I know were killed by them. My father fled them into exile, they broke my ribs, tear-gassed me, machine-gunned children in front of me. They bugged our phones, raped our friends, dragged black people behind their bakkies and wiped out civilian villages dressed as freedom fighters. Think white Interahamwe, and you're on the right track.'

We stared at each other, separated by the gulf of our different experiences. I just could not reconcile the Nick I knew with the man people assumed he must be – and I didn't want to try. Our shared experience in Liberia was far more powerful than other people's memories.

Thereafter, I became increasingly defensive of my friendship with Nick, justifying the whys and wherefores of our relationship in professional, logistical terms, rather than trying to describe the simple bond that had grown between us.

'No,' I said to another journalist friend, who worked in the *Special Assignment* office, 'he doesn't use the word "kaffir", and he doesn't hate black people.'

Agitated, I was responding to genuine suspicion on her behalf. We sat facing each other across stiff table linen and glinting cutlery at a smart restaurant in Johannesburg. From a mixed-race – 'coloured' – background, she wondered why it was that I bristled at the idea he might be a racist. Surely that was just a given?

'Nick', I continued, 'is different. All right, he might not exactly have been a fan of the liberation movement, but he was a soldier, not a murderer. He wasn't bumping people off in hotel rooms—'

'Really?' she interrupted me.

Shifting in her seat, she covered her lips with the palm of her hand – whether it was to hide a smile or a yawn, I couldn't tell.

'You were there, then? In Gaborone, Maseru . . .'

She quoted the names of the capital cities of the former so-called front-line states of Botswana and Lesotho as a provocation: both of them – and more besides – had hosted covert Recce missions that resulted in the deaths of innocent bystanders. Nick himself had led one of the teams on the infamous Gaborone Raid – a Special Forces assault on suspected ANC safe-houses. Among others, a child and a pregnant woman were killed. Nick maintained that his particular squad had simply ransacked an ANC newspaper office for intelligence files and hurt no one. The building was not demolished because, he believed, other local businesses shared the premises. 'I never', he'd said, 'killed anyone in Botswana.'

I pressed on. 'Basically, he was a professional soldier, and he followed orders.'

I sounded like a defence lawyer at Nuremberg. Then she smiled at me. We both knew I had no idea what orders Nick may or may not have followed in the army. It was an article of faith that he was who he said he was. I had no proof either way.

Back home, the film was finally attracting some attention. I attended a huge news media conference in Dublin, where *A Journey Without Maps* was shown on a giant screen in the main events hall. When the film began I sneaked out the back. I was so nervous of this audience of producers, news editors, commissioners and well-known journalists I just couldn't bear to watch their responses.

It went well, though. I was congratulated as brave, original and a future 'award-winner'. The self-belief I'd felt after filming the fire-fights in Tubmanburg might not have been unfounded after all. Suddenly, though, I felt embarrassed; I thought how out of place Nick would have been, how little meaning any of it would have had for him. I was drinking champagne and moving towards recognition; he was back in the jungle, on the front line.

The truth was that he would have been in familiar – if arguably less principled – company. To be able to sit through other people's horror and come out into the bar at the other end: that was what we all wanted – to have experienced, survived and been paid. Some of us did it for real; some of us did it by proxy. At one point I found myself in a corner, feeling ashamed, while men in suits approached like lizards, tongues out, licking the air around me for a vicarious, bittersweet tang of the jungle.

I had no idea if I would ever return to Liberia: the film was working, my career was gaining pace. Every conversation, every encounter, nudged me further into the world of the broadcast media. For the first time, I was forced by a professional audience to answer questions about my motivations for the trip. They wanted to know what it was like going to war, and why I did it. Their questions put me on the spot. Was I on a moral crusade, or merely rubber-necking an accident so that others could rubber-neck it, too? Was the entire trip a rite of passage – a simple surrender to a young man's compulsion for adventure? Or was it a quest for Truth? Unprepared, I made up the answers as I went along.

'To bear witness without accepting responsibility is to create entertainment,' I thought out loud as they scribbled in their notepads. Yes, that was it. 'Witnessing warfare brings with it a responsibility to the story, and, most importantly, to the people whose stories you're telling.'

People seemed pleased with that. I thought of the dying man in the dust, executed by Deku, and the proud, hungry women winnowing the last of their precious rice crop. 'I mean, basically, that's the difference between war reporting as pornography and war reporting as truth. The story that you tell – it has to be honest, which means it has to be their story, not yours. I went without a sense of that – but I learned it. If you don't discharge your responsibilities . . .'

They stared at me, as if silently guessing what I would say next. I was wearing a suit and had a pint of Guinness in my hand, and *was* telling my story. It was absurd. I changed tack slightly. I wasn't sure exactly how I was supposed to discharge my responsibilities as a war reporter. Telling the truth seemed like a good – the only – place to start.

'I went because it's my job to tell stories. I was brought up on stories. I like telling them. I think there is a compulsion to do it,' I continued. 'I couldn't write about economics, or sport – but I can do this, I went and I survived. There are very few people who can do that, who *want* to do it. So if I'm not going to do it, who is? Who will tell those stories?'

My argument was gaining pace, and I liked the sound of it, too. 'There is a moral imperative to this. Just because someone lives in a place where it's hard to hear their voice – because they're being silenced by an oppressive government or caught up in a war – doesn't mean that their voice is somehow less worthy or less deserving of being heard. Quite the opposite. Those are voices that we don't hear often, or loudly, enough. My job is to help interpret those stories, to give them context and clarity and make sure they are heard. That's all. I'm a conduit. My camera is a funnel.'

They believed me; and I started to believe me, too. It seemed as good a justification as any.

* * *

From Dublin, armed with this new mantra, I flew direct to Amsterdam for the International Documentary Film Festival. I met up with Jonathan, the American director from the last trip to Liberia. Profoundly affected by his experiences in Voinjama, Jonathan had a simple proposition. He thought there was a much bigger film to be made in Liberia. Despite the beheading, Jonathan said he'd enjoyed his time in Voinjama, and loved the quirky nature of Liberia and the Liberians. He'd got the 'bug' because of it, and because of the country's unique history.

'I mean, are the rebels really finished, or what? It seemed like maybe they were waiting for the right time to move on Taylor again.'

Jonathan and I were queuing in the foyer of the main cinema to see what other productions were coming out of Africa.

'Yeah, I think that's right,' I said. 'Nick's with them now. He's, er, on a recce trip for me – so I'll get some up-to-date info pretty soon. If they get their act together, they could take the capital. I'm sure they can.'

Later that day we met a producer from the Discovery Times Channel, who liked the idea of a longer film about the rebels, and we arranged to meet again soon to discuss a commission. Drinking coffee in between film screenings, I also met another of Jonathan's contacts – a woman called Kathi Austin.

'James, Kathi. Kathi, James. You two should talk. You've both got this Liberia thing going on. He's a crazy dude, just so you know.'

And with that Jonathan plunged into conversation with another director.

'So you just got back?'

Her accent was hard to place, southern USA perhaps, but with a slightly harder edge than the clichéd dialect I was used to hearing on television. She hoisted a teabag out of a dull green herbal infusion and then removed her jacket. She was petite and beautiful and in her forties. She looked at me, and smiled. I realised I hadn't answered.

'Long trip?'

'Yes . . . no. I mean, yes. I got back from the trip with Jonathan a month ago. I've been cutting a film about my first trip down in Jo'burg, but I just got here. It's Tuesday, right? So I must be in Holland. It's a bit like that. I don't know if I'm coming or going.'

Kathi explained she was a researcher, a sort of investigative activist who worked on exposing players and transactions in the international arms trade. She lived in San Francisco, but was on her way to Frankfurt to interview a man in prison connected to a South American arms-smuggling case. Apparently, it was a huge breakthrough for her, but the details were hard to understand. Most of what she said was vague and suggestive. She seemed to be implying that the man in jail was there partly owing to her investigation, but I was only half-listening.

Nick, I thought, *is an arms dealer. Be very careful what you say.*

'What's the Liberia connection?' I asked, tentatively. 'Did you do something very bad in a previous life?'

'I worked with the UN Security Council's Panel of Experts, looking at arms deals,' she said.

I explained the lukewarm reception I'd had when I'd called the current Panel's investigators on my return in August.

'I really wish I could say that surprised me, but that is just typical. There's so much politics, so much navel-gazing at the UN in general, and nothing really gets done. I'm sorry they gave you a hard time. In the end I wasn't even properly credited on the Panel's final report – they pretty much left my name off. It happens.'

No sooner had we started to chat than it was time for her to go. I asked where her accent was from.

'Virginia,' she replied, hamming it up, slowing down the syllables, 'near Richmond.'

'A Southern Belle, then?'

'Oh, yeah,' she smiled. 'Call me.'

She gave me her number, and said goodbye.

It seemed I was finally getting a name for my work in West Africa. Back in London, I received an unexpected call.

'Ah, yes, hello. Is that James?'

It was a male English voice that I didn't recognise. I agreed it was me.

'Hello, James,' he continued. 'My name is Mick. I'm calling from the Foreign Office.'

'The Foreign Office? What is it?'

'A mutual friend gave me your number. I wondered if we might meet for a chat.'

His inflection was flat and absolutely unreadable.

'Friend?' I repeated, like an imbecile. *Must be Frank*, I thought. The line remained silent. 'Yeah, sure. When suits?'

He gave me a mobile number, a time, and the precise location of a wooden bench by a lake in St James's Park. He didn't give me a surname or an explanation. The line went dead.

Right, well, that was weird. I've just been approached by the Government.

I found him on the bench a week later, just as he'd said I would, wrapped up in a brown trench coat. I wondered if he'd been there the whole time.

'Hello, James,' he greeted me.

'Hi, Mick,' I replied.

'It's a cold day, isn't it?' he said as I sat down next to him. I agreed it was. 'I hope you don't mind meeting here. It seemed like a good idea. It's fairly central.'

I nodded and tried to look over my shoulder without appearing either too obviously amused or paranoid. For several minutes we sat and talked like this about nothing in particular: the weather, the traffic. Then he wanted to know where I'd been in Liberia, whom I'd been working for, whether I was going back. I suspected he knew most of the answers, but I played along, answering in good faith, seeing where it would all lead.

He knew his stuff. He asked a specific question about former pro-Government militia from Sierra Leone fighting with the LURD rebels in Liberia. It was an interesting enquiry, and caught my imagination.

'There are several dozen of them. Ex-Civil Defence Force, mainly,' I confirmed. 'On the other side, Taylor is using the RUF in Foya, re-supplying them by helicopter . . .'

At the mention of the word 'helicopter' we both looked at each other. I wondered if he knew about Nick's plans. Could the British be monitoring his satellite phone calls from Freetown? I pressed on.

'When I was last in Voinjama—'

'In October?' he interrupted.

That freaked me out. I'd not mentioned the second trip at all until then. I continued, cautiously.

'Yes, a couple of months ago, they took an RUF prisoner – alive, for a change. He showed me Yugoslav currency – dinar – that the chopper pilot had given him, and told me that Benjamin Yeatin, Taylor's main commander, was personally handing out the ammo. I'm pretty sure it's coming from Eastern Europe.'

Other than the brief burst of shooting on the outskirts of town, it had been the only other exciting thing to film with the Americans.

'And are the rebels using mercenaries?'

Hmm, I thought, *is this what this is all about?*

'No, they're not. Just the CDF.' Then a thought came to me. 'Listen, I'm happy to talk, but I was wondering . . . I was wondering if, perhaps, if there's anything that I need help with in the future, if we could, er, co-operate?'

As soon as I spoke, I felt foolish – it was as if I was playing a scene in my own imaginary movie but somehow I'd forgotten my lines.

'What kind of help?'

He looked at me as if he might genuinely be interested in what I wanted from him.

'I'm not sure yet,' I said, truthfully. I looked away and stared at a brightly plumed duck that had glided away from the bank near our feet. 'But I'll let you know.'

'Okay. Well, you've got my number.'

As December drew on, with still no word from Nick, Rachel and I went on holiday to Italy. For me it was a final attempt to rescue our relationship. After nearly a week of each other's company in a picture-perfect farmhouse in Umbria, I ran out of things to say. It didn't help that I was obsessed with my career, and my next adventure. Being alone with a beautiful woman in Italy was frankly boring compared to the rush of being with the rebels in the Liberian jungle.

'I just don't understand why you want to do it,' she said, when I explained that I was trying to go back.

I couldn't, wouldn't, explain it to her. There was no common ground. She was too young, and I was too selfish. It could never work. It was over.

At two o'clock in the afternoon of the day I arrived back from Italy, I went to see the head of the Africa Programme at the Royal Institute for International Affairs at Chatham House.

I handed over the photos of the new Kalashnikovs that the rebels had captured from Taylor's army in Tubmanburg. I wanted them traced, to follow the lead back to Europe. To my surprise, while I was there I was invited to write a briefing paper on the LURD rebels, which they wanted me to submit the following February.

London was freezing. The year was drawing to a close.

On New Year's Eve, Nick called.

'It wasn't such a long walk this time,' his familiar voice echoed on my cell phone. He was out of the jungle, and in one piece. 'We went down from the main place to the other town where we wanted to go but the tourists weren't allowed to visit.'

'Yeah, I'm with you.'

He'd been to Kolahun. He'd also seen where Deku had been killed.

'It was a lucky shot. An RPG came through the window of a house he was taking cover in and hit him in the head. There were bits of brain everywhere, all over the walls, the ceiling. They left his body in the bushes.'

'You mean he was killed by Government troops?'

'Ja, that's correct. When we were there the big man didn't want us to know that they were nearly beaten.'

Nick was glad that the film had been a success – he'd heard about it from Piet in Monrovia as well. I told him that I was trying to get funding for another trip to Liberia. He laughed.

'Happy new year,' he signed off, 'regards to your family. I think this could be a very interesting one.'

Things were definitely looking up. Later that week I got a call from a producer at the BBC's *Newsnight* programme in London. They wanted to buy *Journey Without Maps* and re-cut it for immediate transmission in the UK. During the edit I decided to do as Kathi had said, and call her in San Francisco. I told her I needed to fact-check something in the script – in fact, I wanted to find out if she had any plans to visit London. She didn't. I'd been thinking about her since our meeting in Amsterdam. I didn't know any women who were so attractive *and* had compelling histories of working on warfare in Africa. I didn't even know if she was single. In a bid to keep her on the line, I mentioned the Chatham House briefing paper.

'James, you need to be careful. Don't worry, but your work in Liberia ruffled some feathers. You've messed up a few egos.'

'How so?'

'Well, you've reported on things that the UN Panel is supposed to know, but didn't. They claimed it wasn't possible to get into Liberia with the LURD, and then a month later you rocked up in their HQ – *with a camera*. You're kinda beating them at their own game, and some people don't like it.'

'How do you mean, "don't like it"?' I was confused.

'Well, one of them denounced you as a mercenary.'

'What?'

'Yeah, he claimed that you came from the dark side.'

I burst out laughing.

'The dark side? That's fucking *excellent*! Help me, Obi Wan, you're my only hope!'

'James, this is not funny. They accused you of bringing weapons across the Guinea border. They've largely dismissed your reporting.'

I stopped laughing.

'I didn't take any weapons across any border.'

My mind was racing. *Except, of course, for the Kalashnikov I took to Frank in Conakry. Shit.*

In the end I decided to pay Kathi a visit. I was due in Los Angeles to do some filming with Robert, and from there it was only a short hop up to see her in San Francisco.

She was waiting for me in arrivals.

'Hi,' I said, and then realised I had no idea what else to say.

I leaned forward to kiss her on the cheek, and fluffed it. She said an awkward hello, too, and then drove me back to her apartment. There were important issues to consider – mercenaries, spooks and United Nations inspectors included – but foremost in my mind was resolving the tricky conundrum of how, exactly, I was going to get her into bed.

I had only a few days before my next rendezvous: Robert, the writer, had arranged for me to attend a training course for journalists at a Marine Corps base in Virginia, and from there I was due in New York for meetings with Jonathan and the Discovery Times Channel. To my surprise, the television commissioning log-jam had been broken, and funding was agreed – if the rebels looked like they stood a genuine chance of attacking Monrovia. The idea was to film their assault from both sides: Jonathan inside the city with Taylor's men, and me running with the rebels. For that to happen, the LURD needed to recover a lot of territory. According to Nick, they had barely been able to claw back the area around their headquarters on the Guinea border.

I was surprised and delighted to discover that Kathi's old-fashioned, high-windowed apartment – that looked out over Alcatraz Island and the Bay – had only one bedroom.

'There's a sofa bed,' she conceded, waving her hand half-heartedly towards a couch visible through the open doorway to the living room, 'but you might be more comfortable in here.'

Thirteen years older than me, and deeply professionally involved in the most important story of my life, she was not an obvious choice of lover. She was, however, straightforwardly irresistible.

Over the following days we nosed around the city's tourist sights, drank a lot, and chatted over lengthy meals in countless restaurants. Our conversation was always about West Africa, mercenaries and arms dealers. It was hardly romantic, but it was exhilarating. She knew a great deal – and asked an awful lot of questions. Here was the common ground I was missing with Rachel. Sipping bottles of Anchor Steam beer and eating barbecued oysters with her by the ocean, I felt like I was falling in love. Her experience, interest and contacts in Liberia proved insightful and concrete enough; but the details of her life, clouded by enigma, remained a mystery to me. As America edged towards war in the Gulf, I became tangled up in her, and her tales of intrigue and betrayal in Monrovia.

I was becoming more itinerant than ever. After meeting Jonathan in New York, I flew back to London in early February, Kathi by my side. I made my way to Chatham House for the Liberia briefing, before travelling to Brussels to meet Nick. The briefing went unexpectedly well, despite an initially frosty reception for Kathi by the host. I sat on a podium with a Liberia expert and delivered a forty-minute speech about who the LURD were, what their objectives were, and how they sought to achieve them. The room was packed with journalists, analysts – and spooks. A couple of Americans who weren't keen on giving out business cards furnished me with cryptic email addresses and British mobile-phone numbers – and a suggestion that I stay in touch. One worked for the Defence Intelligence Agency, the other for the CIA. They had both seen my film, and they both knew about Nick. Kathi worked the room, collecting phone numbers and anecdotes; I smiled at everyone and tried to work out who my friends might be.

As far as getting back into Liberia was concerned, the only friend I could rely on was Nick. My commission with Discovery depended on the rebels getting their act together and launching a credible offensive against Monrovia. Personally, the contract was a huge deal: my own first proper advance commission for a TV film. Although part of me dreaded the physical consequences of returning, the prospect of a third trip filled me with familiar nervous excitement and anticipation. The scope of what we were planning appealed to me as well. With Jonathan filming behind Government lines, I hoped that we would be able to achieve together what I had failed to do alone: create a rounded, balanced picture of the real nature of the war, and its impact on the civilian population.

It was impossible to predict what might actually happen in Liberia, but just being on the ground with Discovery's endorsement promised a breakthrough for my career. It was also a risk: if the rebels failed to attack, there would be no film. Getting any sense out of Sekou Conneh was almost impossible. My only, vital, source of information about the rebels' prospects of victory was Nick.

We met in central Brussels and ended up in a large-windowed café where we ordered a late breakfast. I was dying to know what Nick had been up to; I filled him in on Chatham House, then he briefed me on his latest trip. He'd been back to Liberia again in January. It was now 7 March.

'On that first trip I only went as far as Kolahun. That was a bit of a fuck-up. No diamonds and a lot of walking at night. Mostly it was just waiting around.'

'No change there, then.'

I was relieved. The diamond exploit in Liberia was an unwelcome and complicating factor in my relationship with him. I suspected, nonetheless, that he was sugar-coating the truth. The United Nations was monitoring both Taylor and the LURD – both of whom they knew were dealing in contraband stones. There was more good news.

'Sekou's forces has made huge advances. Foya is still under Government control, but it's completely isolated, an island.

They've re-occupied all the land they lost when we went down there, right to Tubmanburg.' He held his teaspoon daintily, making concentric circles in the foam. 'This time, though, they're doing it properly. Sekou says he's going to finish off Foya before they try and hit Monrovia.'

'What about supplies?'

'Ag, well, that's the problem. They've got enough for now, but they realise it's impossible to win while they're carrying everything south from Voinjama over that fokken river. Foya makes their supply lines very vulnerable, too. Their main plan is to take Robertsport. The harbour is quite good there – silted up, but still able to take a shallow-draft cargo ship if it's unloaded with canoes. Dragon Master says that Guinea will give them what they need. If they can get a ship in, then they've got a straight run to Tubmanburg and the capital.'

'And if they can't?'

'Ja, well, I'm working on that with Piet. He's trying to arrange an ammo drop for Taylor. It's hard landing planes at Robertsfield at the moment – the UN are monitoring Taylor much more closely now. He managed to land over two hundred tons of weapons while we were there last summer, though.'

'You know, I think our film might have had something to do with the UN's interest. It's really ratcheted up the pressure on him.'

'Ja, quite likely. You've been very busy. Well, it works for us anyway, because if the only way to get Taylor ammunition is to drop it from an aircraft, then we can make sure that the pilots get the wrong co-ordinates and just drop it a little bit further on our side.'

I couldn't help but admire the sheer audacity of the plan: Nick supplying the rebels with weapons bought by Taylor for the Government army. It was cunning – but also very dangerous.

'Piet would really do that?'

'Ja, he really would. He's looking at what happens when Taylor leaves. I think he'd like some new friends. Besides, it's safe. The nearest upper radar coverage is in Ghana, miles out of range.'

'And what about the diamonds? Really nothing?'

My curiosity was getting the better of me.

'Useless, man. Very low-quality, no one is interested. I've just been in Zürich, trying to get some investment money. Actually, that was fokken great. They took us, me and Henri, my new business partner, to a bar with these dancing girls.' He raised his hands, cupped inwards to his chest in imitation of an impressive cleavage. 'Ja, it was all very nice, but no diamonds. I'm still working on the helicopter.'

For a moment, the modest, hard-working man I knew from the jungle looked lost. It seemed he was enjoying life, or perhaps he was just trying to live more how an arms dealer was expected to, to impress his Russian buyers.

I steered us back onto more familiar territory.

'What about this Congo job? Is that still on?'

'I think so. My contact has got some big plans connected to the rebels in Katanga. It's going nicely.' And then, almost as if remembering the final item on a shopping list, he added, 'I'm trying to get hold of some SAM-16s, too. It's quite difficult. They're quite sensitive, much better than those SAM-7s we found, with a dual infrared tracking system.'

This was something else entirely. Highly effective surface-to-air missiles, SAM-16s are more than capable of downing not only airliners, but modern fighter planes, too.

Quite sensitive? I thought. *Fuck me.*

'Mate, if it's all the same, I'd rather not know. Fucking James Bond has got my mobile number and my girlfriend would wet her knickers if she even had the faintest idea we were having this conversation – which, by the way, she never will.'

'That's probably just as well. You wouldn't want to upset her.'

He wrote a name and number on a piece of paper, and pushed it across the table to me.

'Here, if she wants someone to fuck, she can screw this guy. He cheated me on a deal a couple of years back. He's no good.'

'Thanks. I'm not quite sure how I'm going to explain how I came by it, but anyway . . . When is this Congo gig going ahead?'

'The one in the east, or the one in Katanga?'

'Bloody hell, you're going to keep me in work for years at this rate. Either of them.'

There were no fixed dates, but he promised to let me know. His Congolese contact was, by the sound of it, nothing if not shifty. The entire enterprise seemed at best fanciful, and likely impossible. The days of mercenaries marauding around Katanga were a distant memory.

Our shadows moved across the table, and we ambled to a restaurant for a late lunch. Glasses of strong Belgian lager made me light-headed, and more relaxed. Mainly, we chatted about getting back into Liberia, and the new film I wanted to make. This time I wanted to document very carefully the movement of weapons from Guinea to the LURD, as well as getting to grips properly with the rebels' command structure and political agenda. If they did make it into the capital itself, I thought it was very important that the assault – and its consequences – be filmed. Conneh maintained that I would be the only journalist allowed in, which conferred a unique burden of responsibility to make sure I was there to capture it.

Nick was enthusiastic, and his general prognosis was positive. Now tight with the rebels, he would work on securing arms, or at least the means for arms to be delivered, for them. As soon as an attack on Monrovia seemed imminent, we'd get to Conakry, and then make our way to the front line.

'A guy who was with me in the Recces has been up in Ivory Coast, fighting Liberian insurgents in the west, near Man. Taylor invaded to try and fuck up their president, Gbagbo, but he's pushed too far in and seems quite weak. There's another group, MODEL, that's been trained by South Africans there who are pushing into Liberia now.'

'Another Liberian rebel group, you mean?'

It was news to me. The war was escalating.

'Ja, it seems that way. I think they were part of the LURD, but belonged to that Christian – what's it, Krahn? – group. They've formed their own unit – lightly armed. Gbagbo used them against Taylor. Their main objective seems to be a port south of Monrovia.'

Taylor's forces were over-stretched, and now possibly encircled. Worse, he faced two rebel groups, both of which were being supplied by neighbouring countries. He was swallowing a bitter dose of his own medicine.

After lunch, and more beers, we shook hands and then wished each other well as I bundled myself into a taxi.

'See you in Conakry,' I said, as the car pulled away.

'Ja,' he replied, 'and good luck with that woman.'

My life was becoming a complex web of deceit and uncertainty. My only confidant about the fighting in Liberia was Nick, who was increasingly involved in the rebels' war and now helping their push towards the coast in preparation for their assault on Monrovia. From Kathi, I withheld all but the most innocuous details of my relationship with him. From Nick, I hid my deep unease at his diamond dealing, and uncertainty at how I would reconcile his support for the rebels with the truthful telling of the story of the war that I was beholden – both professionally and morally – to recount. It was like being stuck in the middle of some preposterous intelligence *ménage à trois*.

At home, Kathi took a great deal of interest in my phone calls and comings and goings. I didn't mention Mick, or two other subsequent meetings with US Intelligence operatives who had approached me in London. Despite the compulsive nature of our relationship, there was part of me that instinctively mistrusted her. Nothing was as it seemed. I had no idea what Nick might really be plotting with Piet and the rebels, and Kathi was absorbed in her own, mysterious, work – at times to the exclusion of all else. Nothing and no one could be relied upon absolutely – with the exception, as always, of my grandfather, Don. By phone, and fleeting visits to the bungalow in Kent, I kept him up to date with my plans, and, along with my mother, urged him to see a doctor for the cough that was troubling him.

As a return to Liberia loomed ever larger, I called Mick at the Foreign Office. We agreed to meet in a bistro tucked away in St Martin's Passage – a quiet alley in the bustling heart of tourist London. The manager, a close friend of mine, sat us at a private table near the window. I felt comfortable there, and safe.

'So, Mick,' I began, after the menus had been tidied away, 'a little bird tells me that the British Government thinks I'm a mercenary. Apparently, I've been gun-running over the Liberian border.'

As I spoke, I felt a curious mix of emotions: fear, excitement and gnawing uncertainty.

'I think there was, certainly, that impression. Yes.'

He looked at me with dull grey eyes. He was the most ignorable, forgettable man I'd ever met.

Bloody hell, I thought, *Kathi was right. Where do I even begin with this?*

'Well,' I said, 'it's ridiculous. I went in with a professional soldier – which, as you know, is not unusual. The BBC hire ex-SAS bodyguards all the time. It's an industry norm. He picked up a weapon in-country, and never used it.'

I thought of the ambush on the back road, the long grass scythed by machine-gun fire. Mick fiddled with his napkin, and drank some water.

'As I expect you know, I have quite a close relationship with the Americans, who were interested in what I was doing. What I don't understand is why no one else is. All this mercenary rubbish is very damaging, and I want it to stop. I'm a journalist.'

He said nothing.

'I'm just trying to do my job,' I added, for good measure.

'Like I said,' he countered, with monotonous exactitude, 'there *was* that impression. But I think you could interpret the fact that you were invited to submit the Chatham House paper as a sign that you've been brought in from the cold, as it were.'

I stared at him in disbelief. *Brought in from the cold? What is this, a plot from a fucking thriller?*

'I expect you'll find that all has been forgiven. Giving a briefing paper like that is very . . . mainstream.'

'I see. It was quite valuable information, I suppose. I expect some people are quite interested in that information.'

'Yes,' he concluded. 'That is, after all, the nature of the beast.'

It was impossible to like or dislike Mick – his personality was impalpable and his riddles impenetrable. He seemed to be suggesting that whatever problems there had been were now in the past – which was a relief, as I knew that back in Liberia I might very well need the help of the Foreign Office if I got into trouble.

We finished our drinks, and shook hands.

'I'll be in touch,' I said. 'I might have something interesting for you soon.'

In fact, by now I was quite enjoying myself, revelling in the deception. It was like playing an exciting game to which no one knew the rules.

As I considered my next move in Africa, American troops and their Allies invaded Iraq. War reporting – once a rare treat on nightly bulletins – became the mainstay of television news as the press corps scrambled to get embedded with combat troops and film the bloody progress of the occupation. Meanwhile, all I could concentrate on was a small, fetid corner of West African jungle. Planning the next trip to Liberia became all-consuming. I packed and re-packed cameras, and spent hours poring over maps and what few reports were available from other journalists. The more remarkable the onslaught in Iraq became, the more completely I immersed myself in the quest to get back into Liberia. If the rebels did attack Monrovia, the film would have to be powerful and original to break through the saturated coverage that accompanied the 'Shock and Awe' of Operation Iraqi Freedom.

Back at home, Sekou Conneh had taken to calling me frequently and randomly from his satellite phone. He liked to brief me about the progress of the war, or the status of the rebels' latest weapons deliveries. On one occasion, straining to be heard over the crackling line, I excused myself from the table at a friend's house and headed into the hallway.

'How much ammunition do you need?' I bellowed into the receiver, straightening the frame of a painting in the white, up-lit corridor.

Sekou was having difficulty in getting hold of Nick again, and was explaining what he required to begin the assault.

'Jay, we nee' too much. Fi' hundre' plastic, an' mo' bom'. We don' have sufficien' ammunishan to attack a' dis time,' he cautioned.

'AK or PKM?' I clarified.

We continued shouting at each other over the unstable line. His bizarre inflection rose and fell.

'And how many heavy machine guns do you need?' I roared as a young woman in a ridiculously short skirt appeared and handed me my glass of wine.

Our conversation continued for several minutes. I returned to the meal to the dumbfounded silence of my fellow guests. One of them laughed as I sat down, and asked me:

'Are you filming this war, or fighting it?'

12
THE REVOLUTION WILL BE TELEVISED

A year ago to the day that I'd first arrived in Conakry, I strode into the arrivals hall of the notorious airport, armed with my commission from the Discovery Times Channel to make a feature-length documentary about the forthcoming battle for Monrovia. This time I arrived with a photo-journalist called Tim Hetherington.

Two years older than me, Tim was represented by Network – a leading photographic agency in London. When he first contacted me and asked if we could work together, I'd turned him down; but as the scope of this new film became clear, it was evident I would need all the help I could get. Although he'd never been in combat, a chance assignment had taken him to Liberia in 1999; he'd then worked extensively in Sierra Leone and across West Africa. His photographs were disarmingly intimate, different from anything I'd seen shot in the region before. Tim's route into photography had been as odd as mine into television. After graduating from Oxford, he'd got enough money together to travel to India. Two years later, he returned to London, picked up a camera and had an epiphany. After working through night school, learning his craft, he went on to work at first for the *Big Issue* and then the *Independent*. Now carrying a video camera, he was going to help me shoot from behind rebel lines – while Jonathan Stack shot simultaneously in Monrovia with President Taylor. It was his first television production.

Nick was waiting for us with a smile and a welcoming committee of red-bereted presidential guards.

'Nick, this is Tim, who I told you about. Tim, Nick.'

The two men locked palms, and sized each other up.

'Great to meet you. I've heard a lot about you. You seem to have this place pretty much under control.'

Tim spoke confidently, but I could see his eyes darting around, taking in the details of the scene: the harassed passengers, the arrogant smirks of the soldiers. No stranger to African airports, he was looking for whatever trouble might arise before it was too late.

'Ja, well, it's getting easier. Let's head straight to the hotel and we can have a briefing. How was the flight?'

'Brutal,' Tim replied. 'We flew via Nouakchott, where I think one of my bags is having an unscheduled holiday.'

'That's a great start. I think they're about to have a coup. The army isn't very happy,' Nick mused, as the president's soldiers took our passports away for stamping. *How does he know this stuff?* I wondered. 'So, ja,' he continued, 'it could be worse: you could be in Mauritania with your bag.'

After the short, and by now familiar, drive to the outskirts of town, Tim and I checked into the dilapidated safe-haven of the Petit Bateau hotel. Nick had made his own arrangements, and was staying with the rebels' national chairman in town. The three of us sat down to a late breakfast on the terrace while Nick filled us in.

Freshly re-supplied with ammunition from Guinea, and assisted by the emergence of the new MODEL rebel group also battling Taylor in the southeast, the LURD rebels were poised – we hoped – to strike a hammer blow against his regime.

'They have Robertsport – it's under their control – and the chairman says they've finished with Foya. Ag, you know they might still be cleaning up there, but it's not a threat.'

From almost being defeated in Lofa County, their home region, the previous October, the LURD were back in control of more territory than ever before. 'They took a delivery of around three hundred thousand AK rounds just now, and there should be another one coming with more RPG bombs and fuses.' He looked at Tim. 'They won't fight without RPGs – it's fokken irritating.'

It seemed as if the Guinean president – Lansana Conté – was finally prepared to give the rebels what they needed to finish the job. An illicit airdrop of ammunition was not going to be needed, after all.

'Mr B, what's the situation with our American friends? Are they still helping, or what are they doing?'

Nick looked at me cautiously, probably wondering what I'd told Tim.

'Tim knows about this,' I said. 'I'm meeting with one of their guys here tomorrow morning. I don't think the film did Frank any favours. Apparently, it was quite widely watched in Washington. The idea of supporting cannibals is a bit of a no-no. Basically, it put the kybosh on Frank's little mission. I got the impression that they've been told to back off.'

'And what about Conté?' Tim asked. 'Are the Yanks still supporting him?'

The position of the Guinean president was as mysterious as ever, though there were political moves in Washington to try and contain his regional aspirations as well.

'Kathi says that the US ambassador to Guinea issued Conté with a strongly worded diplomatic *démarche* and demanded he stop supporting the rebels. Apparently, she saw it, or a copy of it. I can't imagine it's going to make a blind bit of difference, though.'

Nick agreed it wouldn't.

'Conté hates Taylor,' he said, matter-of-factly. 'He'll do whatever he can to fuck him up.'

Tim was nodding as he pieced together the fragments of the story. Nick was scribbling into his notebook, as usual. Coffee and croissants arrived. Tim ordered fried eggs. Nick doubled, and then I trebled the order. We were all ravenous. The sun climbed higher above us, the edge taken off the heat only by a strong breeze rolling in off the Atlantic.

'When are we going to move?' Tim asked.

'It should be quite soon, I hope – within a week, I expect. Sekou is going to give you an update in the next couple of days. He says he has some internal squabbles to deal with.'

Nick was also anxious to get in and see what the situation was really like. As soon as the area around Lofa Bridge was secured, his diamond operation would become theoretically feasible.

'Okay, that's great, a week's great.' Tim looked relieved. 'I need a bit of R-and-R. My sinuses are fucked. I think it's the flight and the dust, but I'll be okay in a few days.'

That night – for the first time in a long time – I slept soundly.

With Tim on board, the filming seemed less daunting; and with Nick there as a volunteer and not my employee, I felt liberated from the anxiety that I was somehow aiding his business plans with the rebels. My only real concern was how the rebels would react to me, personally, now that *A Journey Without Maps* had been broadcast. It was not a flattering portrait of their movement. One former commander, who had moved to Washington to lobby the United States Government on behalf of the LURD, had sent a thinly veiled threat for the lies he claimed the film had propagated. At the time I'd dismissed it as the ranting of a madman – but I had no idea who, or what, was waiting for me over the border

Tim failed to materialise the next day. His sinusitis had knocked him out. In his absence, Nick and I sat and drank *grandes pression* beers until dusk at our favourite table on the terrace. It was a close day – the relief the breeze had brought the day before was gone, so we sat wrapped in a cloak of sweaty conspiracy, dissecting the war as the tide washed in beside us. Small, grey-headed sea gulls picked their way across the receding, rancid belt of mud that ringed the hotel. It was turning into another unremarkable, interminable day of waiting and plotting, like so many we'd passed together over the previous twelve months. And then Nick raised his glass and led our conversation down an altogether darker and more unpredictable path.

'So, you won't believe what I've been getting up to now, Mr Brabazon.'

'Oh, no, what is it?' His face looked suddenly mischievous. 'This doesn't involve jumping out of a cargo plane over the Congo, does it?'

'No, man. This is altogether a different mission. It looks like I'm getting involved in regime change now.'

Regime change? I thought. *That's weird. I can't really see Nick enjoying Iraq much.*

But it wasn't Iraq. Grinning from ear to ear, Nick explained that a 'business associate' had contacted him with the offer of a job the likes of which had not been seen for a generation.

'I've been asked to help overthrow a government.'

'Seriously?' I wasn't sure I'd heard the words correctly.

'Ja, it seems so.'

'Where?' *Here?* I thought. *In Conakry?*

'Just along the coast,' he said, nodding to the rising tide.

'Oh, Jesus,' I muttered.

He looked serious. The grin was fading. There was, he explained, a small country rich in oil, happily guarded by a tiny, hopeless army 'not far from here'. He'd been asked to assess the feasibility of overthrowing the Government in a mercenary-led seizure of power.

'Guinea-Bissau?' I interjected.

'No,' he replied, 'wrong direction.'

It was like playing a bizarre game of Twenty Questions. That left São Tomé and Equatorial Guinea as the most likely candidates. Nick was suddenly coy.

'I can't tell you now. A few things have to be put in place first.'

He took a swig of beer, looked at me from across our table. A ripple of nervousness washed through me.

'Sekou is going to help. He's promised weapons and agreed that we can pick some of their fighters for the main attack force.'

Sekou, in turn, was to be paid in cash and equipment – particularly the provision of a helicopter.

Despite guarding the secret of the target country, Nick began to delve into the specifics of his fledgling plan. The operation would be seaborne. A boatload of rebels, specially trained and led by Nick, would be joined by a small contingent of South African mercenaries who would then set out from either Guinea, or Liberia itself – if the rebels could hold on to Robertsport. The mercenaries would then disembark at sea into several smaller boats and storm the 'island' at night in a classic beach-head operation.

'They aren't going to know what's hit them. We'll just equip our guys with small arms and a few PKM machine guns. The South Africans will put down a barrage with 60mm mortars once we're close enough. Sekou is taking delivery of some in the next run. Then we lead them in. Ag, it's pretty simple. Very much like the ops we did in the army.'

I didn't know what to say. It sounded like a recipe for a bloodbath.

'What kind of resistance are you going to meet? Do they have helicopters, or artillery?'

'No, man, it's just like all these places,' he said, casting his eyes along the darkening shoreline, 'they don't have the military capability to mount a proper defence. The standard of their army is most likely *very* poor – which is lekker, otherwise it would be a moer of a fight.'

He explained that the current president, alleged to be a psychotic cannibal whose secret police were renowned for abhorrent human rights abuses, was not co-operating with the oil industry. Once toppled, his exiled political arch-rival would be installed in his place. The pay-off would be lucrative oil contracts for the plotters, and security contracts for Nick. Not only would he train the new president's army, he'd supply their weapons, too. From what little I could recall, São Tomé didn't fit the bill; but Bioko, the tiny island province of Equatorial Guinea that sat on top of Africa's third-largest oil reserves, did. I kept quiet.

'Vok, James, this place is rich. It could be incredible – it's so small, they could transform it. They have big plans. The guy I'm doing this with says he wants to turn it into the Switzerland of Africa.'

I sat and digested the information – or at least tried to. *Overthrow a country?* It was hard to think straight. *Is there,* I wondered, *a moral, or even a legal duty to tell anyone?* What Nick was suggesting would break laws in at least four countries. It might even be considered an international war crime. I lit a cigarette. Then another thought crept up on me. *You aren't going to be able to tell anyone – ever.* As soon as I opened my mouth to talk about it publicly, Nick would be arrested. I blew a plume of blue-grey smoke into the thick evening air. As well as the moral and legal dimension, there was a professional angle, too. Exposing the operation would be a major scoop: but there was nothing I could do, other than betray my friend, to capitalise on it.

I didn't see Nick's next suggestion coming at all.

'You can film it.'

'I can film it?'

'Ja.' I must have looked incredulous. 'This will be a real bloody film for you. You can ride in the boat, up front. It will be a real scoop. It'll be great for you – an exclusive.'

I still didn't follow. Why would Nick want anyone to film this coup? Nick explained: if the exiled president's new government was to gain international recognition, the operation would have to look like a heroic local uprising.

'And that's where you come in,' he smiled, and then laid out the plan.

As well as the LURD rebel fighters led by a small vanguard of notorious white mercenaries, Nick was going to recruit Portuguese- and Spanish-speaking black African troops. Some of these had been with Nick in the Recces, but most of the men he planned on enlisting had previously served in 32 'Buffalo' Battalion. Nicknamed 'The Terrible Ones' by their enemies, they had also provided the bulk of the fighting troops for Executive Outcomes.

My job, Nick informed me, would be to film the arrival of the new 'president' and make him look like the head of a rebellious local army – rather than the protégé of an apartheid-era Special Forces unit. There would be a set-piece handshake at the airport and a victory parade once the fighting had died down – and no white faces on camera. This footage – the only television pictures that would exist – would then be released to the world's media, buying the new regime crucial time and credibility while it took over the institutions of state, hopefully helping to avoid interference from neighbouring countries. In return, I would have exclusive access to film 'every aspect' of the coup from the inside for my own documentary – which I could release (only) once Nick and his pals had been paid by the new president and given diplomatic passports. More than just offering me an opportunity as a journalist, he wanted to co-opt me as a conspirator, making me the propagandist, the Leni Riefenstahl, of his coup d'état.

'It has to look like it's one hundred per cent a local thing. What do you think? I'm calling it my *African Adventure*,' he said flippantly.

I took another drag on my cigarette and we looked at each other across the table. He was asking me a huge favour – and offering me a huge opportunity. After the months we had spent together, he had learned as much about me and my profession as I had about him and his. He understood that a war reporter is as opportunistic as a mercenary. I needed a war; Nick needed a war. I protected us with the quest for truth my cameras represented; Nick protected us with an assault rifle.

He was offering me the chance to direct the movie of his own private war – an opportunity that, on the face of it, no sane journalist could agree to.

I held my tongue. Despite the heat and the sweat and the excitement of going to war, I knew that what I said in the next few seconds could have serious consequences – for my future and our friendship.

On the one hand, I couldn't possibly accept. It was illegal; blood would be shed; innocent people would be killed. To partake in the coup, even just with a camera, would mean I'd have blood on my hands, too.

To broadcast propaganda was unthinkable: it was both morally wrong and would destroy my hard-won credibility. 'Tell the truth' had become my mantra after the butchery in Liberia. To become a liar now threatened professional and personal ruin.

On the other hand, I had been given an open invitation to film what might be the defining event on the continent in a decade, a coup that could affect thousands of lives. If there was no credible voice to document it, the true story may never be told – even though doing so would inevitably mean exposing Nick.

Deep down, I wanted to find a way to accept. It was just too extraordinary to let go. There was only one possible compromise:

if telling the true story was *so* valuable that it might exonerate me from temporarily supporting the coup propagandist – I could agree.

A professional compromise, though, wasn't enough: I needed moral self-justification, too. And for this I borrowed one of Nick's arguments: if the president was a monster, and removing him might lighten the burden on his brutalised citizens, then on one level the coup could be justified. The great unknown was what would come after the president, and who, ultimately, would be calling the shots.

There was, however, one last crucial factor to consider: the operation was highly unlikely to go ahead at all. It would be an expensive undertaking, and I thought the chances of Nick actually financing the operation were almost nil. It was a comforting thought, a way of insulating myself from what I was about to say. I opened my mouth to speak.

I thought of my Irish grandfather. He liked a 'wild card'.

'Okay,' I agreed, 'I'm in.'

This, I thought, *is insane.*

'Ah, that's great. It should be quite an operation.'

More beer arrived. I drank deeply as Nick toasted the plan. My mind pictured the scene in perfect, fantastic detail: the hushed voices, the lapping of waves against the side of the boats as we approached the shore; the crunch and slide of the hull on sand as we glided onto the beach; the roar of tracer fire arcing up over us as we stormed forward. There was only one problem: this D-Day fantasy was taking place at night, and therefore almost impossible to film.

'Is there any way we could do this at dawn?' I wondered out loud – sounding like some mad Hollywood film director. Drunk at midnight in the bar of the Petit Bateau, anything was possible.

* * *

Attempts to end the Liberian war through negotiation were gaining pace, if not credibility. Two days after Nick had dropped his bombshell, Tim and I went to Conakry airport in the early morning to film the LURD rebel delegation embarking for peace talks in Accra, Ghana. The VIP waiting room in departures was filled with 'the politicians', as Sekou Conneh called them, whom I did not recognise. They weren't happy to see me: *A Journey Without Maps* had upset a lot of rebel sympathisers. But these were not fighting men, or at least if they ever had been, then they'd exchanged their weapons for sharp suits and crooked tongues long before.

They talked about reconciliation and dialogue, and of overcoming 'internal difficulty'. Nick had warned us en route that Conneh had just faced a serious challenge to his authority from these mealy-mouthed negotiators; but as long as he was the man who controlled the guns on the ground, there was little, if anything, they could do to unseat him. Conneh's original plan hatched all those months ago, to make sure he was publicly identified as the head of the rebel forces, on TV, by the world in general and his own fighters in particular, was paying off.

As I walked, filming, onto the runway while the men who would represent the LURD at the peace talks embarked onto a Ghanaian military plane, one man began barking at me to stop filming him.

'Who ga'e you de autority, heh?' he shouted. 'Who ga'e you de autority to film me? Who de 'ell you tink you are?' he remonstrated, covering his face with a notebook.

'It's okay,' I said, 'Sekou said it was okay. I'm here with Sekou.'

Obdurate, I kept filming.

'Who is Sekou?' he screamed back at me. 'Who is Sekou? Nobody!'

Sekou Conneh, it turned out, was a man who could unleash sheer bloody hell. That day, during President Charles Taylor's visit to Ghana, the Sierra Leone Special Court unsealed Taylor's indictment for war crimes, including charges of murder, rape, sexual slavery, conscripting child-soldiers and terrorising civilians during his support of RUF rebels during Sierra Leone's civil war. It behoved the Ghanaian Government to detain him. They didn't. Conneh had sat by his radio all day. If Taylor was arrested, the war would be over.

Tim and I filmed as the report came in on the BBC World Service. Taylor was on his way home. Conneh spun the news to his advantage: the LURD were no longer just a rebel group trying to oust a democratically elected head of state – they were freedom fighters battling against an indicted war criminal.

'Nah Taylah i' back home, de battle continue. We wi' overrun de city,' Conneh said, emphatically, and then, as if to convince himself, 'We ca' assure people da' we wi' overrun de city.'

His eyes shifted from side to side, as if looking for agreement from us. Tim and I continued filming.

'We ge' de military capability boh we bee' delay' becau' we bee' afrai' o' bloodshe' an' we wan' to protec' our civilian',' he said, disingenuously, 'boh we go' no uddah alternative nah boh to move into de city.'

'So when does it begin?' I asked. 'When does the assault on Monrovia begin and will you wait—'

Conneh cut me off. He stretched his hands out towards the camera.

'De battle goin' to begi' today. I' goin' to pass de ordeh nah.'

Tim and I breathed out long, quiet sighs of relief. The Ghanaian Government had not only saved Taylor's skin, it had saved ours, too. If Taylor had been arrested, we would, in all likelihood, have been on the next flight home. No Taylor meant no war: no war meant no film. This time no one was asking for a bribe: Conneh wanted us on the front line as soon as possible. Nick and I smiled at each other as we spread out a regional map to look at the possible routes into Liberia. For different reasons, we all needed this war.

At nine o'clock, under a bright full moon, I stepped into a canoe on the vast Mano River. The pilot, an elderly fisherman, dipped an exquisitely carved oar into the spiralling black eddies that lapped the shore. Tim and Nick crouched under the trees at the waterline, waiting.

'I'll see you on the other side,' I whispered.

'Ja, go well.'

The pirogue slipped into the strong current. The thick funk of the forest ebbed for a moment as we nosed out into open water. It was a beautiful night. From Conakry we'd flown to Freetown. After a clandestine drive eastwards with two rebel sympathisers, I was finally leaving Sierra Leone and gliding towards Liberia. I had no idea who was meeting us on the other side, or how well disposed they were likely to be towards the author of a film that had exposed their human rights violations. It was not, as Nick had pointed out somewhat unhelpfully, beyond the bounds of possibility that they might execute us. 'Accidents' did happen, after all. Worse still, our guides weren't crossing with us, and there was no way of guaranteeing that the rebels actually controlled the other bank. Given how quickly the front line could shift, it was entirely possible that we might be delivered up to Taylor's army.

The boatman and I made landfall a hundred yards downstream. Out of the darkness an outstretched black hand emerged to pull me clear of the canoe.

'Wehcom to Liber'a,' the hand said, 'we Lor' Forces. Everyting undah contro'.'

As my eyes grew accustomed to the gloom under the trees, I could see I was surrounded by a dozen or so young fighters,

Kalashnikovs in their hands, wide grins on their lips. I shook hands with all of them, smiling back for all I was worth. It was, unexpectedly, great to be back.

Fifteen minutes later, Nick and Tim joined me on the bank, and the heavens opened. Even under the canopy of the trees, it was like standing under a waterfall.

'Jesus Christ!' hissed Tim. 'This is nuts.'

'Yeah, it's all good, though. These guys are cool. We're going to walk for a few hours now to their base – it's in a village in there,' I said, trying to sound encouraging.

The three of us stared at the apparently impenetrable undergrowth. Tim was laughing in disbelief.

'Great! Well, at least it's not raining or anything. That would suck.'

'Yeah,' I agreed, shouldering the heavy camera bag, 'it could be worse. I mean, there could be a war on.'

And then, from the back, in that dry Afrikaner drawl:

'Vok! Ladies, please! In your own time' – and we trudged our way back into the war, lashed by a tropical storm of ominous ferocity.

The next afternoon, Tim, Nick and I stood on the balcony of our old house in Tubmanburg. Feeling an absurd sense of proprietary pride well up in me, I took Tim on a guided tour. Our old bedroom was now a lounge of sorts that led through to our new sleeping quarters – an old store room at the end of a corridor that twisted round into the back of the house. Apparently, every piece of furniture in the place had been looted by retreating Government troops, so the three of us would be sleeping on a mattress on the floor.

'And this', I announced, 'is the bathroom.'

'You weren't joking, were you?'

Tim looked trapped between amusement and desperation. The white porcelain toilet had been dealt a savage blow that had fractured it like a broken skull.

'Apparently, we can shit downstairs in the wives' quarters. They'll do our washing and cooking, too. Actually, that's a good point. Remind me to give them some cash later – no one else seems to. It really goes down well.'

We went back to the balcony. Nick was making a call on his satellite phone beneath the fruit tree outside. The town was haunted. Everywhere I looked from my old perch on the balustrade were reminders of the battles and murders that had engulfed Tubmanburg on that first trip.

'Nick's got a big job coming up after this,' I confided, trying to break the flow of memories. 'It may roll straight into this one. It's a mercenary op, a lot of bang-bang, I expect. How are you fixed for the next couple of months?'

Since Nick had co-opted me for his *African Adventure*, I'd been dying to tell Tim what was on the cards – partly because I wanted to share the burden of the secret, and partly because Nick's plans might affect what we were doing in Liberia. I didn't want to spring any unpleasant surprises on him, but I couldn't tell him the whole truth.

'Yeah, that sounds okay. What is it, more rebels?'

'Not exactly. I can't really go into it at the moment, or rather he can't. It's absolutely not kosher, but if it does go ahead we'll be in good hands. I trust him.'

Nick finished his call and walked up the side steps to the balcony. He looked me straight in the eye and cleared his throat.

'The ammunition has arrived in Robertsport. I'm going to go down there with the new chief of staff, Cobra, tomorrow and then go back to Conakry. I have a contact to meet, and then

I need to go back to South Africa. It's shit timing, man. I'm sorry.'

'Fuck. Really? Is there no way around it?'

Tim and I looked at each other.

'No, man. Sorry. I've got to go. I'll help supervise landing the next delivery and let you know what they've got.' He inclined his head towards the satellite phone. 'We can talk while I'm down there. It messes my plans up, too. It's kak, man.'

An immediate flush of anger quickly drained away. I was quietly confident that Tim and I would be able to look after each other. Besides, the blow of his leaving might just be compensated for by his intelligence updates on rebel armaments.

'Well,' I said, turning to Tim, 'this *is* going to be exciting. I'm afraid you're stuck with me.'

'Don't worry,' Tim replied, looking at Nick, 'I'll keep him out of trouble.'

As if on cue, Dragon Master appeared on the balcony, accompanied by half a dozen other gun-toting commanders.

'Jay, mah man!' he cried. 'Goo' t' see y'. How you bee' keepin'?'

I stepped forward and we embraced each other.

'I've been good, I've been good. It's great to see you, too, man. You look fine.'

Dragon Master was dressed, as ever, in smart camouflage fatigues, topped off with a bright red beret. It was true; it was great to see him. One of the cleverer, and certainly one of the more humane commanders, being with his troops was a real blessing now we'd lost Nick.

Wiping the sweat from his face, Dragon Master filled us in on the latest exchanges with Taylor's army. While we'd been crossing into Liberia through Sierra Leone, a group of LURD rebel fighters had attacked the outskirts of Monrovia. The battle had lasted for a day and a night.

'Some o' ou' men attack Klay Junction. Dey broke trew and Taylah' boy' jus' ran all de way back to Monrovia. Our forces follow dem all de way pas' Po River.'

'All the way into Monrovia? What happened?' I asked.

'Dey finish all de ammunishan, an' com' ba'.'

Nick looked at me quickly.

'They finished the ammunition?' I repeated. 'What, *all* of the ammunition?'

'Yeah, das righ'.'

It was an astonishing admission. A hundred teenagers had managed to fire more than 300,000 rounds of ammunition in less than forty-eight hours – for precisely nothing. Now the supply boat that Nick was hoping to hitch a return passage on was not just useful for the rebels, it was absolutely essential: without it they were defenceless. Dragon Master knew it, too.

'We go an' try delay Taylah, an' agree to ceasefire in Accra.'

Suddenly bashful, Dragon Master looked at me in the evening gloom.

'Ca' I use yor satelli' phone? De moneh fini' on ou' phone. I wan' talk to de Lady in Conokry.'

Sekou's wife, Aicha, was still running the military effort from Guinea.

'Here, use mine.'

Nick handed over his phone instead, and we sat and listened to the sporadic bursts of gunfire that rang out across town while Dragon Master tried to shore up the rebels' defensive positions.

'So it looks like we could be in for a longer wait than we planned?' Tim asked.

'Ja, and waiting is something that James and I learned a lot about in Liberia. Remember, they won't attack properly until they've got a *lot* of RPG bombs – so until that boat comes in, they're stuck here. If they're attacked, they will most likely be able to repel Taylor's men for a while, but you should try and get out the way we came in before they get surrounded here. It's a fokken long walk to Guinea.'

Suddenly, I was less confident of staying on without Nick. I knew only too well how easy it was to lay siege to the town, and how hard it would be to get out. The lack of ammunition posed a potentially serious problem for the film, too. If all the rebels could manage was to maintain their position in Tubmanburg, Discovery was going to be very disappointed. I'd sold them the battle for Monrovia, not a re-run of my first trip.

In the morning, Cobra, the new acting chief of staff whom I'd met in Bopolu in 2002, agreed to an interview. From underneath his olive-green forage cap, he announced on the balcony of our house that Taylor 'mus' com dahn'.

'You've agreed to a ceasefire,' I reminded him – although we both knew that was simply a tactical ploy. 'So how long do you think you'll stay on ceasefire here?'

'I have given dem seventy-two hours, as caution. Cause we wi' not wai' fo' long fo' our civilian population to soffah,' Cobra informed me, somewhat menacingly, as if daring me to disagree. 'Wi'out him steppin' dahn or any agreemen' fruitfu' to de Liber'an people, we wi' take ac'shan.'

He and Conneh were running the war on the ground. The rebel negotiators in Accra were their pawns at that moment: they were entirely powerless without the fighting men in Tubmanburg behind them.

'I have enough men to take over Monrovia,' he continued. 'Enough. An' I have de military capability to take over Monrovia.'

'And that seventy-two hours begins now?' I wanted to clarify.

'Nah, fro' today' date,' he confirmed.

When the interview was over, Nick joined us to say goodbye. He was carrying a small shoulder bag, and was dressed like a civilian. He promised to return as soon as he could, and left his big rucksack behind in our room.

'Is this about the other job?' I whispered apprehensively as we walked to the vehicles.

'Yes. I'll let you know how it goes.' Our bar-side conversation in Conakry was real. We looked at each other briefly and then continued to the car. I was full of questions – who was putting the money up for the job, and who was going to make the real money out of it? Those were the people, more than Nick, that I would be relying on to protect me if it all went wrong. But I let my questions drop.

'Take care, yeah? Good to meet you.' Tim shook his hand.

'Look out for yourself, mate. Keep your head down,' I added, shaking his hand, too.

'Ja,' he replied. 'Stay well.'

Cobra's driver gunned the engine of the pick-up truck, and Nick and the general climbed on board. In a cloud of black diesel smoke they were away, and quickly out of sight.

'Come on,' I said to Tim, 'I'll show you around town.'

We meandered around Tubmanburg – greeting fighters I knew and acquainting ourselves with the ones I didn't. All normal civilian life had stopped: the town was a garrison, nothing more. Several hundred rebels occupied what remained of the houses. Together we collected mangos and avocados from trees near the spot where previously I had filmed the butchering of the captured Government soldier. As we gathered fruit, I told Tim about the brutal murder.

'Do you think it will happen again, if they go into Monrovia? The executions, I mean,' Tim wondered, looking around the old killing ground.

'Yeah, I think so. Exactly the same.'

'And us, do you think we're safe with them?'

It was a question I'd been asking myself, too. Only one commander in the town had appeared unhappy with the film. I was sure none of them had actually seen it, though they would have known what was in it. There was only one real explanation why no one had tried to kill me yet.

'The reason that none of these guys is pissed off with me about the film is because none of them thinks that I filmed them doing anything wrong,' I explained to Tim. 'That's just what you do to prisoners. One of these days I'm going to be asked to testify against them, though. I can see that coming a mile off. I don't think they've thought about that.'

'Would you?'

'Yeah, probably, though I don't know what more I could say than is already in my film. It says it all, really, and Deku is dead, don't forget. He was responsible for a lot of what happened here.'

'And Nick, would you testify against him?'

The possibility was still fresh in my mind. I fudged an answer. I had no idea how much blood was already on Nick's hands from his career in Special Forces.

'If he murdered someone, then yes. Yes, I would. Fuck, it would be hard, but yes. I'm not really sure what murder is here, though – or even what an accessory to murder looks like. I mean, we're all on fucking thin ice, man.'

I glanced sideways at Tim as we walked, weighed down with fruit. Perhaps he was calculating what compromises he'd already made or would have to make as we went further into the war.

'Or I am, anyway,' I continued. 'The Americans, the Brits – everyone's in it up to their eyeballs. The UN could end this war in a day, but no one wants to. Does that make them, their commanders, accessories to murder, too? Nick's a good guy. He's a mercenary, but he's honest in his dishonesty, which is more than you can say for anyone else here.'

Once we had unloaded our stash back at the house, we prepared a light field bag for the impending journey. We had one small black rucksack – our emergency grab-bag – in which, packed between layers of waterproof plastic, we put fresh tapes and shot tapes, spare batteries, chargers, a torch, our satellite phone and a small medical trauma pack. I managed to squeeze in two bags of intravenous fluid in case either of us needed serious attention. We also had a waterproof canoe bag each, to keep the cameras dry in the torrential rains, and two water bottles with integral purifying filters in pouches on our belts. Everything else we carried in our pockets. We would have enough to keep us going for ten days, flat out.

That evening, as we sat on the balcony and imagined what might lie ahead of us, rebel troops paid us regular visits, hawking the wares that they'd looted from the outskirts of the city. Would we be interested in buying a satellite phone? A calculator? Or perhaps a broken video camera? We sent them away disappointed, with American cigarettes as consolation prizes. The last rebel of the day approached us – a shaven-headed youth with a cut-down AK tied to a piece of string slung over his shoulder – with a brand-new electrical appliance that he'd filched from someone's house a few days before.

'Wha' dis?' he wanted to know, excited that he may have bagged some valuable swag.

'These', Tim informed him, 'are curling tongs.'

The youth looked blank.

'For women's hair,' Tim added. And then, by way of compensation: 'Here, have a Marlboro. Better luck next time.'

The teenager slunk off, puffing on the glowing tobacco in the gathering gloom.

That night didn't go well. I lay half on a mattress, half on a concrete floor in the pitch black. Tim had crashed out, balled-up in a sleeping bag next to me. Fully clothed, sprawled under a mosquito net, I was still awake, identifying different gunshots echoing across town by distance and direction. Government troops had attacked the village of Bar that afternoon, around ten miles away. The rebels' position was not at all secure. In the room next door, someone was dying.

Low moans gave way to louder repetitive screams, which drowned out the Kalashnikovs tearing up the night outside. Tired by the journey in, the suffocating humidity and the uncertainty of Nick's departure, screams in the night didn't scare me so much as annoy me.

Disturbed to the point of irritation, I jumped to my feet, wiping the sweat out of my eyes, tasting its salt on my lips. My torch found a doorway along the corridor, a shuddering hole in the black wall, illuminated from inside by a flickering palm-oil lamp. Curled up on the floor was a teenage boy, incoherent with pain, bellowing something instinctual. He was thin, emaciated; his damp clothes gave off a sharp smell of urine that made the thick atmosphere nauseating. A rebel soldier was crouched over him, silent and still. I kneeled down.

'What happened?'

'He koll' Rocket,' the fighter said quietly. 'I don' tink he ca' mak i'.'

Rocket, he explained, had taken part in the first rebel attack on Monrovia two days earlier – the aborted shambles that ended in looting and retreat. Barely sixteen years old, he was a radio operator, so he didn't carry a rifle. During the attack, Rocket had been shot in the head by a Liberian Government soldier. Entering his cranium an inch above his left eye, the bullet, an 8g lump of copper-covered lead, travelled through his brain at over 2,000 feet per second, before punching out a hole the size of a matchbox at the back of his skull.

Squatting over him, inhaling the rank fumes emanating from his body, I tried not to vomit. I could see the head wound clearly. Someone had put a clumsy suture through the entry wound.

He was lying on the exit wound. I turned him over. A fistful of wadding was taped to the back of his head. The humanity of this child had almost completely evaporated with his screams. Tim crouched down next to me, trying not to gag. Half-asleep, I fumbled through the contents of my medical bag.

'What do you think?' Tim asked, looking at me through the unstable lamp light.

'I don't know,' I said. *I'm tempted to put him out of his misery*, I thought. In my hands was a small, glass phial of synthetic morphine, enough to relieve his pain for hours. In my bag there was enough to relieve his pain for ever.

Rocket was clawing at the ground, howling with pain as my thumb tensed against the neck of the tiny, delicate phial. The nearest medical facility that could treat him was hundreds of miles away – over a front line and a national border. It was hopeless.

He probably won't last till morning, I thought. *You wouldn't let a dog die like this.*

Although the moral ambiguities of conflict were beginning to blind me, as I felt Rocket's weak pulse I heard my own conscience, clearly, at last. *There are already too many executioners here. Stop. There is no difference between giving a child a morphine overdose and beheading a prisoner.* I imagined a bayonet in my hand instead of the morphine, and put the phial back into the bag. Instead, Tim and I helped Rocket to swallow a powerful cocktail of tablets. He stopped screaming almost immediately, and, eventually, slept. The animal departed, leaving a brain-damaged boy in its wake, limp on a damp sheet.

I lay awake for a long time afterwards. The further my professional life became entwined with Nick, the harder the choices I faced were becoming. I feared that my solutions were becoming morally unhygienic – compromises, not robust responses. I had seriously considered killing a child. I had agreed to film Nick's coup. I had thought I was unrecognisable to myself in the mirror when I first escaped from Liberia. In retrospect, that was just the beginning.

I considered my conversation with Tim, about murder. I had once told myself there could be no moral relativism in war – that it was the first step on the road to genocide. I was no longer sure that was true. Perhaps doing the right thing was doing whatever it took to survive. I thought of Deku shooting the prisoner: was it really *murder*, or was it just part of his attempt to survive the ongoing, indivisible obscenity of war?

I thought about the conversation with Nick in Conakry, too. I was worried that I'd crossed a line when I said yes to getting in an assault boat with Nick and the other mercenaries. But the truth was that the line had been crossed when I sent out that ambush in Tubmanburg; agreed with the Americans not to expose the Guinean Army; discussed shooting down helicopters. I was already an accessory to war.

As first light crept into the sky outside the window, I finally admitted the truth to myself. Saying yes to the coup wasn't just about telling an untold story and giving a voice to the people whose lives would be affected. There was another, more troubling dimension to my decision. My first-ever film had been shocking, and ultimately acclaimed. But if this current attack on Monrovia failed as a programme, I didn't know where to go next. Nick was offering me a sequel – a film that would be as new, as bold and as raw as anything I could imagine. And that was why I'd said yes.

13
TOO TOUGH TO DIE

On Monday, 23 June 2003, Cobra amassed the bulk of the LURD fighters in Tubmanburg onto the forecourt of the town's blasted gas station for a final briefing. The ceasefire was dead. Freshly equipped with weapons from Guinea, the rebels' offensive was about to begin. Around 400 men, women and children soaked from the rain and bedecked with RPGs, Kalashnikovs and bandoliers full of shiny brass bullets marched out at his command. Tim filmed from one side; me from the other.

'De Liber'an people a' no' yor enemy,' Cobra reminded them. 'Taylah i' yor only enemy.'

A bucket of water was brought out, and everyone gathered round. Verses from the Qur'an were recited in Arabic, and then the Lord's Prayer was chanted in English. I mouthed the words *Deliver us from Evil*, and framed tight close-ups of the kids who were off to battle. After the last *Amen*, everyone rushed forward and dipped their hand into the bucket, splashing themselves with the blessed water in a frenzy of excitement. It was a surreal sight. One man ran around in a green dress, sporting a huge, bushy wig; another streaked past, grunting wildly, wearing only tight red underpants. Sweat was pouring from his forehead; his hands brandished a loaded Kalashnikov.

'De operashan i' call' "Butterfly",' Cobra explained. 'De secon' stage, when we attack de Executive Man*shan*, wi' be call' "Web".'

Cobra had christened his own bodyguard force 'The Wild Geese'. The troops who were joining us from Robertsport were somewhat less romantically named 'The Taliban Brigade'.

'You know, sir,' I said, choosing my words carefully, 'if you're keen on US support, that might not be *the* best choice of name.'

He looked at me as if I was an idiot. Before he went back to his men, he explained the name just meant that they were fierce fighters. Anyone knew that.

'Taylah will ron,' he assured me. 'He wi' ron, or he wi' be arreste' . . .' And then he added, after a moment's reflection, '. . . or kill'.'

Tim and I went back to our room to pack – and wait. Dragon Master had gone ahead a day earlier with 200 men. The plan was to form a bridgehead on the Po River outside Monrovia; Cobra's forces would follow up, and push through into the city.

Forty-eight hours passed, and we had heard nothing. Cobra was nowhere to be seen. It was a typical rebel cock-up, I explained to Tim. I began to feel foolish for ever having believed the rebels would reach Monrovia. Dragon Master must have been pulverised by now. As I lit a cigarette and considered what to do, a junior commander jogged up the steps to greet us, his AK cradled against his chest.

'We leavin'. Everybody in town. Y' wan' com'?'

Tim was on his feet, peering over the edge of the balcony through the heat haze.

'What, now?'

'Yeah. Now, now, now, mah man! We goin' fo' Taylah!'

'What?' I asked. 'We're going to Monrovia? Right now? Where's Cobra?'

'He leavin'. Y' bedder ron.'

And with that he turned on his heels, and jogged back into town.

'Have you got everything?'

I was in shock, but I was wearing everything I needed. The pockets of my photographer's vest bulged with all the kit required to film on the run. I picked up the camera and stuck my head around the door into the lounge. Rocket was there, lying on a dirty mattress, moaning and intermittently listening to a radio blaring the news in French. Somehow he was clinging onto life. *Good luck*, I thought, and then I followed Tim into town at a run – just in time to catch Cobra striding down the main street, heading south.

We walked out of the once-prosperous iron-ore mining town of Tubmanburg thirty-five miles southeast to Monrovia. We walked through baking sunshine that made our skin blister, and then through rain so unrelenting that it was hard to stand upright. Acres of trees, grasses, full and broken canopy jungle and swamps – populated by islands of fire-blasted houses scarred by nearly thirteen years of war – fanned out to the horizon on either side of the miraculously intact, metalled road that dragged the rebels towards potential oblivion. We walked at the front, with Cobra, followed by around 300 men, children and women – the vanguard of the LURD's 3,000-strong guerrilla army that by now controlled over two-thirds of Liberia. We walked for ten hours straight.

Crippled by dehydration and the lack of salt in our diet (what little was available was used as currency, and not for cooking), our thighs cramped and burned with the effort of the march. We crunched chalky Valium tablets to relax our aching muscles, and spoke only when necessary. Quickly exhausted, we took it in turns to run ahead and shoot panoramic footage of the advance, or film short sound bites of the rebels on the move. For the last hours we marched in pitch blackness, relying on the tarmac conveyor belt of the road to guide us.

'Who der? No creep!'

'What the fuck is that?' Tim whispered, as I put out my hand to hold him still.

In front of us a disembodied voice in the darkness called out. Men moved around ahead of us, unseen in the bushes, accompanied by the ominous metal *click-clack*s of rifles being made ready.

'Shit!'

Other rebels immediately behind us stopped in their tracks, too. We all turned and ran, and dropped into a group crouch back on the road. It was hard to see more than a couple of feet in any direction. *Please don't start firing*, I thought. *We'll be cut to ribbons*. Then Cobra was there, and flicked on his torch. The failing beam was just powerful enough to illuminate the iron supports of a bridge and the glinting barrels of the rebels defending it. Hushed greetings were exchanged; Tim and I straightened up and exhaled loudly.

'I think we've made it,' he said, clicking on his own torch. There was more than a hint of incredulity in his voice. 'How are your knees?'

'Pretty fucked. I strapped them up really tight, but that last run bloody hurt.' I was so shattered, it was hard to sound coherent. 'They are actually going to attack Monrovia. Fuck, this is intense.'

We both stood, grinning stupidly while we considered our position. Then we crossed the bridge. On the far side there was a sentry box protected by a large .50-calibre machine gun. Tim, the officers and myself trooped inside.

'We sleep here tonigh',' Cobra said. 'Tomorro', Monrovia.'

There was no food, no ceremony – almost no talking – from the rebels. There was really nothing to be done except rest.

I woke up at first light. A drizzle of rain, blown in through an observation hatch, brought me to my senses. The atmosphere in the squat concrete building was palpable – a stinking miasma of stale sweat, rank breath, farts and putrid feet. Locked in cramp, my left leg had twisted itself over Tim and was jammed up against the sleeping figure of Cobra. Today would be one of the most testing days of the 43-year-old major-general's military career. I extracted myself carefully and hobbled outside.

We were on the east side of the Po River; 300 rebel fighters crouched, lay, slouched, stood and dozed among the trees and in the buildings around us. I took a long draw of water from the bottle on my belt and lit a cigarette. There was nothing to eat. One by one the other ten men, Tim among them, emerged from the bunker. It was a still, eerie morning: mist clung to the road like a thick, wet blanket, muting the tell-tale clatter of an army preparing to move.

'You know, man, if this gets really nuts, just tell me what to do, okay? No bullshit. Don't hold back.'

Tim was quiet, and serious. I could sense him going down into himself like I did before a battle began. I wanted Nick's AK trained on the bush around me: if it came to a rout, there was no telling what might happen to us. *Fuck you, man*, I thought. *Why couldn't you be here, now, when I need you?* Part of my anger came from jealousy, and I knew it. However extraordinary the situation I was in now, I knew I was missing out on Nick's secret meetings to plan the coup. I reassured Tim as best I could.

'Yeah, don't worry. It will be okay.'

We'd talked at length about the ambushes I'd filmed the year before, and how best to survive them, but there was no way to prepare for the chaotic violence of the fighting.

'Just stay back, and stay low. If all else fails, lie down. Watch me, but watch out for me, too. Once it kicks off, it's hard to see anything that's not right in front of you. Tell me what to do, too – and what to film. I may not have seen it. I mean, grab me. Physically grab me and show me if you need to.'

Tim nodded.

'Right, let's do it.'

He handed the grab-bag to our appointed bodyguard – an older, wiry fighter not best pleased with his babysitting detail – and started to film as the rebels began to march.

As the light grew stronger, so did the sounds of explosions towards the city centre. After an hour of hard walking, head-down in the rain, the bush had begun to retreat, giving way to a steadily increasing concentration of villas and houses, schools and churches. The city spilled out to greet us, monochrome in the flat morning light of the rainy season.

The first contact caught us during a heavy downpour, trapped in a cutting in the road. There was no cover of any description. On either side of us there were muddy six-foot banks, slippery as glass from the rain. I threw my camera, sealed up in its canoe bag, up and over my head. I heard it land with a crunch as I dug my fingers into the soft, red earth. Tim helped pull me up, and was quickly ahead of me on all fours, scuttling through someone's cassava crop towards a house where a group of rebels were making a stand. What the fighters on the road were doing – how they were reacting – I didn't know. We reached the house, covered in mud. Tim stood up.

'Mind the window.'

I thought of the lucky shot that killed Deku. Tim squatted down again. We weren't filming. I fished my camera out of the blue bag and switched on. It seemed okay.

'You mus' no' be scare',' our bag-carrier chided us. He'd caught up with us, standing by the open window. 'Move forwar'! You don' got to be scare'.'

'I'm not scared,' I replied. 'I just don't want to get shot.'

Tim was peeking round the corner, up the road. All around us rebels were flat on their bellies while AK rounds screeched uphill, over us.

'What's going on?'

'Dunno. Hard to tell.'

Minutes passed, and then the firing ceased. We emerged back onto the road. No one seemed to be hit.

'Okay?'

Tim agreed he was. We changed tapes, and kept marching.

Another hour passed and then, half-expectedly, the air filled with a sound like hailstones pinging off a zinc roof. A hundred yards ahead a Government ambush found us: the first volley tore into the trees to my right. Bits of bark rained on me. There was no time to film. At first down on my haunches, then up and running into a storm drain, I saw a school building twenty yards off the road that looked like it would provide good cover. Tim had the same idea. A whistle overhead heralded the arrival of something else. *Thump! Thump!*

'Fuck. Mortars?'

Tim was ashen. We were still half in the open.

'No, RPGs,' I replied.

We kept going towards the school as the contact exacted a severe toll. The rebel in front of me was shot straight through the torso. He crumpled, gurgling blood, like an obscene rag doll, lungs hissing as his breath escaped from a hole in his chest the size of a watch face. I looked down at him, and filmed. His eyes lost their focus. Other fighters hauled him up onto a truck. Tim was bent over him, shooting stills, while more bullets whipped up the air around us. Tim's bag-carrier was shot in the head, behind us. A lump of his skull lifted off; part of the left side of his brain was blown out. I had blood on me. Tim was running, filming.

Children carrying guns began crying. Bushmaster, a senior officer in charge of the heavy machine guns, was shouting at them.

'Wha' happen? Eh? Y' nevah see a man die? When de Go'ernmen' fire you, you reply. You reply!'

He was waving his Kalashnikov towards Taylor's troops. Droplets of sweat and rain dripped from his beard. The children stopped crying; the soldier's chest wound stopped hissing. Around us Government bullets mauled the earth, and the children started firing, too. Finally, Tim and I were crouching by the school, breathless.

'All right, man? This is fucking bonkers. It's almost impossible to film anything. Are we doing okay?'

I thought we were. Tim was frantically re-loading tape while I caught my breath. At the same time, Bushmaster climbed up on the back of the truck laden with bodies, swinging the rebels' .50-calibre machine gun, mounted Somali-style on the roll-bar, into action. Taking direct fire, he calmly racked a round into the breech, and let rip. The thick black barrel began singing its deafening bass reply to the Government's chattering rifles. In less than two minutes, miraculously unscathed, he ended the ambush.

By then we were out of the bush completely; the environment had morphed into a perfect urban film set. The perfume of the forest had vanished, giving way to the damp smell of plaster and abandoned houses. Visibly disconcerted, the rebels, many of whom had never set foot in a large town, eyed the buildings suspiciously. Everyone was tired, sweating, on the verge of wanting to surrender, but it was time to move on.

We were now in the outer suburbs of Monrovia. The rebels' plan had been to infiltrate the flanks of their main attack with smaller groups of LURD fighters coming in from other forward positions: they hadn't shown up, and Dragon Master had not left any soldiers behind in the wake of his earlier advance, so the Government army still owned all the territory off the main road. Dragon Master's party had been swallowed behind enemy lines. Taking back-routes and getting lost in the unfamiliar side streets would have been suicide for Cobra – who ploughed headlong into another ambush before the hour was out.

'Down, down, down,' I shouted at Tim, who, two paces ahead of me, was drawing a lot of fire from the front.

A belt-fed machine gun was strafing us. Several of the 300 men and boys who had shortly before been shaking sleep and rain from their bodies were opened up like prime cuts of meat by white-hot shrapnel from RPGs. Wired with adrenaline, I went to look for Cobra. We were being shot to bits. Our defence was unsustainable.

I caught up with him at the back of a house on the shifting front line. He was armed with only a length of electrical cable, and was literally whipping his younger soldiers onwards with it, forcing them out into the field of fire.

'What's going on here?' I asked.

Cobra seemed very calm. He talked so quietly that my camera microphone hardly registered his harsh whisper.

'We near Iron Gate nah. My men den deh, we wi' soon mee' dem.'

I don't know if Cobra was a good man or not. I don't know if he was a particularly clever man or not. But I do know that he was a good commander, or at least that he had the qualities of one. Strolling casually out into the arc of Government fire, he now walked calmly in front of the men whom he had just whipped. At that moment, I felt – knew – that as long as I was with him nothing would touch me, because I knew this man would survive.

'Ready?'

Tim nodded. We sprinted between two houses and then out into the open, aiming for a road bridge that led deeper into the city. It was a couple of hundred yards across open grass to the cover of the houses on the other side. At the halfway point, the shooting began. Cobra was grazed by an AK round. So it goes. Behind me Tim grunted and then fell heavily. *Shit,* I thought, *he's been hit*. I kept running. *Stop!* My mind barked at me, *Go back!* But the incoming rounds were close, and for once well aimed, and my legs automatically carried me – running, running, running – to the safety of the house. Turning round, consumed with guilt for having left him, I saw with relief that Tim was up again, and not far behind me.

'I slipped,' he said. 'I've lost the mic cover.'

Shame burned deep in my chest. I'd left him behind.

'I'm sorry,' I said. 'I was scared.'

I was. I was petrified. I didn't know how we'd survived.

'No, that's cool,' he replied, but I didn't think he'd understood.

'Let's go get it,' I suggested.

'What, the mic cover?'

'Yeah. We need it.'

Doubled over, I walked back out into the open, scouring the ground for the tiny foam windshield. Tim followed.

'All right, this is crazy. Do we *really* need it?'

We were being shot at again. Rebels behind the house were shouting and waving at us to get down. Impervious to their requests, we carried on looking. *I am not scared*, I told myself. My mind was a blank. The war had been put on pause. All the noise seemed to fade away while I searched the grass for the missing piece of kit. After a minute or so, two fighters joined us.

'Found it!' cried Tim.

And we all darted back to the safety of the house. Happy with our small triumph, I came to my senses. The war crowded in again, deafening and terrible.

From there we ran again, to a breezeblock wall this time, behind which several of the commanders' wives had taken refuge. Just beyond them lay the LURD's advance party. Tim photographed me squatting down as RPGs exploded behind us. We stayed hunched behind the wall while boy-soldiers cowered in the mud beside us. A salvo of rebel RPGs streaked overhead. After what seemed like an age, the *tick, tick, tick* of incoming rounds diminished and then died. LURD fighters peered above and around their cover, and then apprehensively stepped out into the open. Tim and I braced ourselves and rounded the wall to find the corpses of Government troops lying in the grass around us. Across the wide tar road the brown T-shirts of the rebels fanned out in victory. Dragon Master broke away from them and ran up to greet us. We had broken through. We were in the city.

Cobra handed me over to his deputy field commander, Iron Jacket, and we sped off towards the centre of town in a looted four-wheel-drive as scores of civilians lined the roads in a slow procession back from the front.

We made it as far as Freeport, where the rebels had been blocked. Fighting raged over New Bridge – control of which would allow or deny access to the presidential palace. Refugees picked their way through the debris, leaving the area as fast as they could manage. Iron Jacket – dressed in a resplendent yellow T-shirt – fired over their heads, shouting and laughing, forcing them to keep moving. We filmed briefly, and then followed Iron Jacket as he returned to the rebels' headquarters at a beer factory on the edge of the city.

The scene that greeted us at their HQ was one of devastation. Thousands of refugees had been crammed into the store rooms and loading areas of the beer factory. Terrified, they huddled against each other as the flat booms of the explosions in town echoed off the walls. There was no toilet, no food and no water.

One area had been set aside as an emergency field clinic. The rebels had paid a terrible price to enter the city. Tim and I inspected the rebel wounded from the day's fighting. The smell of stale beer mixed with a sharp smell of ammonia from soldiers who had wet themselves, and occasionally a suffocating whiff of blood. Several fighters had shrapnel wounds to their legs, where RPGs had detonated on the road in front of them; others had taken AK rounds in their arms or thighs; some had been shot through or disfigured by the explosions that dogged our progress into town. Tim's bag-carrier was still alive, but as wrecked as Rocket had been. Tim tried to force-feed him a watery rice soup so he wouldn't vomit the painkillers he'd been given. Beside him lay a dead young man, partly covered by a sheet, his body already twisted from rigor mortis. He wore a brown T-shirt. Printed on it were the words: *Too Tough To Die*.

I didn't sleep that night, but the Valium knocked me out enough so that I felt as if I had. When dawn broke, shooting began almost immediately. I called Colonel Frank at US Intelligence, who was still operating in the region. If the LURD were going to try and cross the bridge today, I wanted to know what they might be running into.

'Hey, James!' cried Frank across the wheezing connection. 'Great to hear from you. What's going on?'

Frank knew perfectly well what was going on. I gave him my position, and filled him in on the fighting so far.

'It's really good you called, James. Actually, I've been trying to reach you, but your phone's been down. I would really strongly urge you to leave if you can. Seriously.'

His normally jovial tone was suffused with a serious edge. I hadn't heard him talk like that before, and I didn't understand what he meant.

'What, leave Monrovia? Man, that's a big ask. I can't go anywhere without these guys, unless you want to come and get me. Anyway, the channel would go nuts. Why?'

There was no reply. The line dissolved into a mass of static. Whenever a connection became unstable, I did what Nick had taught me and used a sort of pseudo-military radio-speak – that

I only half managed to get half-right – to make sure nothing was misunderstood.

'Frank,' I shouted, 'are you receiving me? Over.'

I suddenly felt stupidly self-conscious. It was like being in a movie.

'Roger that, James. Yes, good copy. You need to leave Liberia. We've picked up an intercept. Taylor wants you and Tim dead. Our information is that he has dispatched two units to find you. He has ordered your execution. You need to leave immediately. Do you copy? Over.'

I felt the blood drain from my face.

'Yeah, roger that. Good copy.'

The previous evening Taylor had claimed to the international media that Freeport was back under Government control. I had been interviewed on my satellite phone shortly after, and immediately exposed that for the lie it was. What was more, the latest report by the UN's Panel of Experts on Liberia had been released the month before, and drew, in part, on the evidence I'd collected the previous year. Taylor had clearly had enough. I looked around me, and saw Tim filming a hundred yards away.

'I'll let you know what my movements are. It's impossible to say at the moment. Look, if we get cornered, can you send a chopper? Over.'

'Good copy, James. No, that is a negative at this time. Over.'

'Great. Thanks. Can you liaise with the Brits and get them to open the bridge at Bo Waterside? Over.'

The bridge was one of the only crossings over the stretch of the Mano River that formed the border between Liberia and Sierra Leone. We had crossed by canoe seventeen days earlier a few miles upstream. An added complication was that, according to a regional treaty, the centre of the river was sovereign Guinean territory, and the bridge was also manned by their soldiers. The bridge had been closed for most of the war. Opening it would be a major diplomatic headache.

'Good copy. That's an affirmative. I'll see what I can do, though I think you'll find we're more amenable to you than your own countrymen. Over.'

'Okay, good copy. Thank you. That doesn't surprise me.' I paused for a moment. 'Frank, one last thing. The rebels want to cross New Bridge. Is that a good idea? Over.'

'Good copy. Jesus! No. That is a negative. Repeat, a negative. It will be a massacre. Try and persuade them not to.'

'Roger, copy that. Over and out,' I said, just in case he was still there, and then hung up.

Nick was out of range, travelling, so I dialled Piet, Nick's contact in Monrovia. He was with Taylor's son, Chucky, in the Executive Mansion. I explained that we'd been advised to leave, but gave away nothing specific.

'Look, James,' he said, calmly, 'I'm not advising, I'm *insisting* that you leave within the next seventy-two hours, for your own security.'

That sealed it. I walked over to Tim and took him lightly by the arm.

'Sorry, mate.'

He stopped filming and looked at me quizzically.

'What's up?'

'I'm afraid we have a bit of a problem.'

I led him to one side. Eight hundred yards behind us, a fire-fight crackled away. Front-line commanders rushed in and out of the compound.

We sat on a low wall and I gave him the news from Frank and Piet. He took it in much the same way I had: it was shocking, serious – and posed a conundrum. How *were* we supposed to get out of Monrovia?

'This wouldn't be a problem if Nick was here,' he concluded.

The fighting behind the compound spooked the civilians in the beer factory. An exodus began that the rebels could not stop. Within minutes, 2,000 women and children vanished into the burning suburbs. The contact was only a few streets away now. I went and found Cobra.

'Look,' I said, 'I've just spoken to the Americans. Taylor's got a lot of firepower on that bridge. They're advising you don't cross it now.'

Cobra looked at me, carefully.

'Okay, tank you.'

He turned and summoned his commanders.

Almost imperceptibly, the mood began to change. More fighters returned from New Bridge, vehicles started lining up near the compound. Behind us, the exchanges of gunfire became heavier, with more incoming crackle and fewer outgoing bangs. It dawned on me what was happening. Cobra, walking past the vehicles, smiled distractedly.

'Are we leaving?' I asked.

He looked at me with bemusement.

'Yes, we wi' go. De ammunishan finishe'. Don't worry, I' de solution fahdah.'

A LURD mortar team was setting up to cover the hasty rebel retreat with an indiscriminate bombardment of the houses around us. I held the viewfinder as steady as I could as the third salvo was fired. The charge detonated and the short, hand-held tube collapsed from the recoil, sending the bomb zipping over my left shoulder, an inch away from my ear. I had been able to see right down the tube when it went off. I put the camera down and we were bundled into a car that would not start. We cast around unsuccessfully to find anything moving that had space for us. The fighter in the green dress and wig ran past, grabbing Tim's arm.

He shrieked something into Tim's face, before running off towards the shooting. Tim ran over to me.

'What did he want?'

'He said "I'm going to fuck you up the ass."'

Tim looked, for the first time, genuinely frightened.

'That's great,' I said. 'Let's get out of here.'

But neither of us knew how. Thirty vehicles lined up. Trucks, Jeeps, town cars, even an articulated lorry, were trying to depart simultaneously. Every shape and size of vehicle vied for position, creating a deadly traffic jam. Tim and I were at the very back. Bushmaster, the commander who had cleared the ambush the day before, signalled for us to get in with him as the Government recovered from their mortaring and started putting fire down over our positions. We clambered into his looted red Range Rover. Bushmaster hung on the side, while the driver, Joe T, smoking a reefer, weaved through the crawling rebel trucks laden down with fighters.

The convoy ground to a halt at Iron Gate under its own weight. We were caught out in the open. From behind us a long screeching sound, like a sharp sonic corkscrew twisting its way through metal and glass, pierced my ears. I looked in the wing-mirror.

'What the fuck was that?' Tim shouted from the rear passenger seat.

'Believe me, you don't want to know,' I replied.

The truck behind us had taken a direct hit from an RPG. Under the rattle of machine-gun fire, I could hear Tim swearing.

'Fuck. I can see them. They look so calm. It's incredible.'

Tim could see Government soldiers eighty yards away, firing at us. He was still clicking away with his Rolleiflex – an old-fashioned stills camera that needed a fiddly new roll of paper-backed film loaded into it every twelve frames.

'Here,' he said, handing me another shot roll.

I licked and glued the paper leader closed, and put the shot roll between my teeth like a yellow cigar as I changed videotape myself. We lost some window glass as the Range Rover was strafed by rifle fire. With the near-side doors wedged shut with sacks of looted rice, there was no option other than to exit the vehicle by opening the off-side doors onto the oncoming rounds. There, off the road and up a slight incline, sat a line of Government soldiers plugging away at us. We danced around the vehicle, and then flattened ourselves behind a wall.

'Shit, the tapes,' Tim said, getting up again.

We'd forgotten the grab-bag.

'No, man,' I cried after him, but it was too late.

Sprinting round the car, he opened the door again and reached in for the precious black rucksack. Bullets snapped overhead as he vaulted the wall, bag flying in front of him.

'Please don't do that again,' I begged, 'that was ridiculous.'

By this point, even experienced rebels were at the point of despair. The retreat had become a turkey shoot. They were taking casualties right down the line, not just up front. Engulfed by clouds of acrid blue cordite smoke, almost every rebel was now firing a Kalashnikov assault rifle on fully automatic into the bush by the side of the road. Over the deafening roar of their last remaining rounds of ammunition, Tim and I ran for cover behind a row of houses. I braced for impact. None came. We made it to the houses. A young man, a refugee, ran up to me and clung on, desperate.

'Save me,' he begged, 'save me. I nah wan' die. I nah sol'iah man.'

He was crying; his arms were closing around my waist. He was hysterical. I could smell the sweat and fear on him.

All I could think was *Execution Squad*. Any one of these civilians could be contracted to kill us. A surge of anxiety gripped me. I slapped him hard across the face with the palm of my hand.

'Pull yourself together,' I shouted. 'Get a fucking grip.' A rebel saw what was happening. 'Get this guy off me, will you?'

The armed teenager pulled him clear and stuck the barrel of his Kalashnikov into the crying man's guts.

'You wan' me shoo' 'im?'

In my panic, for a split second, I wanted him to pull the trigger.

'No, no, no,' I said, coming rapidly to my senses, 'just get him out of here.'

I looked at my potential assassin and saw a frightened, shell-shocked man. I put my hand on his shoulder.

'It's okay. You're going to be okay.'

Finally, we rejoined the vehicles as Bushmaster sprinted to his .50-calibre machine gun and went to work. The convoy punched its way out of the ambush, and over the bridge. We sped clear of the city as the rains came with a vengeance. A looted World Food Program truck, loaded with civilian refugees, overturned on the slippery highway, crushing to death dozens of women and children hitching a ride in the back. The city that had seemed to teeter on the edge of defeat, before half-swallowing us, had spat us back into the bush.

Within another hour we were back in Tubmanburg, exhausted, confused, embarrassed that our own relief to be alive contradicted so sharply the rebels' sense of defeat. Dragon Master walked past us, and we gave each other mock, unsmiling salutes.

My nerves were drawn tight by those last hours of filming. Tim was pale. He sat in the rain by the side of the road, silently smoking a cigarette. I knew then that we had to leave, death warrant notwithstanding. I couldn't go back in; even if I'd wanted to, I couldn't send Tim back in. I'd kept the war as my own private affair for so long. Perhaps it was finally time to give it up.

Back at the house we found Rocket. Miraculously he was feeding himself, spooning rice into his mouth, dribbling a bit. His eyes were focused, and the screaming, we were told, lasted only for an hour or so a day.

'How's it going, Rocket?' I asked.

He looked at me and smiled. I wanted to cry: for him, for me, for the dozens and dozens of people whose lives we'd just seen ended – but no tears would come.

Forty-eight hours later Tim and I left Liberia, and the war. I called Jonathan Stack in Monrovia. He had access to Taylor, and was filming his part of the documentary as per plan. I told him that Tim and I had enough on tape to make the film work; everyone agreed it was time to go. I called Kathi, too. We hadn't really spoken since I arrived in Liberia; she was beside herself with worry.

'Come home, sweetie,' she said, 'and tell me all about it.'

But home was, in truth, not where I wanted to go. I was high on the rush of our escape, and preoccupied with the thought of joining Nick's coup – and investigating the plot behind it. Even the thought of the stuffy flat in London made me feel claustrophobic.

'I was about to call the Americans, I've been so worried,' she continued. 'I think they *would* have sent a helicopter for you, you know, if it had come to it.'

There was no need. Negotiating with the British embassy, Frank had fulfilled his promise – and the Mano River Bridge was opened specially for us. We bade our farewells; Cobra remained defiant.

'Lor' Forces wi' bring Taylah dahn,' he assured me. '*I* wi' brin' Taylah dahn.'

I had lost count of the number of times I had heard the rebels promise to bring Taylor down. LURD's prospects were better than they had ever been, but with the American Government now directly engaged in efforts to secure a ceasefire, it looked increasingly likely that Cobra and Conneh would be allowed to seize an outright military victory. What was more, ammunition re-supplies from Guinea were still erratic – especially RPGs and large-calibre bullets. While the rebels looked firmly entrenched in Tubmanburg, it wasn't clear that they would ever be able to break through Taylor's defences.

As we were unloaded into the hands of the suspicious Sierra Leone authorities, one rebel commander waved a long goodbye from behind the barbed wire on the bridge, wishing us a safe return.

'Nex' time Monrovia!' he cried.

His black T-shirt blared in clean, white letters: *This is Not the Life I Ordered.*

14
ARMS AND THE MANN

I found Nick in the tiny bar of the Comfort Hotel, hunkered down five kilometres from Paris Charles de Gaulle Airport's busy runways. He was back in his chinos and-checked-shirt look – notepad and pen poking out of his breast pocket. I'd last seen Nick only four weeks earlier, as he climbed into a battered four-by-four with General Cobra in Tubmanburg. It felt like a lot longer. My anger at being abandoned by him had been assuaged by the simple relief of survival. It was good to see him.

'Mr Brabazon, I presume?'

Nick stood up, and we shook hands.

'Nick, you really do take me to some wonderful places.'

The best that could be said of the hotel bar was that it was functional. Its wipe-clean atmosphere was designed to be passed through, not relished. Nick rolled his eyes and ordered me a beer.

Nick had called me less than forty-eight hours after I'd got back from Liberia. He was travelling to Paris and wanted me to meet him there, immediately.

'There's a friend of mine I'd like you to talk to,' he'd informed me. 'It should be very interesting. Can you make it?'

I was exhausted. The day before, Mick at the Foreign Office had called to arrange lunch. Then I'd cut and voiced a special report on the battle for Monrovia on the BBC *Six O'Clock News*. Liberia was no longer a hard sell: it was lead news. Tim's agent had also managed to wrangle us a major front-page article in the *Guardian* magazine, which they wanted immediately. By the time Nick called, I was already looking forward to escaping London.

Irrespective of the meeting he had planned, I was glad I'd flown out to meet him. It was unlikely I'd be making another trip to Liberia, and it was good to chew over the fat of the last month with him. I filled him in on the two-day fire-fight in the capital.

'Jonathan's still there,' I told him, 'you know, filming on the other side. Taylor doesn't know we're working together. His updates make for grim listening: the city's under siege – it seems Taylor controls almost no territory outside the capital except for isolated pockets here and there, like Ganta, up in the northeast. Despite all the press coverage, the Brits are still after me. I had lunch with that guy from MI6, or wherever, yesterday. They're mad keen to work out what Sekou's plans are.'

Mick had also quoted to me the name of the ship that the rebels were using to ferry ammunition to the front line. I'd pleaded ignorance. Nick took the information in and smiled.

'Ja, it's a big fuck-up in Monrovia. Everyone is being watched. I've just got back from there myself.'

I smiled, too, and nodded, and then realised what he'd said.

'What, Monrovia? Are you insane? What on earth were you doing there?'

Nick and I both risked arrest and execution if we were caught there – a privilege I'd extended to Tim as well. In fact, Tim and I had enjoyed a narrower escape than we'd appreciated at the time. Back in Freetown, Colonel Frank met us and went into more detail about the contract on our lives. Taylor had offered $10,000 each for us. The call ordering our assassination had been picked up by British Intelligence at GCHQ in Gloucestershire and relayed to the people most likely to get us the message. Frank had been wrong in one respect – the British had done as much as they could to help, after all. Mick had possibly been more helpful than he was admitting, having claimed himself over lunch not to be aware of the origin of the tip-off. Looking for me during the LURD rebel retreat, Government soldiers had found a badly wounded Lebanese man hiding in the ruins of his shop and hauled him back to their HQ believing they'd bagged me, instead. He didn't survive.

'Ja, well, it was quite uncomfortable to say the least. Piet brought me in and I hid in a hotel for two days.' He took another sip of beer. 'And then he introduced me to Taylor's son, Chucky.'

Chucky, a renowned sociopath, was the commander-in-chief of the Government army's infamous Anti-Terrorist Unit, whose initiation rituals, the rebels assured me, boasted – among other delights – the drinking of human blood.

'Bloody hell! Did he know who you were?'

'Ja. He knew, and I told him about you – that I'd brought you in – and that I'm working with Sekou. Taylor wants me to spy for them. Sekou already knows. He's going to give me some info to pass over, to make it look real. It looks like I'm becoming a double agent,' Nick explained, coolly. 'Sekou's been flown to Nigeria, by the way, on Obasanjo's private plane, to discuss peace terms. After that he's asked me to go with him to the next round of talks in Italy and then Ghana.'

'Right. I see. They're really relying on you. Did Chucky have anything to say about me?'

'I wouldn't recommend a trip there yourself. I don't think they found our film very amusing. It was not a good feeling. I was quite paranoid, even. You never know what these guys are going to do, or when.'

I was as perplexed as I was amazed.

'But why were you there? Man, they could've had your nuts clean off.'

'Taylor wants to buy a helicopter gunship. Piet brought me in to discuss a deal with one of Taylor's women called Fina – I'm not sure if it's his wife or what – but we can use her for our own purposes. The Russian Government has ten HIND helicopter gunships – six of which are fully operational – sitting in a factory in the Ukraine. They've been re-fitted like new, but the end-user purchase fell through, so they're stuck in the factory.'

I wasn't sure where this was going.

'If Taylor gets a gunship up and running, the LURD is fucked,' I thought out loud.

'Ja, they'd take a moering for sure. But now I know he wants one, I can stop him from getting one. We can slow down the whole deal. It's a great opportunity.'

Nick was smiling now.

'These are full-spec, combat-ready Mi-24s. They're being sold off *very* cheaply by an arms dealer I know who is friends with the Bulgarian president. They're around four hundred thousand dollars each, with all the paperwork included. The idea is to get two of them for ourselves, to support the other job we discussed, and base them at that big airfield in Conakry. Sekou's cleared it with the president.' Nick drank a mouthful of beer, and added as an afterthought, 'I'm also looking for an Mi-8 or Mi-17 for the rebels so they can clean up the Government lines and re-supply their troops easily. We've made arrangements to move aviation fuel to Voinjama. We would re-fuel there, and then fly straight to Monrovia or wherever.'

My crash course in arms dealing was going up a gear. I glanced around the room. Except for a middle-aged couple chattering in French at each other over tiny cups of coffee a few tables away, we were alone.

'So, basically, Taylor's never going to see any hardware – and the troop-carrying chopper for the rebels would be a kind of part payment for using their support in the other operation?' Nick nodded. 'And then you would use the HINDs on the other attack. Isn't range a problem?'

I never mentioned the name of the 'other place'. I wanted neither the embarrassment of putting him on the spot by asking directly, nor the possible legal responsibility of formally being told where the operation would take place.

'The gunships – one or two of them – would be put on the ship from Conakry. The other possibility is that we put one inside an Ilyushin cargo plane and fly it in.'

We both thought about that for a moment.

'We used the HIND very effectively in EO in Sierra Leone. It would be lekker to have them, but it's not completely necessary. It's just extra insurance.'

He confided that he now had a serious financial backer for the purchase. Nick seemed both delighted and slightly bemused by the implications of what he was proposing.

'Vok, I can hardly believe all this is going along so well. Every week brings a new mission now,' he laughed.

'So this operation is definitely going ahead – the *African Adventure*?'

'One hundred per cent.'

The order had been placed, and the helicopters would be available in six weeks. Regime change was what the meeting with his friend tonight was all about. The Americans and Nigerians were onside, he thought.

'I'm not sure of the exact details. They'll use "oil unrest" as an excuse for intervention in the place we're going.'

Nick was letting me know only as much as he wanted, while reinforcing the idea that the operation was not only viable, but bankrolled. I was trying to work out if all his planned operations were linked – and if so, how.

'And the Congo job, is that still on?'

Nick's original plan of arming rebels in the Congo had seemed a lot more plausible after Kathi had confirmed that the capital, Kinshasa, was a hub of illegal weapons transfers – often facilitated by Russian dealers, sometimes en route to Liberia.

'Ja. I'm calling that my "American Coup" now.'

'Oh lord, really? Do I want to know this?'

'Ja,' Nick laughed again, 'you do. We've had some interesting conversations with them about it. It seems the North Koreans are busy trying to smuggle uranium out of a mine near Lubumbashi in Katanga. The people I'm dealing with want to run the place as an independent country, and the Americans are very interested in the North Koreans.'

'And they'll support the Katangese if the Koreans get the boot?' I cut across him.

Southern DRC was a war zone – with different neighbouring countries, particularly Zimbabwe, plundering its resources for all they were worth.

'I hope so,' Nick chuckled.

My head was starting to spin with the geo-political ramifications of Nick's plans. Even if the operations went wrong, the consequences could be huge. We finished the drinks and went back to our rooms to rest before our evening meeting. Everything Nick was suggesting was unquestionably illegal, supported by the Americans or not. As I put my card-key to the lock I imagined a masked assassin inside, waiting for me with a silenced pistol. There was already one definite contract on my life, albeit one unlikely to extend outside of Monrovia. If word of my connection to Nick's plans spread, who else would want to have a go? I was already known to the Americans – who could easily get Frank to tell me to piss off, or shut up. But the Congolese? The Equatoguineans? The Nigerians? My only solace, as I turned the handle and entered the tiny – and, mercifully, empty – room, was that the governments of the countries in question couldn't run a bath, never mind an intelligence service.

At around eight o'clock that evening, Nick and I wandered over to the only restaurant in the village to find his friend already waiting for us at the table.

'Hello, I'm Simon Mann.' The bespectacled, slightly built man in his late forties shook my hand and smiled in welcome. 'How d' you do?'

'Pleased to meet you.'

'Yes, you too. Nick's told me a lot about you.'

His accent was clean and crisp, infused with the camp lilt of the British upper class.

'Yeah, we've had some interesting adventures over the last year. Pretty intense, actually.'

I pulled up a chair, and made to sit.

'Excuse me,' Simon said quickly, 'I'll be back in a minute.'

He turned his back on the table and threaded his way to the lavatory.

'Nick,' I hissed, 'is that the guy from EO?'

Nick nodded. One of the brains behind the Executive Outcomes mercenary army, Simon Mann was a legendary professional soldier – and political deal-maker. Ex-G Squadron SAS, he'd also co-founded Sandline International, a private military company that had famously been implicated with the British Foreign Office in supplying weapons to Sierra Leone. He was, by reputation, very experienced in African warfare. I was astonished. I'd had no real idea whom I'd be meeting, or why – another soldier, perhaps, or a contact like Piet in Monrovia. Simon was in another league. Nick, it seemed, was serious.

'How much does he know that I know?' I asked as Nick sat down and folded his napkin across his knees.

'Absolutely nothing,' he beamed at me.

'Okay, wow. This is going to be a fun evening. What do I do?'

'Be careful.' Still grinning at me, his eyes flicked over my shoulder, warning me of Simon's impending return. 'Let's get a bottle.'

Simon wanted to drink rosé – a lot of rosé. The evening was hot, the wine was cold, and we put away the first bottle before the menus were even opened. We occupied three-quarters of a snug, round table. Nick was seated to my left, Simon to my right: I was stuck in the middle.

Simon suggested that we order before the kitchen closed. He wore an expensive watch; his pale, cotton shirt was carefully pressed; in fact, his whole demeanour said *I am very rich, and effortlessly so*.

We all touched glasses, and then Simon got down to business and asked me what Liberia was like.

I began to talk. And talk. I recounted tales of Nick and me in Liberia together, how we got in, what we'd accomplished. I talked about the films I'd made and planned to make. It was clear to me that I was being vetted for a job – presumably the role that Nick had outlined to me in Conakry – and I presented myself to him with as much care as the third bottle of wine would allow. I stressed the delicate nature of the work we'd done, the relationship with US Intelligence and my own encounters with British Intelligence; most of all, though, I was careful to let him know not only what I had reported, but also what I had not.

'It was quite tricky with the Guinean connection,' I told him. 'My access to the rebels was agreed specifically on the basis that I would not broadcast any details of the assistance they were getting from President Conté and the Guinean Army – it had to look as if it was *entirely a local, Liberian uprising*.'

I stressed these last words. It wasn't quite true, but I wanted to hammer home the point: I'm a safe pair of hands, and I've done this before. Nick gave me a sidelong glance. He was being very quiet.

'Of course, I filmed everything, because there'll come a time when all that can be said openly. It's a question of not biting the hand that feeds you, while still being honest. You're nothing without credibility in my industry. When you've been seen to tell uncomfortable truths once, the audience – and the commissioners – will believe anything you tell them thereafter. It's just that some stories take a long time to be told in full.'

The subtext was, I hoped, abundantly clear.

Simon poured the last of the bottle and raised his glass, looking at me and Nick.

'Here's to your successes in Liberia,' he proposed. 'Long may they continue.'

We drank the toast and beckoned the waiter over. The plates were cleared and desserts piled up, followed by glasses of whisky and Armagnac. Simon rejoined my monologue with one of his own. His dialogue was focused on Iraq, the need for oil security and regime change – and the use of private military companies to guarantee it.

He seemed to think that the era of all-powerful national armies dominating international diplomacy was over – and had been for a while. He cited the achievements of private armies – his private army – in Angola and Sierra Leone by way of example. 'Resource security' was the main game. Oil-fields – African or Middle Eastern – were hugely important for the West. But while the Chinese made rapid gains with their quiet diplomacy, the Americans were still working out what to do next on the continent.

He talked about good governance in Africa (apparently a rarity outside of a few isolated oases of best practice, such as

Botswana), and how the rise of Nigerian influence in the north of the continent allegedly matched the resurgence of South African power in the south. Well educated and well informed, it was undeniably fascinating to listen to him hold court. Indeed, almost everything he said was perfect primer material for announcing the coup – and despite the growing fog conjured by glasses of spirits on top of the wine, I clung on nervously for the dénouement.

At the beginning of the evening I had felt compelled to be on my best behaviour, in the same way I might if having dinner with a friend's well-to-do father: scared of saying the wrong thing, or making myself look naïve. By the time we left, though, we were all tipsy, and almost the last guests to leave. As we made for the door, one of the remaining diners got up and took hold of my arm.

'Monsieur, I know what you are up to, I know who you are,' he said in quiet French, tapping the side of his nose. 'Yes, I know what your game is.'

'Oh, good,' I replied in French, 'I'm glad someone knows what's going on.'

As we stumbled into the night air, Simon turned to me.

'What did he want?'

I recounted what the man had said.

'He's probably French Intelligence,' I suggested.

Laughing, Simon shook my hand goodnight, and then we peeled off to our respective hotels. The drop punch hadn't come, and I began to fret that I'd said something to rule me out of the operation.

Back at the Comfort, I fumbled for my key.

'Nick?'

'Ja?'

'How do you think that went?'

'Perfect, Mr B. Spot on.'

It was too late, and I was too tired to pick his brain any further.

The shower in the moulded plastic bathroom was freezing but invigorating. I had been mulling over the previous night's conversation. The weirdest thing of all was that I'd been there at all. Everything I had done in Liberia had been defined by impeccable planning, by my almost obsessive desire to maintain absolute control over the project. Now I was up to my eyes in a scheme that was too opaque to understand, never mind control.

As I got dressed and prepared to head back to London, I considered the meeting with Simon. Despite his clubbable good humour and impeccable manners, what Simon had manifestly failed to do was offer me a job, or mention the coup – any coup – at all. I'd surprised myself at how disappointed I'd been when he hadn't offered me the film rights to his operation outright, despite Nick's assurance that the dinner had gone well.

The more I considered Nick's original proposal, the more I worried about my own personal role in the operation. Sweeping aside the moral complexities of what I would be asked to do looked increasingly difficult. When it came to it, I knew I would not be able to refuse Nick's demands to broadcast propaganda in the way that I had refused the rebels in Liberia. I clung to my original, mercenary, justification: that the ends excused the means. My sustaining comfort was hope – hope, for all our sakes, that Nick and Simon knew what they were doing.

As I headed down the stairs to the lobby – and the waiting shuttle bus – I tried to console myself with another thought, too: much of what Nick had told me could just have been wishful thinking on his behalf. *Perhaps there is no coup? Even if there is, who knows if he's even told Simon that he's asked you to film it?*

It wasn't unreasonable to expect that I might never see the minted Mr Mann again.

Downstairs, the bus was waiting. So was Simon. We put our bags into the luggage racks, and sat together, nursing our growing hangovers.

Simon blamed the whisky. Nick joined us on board, and then, after the short drive to the airport, we waved him off at eleven o'clock, bound for Conakry. I wished him a safe trip.

'Ja, you too. I'll be in touch.'

We shook hands. He and Simon said goodbye, and then Nick's back disappeared through the door leading to the terminal shuttle link. I turned to face Simon.

'Well, it's been good to meet you, thanks again for dinner.'

Simon said it was a pleasure. We shook hands and he vanished into the terminal. *Damn*, I thought. *I need time alone with this guy.* I walked through the door, and went to check in. Simon was in the same queue: we were on the same flight. Once through immigration, he invited me to have breakfast with him in the British Airways VIP lounge. The smiling hostess waved me through at his request, and we sat and chatted over black coffee and biscuits.

He thought that 'good men like Nick' were hard to find. Crucially, he thought they were 'very loyal'. Simon said he trusted him.

'Me, too,' I agreed. 'You know, I've trusted Nick with my life. He saved me in Liberia, that's for sure. Actually, I think he's the only person I would trust in that situation.'

Simon nodded. I went on.

'It's funny, though. Despite everything he's been through, there's something about him that's quite naïve. Or maybe it's just optimism. Once he's decided that he trusts you, he's very open, almost to a fault. I think he wants to put the people he's responsible for at ease, so they believe everything's going to work out okay.'

Simon agreed that might well be true. He and Nick, he told me, were developing some interesting plans – business plans – in Africa. I looked at Simon, wondering if *this* was the moment to ask what businesses it was *exactly* that he and Nick were in. I opened my mouth to speak.

'Is there a number I can reach you on?' he interrupted.

I gave him my card, and punched his number into my mobile.

The moment passed. After we'd swapped numbers, Simon and I exchanged anecdotes about Nick and our own military experiences. We kept chatting until we reached the taxi rank at London Heathrow. We shook hands again as his cab pulled up.

'Stay in touch,' he urged, with his characteristic half-smile. 'I might have some work for you shortly.'

I waved him off, and headed home to Kathi.

'Everything okay, sweetie?'

Kathi and I were standing in the living room of the flat in London where we were staying. I looked at her and sat down at the dining table.

'Yeah, everything's fine.'

I could tell she could see it wasn't.

'Listen, there's something I need to talk to you about and, well, you know, this has got to stay between us.'

She nodded, looking at me carefully. I had missed her while I'd been away. Apart from my mother and grandfather, there was almost nothing continuous – or dependable – about my life in Britain, and I was going to rely on her more and more. Kathi made a living from researching and writing about all the things that had become the bread and butter of my career: arms dealers, weapons transfers, rebel groups, spooks and mercenaries were her stock-in-trade. She was both the best and worst person to confide in. What I wanted was a confidant with whom I could share the burden of the experiences I was collecting. She was the only person I could talk to openly and intimately who would have understood.

'When I was in Guinea, before we went to Liberia, Nick told me about this new job he's working on. It's not *his* gig as such, but he's been asked – I swear I'm not making this up, by the way – he's been asked to help overthrow a government. You know, a full-blown mercenary operation.'

Kathi seemed to take the information in her stride.

'Where, West Africa?'

She wrinkled her nose, as if sniffing out candidate countries ripe for regime change.

'Yeah, but I don't know where exactly,' I said, almost honestly. 'I don't know if he's got the cash to do it . . . I mean, basically, he's planning a coup d'état, which can't be cheap, and it's just – well, I just met him in Paris with his friend Simon Mann. Do you think that's a big deal?'

'Yes, I think we can safely say that is a big deal. God, you are amazing. Of course it's a big deal!' She exhaled heavily. 'But you need to be careful, James. I know Nick's a good friend, but the people involved in these things don't screw around. If it's real, you need to protect yourself. Have you agreed to anything?'

'Yes.' I conceded I had. 'I mean, informally. I told Nick I'd film it.'

'Okay, well, that's unusual. I'm serious. You need to be more cautious.' She *was* serious. Her gaze flitted around my face. 'I worry about you, baby. I was out of my fucking mind when you didn't call from Liberia. Just . . .' She paused and walked over to me and shrugged. '. . . you know?'

Up until then, I hadn't been worried about Nick's *African Adventure* from a personal point of view: outside of managing the obvious risks of storming a defended beach at night with several

Under fire in the outskirts of Monrovia, June 2003. This was the last ambush entering the city. Several Government soldiers were killed a few feet away. © Tim Hetherington

Tim Hetherington outside rebel headquarters in Monrovia, June 2003. That morning he'd filmed four ambushes in as many hours, after walking thirty-five miles the day before in torrential rain. © Tim Hetherington

LURD rebels use a truck-mounted .50-calibre heavy machine gun to clear an ambush in the outskirts of Monrovia, June 2003. Many of the rebels wore – and were buried in – T-shirts bearing the slogan *Too Tough To Die*. © Tim Hetherington

'Rocket' – a sixteen year-old radio operator – photographed by Tim in Tubmanburg. Rocket suffered severe brain damage after being shot in the head during the rebels' first attack on Monrovia, June 2003. He was unarmed. © Tim Hetherington

A LURD rebel says goodbye to his wife as he sets off for the attack on Monrovia, June 2003. © Tim Hetherington

A LURD mortar team covers our retreat from Bushrod Island, June 2003. Their later bombardment of Monrovia caused hundreds of civilian casualties. © Tim Hetherington

The first LURD rebels leave Tubmanburg on the ten-hour march to the capital, Monrovia, June 2003. © Tim Hetherington

The corpse of a Liberian Government soldier lies by the side of the road as LURD rebels march into Monrovia, June 2003. © Tim Hetherington

Charles Taylor photographed five months after starting the first Liberian Civil War, 29 May 1990. In the presidential election that followed his victory six years later, his supporters campaigned under the slogan 'You kill my ma, you kill my pa, I will vote for you.' © AFP/Getty Images

Severo Moto, the exiled Equatoguinean opposition leader that Simon Mann wanted to install as President. In April 2008 Moto was jailed in Spain for possession of weapons which he planned to send to Equatorial Guinea. © AFP

Zimbabwe's President Robert Mugabe (left) holds hands with his new best friend, President Teodoro Obiang Nguema of Equatorial Guinea, in Harare. Mugabe announced in March 2007 that Zimbabwe had begun importing oil from Equatorial Guinea; in January 2008 Simon Mann was extradited to Equatorial Guinea. © AFP/Getty Images

Inspecting one of the two Dakota DC-3s used on the first coup attempt in February 2004. Filmed in November 2004 at Wonderboom airport, Pretoria, outside the hangar of its owners, Dodson International Parts SA Limited, for the Channel 4 documentary *My Friend the Mercenary*. © Hardcash

Flight N4610. The Boeing 727 that Simon Mann used in the second coup attempt in March 2004, pictured here impounded at Harare International Airport, Zimbabwe. It has been claimed that the aircraft was flown to South Africa from the United States by a pilot who worked for the CIA. © Reuters

Pictured right to left: 727 pilot Neil Steyl, Simon Mann, Hendrik Hamman and Lourens 'Loutjie' Horn in court in Zimbabwe, with the other men arrested in Harare, March 2004. © Associated Press

Simon Mann (front, left) handcuffed to flight engineer Ken Paine in Chikurubi maximum security prison, Harare, Zimbabwe. In between them, walking behind, is Simon Witherspoon, the former 5 Recce operator who led the reconnaissance of Kolwezi airport during the first coup attempt in February 2004. © AFP

Nick on trial in Malabo, Equatorial Guinea, 18 November 2004. He remained almost permanently handcuffed for the five years and eight months he served in Black Beach prison. © AFP

Simon Mann addresses the media after being released 'on humanitarian grounds' from Black Beach jail in Equatorial Guinea, November 2009. Nick is seated behind him to the left in red. In prison, Nick lost forty per cent of his body weight, often eating only leftover scraps of food. Simon's wife, Amanda, later claimed that Simon had been so well treated in jail by 'that lovely, lovely man' President Obiang that her husband had chosen to go on a diet 'to stay trim and slim'. © Associated Press

Nick and I at his new home in Pretoria in the week of his release from Black Beach prison, November 2009. © Marzaan du Toit

dozen paid killers, it had seemed like a fairly straightforward military proposition. Kathi's reticence gave me cause for thought.

'Simon's a very big deal, if they're really in this together. He's very well connected and you know – I mean, sweetie, you of all people should know – that he was basically the brains behind Executive Outcomes. I'm not saying you need to be careful of him, I mean he's not a stupid guy, but somewhere there is going to be someone involved in this who will not want to be identified by you.'

I lit a cigarette and stared back at her.

'Is there something else? You seem a bit troubled.'

It was as if she could see straight into me.

'Yeah, there is something else. It, ah, well, it makes all this running around after stories seem a bit fucking stupid.'

I looked at her and almost couldn't say it out loud, because the moment I did it would become real. The man who had helped to bring me up with such care and love was dying. I crushed the cigarette out.

'I spoke to Mum while I was in Guinea. Grandad has been diagnosed with lung cancer. You know, he's being really stoical about it, but from what I can tell it's quite bad. He doesn't want to upset Nan, but they're worried it's going to spread into his bones.'

What had started off as a persistent cough had led to a biopsy. At first the tumour seemed contained, but it had been festering for longer than originally suspected. With the right therapy, he might be treatable. But now he was having scans on his legs. If the cancer attacked his bones, his condition could deteriorate rapidly. The thought of losing him was too much, and I told myself that he'd pull through okay. Kathi wove her fingers through mine, and I hung onto her, desperate for reassurance.

* * *

Nick called from Conakry to confirm that helicopters would be ready in six weeks. As far as Nick was concerned, I was definitely on board – despite Simon's reticence in Paris. That gave me until the beginning of the third week of August 2003 to prepare. I kept a bag packed, ready to go – and considered my other professional options. After the unexpected success of the *Newsnight* piece, the BBC invited me to shoot and direct a four-part series for BBC Two called *The Violent Coast*. It was planned that I would travel to Sierra Leone, Liberia, Ivory Coast, Benin and Nigeria for what the series producer said was a mixture of current affairs and entertainment. If nothing else, it would be a great way of keeping up with developments in the region, and working with Tim, who was hired as the assistant producer. If the series went well, I reasoned that I might be able to court the Beeb as a client for the film of the coup. The contract was due to begin on 18 August. I called Nick to make sure I wasn't ruling myself out of the operation by accepting.

'No, man, that's great for you,' came his enthusiastic response. 'A team of my guys have gone up to the place we're looking at to do a recce. We're setting up some businesses there as a cover. It's very interesting. It looks like we are going to be very busy indeed. There's quite a few opportunities.'

He promised to give me as much warning as he could, and keep me up to speed with events. Just as I signed the BBC contract, Sekou Conneh called me. His forces were preparing to attack Monrovia again.

'Dis time,' he said, 'we goin' to bombar' de city an' make Taylah ron.'

It had been long-standing military strategy on behalf of the rebels to force a Government surrender by mortaring Monrovia. As early as June 2002, Conneh, Cobra and other commanders had agreed that it was the best way of forcing a mass rout with the relatively few troops at their disposal.

'When y' com' ba'?' he asked.

I told him I wasn't sure I could. To placate him, I told him that Tim might come instead. The truth was that there was nothing to be gained from going back, unless something radical and unexpected happened – like a new front opening up in the war, or a surprise Taylor victory.

Every day, I listened to the World Service, following the rebels' progress. Two weeks later, on 16 July, I switched on the radio to hear not that the rebels were in sight of Taylor's office, but that a coup had been launched in São Tomé – a tiny group of islands in the Atlantic, off the coast of Nigeria and 300 miles southwest of Equatorial Guinea's capital, Malabo. I called Nick immediately, and asked him if he'd seen the news.

'Yes, that was a bit of a surprise,' he said, chuckling on the phone. 'It's caused us a little bit of a problem.'

The Nigerians had waded in – resolving the crisis almost immediately. Their diplomacy was being backed by the real threat of military intervention: Nigeria's share of São Tomé's deep-sea oil reserves was reported to be worth $162 million.

'There's been a slight delay on the funding, too, but there's a Lebanese investing now so there's no rush. I'm going to Conakry in a week. I'll let you know what the situation is like when I've spoken to Sekou.'

Five days later, the LURD had reached Monrovia again, freshly re-supplied by boat from Guinea, and their barrage of the city began in earnest. The US embassy's Greystone complex received a direct hit. Upwards of 10,000 displaced civilians had sought refuge in tents in the compound: nineteen people were killed and sixty were wounded. Distraught parents, husbands, mothers, brought the dead to the front entrance of the US embassy and heaped them up as a symbol of their grief, demanding intervention. US Marines were flown in to secure the building, and evacuate some foreign nationals – but nothing more. Instead of hope, the Marines carried with them a case of beer and shut themselves away out of sight behind the embassy's high walls and razor wire.

On 25 July, two days after the Nigerians oversaw the return of the ousted president in São Tomé, the LURD fired more than thirty 81mm mortars in a ten-minute barrage of the Newport Street and Mamba Point areas. The Newport High School campus was hit. Eight refugees were killed. A further twenty-five people were killed in and around the Holiday Inn Hotel on Carey Street in central Monrovia, where an estimated two hundred civilians had gone to seek shelter. The following day yet more bombs rained down on the city, this time hitting the Greater Refuge Church, where around three hundred people had gathered: five were killed, many more injured.

On the 27th, John W. Blaney III, the US ambassador to Liberia, announced that President Bush, who had already called for Taylor to step down, had ordered three warships to sail for Liberia, laden with a fighting-force of 3,500 Marines. They were expected to arrive within two weeks. As well as the pressing humanitarian crisis, about which the United States Government had so far done almost nothing, Ambassador Blaney also reminded Jonathan – who was still in Monrovia – that the US did now need to act, not least because Liberia was severely destabilising Western Africa, a region which supplied America with around 20 per cent of its imported petroleum. Demanding a ceasefire, they called on the LURD to stop their attacks, and then called me.

Frank from US Intelligence wanted to know if I could call Conneh and urge him to agree to a ceasefire. At the very least, he wanted to know if I could help stop the LURD from launching more mortar attacks.

'Man, we know exactly where those mortars are being fired from,' he said, 'and they're just not going to be allowed to carry on doing that.'

'So there are circumstances under which you'd take them out?'

Frank confirmed that that was the case, that they had the capability to do so and that the threat would be made directly. He also knew, he told me, that the LURD were transporting arms to Liberia from Guinea by ship.

'Frank, you know our mutual friend? The one who's travelled with me a lot?'

'Roger that, yes.'

'Er, he might possibly be on the ship. If it was going to be sunk, could you warn me?'

'Roger that. Yes, I could do that, James.'

I had taken his call in the street. I stopped and looked at the cars passing, couples window-shopping for diamond rings along Bond Street. Everything seemed so normal. I walked down to St James's and found a quiet spot on Jermyn Street to make the call. A besuited gentleman trotted past, muttering under his breath at the dawdling tourists clogging the pavement. I dialled Conneh's number. He was in Conakry.

'Listen, Sekou,' I said, still wondering how best to broach the subject, 'the mortar attacks on Monrovia are getting very negative publicity. You'll get a lot of international praise if you announce that you've stopped them. Say it's for humanitarian purposes. It'll make you look good.'

I knew it was the only argument that might work. With power so nearly in his hands, Sekou was not going to be easily persuaded to stop – and he wasn't.

'We wi' continue to figh',' he insisted.

The peace talks in Accra were evidently a sham. Every concession the rebels gave, or promise of a ceasefire they hinted at, was a tactic to buy more time or territory.

'We jus' talkin' while we ge' mo' RPG bom' fro' Guinea,' he informed me. 'Den we ca' sta' de attack again.'

I gave up and called Nick, who was already in Guinea. I suspected that Nick might be due to start shepherding weapons deliveries by boat to the rebels.

'Nick? It's James. Listen, man, I've just spoken to our American friend.'

I recounted the conversation with Frank.

'Okay, thanks, man, that's very helpful,' Nick said. 'I'll do what I can with Sekou. I don't think they realise how many civilians are being killed.'

Nick didn't realise how many had died, either. He was shocked by the news of the direct hits.

'That is kak, man, the people will never support them if they carry on with that shit. And anyway, it's stupid, they can't see what they're doing. If they're not killing Taylor's soldiers, then it's just a fokken waste of time.'

Nick also confirmed that the peace talks were a ploy – at least for Sekou. The last 'ceasefire' had been agreed to so that the LURD forces outside Monrovia could re-supply MODEL rebels coming up from the southeast, who had – in true Liberian style – run out of ammunition. I had only a very sketchy idea of what Nick was now doing in Guinea with Sekou. It was frustrating and alarming. I'd brought him into the Liberian war, and he'd co-opted me into the coup – but our relationship was anything but equal. Nick was clearly in danger, but without full disclosure from him about what he was planning, it was impossible to protect him.

When we finished talking, I realised that the implications for Nick's *Adventure* of both the coup in São Tomé and the LURD rebels' indiscriminate bombardment of Monrovia could be substantial. The presence of US naval firepower in the region, and the Nigerian military response to the São Tomé coup, had ushered in a set of unintended consequences: Guinea and Liberia *per se* were more than likely fatally compromised as operational bases. More than that, it was probable that any seaborne operation to launch

Nick's operation was off the cards. I might have a long wait on my hands.

In the end, the war in Liberia came to a quick resolution. Sekou, who had been accompanied by Nick to the last round of peace talks in Ghana, was frozen out of the final negotiations by the 'politicians' from Conakry. He remained the titular head of an army that could no longer fight unless it took on the Americans, and of an organisation that was all but unelectable. His wife, long the source of the rebels' military power, began to move against him – splitting away senior fighters and shoring up her own power base. On 31 July, the LURD agreed to a ceasefire, still only having reached Freeport. Not one rebel fighter had managed to cross New Bridge into the centre of town.

By 3 August, American warships had arrived off the coast of Liberia. Two days later, 700 Nigerian peacekeepers deployed by air into Robertsfield airport and occupied Monrovia without a shot being fired. The war was over, and the front line fell silent.

I watched the pictures on the evening news. Journalists, dozens of them, swarmed around Cobra, spilling out into LURD territory. Government fighters and LURD rebels held their forearms up to each other and shouted 'same skin, same skin', calling each other their 'Liberian brothers', while embracing and sharing cigarettes and hooch. It was strange to watch. Only a few days before, LURD fighters had been hacking the arms off Government soldiers whom they captured near the bridges. Now, suddenly, the years of war and slaughter had all apparently dissolved in an afternoon.

As soon as the fighters began to re-discover their shared humanity with the enemy, the LURD high command began to fragment. Cobra was bought off by the promise of a command position in the new Liberian Army, and the knowledge that he could pay himself a generous slice of the money the United Nations would offer for buying up the rebels' weapons in the ensuing disarmament programme. In total, the UN paid to demobilise more than 100,000 combatants in Liberia (including more than 10,000 children), despite accurate estimates that there could have been no more than 4,000 or 5,000 rebels and a similar number of Government troops and militia. The commanders on both sides made small fortunes: Cobra invested some of his in a diamond-mining operation near his home of Bakedu.

On 11 August, Taylor went into exile in Nigeria. A week later LURD, MODEL and the Government of Liberia signed the Accra peace accords, and established a two-year National Transitional Government – which excluded Sekou Conneh – and agreed the demobilisation of the armed factions.

It wasn't clear who the real winners would be, though I suspected that the true beneficiaries would be the people who took power once the Transitional Government ended. For the time being, the LURD and MODEL 'politicians' had stolen a march on Conneh and the fighting men. Joe Wylie, who denounced Conneh as being xenophobic, incompetent, disruptive and dictatorial before the attack on Monrovia began, landed a position in the Ministry of Defence. What was clear was that the fighting men themselves would be left with nothing, least of all their weapons.

Nick dropped off the radar. Guinea's territorial waters were being closely monitored by the Americans and Nigerians. It was no longer possible that Nick could use Liberian rebel fighters – who would have to disarm, anyway – on his planned raid.

In addition, the failure of the São Tomé coup had confirmed that the target of Nick's planned regime change must surely be the president of Equatorial Guinea. In Nick's absence, I sat down to research the sordid, seldom-reported facts of the Equatoguinean regime. In the same way that reliable information about Liberia had been hard to come by eighteen months beforehand, verifiable details about the government of Equatorial Guinea were equally difficult to source. It seemed that the only point at which the former Spanish colony had broken into popular political consciousness at all was after Frederick Forsyth published his bestselling novel *The Dogs of War*, a ripping yarn that was, in fact, a fictionalised account of his own close personal involvement in a foiled coup there in 1973.

President Obiang of Equatorial Guinea, or Teodoro Obiang Nguema Mbasogo, to give him his full name, was indeed no stranger to the idea of taking power by a coup d'état. In 1979 he deposed his own uncle in a bloody rebellion that saw him installed as one of Africa's most brutal dictators. He had exemplary training: before grabbing the top job, he ran the country's renowned Black Beach prison – an institution feared across the African continent for its extreme violence and depravity. Executions, which were said to be commonplace, reportedly involved forcing the condemned man to lie face down, and staving in his skull with an iron bar.

During his near-quarter-century of mis-rule, hundreds of opposition activists had been tortured, murdered and possibly even eaten by his security services, who were accused, along with the president, of cannibalism by political opponents. Even his deposed uncle was put in front of a firing squad – but not before his protégé had taken safe delivery of the former president's extensive collection of skulls, rumoured to confer magical powers. The macabre good-luck charms seemed to be working. His grip on power was complete. Presidential elections in 1998 and 2002 had seen Obiang romp home with 98 per cent of the vote. A coup, it seemed, was the only way of getting rid of him.

The 61-year-old President finally denied that he ate people, insisting that he was a 'Catholic and a humanitarian'. He also declared himself to be a living god. Equatoguinean official state radio repeated Obiang's claim that he was 'in permanent contact with the Almighty' and 'can decide to kill without anyone calling him to account and without going to hell'. Self-deification notwithstanding, Pope John Paul II, at least, took his claim to be a sincere Roman Catholic at face value, and celebrated Mass with him in 1981.

Enjoying life as a god incarnate clearly offered other fringe benefits. Reports on the financial pages estimated that his personal net worth weighed in at an extraordinary $600 million, making him one of the richest heads of state in the world. It seemed likely that Obiang's personal income from the granting of oil-exploration licences to international companies was exceeding $10 million a week; meanwhile, the majority of his citizens struggled to find clean drinking water, electricity or healthcare. According to the World Health Organisation, life expectancy for the majority of the population was a mere forty-eight years – only a slight improvement on war-ravished Liberia. At the same time that Obiang re-affirmed his divinity, he also felt compelled to take full, personal, control of the National Treasury, a measure, he explained, designed to stop 'government corruption' whittling away oil revenues. At the same time, his son, heir-apparent and LA rap music producer, Teodorín, had managed to accumulate an impressive fleet of Lamborghinis, Ferraris and Bentleys, despite claiming to earn an official salary of $50,000 a year. His favoured status as Obiang's successor sent shivers down the spines of the Western governments who imported increasingly large amounts of West African oil, and needed stable regimes in the region to keep the wells flowing.

Equatorial Guinea's oil reserves were vast, to say the least. The third-largest oil producer in Africa, the fetid equatorial island of Bioko sat on an enormous reservoir of premium-quality crude: proven reserves were estimated at 1.1 billion barrels. Equatorial Guinea was producing 250,000 barrels a day. The United States alone imported nearly 5.5 million barrels in 2001. In the first six months of 2002, they had imported almost as much oil from Equatorial Guinea as they had done in the whole of 2001 – when US direct investment already stood at $1.7 billion.

The keys to the presidential palace were a licence to print money – as much money as a mercenary could imagine.

Three weeks passed. Simon Mann called out of the blue. He was trying to track down Nick. We both were: neither of us had heard from him for weeks. I said I'd pass on the message and immediately dialled Nick's numbers. None of them connected.

I was a month away from heading out to Sierra Leone for the BBC. The preparations were unlike those for my previous trips to West Africa. The culture at the BBC was one of legal protocols, risk-assessments and heavy printed tomes of *Guidelines for Producers*. I learned to phrase the challenges that I might face on location in optimistic, non-threatening language. Liberia, for example, was represented as 'a hostile environment in which a number of threats to the production personnel had been identified, but that with proper planning and contingencies did not present risks that could not be sufficiently mitigated to ensure the successful completion of the brief'. Despite the miles of red tape at the BBC, I was looking forward to getting back out to West Africa again, and seeing what had happened in Liberia after the guns fell silent.

Finally, on 9 September 2003, Nick re-surfaced. In response to my enquiry about the timing of the coup, he wrote an email: 'James, Movements not yet set. Will keep you posted.'

The operation was still on.

At the end of the first week of October, I set off for the first leg of my long slog around West Africa. In Monrovia, I walked across bridges the battles over which had killed dozens of young fighters and hundreds of civilians. I walked past the spot where Tim and I had filmed Iron Jacket firing at looters on the far side of the bridge, and where later that evening we'd drunk bottles of stolen, warm Club beer amongst the corpses that littered the highway.

In truth, *all* the fighting had been about getting over those bridges; they spanned the deaths of maybe 3,000 or 4,000 people in those last four years of fighting alone. Exact figures were impossible to calculate. Almost all of the rebels I asked after had been killed on the bridges, or executed by their own comrades – often for looting. Dragon Master was in hiding somewhere in the city; Deku had become posthumously lionised as the rebels' harbinger of death. A popular peace slogan ran *No more Deku, no more Taylor.*

It was a sad city, filled with people displaced from their homes, desperately pinning their hopes on an awkward and corrupt United Nations peacekeeping mission and a kleptocratic Transitional Government. The adrenaline and hubris of the battles they had endured were dissolving inexorably into the squalid reality of urban poverty.

I returned to Tubmanburg and met with Conneh, an almost-tragic rebel without a cause, who, it turned out, was still trying to cement a business deal with Nick. But with peacekeepers fanning out across the country, and the Americans watching everything closely, the chances of setting up a joint mining operation were increasingly slim. Liberia's players were moving on, positioning themselves for the elections: but the soldiers in his compound were listless, still armed and getting younger. Dozens of children clutching AKs hung around, while Conneh sat, guarded by Guinean soldiers, like some surreal Hamlet.

As I walked through the town, I was mobbed by people wanting to say hello – civilians who remembered me from the war, rebel soldiers I'd filmed fighting. The market was working again, as was a small cinema. People had crawled out of the forest and reclaimed their homes, and their lives. Everything looked different. Roofs were patched with zinc or sheets of United Nations-issue blue plastic, and blasted walls were hung with loosely fitting tarpaulins. I walked to the spots where the prisoners had been executed, where I'd dived for cover, or sat, exhausted and smoking, astonished at my own survival. Drying clothes and children's voices wafted from the balcony of the house where first Nick and then Tim and I had passed so many hours. I squatted down and wiped the sweat out of my eyes, and put my palms onto the hot, dusty ground. It was impossible to get Liberia out from under my skin. Its mark festered inside me. I was glad I'd come back to see Conneh and re-trodden the ground I'd run over during the fighting, but the shabby politics and double-dealing of the peace settlement demeaned the deaths of the people I'd filmed and become friends with. When I left a week later, I knew I wouldn't return.

During a break in filming, I finally got hold of Nick. His plans were developing rapidly. The original reconnaissance of the target had gone well. Now he was in business with the brother of the president he intended to overthrow. In addition to negotiating a sea-fisheries protection contract (to which end he was purchasing a boat from Cape Town), he was working on agricultural projects and hoped shortly to sign a contract to start up an aviation company. These businesses were cover operations – fronts that allowed him to conduct an in-depth reconnaissance of the island, in textbook Special Forces style. The companies had two other purposes: first, they provided a pretext for importing men, machinery, boats and – in the case of sea-fisheries protection – even guns; second, they could be profitable in their own right – in effect, an insurance policy in case the coup failed to happen. He'd moved his men into permanent accommodation and was travelling 'there' more frequently himself. He sounded genuinely excited, and was either astonished at his luck in business, or playing the consummate actor over a telephone line that we both knew must be monitored.

'But the *Adventure*', I asked, trying not to sound too insistent, '*is* going ahead?'

'Ja,' he replied, 'I'll keep you informed.'

We chatted about the situation in Liberia, and I filled him in on the BBC series and my schedule. No explanation was given for his long absences: I assumed they were taken up with gathering intelligence on the targets to be attacked. I also asked him for Simon's number. My phone had been stolen a couple of weeks before, so I plucked up the courage to ask for it again.

'I'm sorry, I don't have it.'

His reply caught me off-balance.

'What, you don't have Simon's number?'

I wasn't sure I'd heard him right. He became uncharacteristically evasive, and the conversation was punctuated by an awkward pause while he seemed to collect his thoughts.

'No, I don't have it,' was his final, emphatic answer.

We finished the call. I stood in the study of my new flat in London and looked out over the rows of gardens spreading across my quiet corner of North Kensington. Nick was lying to me – the first time I'd known that he'd done so. *Perhaps they've fallen out? Or maybe he's trying to protect me from something?* In comparison to navigating my way through the twists and turns of Nick's planned coup, Liberia had been remarkably straightforward.

As I travelled back and forth to Africa, I became further accepted as part of the respectable face of television journalism. At an awards ceremony in London, I won two Rory Peck awards – the industry's highly prized gongs uniquely for freelance cameramen. Other nominations and awards followed. It was hard to justify the price. A lot of blood had been spilled for the professional recognition they brought, not to mention untold turbulence in my personal life.

After returning from the latest BBC trip, I'd gone down to Kent to see my grandfather, Don. As soon as he walked into the room, I knew he was dying. My mum and grandmother were positive, supportive, and apparently blind to what was happening in front of them. Perhaps it was because I'd spent so long among the dead and dying in Liberia that it was so obvious. No one spoke the word 'cancer', least of all Don, who didn't like to talk about it in case it upset my grandmother.

'How is everything with Kathi?' he asked instead.

I told him everything was fine. I thought it was.

'I mean, obviously, you know, she's much older and everything . . . but she's very grounded. We're dealing with the same people, doing the same things, but from different ends of the spectrum. She knows everyone. It's pretty amazing.'

My grandfather raised his eyebrows almost imperceptibly.

'There's more to her than meets the eye,' he'd replied. 'Still, I'm glad it's working out.'

As the winter wore on, my grandfather's health deteriorated. On Christmas Day he sat with us for dinner, eating a tiny portion of the feast that Mum and Nan and Kathi had prepared. The tumour in his lungs had spread to his thigh bone, devouring him by degrees. By January it was clear, to Kathi and me at least, that he didn't have much time left. Increasingly reliant on morphine and the constant care of his family and specialist nurses, he began to slip into long narcotic daydreams that insulated him from the agony of his body's collapse.

For as long as I could remember, Grandad had been exactly that – a Grand Dad. When I had nightmares as a small child, he would sit with me and make me laugh, or tell me stories until I fell asleep. He spent hours on a windswept pier jutting into the Channel as I tried, and occasionally succeeded, to catch something for supper. He let me blast holes in almost anything in the garden with my air rifle, and showed me, very patiently, how to grow potatoes.

He taught me to recite my times-tables and then he taught me how to drive. And when I left university he took me on one side, to make sure I understood what my responsibilities were as a man towards my family.

When I started to work, he helped. When I was travelling alone in Palestine, and taken seriously ill, it was Don's telephone number that I repeated over and over again to the medics who rushed to treat me; when my car broke down in a refugee camp at night on the Afghan border, I called Don; when I blew a tyre in the Kalahari Desert, I called Don, because he knew what to do.

He watched me make mistakes, and helped me learn from them. And when suddenly I got my break, he enjoyed every minute of it with me.

I took rough edits of the BBC films I was working on to show Don, and he watched them when the opiates wore off, propped up in bed. I told him about my nomination for the Royal Television Society's best cameraman of the year award. He held my hand and nodded.

'And they can't take that away from you, can they' he assured me.

My grandmother brought in a small blue album of black-and-white photographs from the Second World War, and we sat together while he guided me through his days in Palestine, El Alamein, Tobruk and Italy. His handsome face peered out from the burning desert across sixty years of hard work and achievement: an example I had tried hard – and mostly failed – to emulate.

I took notes with a pencil while, completely lucid, he pronounced the almost-forgotten names of his comrades deliberately and with a warmth that blew a breath of life into them for a few hours more. One photograph, blurred and lopsided, showed rows and rows of Italian prisoners of war lined up by the side of the road.

'That was taken from the back of our truck. We were going up the line, in Libya.'

He put the photographs down and held my hand again. His eyes were glassy with unshed tears.

'You know,' he said, his voice still strong but starting to crack, 'I don't know if I'm going to make it.'

It was a question, as much as a statement. I could neither lie to him, nor tell him the truth.

'No, I don't know either. It's hard. It's such a hard fight, this one.'

And then I saw what it was in his eyes, that same look that I had seen in countless other faces in Africa. He was going up the line again, not knowing if he was coming back.

Back in London, the New Year had hardly begun when Kathi and I split up. Our relationship crumbled in a night fuelled with accusations, recriminations – and a lot of alcohol. By the time we sat down to dinner in a local journalists' club, I was drunk enough to have difficulty walking straight; thinking straight was out of the question. Fundamentally, I wanted to be alone – and her company, with all the intrigues of her work, had by degrees made our life together one of the loneliest places to be. My relationship with Kathi felt like a game, and I was too tired to play any more.

It was an ugly scene. I struggled out into the night air, enraged by her politely evasive responses. I stumbled across an always-busy main road outside the club before collapsing. Slumped on the pavement, I called Tim. He thought I sounded a bit rough. I told him I'd left Kathi. And then suddenly I changed the subject. A memory of our trip into Monrovia, of a particular episode whose true meaning I had suppressed for so long, hit me hard.

'Tim, man, I need you to forgive me, I need you to forgive me,' I repeated over and over. I didn't know where the words came from. 'In Monrovia, I left you. I thought you'd been hit, man – and I just left you. I was so scared, I was so fucking scared, man. I didn't want to die. I'm sorry. I'm so sorry.'

He cut across my ranting, gently, feeling his way cautiously into my hysteria.

'We were both scared. It's okay, it's really okay. I'd forgotten about it, it didn't mean anything. It doesn't mean anything. You're my brother, we're brothers. No one understands. No one will ever understand what it was like. It's okay.'

'It's not okay. It's really not okay. My grandfather is dying. You know? He's going to die very soon, and no one will admit it or say anything. No one understands that, either, no one understands why it hurts so much. He's just an old man, right? He's lived a good life.'

I was crying uncontrollably, shaking on the freezing January ground.

'He wasn't a coward. He was always there, he never left me. No one else gets it, man. I'm just a coward.'

I don't know how long he talked me down for, but at some point I stopped crying and stopped talking. I curled up on the pavement and slept. When I woke up, it was still dark. I went home to find Kathi waiting for me, shaken, but apparently ready to forgive – but something had snapped. The next morning she left. I never saw her again.

At last I felt as if I was in control of my personal life. The BBC job had wound up, and I looked forward with anticipation to my *African Adventure*. I called Nick – who was in South Africa for once. He had surprising news.

'Ag, well, it's quite an interesting story,' he began. 'The businesses have gone very well. I've got a joint venture now with the president's family under way, and there are a lot more plans in development. We might not need to do our operation after all. We're looking at making so much money here, it might not be necessary to remove him.'

After waiting to go for eight months, his news was a terrible anticlimax. I was out-of-contract at the BBC, and his coup was the only meal ticket I had. I was counting on him.

'Okay. Well, if it does go ahead . . .'

I paused while I chose my words carefully. We always spoke in a loose code that seemed to evolve from month to month.

'If you do decide to go ahead, how much notice will I get? My bags are packed. I think it would be a very exciting holiday, and I've got someone lined up to buy the souvenirs afterwards.'

In fact, no one had commissioned the film of the coup. I planned to shoot it on spec and sell it afterwards.

'Forty-eight hours,' Nick replied.

'And what about the big country, in the middle? Any news there?'

We had not talked about the Congo job since Paris.

'Ja,' he confirmed, 'that is still on.'

My spirits lifted. Somehow, somewhere, we were going to go into action together again.

He signed off, as usual: 'I'll let you know.'

I waited in nervous ignorance, texting and emailing in the hope of some movement. And then my grandfather died.

On his last morning, as I prepared to go to London for a meeting, my mother suggested I say goodbye to him. It was the day before his eighty-third birthday. I understood what she meant; there was no way to know the day, nor the hour. Leaning over his emaciated body, I wrapped my arms around him. Six-foot-one and light as a child. Conscious, lucid, he looked at me through his watery blue eyes that now sank back into his skull.

'Most people think they're lucky if they ever meet their heroes,' I said. 'I've lived with mine all my life.'

Deep breaths rattled in his ravaged lungs. I kissed his cheek, and told him that I loved him. He held my hand as tight as he could.

'We're the same, you and me.'

It was the highest compliment I could ever be paid. He looked at me and I kissed him again and said goodbye.

On 4 March 2004, my grandfather Don Sim was cremated at a small family service near to his home in Kent. For four days my mother, grandmother and I sat and nursed our grief, recounting memories, sharing the burden of remembrance. On 9 March I returned to London. I hadn't looked at a newspaper, heard the news or checked my email for eleven days. Not even my mobile phone worked at the house in Kent. Back in my London flat, I drew the curtains, switched on the heating and made a cup of tea in the chilly, empty space. Then I turned on the radio, and got the shock of my life.

On 7 March, a Boeing 727 had been seized at Harare airport in Zimbabwe, carrying sixty-four suspected mercenaries and military equipment. Eighteen hours later, fifteen other suspected mercenaries, including several South Africans, had been rounded up in Equatorial Guinea on suspicion of being an advance guard for the Zimbabwe force. Together, they were believed to be plotting an imminent coup d'état in the Equatoguinean capital, Malabo.

I picked up my phone and called Nick.

PART THREE

15
SIMON SAYS

'Hello?' It was Nick. My shoulders dropped in relief. *Thank God.*

'I've just heard the news. Are you okay, man?'

The line fizzed and then echoed with a sharp tap. It sounded like a scuffle or Nick dropping the phone.

The line went dead. I tried again, standing nervously in the box-room office at the back of my flat, surrounded by piles of prints from my old photographic career. The call connected.

'Who's this?'

It was another man speaking now, with a strong accent and African intonation. He sounded almost Spanish.

'It's James,' I said. 'James from London.'

'James who?'

My gut tightened. Something was wrong.

'I'm a friend of Nick's. May I talk to him, please?'

A long pause elapsed, filled with crackles and hisses.

'Nick cannot come to the phone right now. He's in the shower. Can you call back in an hour?'

I agreed reluctantly and hung up. Sixty minutes later my call was answered again, but when I asked for Nick the line went dead. My third attempt went to voicemail. Thereafter, Nick's number was unobtainable. He was gone.

I paced around the tiny room, trying to collect my thoughts. I knew a great deal about the coup, but not quite enough to help him now. In fact, the best I could hope to do for Nick was to shut my mouth, and keep it shut – destroying in the process any chance I had of reporting on the story myself. I switched on the radio, opened my email, and prepared to become part of the audience for the story I'd hoped to be directing.

Within an hour my phone rang. It was a man from the US military's Joint Analysis Center at Molesworth in Huntingdon – a top-secret facility in eastern England from where the CIA, DIA and a host of other military intelligence entities (including MI6 and other foreign agencies) co-ordinate jointly on intelligence from Africa, Europe and the Middle East. He had one urgent question:

'James, what the hell is going on?'

I had to confess that I didn't really know. I pressed him to see if he knew *anything* – but he claimed that the entire event had caught 'everyone' unawares. Very politely he asked me to check in when I did know, and rang off. I called Frank, my US Intelligence contact, but to no avail.

There was no breaking news that mentioned Nick or Simon by name. I started to search the Internet for clues. Journalists were filling up pages of speculative copy online. Alibis started to appear. A man calling himself 'Charles Burrows' telephoned the Reuters news agency. He was, he claimed, a representative of Logo Logistics Limited, the company that owned the impounded jet plane. It was all, apparently, a 'dreadful misunderstanding': the men were not mercenaries at all; they were security guards who were on their way to guard a mine in the Democratic Republic of Congo. As if to corroborate this, state television pictures from Zimbabwe showed army personnel sifting through the equipment confiscated on the plane, including sleeping bags, army boots, satellite phones and radios – though no weapons.

As the day wore on, it dawned on me that there was only one person I could really call. I scrolled through the numbers on my phone, and dialled Nick's home number. His wife answered. It was the first time I had spoken to her, the first time I'd had any contact with anyone Nick knew other than Cobus, Piet the spy in Monrovia and Simon Mann. She was distraught, but claimed to know little. Nick had been in Equatorial Guinea and now he had vanished.

'James,' she fretted, 'what is going to happen to him? You've been to these places, you know what these people are like. They aren't like us. They aren't going to give a damn about anything.' She was crying, her voice cracked and distorted as the shock took hold. 'They can just kill him,' she declared. 'They can just kill him. James, do you think they will? Will they kill him?'

'Well,' I said, thinking on my feet, 'the best way to make sure Nick is not harmed is to make this as public as possible. You need to make as much noise as possible. You don't know he's been tortured or mistreated – so right now the best thing to do is hope for the best and plan for the worst.'

I chose my words carefully. It occurred to me that I had no idea what she knew about Nick's *African Adventure*. I also had no idea whether her phone was tapped.

'Whatever Nick may or may not have done – or been planning to do – he has rights. It doesn't look like he's actually *done* anything, which is handy, but even if he was planning to do something illegal – which we know he wasn't – he would still have rights. You know, a right to be treated properly, to have a lawyer, a right to have a fair hearing – all that kind of thing.'

She didn't sound convinced, but I carried on regardless.

'Now, it may well be the case that he'll be released very soon – but on the off-chance that he's held for a few days, you should get onto Amnesty International now, and every other human rights organisation you can think of, and help them to publicise his detention. I'll email you a list, too. It's very important that this happens quickly.'

It was only later that evening, after I'd hung up, that the implications of Nick and Simon's arrests finally sank in. The news reports online and on the radio made it seem so remote that I had forgotten for an instant how close I'd been to being with them when they were seized. It could just as easily have been my mother, or Tim, making desperate calls to Amnesty International. I had escaped. My grandfather had saved me.

The following day Simon Mann was officially named as one of the Zimbabwe detainees – arrested at Harare airport with two other men as he met a Boeing 727 jet airliner carrying the sixty-four mercenaries and three crew. Simon Witherspoon, a white South African former soldier (and erstwhile member of Executive Outcomes), was identified as the spokesman for the men on the plane. Meanwhile, Nick had been named as the leader of the contingent seized in Malabo, the capital of Equatorial Guinea. It wasn't looking good.

I tried Frank again, and finally managed to get through. He was in West Africa and professed ignorance of the operation – claiming to be as much in the dark as everyone else.

'Frank,' I pressed him, 'you are a senior Intelligence field officer. Are you seriously telling me that the first you heard of this was when Simon was arrested?'

He insisted that was the case. Frank asked me what I knew, but I was cautious again – and pleaded ignorance of any foreknowledge. I had no idea where a report of my conversation with Frank might ultimately end up. At that crucial stage, any seemingly harmless scrap of information had the power to implicate

Nick in treason – in a country renowned for its predilection for torture and execution.

'Do you have any information about the guys arrested in Zim?' I followed up.

It turned out that Frank had a personal interest in the story: several of the men arrested with Simon were friends of his, and at various times in the past had been employed 'on legitimate US Government business'. His network of South African guns-for-hire had quickly furnished him with some of the names of the other men picked up.

Simon Witherspoon, and another South African soldier, called Raymond Archer, had been hired in West Africa a year after the same operation to evacuate the anti-Taylor rebels from the US embassy in Monrovia in 1998 that Cobus had told me about when we first discussed the Liberia film. Several of the other white men detained in Harare – including Louis du Preez – had also worked on behalf of the Americans; all of them had been employed by Executive Outcomes, and, Frank pointed out, most of them had been in the Recces with Nick.

As well as these past US Army connections, there was another American military link to the mercenaries arrested in Zimbabwe: the Boeing 727 that flew them there from South Africa was registered in the US and until recently had been used by the American 201 Airlift Squadron of the National Guard. It had only been sold by the Government to the company that supplied it to Simon in 2002. Frank thought that was an amusing coincidence – and believed that following the aircraft's history might be enlightening.

What certainly wasn't a coincidence was that of the sixty-four soldiers arrested on the plane in Zimbabwe, many had formerly served with 32 'Buffalo' Battalion, the so-called 'Terrible Ones' who had provided the bulk of Executive Outcomes' fighting men. Diplomatic sources were claiming that twenty were South

Africans, eighteen were Namibians, twenty-three were Angolans, one was a Zimbabwean travelling on a South African passport, and that there were also two men from the Democratic Republic of Congo present. It sounded like an EO old-school reunion.

'Frank,' I asked, before we hung up, 'if the reports are correct, and Nick had tried to topple Obiang in Equatorial Guinea, how far do you think he'd have got?'

Frank laughed.

'What you have to ask yourself, James, is how could he have been stopped? Obiang has no anti-aircraft artillery, and most of their army is drunk and untrained. Nick and his guys could have rolled that bunch of momos up with their eyes closed.'

That evening Nick appeared in my living room. On television news reports he looked strangely young: clean-shaven, and wearing a dark green shirt, he showed no obvious signs of mistreatment. His hair was wet and matted, and sweat gleamed on his face. The only similarity between what he'd planned and what had subsequently happened was that he'd ended up starring in a propaganda broadcast after all.

He was talking to an unseen interviewer from the Equatoguinean Government. He claimed to be talking freely, and that he had not been tortured. I wanted to see him clearly, for him to turn and look me in the eye – *Then I'll know if you're lying*, I thought. What he said next shocked me.

'Half an hour after the people landed with the force from South Africa,' Nick explained in clear, precise English, 'they will fly in Severo Moto and a new government from Spain.'

Moto was an Equatoguinean political exile. He was supposed to land in Malabo airport under the cover of darkness.

'They will land here and then he will be here on the ground, then he can take over the government,' he re-affirmed. He seemed unflustered – relaxed, even – as he implicated Simon and the other men arrested in Harare.

Oh, mate, I thought, *what have you done?* It was impossible to imagine Nick selling anyone out, or cracking under pressure. *Perhaps they've threatened to shoot him,* I reasoned, *or perhaps he's cut a deal with them?*

Other news coverage showed photos of Simon Mann as a schoolboy at Eton and, bizarrely, playing the role of British Army colonel Derek Wilford in Paul Greengrass's drama-documentary *Bloody Sunday* – looking, one commentator remarked, not unlike Richard Burton's character in *The Wild Geese*.

It was hard to reconcile the image of the two professional soldiers I'd had dinner with in Paris with the men now under arrest: their confidence in victory had been unfounded, and the plot was unravelling faster than anyone could keep up with. The excitement they'd shown over their *African Adventure* had ended up as a public-relations bonanza for two despicable regimes – spokesmen for whom were now busily, and not implausibly, ranting about taking revenge on 'colonial powers', 'MI6' and 'the CIA' for meddling in Africa's business. While Nick faced a trial for treason in West Africa, Simon and the others were similarly threatened with the death penalty by Zimbabwe's foreign minister. Even South Africa's Department of Foreign Affairs seemed to be jumping on the anti-mercenary bandwagon, emphasising that if the men on board the ill-fated 727 did turn out to be 'dogs of war', then they would be abandoned to the justice of Zimbabwe's President Robert Mugabe.

In fact, a lot of people had been abandoned by Nick and Simon's big *Adventure*. As well as Nick's wife, and his cherished eleven-year-old daughter, there were the families of more than eighty-five men who now faced either capital charges or a lengthy stretch in prison. Alongside one of the greatest news stories of the decade was unfolding a series of painful, personal tragedies. The reality of my conspiratorial confidences with Nick was beginning to hit home.

'I managed to talk to him by phone,' Nick's wife told me, strangely sanguine when I called after the broadcast.

His captors had allowed him to make a closely monitored call to her in order to ask for information about the coup from the files in his office. It was clear that she now knew why he was in Equatorial Guinea, and had access to details about the operation. Nonetheless, hope and expectation lifted the timbre of her voice.

'He assured me he's okay, really.'

It sounded as if she was trying to convince herself. Either Nick's role was not what it seemed, or he was lying to protect his wife.

'Perhaps he'll be back soon, James. We must pray, anyway.'

But Nick wasn't coming home any time soon. Along with fifteen other men who'd been arrested with him, he was heading for Equatorial Guinea's notorious Black Beach prison – a crumbling, Spanish colonial-era penitentiary on the main island of Bioko. Renowned as Africa's worst jail, it was more reminiscent of Devil's Island in *Papillon* than of a modern penal institution. The prisoners temporarily vanished into a labyrinth of violence.

It wasn't long, though, before one of the South Africans managed to smuggle out an account of their mistreatment, scribbled onto the back of a cigarette packet. Dated 10 and 11 March, and later quoted in a damning Amnesty International report, it read:

> 10/3 22*h*00–23*h*00 *I was taken to the police station for interrogation. I had no lawyer. I was asked many questions. I had no answers for them.*

1. *Handcuffs tightened and cut into my flesh, into bone of right hand.*

2. *I was beaten with the fist. I had no answers . . . Beaten on head and jaw.*

3. *They took me to a small dark room down the stairs into the police courtyard. Here I was put on the ground. A dim light was burning. I saw Sérgio Cardoso hanging, face down, in the air with a pole through his arms and legs. The police guard started asking questions which I still could not answer. Every question a guard would stand on my shin bone, grinding off the skin and flesh of the right leg with the military boots. This carried on for at least 30 minutes. I was shouting, begging them to stop.*

4. *Later I begged them rather shoot me for I could not take the pain and agony any more . . . After no answers it stopped. I was taken back at 2 o'clock.*

5. *11/3 about 15h00 I was tied to a bed with cuffs on my right hand. I was beaten and slapped . . . my right thumb broke.*

6. *At my bed . . . I was beaten with a blow unconscious.*

7. *The same afternoon I was burnt with a lighter.*

8. *At 17h00 I was taken to the police station and told to write everything I knew. Anything that came to my mind. I will have the same and worse treatment of the previous evening. I was terrified and wrote down as if I was involved in everything (which I was not) because they were to torture me again.*

Cardoso, while hanging from the pole, was electrocuted and then subjected to mock executions. Many of the men had the soles of their feet burned with lighters. All of them were painfully shackled hand and foot, beaten with rifle butts and told they would be killed.

As well as Cardoso, several of the other fifteen men arrested with Nick had South African military backgrounds – and some had previous form. José Passocas Domingos (known as J.P.) had served with 5 and then 4 Recce, while Marius Boonzaier (known as 'Bones') had been in 1 Recce, before moving on to work in Special Forces intelligence. George Alerson had started off in 32 Battalion, before passing selection for 5 Reconnaissance, where he served with Nick. He'd already served a lengthy jail term in Mozambique for his part in an aborted assassination attempt on Albie Sachs, an anti-apartheid legal activist who was later appointed as a judge by Nelson Mandela. Eventually blown up by a car bomb in Maputo in 1988 by agents from the Civil Cooperation Bureau, Sachs lost an arm, and the sight in one eye.

Gerhard Merz, a German aviation specialist whom Nick had hired through Simon, was altogether a different character: the manager of an aviation company called Central Asian Logistics, he had set up Nick's air operations in Equatorial Guinea. Even by the standards of the mercenary company Nick kept in Malabo, Merz had a particularly dangerous past. The United States Government claimed he had brokered the sale of materials for making chemical weapons between China and Iran from 1991 to 1993; in 1994, Bill Clinton put the presidential signature to an Executive Order denouncing Merz for promoting 'the proliferation of nuclear, biological and chemical weapons'. Nick had certainly collected a motley crew of fellow *African Adventurers*.

On 17 March, Merz was tortured to death. Left in front of the other captured men, his body was covered in bruises; his back and feet burned by cigarette lighters. The Equatoguinean authorities claimed he'd died of cerebral malaria; Amnesty International disagreed. Nick's other colleagues narrowly survived their interrogations in what Sérgio Cardoso – Nick's right-hand man and former soldier in 32 Battalion – described as a dark, blood-spattered 'torture room'.

Nick himself was kept separate from the other prisoners – tied up in pitch-black solitary confinement. The future of all the detainees there looked bleak. A week after his arrest, President Obiang – the former governor of Black Beach prison – denounced Nick and his cohort as 'devils', promising 'the terrorists' 'a fair trial', with the caveat that 'if they have to be killed, they will be killed. Equatorial Guinea has not abolished the death penalty, we won't forgive them.'

The seventy men, including Simon Mann, held in Zimbabwe's Chikurubi maximum security prison also feared for their lives. Ironically, the jail itself had been built by the former white minority Rhodesian Government – a regime previously enthusiastically supported by several of the guns-for-hire who had now ended up behind its walls. Originally built to house 900 inmates, by March 2004 it accommodated more than 3,000 men. One of the mercenaries died of meningitis, and two others were later released on medical grounds. Smuggled out of jail, horrific stories of their confinement painted a grim picture of abuse.

Homosexual intercourse was openly practised by many of the local Zimbabwean prisoners; younger men were raped in return for the 'protection' of older inmates. It was estimated that more than half of the prison population was infected with HIV. Raw sewage piled up in the cells; there was no running water; and the guards savagely beat the detainees with batons. Both the black and white recruits who were brought on board as foot-soldiers for the coup lived in conditions described by one former soldier as being like a 'concentration camp'. Other prisoners died in the overcrowded cells almost every day.

Chained to the bed where he slept, Simon Mann was eventually kept separate from the other men arrested with him – because one of the other white mercenaries, Louis du Preez, threatened to attack him.

As news of the men's condition leaked out to the press, Nick's wife became increasingly agitated. Not only was Nick being held on death row by a despotic government openly seeking his execution, the situation in Zimbabwe, too, contained the seeds of another tragedy for her.

'You see, James,' she explained in one of our, by now, almost daily conversations, 'there's something else, something really bad, that I have to tell you.'

I tried, and failed, to imagine the scale of the horror she was about to impart.

'It's my brother, Errol,' she continued. 'He was on the plane, too. He's in jail with Simon in Chikurubi. He's being held in a cell with two hundred black people, James. I'm asking you – what is going to happen to him? It's a disaster. Those people will tear him to pieces, James. He's never even left the country before. It's the first time he's ever left South Africa.'

Nick's family was falling apart.

As legal proceedings in Malabo and Harare began to gain pace, an avalanche of documents tumbled into the public domain; the lengthy statements from Simon and Nick provided astonishing insights into the logistics of the planned coup – including detailed accounts of who was involved, where the weapons came from and how the operation was launched.

The main evidence used to piece together events was Simon's handwritten thirteen-page confession, which implicated several other co-conspirators. It was dated 9 March 2004 – two days after he was arrested – and was leaked almost immediately, with one page missing. I was given a copy at the end of March by a colleague who was in contact with a source close to Ely Calil, a Lebanese businessman named by Simon as the plot's facilitator (a claim which Calil denied).

Although Simon claimed there was no lawyer present when it was written, and that it was extracted under 'brutal and severe torture and assault for several days', he would openly admit, much later, that while it was 'made under duress' it was nevertheless true.

According to the confession, the leg of the operation that had got Simon and Nick busted in Harare and Malabo was not the first attempt at pulling off the coup d'état in Equatorial Guinea. The original plan of deploying a seaborne invasion force had been abandoned by August 2003, and it had taken a further six months to get the operation up and running again owing to a lack of ready cash that autumn – a fact Nick had corroborated on the phone the year before.

In December 2003, the plotters received the money they needed to proceed, and Simon confirmed that Nick's cover-businesses in the capital, Malabo, appeared to be operating successfully. They were indeed being used for intelligence-gathering and as an insurance policy – 'if the project did not go ahead', he wrote, 'then, hopefully, they would make money'.

Simon said that the schedule for the operation was agreed then. 'A time limit of 16 Feb was set by EC [Ely Calil],' he wrote. 'Since we could only get restarted on 6 Jan we had little time.' The press speculated that the date was dictated by political expediency rather than the exigencies of military preparation: perhaps, it was thought, the plotters had deemed it essential to launch the coup before the forthcoming general election in Spain.

Severo Moto – the Equatoguinean opposition leader living in exile in Madrid, and identified as the plotter's man-who-would-be-king – was favoured as a successor to Obiang by the then Spanish right-wing government of José María Aznar, who may have recognised his premiership after the coup. The general election in Spain on 14 March had resulted in the formation of a new left-wing government much less sympathetic to Moto. The Spanish had much to gain from a friendly regime in Malabo: they had been almost entirely excluded from the riches of Equatorial Guinea's oil boom.

It was clear to me that the fact that Guinea and Liberia were off the cards as a launch-pad had caused other serious logistical issues. First, now that the operation was based out of South Africa, the mission required planes, not boats, to get the men and weapons to the target. Simon's statement described how this problem had, in fact, been resolved by Nick's Pan African Airlines and Trading Company (PANAC) – a joint-venture business with Armengol Nguema (the president's younger brother and head of national security, who was not involved in the coup) – whose planes were supplied by Merz, the first plotter to die in jail. Second, as the initial press coverage of the arrests had shown, with no Liberian rebels available to act as foot-soldiers, a larger number of black ex-32 Battalion members had been recruited, and in a hurry, from Pomfret – the poverty-stricken, asbestos-riddled wasteland in northern South Africa into which they had been re-settled when their unit was disbanded near the end of the apartheid era. Finally, with no rebel armaments to rely on, Nick needed to get guns – fast.

In his written confession, Simon describes in detail the mad scramble to procure weapons for the project. At first Nick and Simon sought help from Nick's business partner – a South African named Henri van der Westhuizen. Together they tried their old contact in Uganda. It failed. Then they discussed acquiring weapons from Kenya, Burundi or Zambia. Those contacts failed, too. As a last resort, Nick opted to purchase the rifles and ammunition they needed in Harare, from Zimbabwe Defence Industries (ZDI) – the country's state-owned armaments company.

It was a shock to read, in Simon's words, how they had settled on Zimbabwe as a source for their lethal hardware. To my untrained eye, that could not, to say the very least, have seemed an attractive option. It was fair to assume that British and South African mercenaries are not exactly beloved of President Robert Mugabe – especially not ones with close ties to Britain's political elite, or those with a two-decade history of undercover warfare against him. It must have been obvious to Simon and Nick that Simon risked becoming the star attraction in Mugabe's war of words with what Mugabe styled Tony Blair's 'gay gangster' government. *They must,* I thought, *have been under extreme pressure to have taken such a risk.*

Yet Simon wrote that he was reassured by the fact that Nick felt it was safe to proceed. Nick had done deals with ZDI before.

I pored over the wealth of information detailed by Simon in his account of the failed operation. He said he and Nick flew to Harare on 8 February 2004 – where a ZDI representative ushered them through customs – much like, I imagined, the Red Berets had whisked Nick and I through immigration in Conakry airport. Simon then described how, at a hotel in town, he and Nick sat down with one of the company's functionaries called Martin Bird, and discussed their military requirements.

'NDT put the order for the EG project to MB,' he wrote, 'who said that he did not see any difficulty. NDT then surprised me by saying that he had a second order of ammunition only. MB saw no problem with this, either.'

When Bird had left, Nick explained that the Equatorial Guinea order was too small for ZDI to take seriously, and it needed to be bumped up to be made worth their while. His second order was for a rebel group in the Congo – and he 'was very adamant that Zimbabwe Defence Industries would be interested in making friendly contact with the DRC rebels'.

Later, according to the confession, Nick and Simon paid ZDI boss Colonel Tshinga Dube a visit at the company's offices. Simon explained that the weapons were needed to guard a mine in northeast Congo, near the border with Uganda. Apparently uninterested, Dube could hardly bring himself to look at the map of the DRC that Simon pointed to, as the men struggled in vain to hold the colonel's attention. Another meeting followed; this time Nick went into see Dube alone, to discuss the ammunition order for the Congolese rebels. Simon said that Nick emerged in high spirits – Dube had reportedly been pleased with the prospect that ZDI and the Zimbabwe Intelligence services would gain a 'direct and positive link to the new rebel DRC rebel grouping'. Contracts were signed on 10 February with ZDI's Group Captain Hope Mutize: one for Equatorial Guinea by Nick and Simon; the other, by Nick alone, for 'the Katanga' uprising in the Congo.

I knew that the mining cover-story was an irrelevant ploy – but the rebel group that Nick wanted to supply wasn't. His planned operation in Congo's Katanga province – described to me in Liberia and Brussels – had evidently become an integral part of the Equatorial Guinea coup plot. The British press passed over the Katangese rebels, licking their lips at the news-feast served up by Simon's increasingly unenviable predicament. I stared at Simon's handwriting in astonishment. Nick had not been planning one operation, but two.

Simon continued that on 11 February he and Nick had flown from Harare to Ndola – a town in northern Zambia near the Congolese border. Here, according to Simon, they met 'Abu who was apparently the leader of the Katanga uprising shortly to occur' – the same man, I suspected, that Nick had talked to me about in Liberia. Abu was told by Nick and Simon that 'he must secure the airstrip at Kolwezi for 24 hours so that his equipment could be delivered to him'. I looked up Kolwezi on the map. It's a small town near the Katangese city of Lubumbashi – site of the Shinkolobwe uranium mine.

The narrative of the plot unfolded like a tragic farce. Every act described seemed laden with premonitions of the failure to come. Simon did not say exactly what was supposed to happen in Kolwezi, but the details emerged piecemeal into the public domain over the coming weeks.

According to aviation records, intelligence sources, insiders and the investigations of journalists on two continents, it eventually became clearer what had happened. A mercenary pilot called Crause Steyl, who had flown for Executive Outcomes, flew to the Canary Islands – an outcrop of Spanish territory in the Atlantic Ocean, off the coast of West Africa – and waited there with three alleged plotters: Greg Wales (said to be Simon's political adviser), David Tremain (a businessman and mining expert), Karim Fallaha (a Lebanese businessman) and another pilot. Their job was to escort the exiled Severo Moto – who was also in the Canaries – back to victory in Malabo once Nick and Simon had mopped up. According to Simon's confession, Moto would be escorted to Malabo to coincide with a local military and civilian uprising. Nick's men were to act as Moto's bodyguard.

Before dawn on 19 February 2004, sixty-four mercenaries – including several of Africa's most notorious guns-for-hire – embarked onto two Dakotas at the Wonderboom civilian airfield just outside of Pretoria. After making the short hop to Polokwane international airport, the men cleared immigration and flew north.

I supposed that in Kolwezi the men and the weapons from Zimbabwe would be paired up on the runway, and cross-loaded onto an Antonov 12 cargo plane belonging to Nick's PANAC company – which, according to Simon, had flown down from

Malabo to meet them. Once all the (now armed) mercenaries were on board, the Antonov would then have returned to Equatorial Guinea – where Nick and his advance party would be waiting to greet them before they stormed the capital.

Up to the departure of the Antonov for Harare, everything went like clockwork. And then wheels came off – literally. Simon's confession fills in the details.

Landing at Cameroon en route from Malabo, the Antonov's nose-wheel broke. Severely delayed, the aging cargo plane managed to take off again. Simon waited in Harare, ready to load the weapons.

In a moment of extraordinary comic timing, the Antonov was then crippled again shortly after take-off and forced to make an emergency landing in Lubumbashi after its nose-cone was struck by a goose. Exactly what happened next in that corner of Katanga was unclear. 'In the meantime,' Simon wrote, 'the rebels had not secured Kolwezi and the whole operation was cancelled.' Either the rebels did not in fact exist – or, in time-honoured tradition, they had failed to show up.

The planes carrying the mercenaries landed instead at Ndola, in sleepy, law-abiding Zambia – presumably lest they be confronted, defenceless, by the infamously inhospitable Congolese Army. Here they waited for three hours at a commercial airport before flying back home again – where most of them were installed in the Hotel 224. Several days later, Moto and the other men on the Canary Islands headed their separate ways. What Nick and Simon had tried to pull off wasn't just a coup d'état: it was a breathtakingly complex enterprise that had involved moving almost one hundred people in six countries thousands of miles across Central Africa on half a dozen flights – the successful outcome of which was entirely predicated on the exactly timed uprising of a hitherto-unknown rebel group in one of Africa's most unstable regions.

What puzzled me most of all was not why Nick's *African Adventure* had failed the first time around, but why – given the extent of his experience in covert operations in the army and his recent experience in Liberia with me – he'd ever imagined it could succeed at all.

And yet, seemingly undeterred by this setback, Simon and Nick pressed on in what appeared to be a stupendous example of the triumph of hope over experience.

Simon related in detail how he and Nick had headed back to Harare immediately after the disaster in Kolwezi, agreeing a $10,000 surcharge with ZDI's Martin Bird to compensate for the inconvenience of messing up the collection. Ditched in favour of more reliable air transport, the goose-battered Antonov was retired in place of the Boeing 727 jet airliner: purchased in haste in the US, it was flown into South Africa, arriving in the early hours of 7 March, three days after Nick had made it back to Equatorial Guinea. In the Canaries, Moto and the gang were in place again, too. On 6 March, Simon – accompanied by former Recce and EO mercenary Harry Carlse and ex-Special Task Force policeman Lourens Horn – flew to Kinshasa, the capital of the Democratic Republic of Congo. Here he met with a man called Tim Roman – an American contractor and confidant of Congo's president Joseph Kabila – while Carlse and Horn stayed with the aircraft. Simon claimed he was looking for a back-up aeroplane – and Kabila's blessing for their operation. Roman knew Colonel Dube at ZDI well; he 'had flown similar missions in his aircraft before', and 'thought he would be able to do it' – and promised to be in contact once he'd chatted to Kabila. Simon flew back to Harare with Carlse and Horn. Simon checked in with the ZDI representatives, and waited.

Here Simon's neat, handwritten confession ended – but I could piece together the rest for myself.

Back at Wonderboom airport, the newly arrived 727 was loaded with non-lethal military kit, including bolt-cutters, boots, sleeping bags, medical kits and radios. Then it was filled with sixty-four soldiers and three crew. Again making the short hop to Polokwane to clear immigration, the plane touched down at Harare airport at seven o'clock in the evening, taxiing to the military zone as agreed with the airport authorities. The weapons would be loaded on site: there would be no need to cross-load in unstable Congo, they would be able to tool up *over* the Congo – the aircraft's hold was pressurised, heated, and accessible from the cabin in flight.

Unbeknown to them, however, the mercenaries had reached the end of the line. It was already over. Simon, Carlse and Horn boarded the plane with customs officials, as the main force of mercenaries simply sat and waited in their seats. Then the three of them were taken by Hope Mutize, the ZDI representative, to the parachute hangar nearby to get their hands on the weapons. They prised open the crates to show the lethal cache within. Carlse complained that the consignment did not match Simon's order. Moments later they were surrounded by soldiers and plainclothes police who had been hiding in the shadows. They were cuffed, and bundled into waiting vehicles. Seized by other Zimbabwean soldiers, the men on the 727 were arrested, and driven straight to jail.

Eighteen hours later Nick and his team were picked up in Malabo.

Do not pass go. Do not collect oil revenue.

My emotions had ranged from horror at Nick's arrest, to disbelief at the plan they'd devised. Then a flash of anger flared up. *You wanted me to risk my life for this shambles?*

It was unthinkable that Nick could have put together a plan that involved taking so many apparently avoidable risks. The idea that Simon, a former SAS officer, could have dreamed it up with him beggared belief. Had I misread it all? I telephoned a friend of mine recently demobbed from the SAS himself – a long-serving sergeant-major with nearly two decades of operational experience, not long returned from Afghanistan. Familiar with the details of the coup plot from the media and his own security industry sources, he gave his professional opinion on the doomed *Adventure*.

'What you have here, mate,' he chirped down the phone, 'is what could, in all fairness, only be described as an astonishing catalogue of buffoonery.'

It was embarrassing to hear his verdict. He knew Nick and I were friends, but he didn't hold back.

'Rule One: never marry up the men with the kit until you're on target – you've got to have cast-iron deniability until the key moment. Rule Two: do not buy the weapons from an overtly hostile, tyrannical regime. Rule Three: if at first you don't succeed, do not try again – you've got to be prepared to walk away. There's no way you could commit to an operation like this until twenty-four to forty-eight hours beforehand – and that would be completely dependent on the intelligence you were receiving.'

'But what about Simon?' I protested. 'Surely a former Special Air Service officer would have considered all that, and made a tactically sound judgement despite the apparent odds against success?'

'James, Simon's reputation is not – er, how shall I put this? – uniformly excellent. He only served two-thirds of his tour with the Regiment. Apparently, there was some kind of incident – a difference of opinion about operational matters – and he decided to leave.'

'Mate, are you sure?'

'Yep. I'm sure. The other thing to bear in mind is that he might have been told he was good to go. But he wasn't, right? So either his intel was compromised, or he was set up.'

Perhaps Simon and Nick had been beguiled by their own previous successes with Executive Outcomes – which had, after all, been the most successful private army to fight in the modern era. In Sierra Leone, their contingent of around 100 men had fought and defeated a rebel army of 3,000–4,000, often psychopathic killers. Their thinking was clear: if 100 of their men could defeat the Sierra Leonean RUF rebels – even if they'd only been up against a hard core of around 600 fighters – then two-thirds that number could take out a despised despot on a tiny island protected by 'a bunch of momos'.

I hung up and contemplated Nick's planning. Doing so posed an obvious, if often overlooked, question: what on earth would lead Simon, Nick and the backers of the operation to think – truly believe – that they could overthrow the government of an independent sovereign nation, install a puppet president and run it as an ongoing business concern?

The answer was a surprisingly simple one: the fact that African history is peppered with the often tragic antics of Europeans and white Africans who have done, or nearly done, just that. Simon, Nick and the other operatives involved in the Equatorial Guinea coup plot were the last in a pedigree of mercenary whose days on the continent looked like they were finally up.

As the days wore on, my anger towards Nick burned itself out. My dismay at his involvement developed into a curiosity about why he'd gone ahead with it at all. In late January, he'd left me with the strong impression that he was walking away from the coup – but ten days later he'd placed the weapons order with Simon in Harare. What was more, Nick had had several hours in which to escape from Equatorial Guinea after Simon's arrest – but his wife had been adamant that he'd been seized at his house the next morning, having made no attempt to run. Perhaps it was just greed and a thirst for adventure that had compelled him to go, and a potentially fatally misplaced sense of his own security that had prompted him to stay; or perhaps he thought that he was being protected – that the operation was being underwritten by one of the players who had enabled similar mercenary operations in the past: former colonial powers; the Americans; and the South African Government.

Severo Moto, pretender to the throne in Malabo, was at least supported in exile by Spain, Equatorial Guinea's former colonial power; the US military also had links to several of the mercen-aries, and the plane that took them to their fate was previously operated by the US Air Force – but none of that added up to proof of external support. The most tantalising question – in an ocean of conundrums – was what South Africa's role had been in the entire enterprise. It was inconceivable to me that Nick – a Special Forces legend, high-profile arms dealer and former Executive Outcomes military commander – would not have established contacts with South African Intelligence: for all I knew, he could have been on their pay-roll himself. The difficulty would be in ascertaining if the South Africans foiled it, or were themselves thwarted.

Prompted by Simon and Nick's confessions, the Government of Equatorial Guinea pointed the finger at the people they believed backed the coup financially – including Greg Wales, David Trem-ain and Karim Fallaha, all of whom had been in the Canaries with Moto in February and March. All of them denied it. The main backer, though, the overlord who they said had brought Simon and Moto together, was, they alleged, the Lebanese oil tycoon named as Ely Calil.

Born in Nigeria, Calil was supremely well connected to the West African oil elite, and estimated by the *Sunday Times* to be worth £100 million in his own right. He was also closely connected to the British political establishment: a friend of Peter Mandelson (to whom he rented a luxury apartment in 1999), he was also reported to know David Hart and Tim Bell (confidants and advisers to Margaret Thatcher during her prime ministership), and was said to be a former financial adviser to the novelist and convicted perjurer Jeffrey Archer.

According to Simon's confession, Calil introduced Simon to Severo Moto in Madrid in May 2003. Calil, Simon maintained, had been funding Moto in exile, and wished to see him returned to Malabo. Calil refused to give interviews (he had not been photographed in public since 1972), and denied having anything to do with a coup. Almost immediately after that meeting – and the ones that Simon said followed soon thereafter – Nick and Simon had begun to plot the violent overthrow of Moto's nemesis: President Obiang.

Trying to establish who might be behind the plot seemed like a daunting task. My connection to the operation was solely through Nick and Simon, both of whom were unable to communicate freely with the outside world, and certainly not with me. Nick had said that a Lebanese had invested heavily into the project – but that didn't prove either Calil or Fallaha's involvement. I didn't know where to start, or even if I should. I suspected it would be very hard to unearth anything that would really help Nick, and comparatively easy to discover a great deal that would be sure to harm him.

Then, on 26 March, I got a call from a man who introduced himself as a friend of Nick.

'Hello, James,' he greeted me, as if he'd known me for years. 'I'd like to talk to you. I'm trying to help the guys in jail.'

His name was Dries Coetzee; he'd got my number from Nick's wife. He spoke carefully with a gruff Afrikaans accent. What he needed to say, he wanted to say in person.

The following morning at eleven o'clock I took myself off reluctantly to see him at the Strand Palace Hotel in London, and braced myself for an interrogation. In his late thirties, Dries looked like an Aryan caricature from a Second World War cartoon. Built like an Olympic shot-putter, he had hands like shovels and a wide-open baby face topped by a frizz of blond hair.

'It's very good to meet you,' he said, slowly rising out of his chair to both greet me and size me up. 'I hear that you and Nick had quite an adventure together.'

My right hand vanished into his gargantuan grip. I agreed that we had, and that we'd almost shared another, less successful one, too.

'Ja, well, James, that's why I'm here.'

His manner was disarmingly direct, his mood affable and his mission clear: he'd come to get money from whom he called 'the backers', to help pay for the cost of legal representation, food and other expenses for Simon, Nick and the other imprisoned men. But no one wanted to play ball.

'If there's anything you can think of that might help,' he said, 'we can make a plan. Simon is writing a number of letters from jail, which I have access to. They are very revealing.'

He said that if I ever decided to make a film about who had betrayed Nick and his men, he would make the letters available to me. It was a potentially explosive offer; I told him I'd have to think carefully about it, and offered to drive him across town for his next meeting.

As we crossed London, he warmed to his main theme again.

'You know who else refused to help?'

His eyes were like saucers; he was getting quite angry at the thought of no one stumping up.

'No, who?' I was only half-listening, busy looking for a parking space.

'Mark Thatcher, that's who.'

'Mark Thatcher?'

'Ja, that's right.'

I stopped the car, and reversed back into a parking bay on Norfolk Place.

'Mark Thatcher is involved in this?'

'Ja. Guess what he fokken said when I rang him and asked for help?'

Mark Thatcher? It was hard not to laugh. *Jesus, no wonder they fucked it up*. The accident-prone son of the Iron Lady was certainly not someone you'd rely on for logistical planning: he had, however, participated in the al-Yamamah arms deal between British Aerospace and Saudi Arabia – the largest export deal in British history, worth in excess of £40 billion.

'No, what did Mark Thatcher say when you asked him for help?' It was like being the straight man in an '80s stand-up routine.

'He told me to vok off. He said he was watching the Grand Prix, and couldn't talk. It's fokken unbelievable. Grand Prix! He told me to call back later. Some fokken friend he turned out to be.'

Dries and I exchanged numbers. He unfolded himself out of my car, and headed off alone into the Underground. *Mark Thatcher.* It was preposterous. If he could be involved, so could anyone. For the first time since Nick had been arrested, I felt that familiar surge of adrenaline. We may have been separated by more than 3,000 miles and the thick walls of Black Beach prison, but I was now determined to get to the bottom of the plot.

As the days after Nick's arrest turned into weeks, I stayed in close contact with his wife. I travelled to New York to finish *Liberia: An Uncivil War*, the by-now feature-length documentary that Tim, Jonathan and I had shot in Monrovia. I drank so heavily during the edit that I managed to scare myself into abstinence. By the time the film premiered at the Human Rights Watch International Film Festival, I had quit drinking entirely, and become teetotal.

With the film put to bed, a year after we'd escaped over the Mano River, it finally felt as if I could begin to put some distance between me and Liberia. Intrusive images, brutal memories, the guilt of survival – these were the threads from the forest that had been woven into a suit I wore every day. Now I was moving on, or so I hoped.

Cutting out the drink seemed like a good place to start. Playing the role of a 'damaged' war reporter was a seductive proposition: women wanted to rescue me; men who didn't know better wanted to be me – or at least get drunk with me. Or so I thought. It was ridiculous and deluded and I'd had enough.

Back in London, I had a series of meetings with Channel 4 which ended in an offer to make films for their international current affairs series *Unreported World*. My travels with Nick had finally coalesced into a viable, respectable career. I'd thought I'd needed to film the coup to survive professionally – but that was not true. The legacy of working in Liberia was not just a brutal memory of the past, but a positive vision of real work as a filmmaker in the future.

Meetings at Channel 4 also offered another opportunity, but one which looked more like a poisoned chalice than a trophy commission: they wanted me to deliver a film about Nick and the coup for their *Dispatches* series. Media interest in the case had snowballed. Letters appealing for help leaked from Simon's prison cell – drafted by him to his friends 'Scratcher' and 'Smelly', said to be references to Mark Thatcher and Ely Calil – ended up on the news pages of British papers. Dries had been right. Other alleged contributors to Simon's regime-change escapade were named, too. These letters, I suspected, came from the stash that Dries had promised me.

Accepting the commission was morally and legally treacherous. Not only would I be profiting from Nick's situation as he went on trial for his life, but also anything I did or said in the making of the film could seriously jeopardise his chances of getting out alive. I was reluctant even to refer to Nick as a mercenary, a position that brought me into immediate conflict with the commissioners at Channel 4. What was more, I had promised Nick that I would never name him in connection with my work in Liberia, and had tacitly agreed not to expose his role in the coup: going ahead would mean breaking my word to him. On the face of it, making a film about him was out of the question.

There were, however, two compelling arguments in favour of accepting Channel 4's offer: the first was that if I didn't make the film, then someone else definitely would; and the second was that it would give me a chance to get to the bottom of Nick's plan. Nick had few enough friends as it was – and it was unlikely that anyone else would make a film that would give him a fair hearing, let alone the benefit of the doubt. I talked it through with his wife, who gave her support, and then called Channel 4 to accept the commission, even though I knew that doing my job as an independent, impartial journalist would be impossible. I explained in no uncertain terms that I would not do or say anything that would further endanger Nick's life. They agreed.

At the core of the film – to be directed by my colleague Carla Garapedian – would be a simple question: Nick had told me he didn't need to go ahead with the operation – so why had he?

Nick went to trial in the third week of August 2004. Nick's wife flew to Malabo and sat, shell-shocked, in the court room. It was almost as hard to watch on television. Standing before the court in a blue shirt, shorts and sandals, Nick raised his voice and challenged the judges. He was shackled at the ankles.

'We've been chained like wild animals,' he said, showing his handcuffed wrists to the Bench, 'we've been tortured by the police . . . we haven't done anything wrong.'

If he had, he reasoned, he would have tried to run away. The three judges were impassive. Only one of them had actually practised law; two of them were related to President Obiang. All of the court proceedings were in Spanish – and were either translated badly, or not translated at all. Nick and all his co-accused had enjoyed, in total, less than an hour with their defence lawyer – who was not allowed to offer his clients advice in court. It looked like a foregone conclusion. And then it stopped.

On 25 August, Mark Thatcher was arrested at his luxury home in Cape Town. The media went into a feeding frenzy, and the Equatoguinean Government postponed Nick's trial while they sought to gather new evidence and attempt to extradite Thatcher. It looked like a reprieve of sorts. The day after, bank details were leaked showing a payment of $135,000 into Simon's Logo Logistics bank account four days before the March attempt crash-landed: it was from one J.H. Archer. Journalists couldn't believe their luck. Jeffrey Archer's lawyers said that the disgraced Tory peer 'had no prior knowledge' of the coup, and that Archer had 'never issued a cheque in the sums mentioned' – neatly sidestepping the fact that the money was paid in by credit transfer. When pressed on that point, Archer replied that he considered 'the matter closed'.

The story ran and ran. Greg Wales – one of the men on the Canaries with Severo Moto – admitted to several meetings with Simon Mann and Mark Thatcher prior to everyone's arrest. Gary Hersham, a British businessman who introduced Simon to Ely Calil, denied any knowledge of the plot though he accepted that he had travelled to Gabon in West Africa with Simon and Greg Wales.

Two days after Thatcher had been arrested, the two men detained with Simon in Harare – Harry Carlse and Lourens Horn – were acquitted and released. It was expected that they would have to co-operate with the Scorpions once home to avoid a custodial sentence under South Africa's anti-mercenary laws. On 10 September, Simon was sentenced to seven years in Chikurubi maximum security prison. Errol and the other men got a year apiece, having finally been convicted for breaking immigration laws by entering Zimbabwe illegally on the Boeing 727.

Before we left to begin filming, I had one last appointment – in the Commonwealth Club on Northumberland Avenue, at the other end of the Mall from Buckingham Palace. A journalist friend who had been busy unearthing the details of the coup plot for the national press had invited me to meet Nigel Morgan – a close friend of both Simon Mann and Mark Thatcher. Morgan had been named by Simon in a letter he'd written from jail asking for help, the same letter that fingered 'Smelly' and 'Scratcher'. He was reported to be deeply implicated in the whole affair – though in what exact capacity was unclear. He was rumoured by the press to be a go-between, linking all the key players of the coup plot with commercial interests and national intelligence agencies. His personal agenda was anyone's guess.

As we walked along the wet autumn pavement, I asked my friend who Nigel worked for.

'Well, that's a good question. He's independent, a commercial intelligence freelancer. He prepared a file about the coup for a big oil company, and I don't think it would be a stretch to say he has quite a cosy relationship with the South Africans.'

We got the to door of the club and stepped into the brightly lit interior.

'Basically, he's a spook?' I asked.

'Yes, basically, but I'm not sure how formal the connection is – definitely an asset, not an agent. He's quite the bon viveur, by the way. His detractors call him Captain Pig,' he smiled at me, 'and Nosher.'

We found Morgan – a ruddy-faced man in a Savile Row suit – nursing a gin and tonic upstairs. A genial former officer in the Irish Guards, he looked like he might every bit live up to his mischievous monikers.

'Ah, James,' he greeted me as we shook hands – him seated on a low couch, me towering above him still wrapped in a fleece and leather jacket – 'good to meet you.'

I sat down next to him and ordered drinks while he dug around in his attaché case for a thick file of papers. He turned back one page of type, briefly showing me the short lines of typed dialogue. The printed black letters revealed details of private telephone conversations I'd had with Nick.

He folded the paper away carefully before I could fully scrutinise its contents. Sitting back, he raised his glass in welcome, and smiled.

'You had a very lucky escape, young man.'

16
LAWYERS, GUNS AND MONEY

I pushed open the door to Nick's office and clicked on the light. The Regimental plaque of 5 Reconnaissance Regiment hung on the wall; a laminated world map covered the desk in front of his computer; filing cabinets jostled for space by the door. I sat down in his chair. Open on the desk was the notebook he'd carried through Liberia, covered in the familiar slanted scrawl of his handwriting. I picked it up like a relic, and leafed through it. Here and there my name appeared, or some detail of our plans. I put it down and felt a terrible sadness. To see the names of the people we'd worked with – Frank and Cobus and Tim – and the names of the towns and villages we'd tramped through and nearly died in brought his absence into sharp relief. It deepened my resolve to find out what Nick had really been up to – whether he had decided to go ahead with the operation, and why. I also hoped to unravel the implications of the arms deal in Zimbabwe. Perhaps, I thought, I might even find something so valuable to Obiang that it might be traded with his henchmen to save Nick.

It was clear from even a cursory glance through his files that what Nick had been up to, primarily, was making money – or at least trying to. Email correspondence between Nick and Simon charted how the businesses that Nick had begun in Equatorial Guinea were rapidly expanding – along with their budgets. By October 2003, Nick's monthly operating budget was just shy of $30,000, including his salary of $5,000 a month. Not a fortune, but nice work if you can get it. By the end of January 2004, that budget had jumped to more than $80,000.

The company they had set up on 25 August 2003 as a vehicle for their investments in Equatorial Guinea – Triple Option Trading – was operating as a genuine and viable business concern, as well as a front-organisation for the coup. Statements showed that Simon's bank accounts were paying for it. The branch of the company incorporated in Equatorial Guinea did so as a joint venture with Armengol, the president's brother, who apparently signed up in good faith, ignorant of their plans.

There were thousands of sheets of paper chronicling Nick's business plans – dozens of files to read and digest. In among all the breakdowns of day-to-day running costs and emails about getting different projects up and running, details about high-value items indispensable to regime change caught my eye.

On 5 February 2004, the company belonging to Gerhard Merz – the German later tortured to death – invoiced Triple Option to the tune of $124,000 for the Antonov and Ilyushin cargo planes and crews; six days later, a $20,000 invoice for 'local cars' was raised. With ground and air transportation for the men arranged, the first coup attempt was launched eight days later. The invoice was marked 'Simon AC Monthly' in Nick's handwriting. On 1 December 2003, Simon guaranteed Nick $2 million for Triple Option Trading. Between 5 January and 2 March, Nick's company received a total of $220,000 from Simon's companies: Nick was in too deep to bail out.

* * *

'I'm surprised you're still alive.'

Nick's business partner, Henri van der Westhuizen, sat across the table from me at Nino's coffee bar in Centurion, a small town outside the eastern suburbs of Pretoria. Named in Simon's confession as the man that Nick had first turned to for weapons, I had contacted Henri as soon as I arrived in South Africa. If anyone could help piece together the puzzle of the coup, it was him. A small man with dark wavy hair and a quick, nervous smile, Henri didn't look like an assassin – though that's what he once had been. He still talked like one, though. His welcome note had been delivered before I'd even managed to sit down.

Research in London had turned up some of the details of Henri's past. The evidence he gave at the Truth and Reconciliation Commission – an amnesty-granting body set up by Mandela's government to oversee a national process of inquiry and healing – was a matter of public record. Henri was a member of the Civil Cooperation Bureau – the South African Army's death squad that was run out of Special Forces headquarters.

Henri was responsible for blowing up the same ANC legal activist in Maputo whose attempted assassination had put George Alerson (now in jail with Nick) behind bars in Mozambique. He also helped establish a target-development group that worked closely with the apartheid government's Counter-revolutionary Intelligence Target Centre. They decided which ANC activists should be assassinated, and provided the information necessary to make sure they were eliminated – often by covert military action undertaken by, amongst other units, Reconnaissance Commandos. Henri was granted amnesty not only for the bombings, but also for gun-running into South Africa's black Ciskei homeland, where he admitted helping to facilitate a coup d'état.

He seemed so mild-mannered and approachable that it was hard to connect the words he spoke with the relaxed countenance he projected.

'Really?' I asked him. 'Is it dangerous for me to investigate this?'

He beckoned over a waitress and looked at me blankly.

'Yes, it is. Look, you might be all right. Nick is very respected, and it's well known what you two went through in Liberia together . . .' He paused to make sure I was following what he said. 'But if you dig deep enough, you're going to start upsetting people. Some of these people are powerful people, and they'll protect their interests.'

Had anyone else warned me, I would have shrugged it off: but target-identification had been Henri's stock-in-trade. If there was one thing he knew about, it was bumping people off. I was fairly sure that he was helping me, and not threatening me.

The waitress took our order for coffee and pastries and sauntered back to the till.

'Is there anyone in particular I need to worry about?'

'No, not a named individual.' His face was impassive. Then he removed his brown leather jacket and leaned over the table. 'Just be careful. I'll do what I can to assist you. Now, what was it that you wanted to know?'

'Well, at the risk of pissing people off that I really don't want to piss off, what I'm trying to work out is exactly what Nick did have planned – and why.'

I confided that doing an arms deal in Zimbabwe had baffled me.

Henri began to talk.

He confirmed that the initial plan, outlined by Nick to me in May, had been to use Guinea Conakry as the launch pad for the operation – the men were to have been trained there and then depart for Equatorial Guinea by ship. When the plan changed, Simon Mann had approached Henri through Nick in January 2004 and asked him to procure the weapons for the coup. A deadline of

23 February was insisted upon because the operation had to be completed before the Spanish general election in March – though why this has been so important, Henri had at the time not been certain. Henri and Nick then travelled to Uganda to source the guns from their old contact in Kampala, but the deal fell through – one of the key players, a senior Ugandan army commander, was unavailable – and the pair returned empty-handed. Simon lost his temper at the news, and Henri walked. From that point, he claimed, he had nothing more to do with the operation.

'Nick had about one month to turn it around. But it wasn't possible to guarantee. Even the weather, anything, could have delayed it. You just can't guarantee that sort of deal in that time frame.'

The deal transferred to Zimbabwe Defence Industries.

As the date for the coup drew nearer, Nick had confided his fears in Henri.

'Nick realised he was in shit, and asked me to go to the Scorpions.'

The Scorpions were a sort of South African FBI, with a reputation for fearless investigations into organised crime and corruption.

'He wanted to talk to the Scorpions about the coup?' I asked. 'What, to get their blessing?'

'Yes. He knew the operation was a fuck-up.'

Henri said he tried to arrange a meeting on Nick's behalf, but it didn't work out. Time ran short and Henri went alone for a meeting with Bulelani Ngcuka, the National Director of Public Prosecutions, on 18 February – the day before the first coup attempt.

I stared at Henri across the table. It was an extraordinary admission. Ngcuka had helped to establish the Scorpions and was closely linked to South Africa's president, Thabo Mbeki. Ngcuka's wife, Phumzile, had been made Minister of Minerals and

Energy in 1999. It was a position that would have made Ngcuka particularly interested in the political stability of Equatorial Guinea – Africa's third-largest oil producer.

'What did they say? I mean, what could they say?'

I was incredulous. Nick had asked that Henri elaborate on the plan to the country's top investigator, knowing, in all likelihood, that it would have been passed to the president himself.

'They clearly knew about the operation already. They didn't ask a single pertinent question. They didn't say if they agreed or not – in fact, they hardly spoke. I was asked to find out more information about the UK angle – Simon Mann and the backers. We agreed they should be investigated.'

Henri felt that by not saying 'no', the Scorpions had given their tacit support. He inferred that it was the backers who were in the Government's sights – and that Nick likely wouldn't face any problems if he went ahead.

Henri's revelation raised serious questions: if the Scorpions already knew about it, who told them – and who else knew? The answer was, apparently, quite a lot of people.

'I knew that intelligence reports were being made on Simon's activities,' Henri told me.

An apartheid-era intelligence operative and freelance spook called Johann Smit had compiled a comprehensive and accurate dossier on Nick and Simon's activities at the end of 2003, and passed it to the Equatoguineans, the South Africans, the British and the Americans.

'I asked Simon if he was aware that he was probably being monitored,' Henri continued. 'He told me he had everything covered – that Nigel Morgan, his contact with the South African Secret Service, was providing him with all the intelligence reports.'

Nigel, whom I'd met only ten days before in London, denied this. Nevertheless he apparently had a central role to play. It was, Henri said, well known in intelligence circles that Nigel Morgan worked for the South African Secret Service – and that he and Johann Smit had once been business partners. The South African Government could have known about the plot for months – which would explain why details of my conversations were recorded in Morgan's files.

The coup, Henri laughed, had even been discussed at a meeting in Chatham House – when a South African national working for Shell in corporate affairs (who was also apparently close to Mbeki) had warned that a mercenary invasion was imminent.

There was one last thing I needed to know from Henri. Had Nick tried to back out?

'I was surprised when he did the ZDI deal. I was strongly under the impression that he wanted to concentrate on the legitimate businesses he'd set up in Equatorial Guinea. He told me that he'd handed over all military planning to Harry Carlse and wanted to walk away from the whole thing – but Simon told him that they couldn't back out because the "investors" wouldn't allow it. All I can tell you is that three weeks before the operation in March, Nick had no idea where any of the key targets were, including President Obiang. You know Nick. Would he really have gone ahead on that basis?'

As we finished our coffee, I asked him about his time in the military. He was, he said, fortunate to have had excellent colleagues to work with. A good friend during his career in military intelligence had been a police colonel called Eugene de Kock – whom Henri described as his mentor.

'Yes, I see the colonel regularly. I still visit him in prison.'

Dubbed as 'Prime Evil' by the South African press, de Kock was serving a 212-year prison sentence for a string of murders.

Henri and I shook hands and agreed to meet again shortly. I left and briefed Carla, the director of the film we were making, who'd been patiently waiting in the car park. On camera, I repeated what Henri had told me. The meeting disturbed me – not just because of the weight of the information Henri imparted, but because of the window it opened onto a world I knew very little about. Nick had been, to me, the model of a professional soldier: despite killing in the service of apartheid, he had been a fighter, and not a murderer. The blood he'd shed had been on the battlefield, not in people's living rooms. 'We were very professional Special Forces,' he always told me, 'we never did anything wrong.' But the men who served in the Civil Cooperation Bureau and the men who fought for Special Forces were inextricably linked, part of the same apartheid-state machinery.

Everything I knew about Nick led me to believe that, although he may have been with them, he was not one of them: because his conscience was clear, I had naïvely thought that mine could be, too. After all, he had never been called to account for his time in the military by the Truth and Reconciliation Commission. Yet the more I learned about the plot, and Nick's role in it, the less certain I could be of his intentions. What did it say about him that one of his closest friends was mentored by Eugene de Kock? If it was the case that a man can be judged by the company he keeps, then we might both have some tough questions to answer.

Three days later I re-connected with Dries. It was time to call in his offer to see Simon's letters. Carla and I sat around a table in a bland lawyer's meeting room with him and an attorney called Bernhard van der Hoven. Van der Hoven opened a file, and Dries spread out a collage of pages torn from *National Geographic* magazines and notebooks. They were covered with Simon Mann's unmistakable handwriting. Carla and I looked at each other. I reached out my hand, and then checked myself.

'May I?'

'Yes, James. You can read them all,' Dries agreed – his wide-open face beaming at us from across the narrow table.

The scrap-book of pages consisted of more than a dozen letters addressed by Simon to a variety of recipients.

'Do you mind if we take notes?' Carla asked. Again, the answer was yes. 'Okay,' she continued, looking at me now, 'you read them and point out the bits we need, and I'll copy them down. You know what we're looking for.'

I dived in, and Carla began scribbling shorthand.

On top of the pile was an undated page in Simon's writing that explained the code names employed in the correspondence. The first part read:

Code *Scratchy is Mark Thatcher* *Gazza*

Smelly = EC *Gary Hersham*

Among the cache were the 'Wonga' and 'Smelly' and 'Scratcher' letters that had already been leaked to the press. These letters indicated that, in order to finance the coup, Simon had approached different private investors to stump up lump sums around the $200,000 mark – presumably with the expectation of large returns at a later date. Most of the letters, though, had not been seen before.

On 21 March, he asked his correspondent, Timothy Robarts (who was not asked to finance the coup), to act as a lender-of-last-resort to his wife Amanda – Simon apparently had no idea how much in the way of ready funds was at her disposal – guaranteeing any loan with his word as a gentleman. 'The first 5 days were very bad & not "Geneva Convention",' he'd written, 'but we are OK and safe for the moment . . . What I was trying to do was RIGHT and the cause JUST. There is a lot of rubbish about mercenaries. At least, mercenaries are meant to fight for something they do not care about and get paid. We were trying very hard NOT to fight in a cause we did care about, and in which I have spent far too much of my own money!'

Money, and the moral justification of his actions, featured highly in much of the correspondence. Couched in the same terms of the means excusing the ends that I had used when convincing myself to say yes to Nick's proposal, it was uncomfortable to read Simon's self-justifications. Also on the 21st, he'd written to his financial assistant James Kershaw – by then turned state witness – saying that 'Your pay can be justified by me alone if you take Hansard and Co. [the trust that oversaw Simon's various financial entities] out of the loop. I hear NM [Nigel Morgan] is helping you manage all of this but you work for me. Do not allow any editing or redirecting of any of these communications.' In a different letter he urges that Kershaw 'should be pushing funds out of project accounts and into our personal account'. 'JK has full power of attorney over all money etc,' he writes. 'He has the £ masterplan from my trusts and co. and the £ masterplan for this project.'

He asked that the letters be seen, initialled and returned to him. In that last respect, at the very least, Simon's wishes had clearly been ignored. On a letter dated 19 March – in which he says he's 'just had a strange interview with the Angolans!!' – Mark Thatcher's email address was written with the postscript: 'Mark – please forward this to Nigel – Please can you help us.' In a separate missive, Simon writes Ely Calil's email address out, and then next to it prints the message: 'E – I am depending on you and trusting you to help us now.' He also asks that Kershaw 'should send the signed Logo/Panac [aviation] contract to Smelly'.

Much of the material was unnervingly direct – and some of it too intimate to describe.

The penultimate letter that Dries showed us apparently nailed the issue of why he and Nick had been so rushed at the beginning of the year. To an undisclosed recipient Simon wrote that 'You should be aware of a meeting at Smelly's Gaff with Smelly, K and Gazza Sunday 23 Feb? At that meeting they said they could only come up with 500 not the 1000 that I had asked for.' 'After some debate, out of desperation,' he continued, 'I asked Smelly if I raised $ or a straight personal loan from a third party [whether it] would be underwritten.' Simon was apparently reassured that 'he would pay me back for sure'.

'We only got the money in time to start real work on 6 January with 16 February set as a deadline – & that after all the stop starts,' Simon complains to the addressee. 'Smelly must take a big chunk of the blame himself. All of last year he messed around with the £. You know that. Smelly ensured that we never had both the time and the £.'

'Smelly' was Ely Calil, the Lebanese oil tycoon; 'Gazza' was Gary Hersham, the British businessman who, also according to Simon's confession, had introduced Simon to Calil in early 2003. There was nothing to suggest that Hersham was involved beyond allegedly being present at the meeting; there was also no indication of where the money originally came from, or proof of what, specifically, Calil thought Simon might be doing with it. Both men denied fundraising for a coup.

As I ploughed through Simon's tatty pile of desperate pleas for help, recriminations and justifications, Nick's name was conspicuous by its absence. In one of the letters, Simon found the space and time to recount a long joke about public schoolboys, but not once does he enquire after Nick's – or the other Equatorial Guinea detainees' – circumstances, treatment or prospects. Now the game was up, it was every man for himself.

Dries gathered up the ragged pages, and then slid black-and-white photocopies of some of the letters across the table to us.

'You asked for some copies.'

'Thanks,' I said, and then asked: 'Who has seen these? I mean all of the ones we've seen, not just these photocopies?'

'Billy Masetlha, the president's national security adviser, has a set of bad copies. Rachel Gaskin has a full set of colour copies and these are the originals. That's it.'

Carla and I took notes as he talked us through it. Gaskin, an American lawyer, was a confidant of the Mann family. Masetlha was South Africa's domestic spy chief.

'And why have you got them, Dries?' Carla wanted to know.

'To keep them safe, and to help the guys in Zim – and to help Nick and them up in EG.'

At this point Dries spelled out his demands. The cost of the lawyer in Zimbabwe was apparently 81,643 South African rand; the Equatoguinean lawyer 30,000 rand; and Dries's personal travel costs so far a further 35,000 rand.

Carla and I looked at him with a mixture of disbelief and grudging respect: he was, if nothing else, straightforward.

'We'll get back to you,' Carla pronounced, finishing the meeting. 'Thanks for your time.'

They shook hands politely over the table. Van der Hoven showed us out. Safely back in Nick's silver BMW, she turned to me as I turned over the ignition.

'What did you make of that?'

'Well,' I said, 'call me old-fashioned, but when people demand cash like that, they should at least have the decency to point a gun at you.'

I looked out the front window, at the door to the office block.

'Fuck it. Let's buy 'em.'

Back at Nick's house I sifted through photocopies and printouts that I had been collecting. Documents had recently surfaced in London and Pretoria that Nick himself would not have seen. They seemed to fill out the financial support – and expected returns – of the coup in specific detail.

The main promise of funding for Simon seemed to come from a group of Lebanese investors at the Beirut-registered Asian Trading and Investment Group SAL. Karim Fallaha, who had accompanied Greg Wales and Severo Moto on the Canary Islands, was a director. In a contract signed by Simon on 19 November 2003, they agreed to invest $5 million into Logo Logistics Limited not for a coup but for projects in 'mining exploration . . . aviation (cargo and PAX), helicopter charter and commercial security in the following countries: Guinea Republic, Sierra Leone, Liberia and Angola'. In return for their largesse, the Lebanese consortium required a 50 per cent interest payment immediately on the realisation of the 'totality of the projects'.

Two contracts dated 22 July 2003 had already come to light, drawn up between Severo Moto, who does not sign them, and 'Captain F' – Captain Simon Francis Mann's regime-changing pseudonym – who does. The first contract makes provision for Simon and three other conspirators (to be named by him) to be paid $1 million. That was also how much Nick was in for – how much he said he'd been promised in his confession in Equatorial Guinea. Six mercenary officers would get $50,000, and the 'seventy-five' foot-soldiers $25,000 each. His demands added up to more than $7 million. For both himself and his guns-for-hire, he insisted on immunity from prosecution and Equatoguinean citizenship. He also employed an old mercenary trick, and stipulated that the plotters would be responsible for providing Moto's presidential guard – thereby controlling the person of the president himself.

I began to understand why Nick had asked Henri to go to the Scorpions – the people who would have prosecuted Nick if he was arrested in South Africa. With investments being made on such a massive scale, and with no idea of the location of the key Government players he was supposed to kill or capture, it was no wonder Nick had sought reassurance. He knew from Henri that the South African Intelligence services were aware of the operation, and possibly even involved in it: if they wanted him to back off, he would have done. His economic future on the island was set – coup or no coup. The only thing that could jeopardise it was a botched coup.

In the second contract to come to light, Captain F goes for gold. Marked 'confidential' – possibly hidden even from the other freebooters themselves – the formally typed wish-list demands $15 million within two months of Moto being installed. Other clauses and demands showed that Simon sought to control all of Equatorial Guinea's security, intelligence and procurement requirements. Not only did he want to control the security forces, he wanted to make sure the plotters were the only ones allowed to profit from equipping them. As well as taking up diplomatic passports (as Nick had described to me in Conakry), the contract demanded the right for the conspirators to oversee the return of hundreds upon hundreds of millions of dollars (minus a commission) that Obiang had squirrelled away in off-shore bank accounts.

Two other pieces of coup literature purported to shed further light on the plotters' intentions. 'Assisted Regime Change', dated the same day as the Captain F contracts, examines how Equatorial Guinea might be run after the coup. The blueprint for the aftermath of the putsch recommended shutting down all international communications and enlisting journalists and businessmen as part of a concentrated campaign to ensure the new government was legitimised and recognised internationally as quickly as possible. In order to boost their credibility, the plotters intended to announce wide-ranging social and economic reforms, whilst ensuring that the foreign oil companies on whom they would rely for continued revenue were not alienated in any way.

The second political document, entitled 'Bight of Benin Company', was apparently drawn up in January 2004 – at about the time when Nick was trying (and failing) to get weapons from Uganda, and expressing his reservations about the wisdom of the operation to me. A version of the Bight of Benin briefing had turned up in Simon's office in South Africa. The author warns that the main problem faced by the plotters is the threat arising from 'bad behaviour; disloyalty; rampant individual greed; irrational behaviour; back-stabbing; bum-fucking and similar ungentlemanly activities' within the conspirators' own ranks. Mark Thatcher's involvement, for example, was to be kept strictly confidential.

The problem of how to deal with Moto once he was in charge was also an issue, as was the role of the United States Government and, in particular, the Nigerians – who, it was feared, may have invaded Equatorial Guinea to reduce it to 'vassal status'. Intriguingly, tied into the perceived threat from Nigeria, one of the plotters' apparent main concerns expressed in the document was the risk that 'E.K.' (presumably Ely Calil – sometimes spelled 'Khalil') himself might pose to their plans. If Calil was the funder and instigator of the operation that Simon had planned, it would have been reasonable to expect that they were all singing from the same hymn sheet. Not so. The author of this briefing fears that Calil may have ulterior motives and, apart from possibly being 'part of the usual Lebo conspiracy (which will involve money-laundering, diamond trading, etc) creating problems with the outside world', he might ultimately be working for 'the Nigerians or a faction of them, a possible view being to destabilise EG, grab some of its oil acreage; [and] shift a lot of oil revenue to Nig'.

The other threat the plotters had identified was Nick. It was feared he 'may be working for, or now or later may be bought, pressurised or threatened by Obiang'. They also worried that he 'may have his own plan'. The ways by which to limit

Nick's powers were laid out starkly: Triple Option Trading's contracts were all to be routed through a company controlled by the conspirators, and the mercenaries and security contractors employed after the 'event' should be of the plotters' choosing – not Nick's. It seemed inevitable that Nick would have known the other plotters' propensity for back-stabbing: although he stood to gain a million dollars from facilitating the coup in Malabo, his legitimate contracts were likely on course to earn him that much, anyway. What I could only guess at was whether Nick realised that they thought he might actually be working with Obiang.

When we'd sat and first discussed the coup in Conakry fifteen months before, I'd imagined the be-all and end-all of it as a dramatic fire-fight and emblematic victory parade; I'd imagined breaking the story and, later, exposing the inner workings of the operation. What I hadn't imagined was the sheer scale of what Simon had been planning. I doubted that Nick knew, either. Turning Equatorial Guinea into 'the Switzerland of Africa' and removing a despicable tyrant from office seemed, on the face of it, like a reasonable, and possibly even justifiable, objective – even if a few foreigners made some money in the process. What was not reasonable, and certainly not moral, was the hegemony that the plotters' manifesto sought to visit upon the country. By forming a company to run Equatorial Guinea, in much the same way as the British had initially ruled India through the aegis of the East India Company, what the conspirators sought to achieve was the straightforward contractual control of an independent nation-state. They didn't want to remove Obiang and install Moto – they actually wanted to own Equatorial Guinea outright. The language of their document is casually racist; their agenda explicitly colonial. Simon may have pleaded in his confession that he was trying to help the 'cause' of the 'good and honest' Severo Moto – but his plan was, at root, dishonest and avaricious.

Despite the clarity with which these documents exposed the moral bankruptcy of the plotters, my natural objections to the real intentions of the operation did not lead me to condemn Nick himself. It did seem unlikely that he would have known any of the detail in the new documents that had been unearthed: indeed, the plotters clearly distrusted him, and planned to move against him, too. Moreover, my friendship with Nick had profoundly compromised my personal judgement in relation to the coup – to the extent that my fears in London had been correct: in the face of Nick's possible death sentence, it was, as a journalist, simply not possible for me to be objective or impartial.

It was time for Carla and I to broaden the story. In the third week of October 2004, seven months after Simon had been arrested, I touched down at Harare International Airport. It was the first time I'd been back to Zimbabwe since working there as a news producer covering the 2001 presidential election for the BBC. I wanted to see if following Nick's trail shed any light on why, and how, the operation had been compromised.

As the plane turned into its parking stand, the mercenaries' stranded Boeing 727 swung into view on the apron. The sight of the dirty white fuselage made my stomach contract. Just being collared as an unaccredited journalist carried a two-year jail term there. If the authorities linked me to Simon, I could expect much worse.

We decided to start by visiting Dumisani Muleya, one of the few independent journalists still working in Zimbabwe. He claimed to have the inside scoop on the arms deal. In the shadow of the ruling party's headquarters, we sat down in a stuffy conference room in the building where he tried to continue reporting the news. He was hanging on by his fingertips: earlier that year he'd been arrested and charged with criminal defamation – his reward for doing his job, and for angering the Government. Whatever strictures I operated under, Muleya's were much more severe.

'Good afternoon,' he greeted us, as Carla unpacked the camera from an innocuous shopping bag. 'I think you've made it without any problems so far. That's a good start.'

We shook hands and briefly lamented the weather – despite the sweltering heat, he was smartly turned out for the camera, in a shirt and tie – before he fanned a folio of signed ZDI contracts across the end of the board table to which we'd drawn up our chairs.

Nick had intended for his men to be well equipped. Annotated in his characteristic calligraphy, the paperwork that Carla was busy filming did not hint at political manoeuvrings in public-school slang – it spoke of cold, military facts. The mercenaries would have been hitting Equatorial Guinea with an impressive arsenal that comprised ten Browning 9mm pistols; sixty-one AK-47s; twenty PKM belt-fed machine guns; ten rocket-propelled grenade launchers; two 60mm mortars; one hundred and fifty offensive hand grenades; and twenty flares. In addition, Nick had requested more than 75,000 rounds of ammunition, eighty mortar bombs and a hundred rocket-propelled grenade warheads.

The total cost of the Equatorial Guinea coup weapons was fractionally over $80,000 – and they weighed in at more than four metric tons. At the top of the quotation, Nick had written the name of the registration of the cargo plane that would make the pick-up from Equatorial Guinea (AN12 EK-11351) and the name of the hapless Armenian pilot, Captain Ashot Karapetyan, who had ended up in Black Beach prison with Nick. The second order – signed by Nick alone – was for six tons of ammunition and rocket-propelled grenades. Destined for the rebels in Congo's Katanga province, it cost more than $100,000.

I picked up the quotation for the rebels' ammunition.

'So Nick actually said, "We want these weapons to give to rebels in the Congo"?'

The criminality of Mugabe's regime notwithstanding, it was still breathtaking that the state-owned arms supplier would openly discuss arming dissident rebel groups.

'Yes,' Muleya replied, dabbing the sweat from his high forehead.

That, according to him, had been when the problems started.

'Simon Mann mentioned a different reason, which was "We're going to protect a mine."'

Nick, meanwhile, had mentioned the rebels, which apparently made the Government very uncomfortable. I looked at the paperwork carefully, and asked if the problem was the Congo rebels *per se*, or just that they hadn't stuck to the same story. It was, he insisted, the Katanga connection.

'Nick apparently thought that it would not matter, that they didn't care what the weapons were used for. He underestimated the possible negative reaction from the Government in Zimbabwe.'

Heavily involved in extremely profitable mining operations in the Congo – where their troops had been deployed after intervening in Congo's civil war – the Zimbabwean Government relied increasingly on profiteering in Congo. What they needed in order to keep a steady flow of diamonds, timber and gold pouring south was a friendly regime in Kinshasa, the capital, and stability in the jungle – not a rebel insurgency that would threaten both. Robert Mugabe and Joseph Kabila (the president of Congo) were close allies. Colonel Dube, the head of ZDI, would, as a matter of routine, Muleya told me, report his deals directly to the Zimbabwe Central Intelligence Organisation. It seemed to Muleya that the chances of the CIO signing off on supplying the enemies of Mugabe's own best Congolese friend were remote in the extreme. So either Nick had made a serious miscalculation in sourcing bullets for the rebels through ZDI, or he had pulled it off against the odds and struck a private deal with Colonel Dube, guaranteeing the ZDI chief's silence with the valuable intelligence rewards the Katangese job promised.

We shook hands and made arrangements for the paperwork to be shipped to London discreetly. Muleya slipped back to his bureau and Carla and I drove across town. I had a letter to deliver, and wanted to hand it over as quickly as possible.

Simon's lawyer, Jonathan Samukange, didn't ask to see our press passes as we filed into his office in downtown Harare. Immaculately turned out in smart trousers buckled with a gold clasp and an open-necked shirt that revealed a gold chain, Samukange was a small, charismatic man who spoke in flamboyantly accented Zimbabwean English. He warmed to the camera immediately – adjusting his cufflinks and leaning back in his chair. Rebels in Katanga were, he believed, the cause of everyone's downfall.

'If Nick hadn't mentioned the DRC rebel movement,' I pressed him, 'do you think the deal would have gone ahead as planned?'

Turning to face me, Samukange, too, laid the blame for Simon's arrest squarely on Nick's shoulders.

'Yes. Yes,' he replied, underlining his certainty with short, sharp nods of the head. 'The only unfortunate statement which he made was that he said, "I'm going to supply the rebels in the DRC." The arrest was never designed, and this is on record, an affidavit,' he continued, wagging his right finger at me, 'it was *never* designed to stop them going to Equatorial Guinea.'

By now he was rocking from side to side, both index fingers aimed at me like the barrels of fleshy brown six-guns.

'It was to stop them from supplying rebels in DRC.'

'So Nick du Toit was to blame for the operation not succeeding?'

'Yes, definitely, definitely. Yes, definitely. If he had not issued that statement, Simon Mann would not be sitting in Chikurubi.'

I was still unconvinced. The governments in Harare and Malabo had both publicly credited the South Africans with the tip-off that led to Simon and Nick's buccaneers being busted: whether that was genuine gratitude, or part of a pre-arranged script, was impossible to tell. I changed the subject and asked Samukange what Simon's chances were of an early release. He thought it was possible. Then I handed him the letter.

'Do you think that you would be able to deliver this to Simon, please? It's not signed, as such, but he'll know who it's from.'

The six sides of writing paper set out the current state of affairs, namely: that the Equatoguinean Government's civil case against Simon and the other plotters looked doomed to fail; that Crause Steyl, the pilot who was to have flown Severo Moto, Greg Wales and the others gathered in the Canary Islands into Malabo, had struck a plea bargain with the Scorpions; and that, in Black Beach, Nick was getting the shit kicked out of him. In the final paragraph I asked if there was any message Simon wanted to convey to the outside world. Samukange agreed that he would see it into Simon's hands – and suggested I call back in a few days to hear his response.

As Carla and I drove back to the hotel, I added up the balance sheet of the investigation so far. I couldn't be certain that Nick had definitely planned to go ahead with the operation – but it seemed very likely that he had. Either he was bullied into it (unlikely), or, more plausibly, he figured it was a win/win situation: if the coup worked – he was made; if it didn't – he had hundreds of thousands of dollars' worth of investment into his businesses in Equatorial Guinea, which might end up being as profitable in the long run. The fact that he possessed no weapons, and no incriminating paperwork, meant he'd either seen no reason to run when Simon was arrested (quite possibly because he couldn't face losing his investments) or thought that trying to leave would look like an admission of guilt, and had stayed reluctantly.

The question now was: where did the information come from that led to the arrests? There was an array of possibilities. The Zimbabweans could have busted Simon all by themselves because they wanted to stop his Katanga project; then again, the Equatoguineans could have blown the whistle after rumbling Nick and connecting him to Simon. Alternatively, the South Africans may have tipped off the Zimbabweans, as many already believed. If the South Africans gave the nod to the Zimbabweans – which was most likely – the question in turn was: where had their information come from? Nick himself, Nigel Morgan, or another intelligence leak? The fact that the entire operation had been repeated sixteen days after the initial failure in Kolwezi gave plenty of scope for operational security to be breached at any number of points.

Despite the permutations, visiting Harare had left me with the bitter taste of an unpalatable possibility: Nick just might have fucked it up.

17
CONGO MERCENARY

I re-trod the footsteps of the coup-plotters around South Africa with Carla. In Pomfret, the scorching, asbestos-ridden town that many 32 Battalion fighters had ended up in, the families of the accused wanted Simon's scalp for getting their loved ones in trouble; in Cape Town, we filmed the luxury playground that Simon (and, indeed, some members of the Equatoguinean ruling family) called home; in Pretoria, we visited Wonderboom Airport, and found one of the DC-3s used in the 19 February operation still sitting outside the hangar of its owners: Dodson International Parts SA Limited.

In Nick's office, I fanned out more sheaves of paper across the floor and exhumed the evidence that he and Simon left buried in their correspondence. Carla was not there to film me; this was an unrecorded, private act. What I wanted was to hear Nick's voice; what I hoped to find was an explanation – something that would exonerate him from the growing accusations of incompetence. I was looking for details of other people involved in the plot – and something, anything, about the Congo operation.

Over the next few hours, as I trawled through hundreds of files and documents, I discovered three key facts. The first was that Ely Calil, the Lebanese businessman whom Simon had implicated in his confession and letters from jail, featured prominently in documents relating to Nick and Simon's project in Equatorial Guinea.

A thick blue folder named 'Toothpick', which Nick's wife said Simon had left in Nick's office one day, contained a handwritten compliments slip. It read: 'Simon, Best regards, Ely Calil.' There followed three emails dated 14 and 15 May 2003 under the subject heading, 'Thoughts re FP and EG'. In them, Simon presents Calil with two different options for a planned 'Fishery Protection' operation in Equatorial Guinea. In fact, the content of the emails concerns Nigeria, the oil industry and different ways of ultimately deploying mobile armed personnel into Equatorial Guinea's territorial waters. In two dense pages of type about the multi-million-dollar proposal, the word 'fish' does not appear once.

Simon proposes two options, including 'the immediate deployment of an off shore asset protection force . . . plus the immediate deployment of a Guard Ship . . . armed and manned with a Quick Reaction Force and a helicopter', and signs off with the question: 'What do you think?'

Calil's reply is short. He asks Simon to brief him on the Nigerians, and gives a one-line answer to Simon's question about the best way to go about securing a 'fishery protection' contract: 'I would go for Option 1: get our foot in the door and start proposing extras . . .' The correspondence ends with Simon reminding Calil that he'll be in Madrid on Sunday – and that he'll see him then.

Whatever the two men were really discussing, exactly two weeks after that email was sent Nick had sat with me in Conakry explaining how a force of international mercenaries would board a boat from Guinea Conakry and set sail for their African Switzerland, where the president wasn't playing ball with the oil companies. A month later, a few minutes before we met up with Simon, Nick had explained how they were now planning to try and get a helicopter gunship onto that boat, too.

The second key fact was that Guinea Conakry and Liberia were definitely intended to be used as bases from which to launch the coup designed to winkle President Obiang out of his palace. It also contained a letter of invitation for Simon to study a mining project from a company in Guinea Conakry, dated three weeks after his planned meeting in Madrid with Calil. On the same day, 8 June, Nick paid South African company Anscad Logistics for a large order of non-lethal military equipment (very similar to that found on the Boeing 727 in Harare) to be delivered to a company called TTK – also in Conakry. Then – on the day when General Cobra reached Tubmanburg with a fresh delivery of weapons by boat from Guinea, and Nick arrived back in Conakry – TTK issued three letters awarding Nick and Simon bogus mining-security contracts. Their purpose was to support Simon's application for a visa, and to facilitate the importation of military equipment.

Nick's 2003 diary dropped intriguing clues to the build-up to disaster. Under 'Goals for May' – which Nick had been filling out when he first told me about the coup in Conakry, and invited me to film it – was the initial list of weapons he wanted: machine guns; AKs; RPGs; mortars; and 80,000 rounds of ammo. The total cost was a shade under $50,000.

Elsewhere in his diary, neatly written out in vertical tables, was a list of code words for the Equatorial Guinea operation. It ran over one and a half pages. The weapons were listed as spare parts for a mechanical digger; uniforms as 'guards' clothing'; Nick was to be known as 'Diver' and Simon as 'Frank' – derived from his middle name, Francis; the Boeing 727 was the 'Truck'; pilots were to be referred to as 'mechanics' and the 'Force Personnel' as 'Dredgers'. I turned the page, and scanned the continuing list. There, sandwiched between 'Recce' and 'Entebbe Military Airport', was my name: code word – 'the Metallurgist'. It was the only time I had seen my name printed in black and white in plans for the coup drawn up by the plotters themselves. Now here I was, right in the middle of it. At first I laughed out loud at Nick's choice. But he understood my profession perfectly. Metallurgists fabricate alloys – giving hard metals new properties, making them easier to manipulate.

The third and final fact was the most significant of all. It concerned details that were buried in another file – marked 'Abu Baker'. Abu was Nick's man in Katanga – the rebel leader who had failed to secure the airstrip at Kolwezi. On 15 May 2003, Abu (as head of national and international affairs for an organisation called the PDD: Peace, Development and Democracy) signed a contract with Nick. In the contract, the PDD granted Nick 'the sole mandate to explore the minerals and manage the mines in the regions of Katanga Province' in return for supplying 'military and financial support' to the PDD. Attached to it was another typed list of code words headed 'Abu Kodes' – to be used during planned military action in the Congo connected to the 19 February Kolwezi attempt at the coup. A detailed trawl of the Internet returned not a single mention of the PDD rebels: they were completely unknown.

The file also contained hand-drawn maps of Congo, Katanga and the town of Lubumbashi (famous for its uranium mine). They were marked with military installations, suggested lines of attack and mining concessions. The overall effect was more *Boy's Own* than Special Forces: the handwriting (which was not Nick's) was urgent, in underscored block capitals, and in a mixture of French and English. All that was missing was an X to mark the spot.

I couldn't shake the feeling that Abu's role was somehow pivotal.

In the back of Nick's address book Abu's name was written apart from all the other numbers, next to that of an American colonel called Smith – Clarence D. Smith, Jr – the US defence and air attaché in Pretoria. Abu's connections and pretensions were impressive: the last code on the list, numbered thirteen, read 'I have malaria'. Its meaning was printed next to it: 'we took Kinshasa'. Nick wasn't talking to me: he was shouting.

Although documents and meetings were shedding light onto the details of the plot, what I wanted more than anything was to talk to someone directly involved in the last days of the operation. Everyone in any position of power in the plotters' hierarchy was either in jail or incognito – and likely to be there for a long time. Even if Simon did write back to me, he was hardly likely to give me the heads-up on Nick's last-minute motivations – not least because I suspected that communication between them had all but broken down as D-Day approached. Only one man was in a position to help me – the man reputed to have taken over military planning of the coup after the February disaster, and who accompanied Simon to Harare to collect the guns.

Former Recce operator, Executive Outcomes mercenary and notorious hard man Harry Carlse had been acquitted in Zimbabwe and was said to be co-operating reluctantly with the Scorpions to help mitigate the sentence he expected to be served at home in return for breaking South African anti-mercenary laws. He agreed to meet me.

He wasn't hard to find. In amongst the Tuesday morning coffee-drinkers and mums running shopping errands, Harry – a dark-haired ball of muscle – sat nursing a cup and saucer at a café in Menlyn shopping mall. Lourens 'Louwtjie' Horn, released from jail with him, was perched adjacent wearing a haunted expression that was immediately unnerving. We shook hands firmly, and sat down.

'It's good to meet you,' I said. 'I've heard a lot about you.'

He looked at me, as if hunting for clues of his own.

'I was in the jungle with Nick in Liberia,' I continued, in an effort to add a little credibility to the enquiries that we both knew were about to follow. 'He invited me along on the operation. Lucky escape, I guess.'

Harry nodded. He appeared, in fact, to be the hardest man I had ever met. *This,* I thought, *is who you'd been expecting two and a half years ago at that pool-side bar in Johannesburg.*

'What I'm trying to work out', I asked, after ordering coffee, 'is what Nick's motivations were. Why didn't he run as soon as you guys were arrested? He knew immediately, right? He spoke to Crause on the phone. It doesn't make sense to me.'

'I don't know why Nick didn't leave,' Harry replied.

His jaw, dark with stubble, worked around a thick Afrikaans accent. It would only be Harry talking. Horn, an ex-policeman, sat quietly next to him. Harry believed Nick was going to be connected to the guys in Zimbabwe – simply via his brother-in-law Errol Harris, who was on board.

'I wasn't happy about Errol being involved, either. That wasn't my idea.'

'I see. There seems to be some confusion about Nick's final motivations. It seemed as if he might have tried to walk—'

Harry cut me off.

'Nick was in.' He spoke quietly. The way he looked at me suggested that he and Nick may not have always seen eye to eye, but he leaned in over the table and spoke precisely and carefully. 'He was definitely in.'

'So what was the plan, then? To land the 727 in Malabo?'

Harry shifted back into his seat.

'Ag, I don't want to get into the detail of this.' He and Horn looked at each other. He seemed to be making his mind up about something. He relaxed, and turned back to me. 'The plan was to insert into Malabo airport at 0200.'

'On the morning of the eighth?'

'Ja. Louwtjie and I devised the plan. It was a good plan. It would have worked.'

I was relieved that Nick hadn't been involved in the planning of the Harare operation, and a tinge of guilt crept up on me for having assumed he'd been entirely responsible for the second attempt.

'And what about Kolwezi and Abu?' I quizzed Harry.

He shook his head and rocked back in his seat. He looked angry.

'The Abu Baker story is bullshit. I won't discuss Kolwezi. It was Nick's plan.'

I nodded, and waited.

'It was a fuck-up,' he continued. 'It should not have happened. The details of that will just get Nick into even worse trouble. The guys who went down to Kolwezi, to do the reconnaissance, they're in prison in Zim.'

Under different circumstances, Harry and I might have rendezvoused on a beach on the island of Bioko, or on the steps of that 727. The operation could have been a blood-bath.

'Okay.' I accepted that there were some issues he just wouldn't go into. 'You know, I really appreciate you talking to me. It's a delicate time – not many people are prepared to discuss it.'

Harry looked at Horn again and then pushed his empty cup away.

'We want to tell the story and expose those to blame. And we want our legal fees paid.'

'Those to blame for what, exactly?'

'We were told we had specific, named, high-level support in South Africa. We knew we were compromised prior to take-off, and we want to get the people who trapped us.'

I wondered what 'getting' them might entail. Harry was someone with whom you clearly did not fuck.

'I want to know what Johann Smit's role was—'

'He used to work with Nigel Morgan . . .' I interrupted.

'Nigel Morgan is an intelligence whore,' he declared. 'They sold us out.'

With that, he stood up and put out his hand. The meeting was over.

'Harry,' I asked, as they prepared to leave, 'what do you think's going to happen to Nick?'

He looked up at me, and grimaced.

'He's a dead man.'

The next day, Carla and I sat down in the breakfast café of the Sheraton Hotel in central Pretoria and waited for Billy Masetlha. Director-general of the NIA – the National Intelligence Agency – Masetlha was South Africa's top spy; he was also national security adviser to President Thabo Mbeki. He was not a fan of interviews, still less of television appearances. He was a real-life African 'M', and we couldn't believe that he had agreed to talk.

'So where do you want me to sit, chief?'

Good-natured, and carefully spoken, 'M''s soft voice wrapped itself around the word 'chief' with a gentle irony that left no uncertainty as to who was in charge. We pulled up chairs, Carla started filming and we began to talk. Interviewing spies – especially chief spies – is a bizarre event: what you want to know, they either won't or can't tell you, and what they do tell you is significant not just for the content of what you're being told, but by virtue of the fact that you're being told at all. The man who sits at the president's right hand does not open his mouth to the friend of a mercenary he's just helped to have arrested without calculating each syllable with absolute precision.

The motivation for stopping the coup, Masetlha began, was borne out of a South African desire to serve the wider interests of the continent.

'The people who were actually responsible for this current coup are non-Africans,' he reminded me, after I'd asked how he'd felt about seeing so many of his countrymen arrested. 'The question therefore arises, "What is Africa going to do about it?"'

To make those governments and those individuals responsible accountable for their actions, was what. No one, he believed, had a right to bring about regime change even in so-called tyrannical or oppressive regimes: aspiring leaders must be forced to go through democratic channels.

'Mercenaries used as liberators? It's a very interesting angle,' he scoffed.

This, though, was precisely what Masetlha – and his comrades in the armed wing of the ANC – had manifestly failed to do themselves when they took up arms against the tyrannical apartheid government. Once you were in power, it seemed, it was okay to have one law for yourself, and another for everyone thereafter – even if they were mercenaries.

So the backers of the plot were the true enemy. Nick, he maintained, was their victim: a willing victim, certainly, but a victim nonetheless. I thought of the stories that Nick had told me about the operations conducted against the men he called 'terrorists', men like Masetlha, whom almost everyone else called freedom fighters, and who had won – and more than once.

'It's reported,' I said, 'amongst the people involved, that shortly before undertaking this operation Simon Mann sought to reassure people by telling them that he firmly believed that he had backing from the South African Government.'

Masetlha's glasses reflected my silhouette in the bright, plate-glass windows behind my back. It was like looking into a fairground mirror.

'He's lying,' he insisted. 'This Government took the decision to liaise information with the Zimbabweans *months* ahead. This Government took the decision to liaise information with the Equatorial-Guineans *months* ahead. We were involved with them throughout until we gave them the detail.'

So they knew well in advance – even though they had reportedly left it until the eleventh hour before informing the Zimbabwean authorities of their imminent arrival. The question was *how* did they know? Masetlha believed that it was simply not plausible that Nick had made details of the plot available to the national prosecutor, and then slightly hedged his bets by stressing that no 'formal meeting' had taken place – which was, at least to the letter, correct.

Slowly, we edged towards what I wanted to know. I knew that Nick had asked Henri to arrange a meeting with the Scorpions. Had it been Nick's desire for reassurance that had compromised the operation? 'M' could see what I was pointing at – but didn't agree.

'We have information independent of all these people you are talking about – your Scorpions, your NPAs, your Nick du Toits – all that. Independent – which still flows to this day, that information. Independent – same sources, same capacity, same ability, same penetration. To this day.'

He waited for the implications of what he was saying to settle before he continued.

'Intelligence, not hard, prosecutory evidence, which we used to advise the governments concerned . . . We are certain, one hundred per cent certain, that that was the only source of information we had which we liaised with those governments that actually caused the arrest of these people . . . There was no information that was provided by Nick *at all* that was used.'

So according to Masetlha, Nick was off the hook as a grass, at least. I thought I'd push my luck a bit further.

'It's been rumoured in the South African and international media', I continued, 'that the National Intelligence Agency and the SASS comprehensively infiltrated the personnel involved in the operation. Is that something you can comment on?'

This, more than anything, was what Harry – along with all the other men arrested, I suspected – wanted to know: was it an insider who sold them out?

'No, I can't . . .'

We looked at each other, or rather, I looked at the silhouette of myself. Then he relented a little.

'All I can say is that we knew for a while what was going to happen, when it would happen, who was involved, why. That's the information we liaised with the governments concerned which resulted in the detention. . . . That information', he reiterated, 'was totally independent.'

There had, in fact, he said, been NIA agents among the men recruited – men who were still in jail, and who had been released; but, in the main, he was 'relying on one independent source inside the operation'.

The only emotion I felt was relief. Nick may have warned the Scorpions in a last-minute bid to protect himself – but he hadn't been responsible for the arrests of his men. The South Africans had known 'for months'. Indeed, the plotters seemed to know that, too. Harry had said that they knew they were compromised – but had gone ahead, anyway.

The implication of Masetlha's carefully worded answer about NIA infiltration was intriguing: only four men had so far been released from jail, and all of them from Zimbabwe. Two black foot-soldiers had been let go on medical grounds; Harry Carlse and Lourens Horn had both been acquitted – and were now, he claimed, helping with the prosecution against Mark Thatcher.

Masetlha seemed to be implying, though, that his main source of information had not been imprisoned at all. Simon's point-man with the South African Intelligence services was Nigel Morgan – and unless Simon had been talking to anyone else connected to the South African Intelligence services or Government, it was looking increasingly like it was Morgan, the red faced former British Intelligence officer, who was in the frame for the plotters' downfall.

There was one other thing I wanted to know from Billy Masetlha: what would Equatorial Guinea's neighbours have made of the putsch, had it succeeded?

'I mean,' I asked, 'can you imagine a scenario in which the Angolans and Nigerians would just have sat there and watched it happen?'

'Yes, they would do that.'

I wasn't sure I'd heard him right.

'They would?'

'Why not? Why not?' he asked. 'They would condemn it,' he smiled, concluding with the same calculation that the plotters themselves had arrived at, 'but you can't reinstate a president who is dead.'

There was one more place that I was keen to visit. I'd always been intrigued by the Hotel 224 – the down-at-heel hotel where most of the men who'd been arrested in Zimbabwe had last tasted freedom in South Africa. I didn't have far to go. Carla and I found it just around the corner from Masetlha's office. Whoever had the idea to billet more than fifty of Africa's hardest guns-for-hire for two weeks in a cheap hotel with a cheap bar minutes from the headquarters of the NIA was, it was fair to surmise, must have been convinced of their immunity from prosecution.

We, too, were coming to the end of our time in Pretoria. In the month I'd spent trying to piece together the narrative of the coup plot, I'd managed to establish that Nick was deeply involved up to the end. I'd also seen for myself that he and Simon were part of a huge international network of conspirators, colleagues and contacts in Equatorial Guinea, South Africa, Guinea, Liberia, Spain, Britain and America. It was also clear that the plot had been comprehensively penetrated by South African Intelligence, who had ensured it could not succeed. Finally, the fantastical details of the Katanga operation had come to life in Nick's study. Integral to the success of the plot, the hugely important figure of Abu Baker had also emerged slowly from the shadows.

What I had failed to do was unearth a single shred of evidence that could help Nick in jail. It was, I concluded, just not possible. His profound involvement was established beyond doubt. After key members of the operation gave lengthy legal statements in South Africa, there was nothing left to barter for his release.

It had also been impossible to unravel the role that Spain, Britain and America might have played in the operation – and exactly what the nature of Ely Calil's involvement was, though Simon apparently thought him a principal player and conduit for funding. Similarly opaque was Nigel Morgan's position: despite being accused by several sources of selling his friend Simon out to the South African authorities, he refused to go on the record and set the matter straight. The only thing about which he was clear was that it was men – not weapons – that had caused the final, inescapable, problem. Even though Nick's ZDI deal had almost certainly had been reported to the Zimbabwe Central Intelligence Organisation, it had not, after all, sounded the alarm: Nick had done too many deals there before, and Dube was too crooked, for the Katangese-rebel issue to raise suspicions. The Tuesday before the coup, the South Africans had sent a team to Malabo to brief Obiang's people; the final call had then been made to Mugabe only after the mercenaries' Boeing 727 had cleared South African airspace on the evening of 7 March.

As I sat in the bar of the Hotel 224, totting up the conclusions of our investigation, one curious fact posed more questions than all the others combined: despite all the leaks, compromises and betrayals, no attempt had been made to stop the operation on 19 February. But why not?

One explanation was that the people who wanted it stopped didn't know it was happening on that date. With the men going via Zambia, and the weapons reaching them in Kolwezi, there might have been enough confusion and deniability to make sure they had the space to get airborne.

'Even Masetlha', I reminded Carla, 'fudged his answer about the details of that first attempt.'

Whoever his sources were, though, it seemed unlikely that they would have been in the dark about the original schedule – the role that Katanga played in the coup, and the date they were due to fly, would have been known by many of the foot soldiers. Another possibility was that the Intelligence services had just screwed it up. Given the South African Secret Service's reputation for bungling and ineptitude, that was all too plausible. The most likely reason, however, that no action was taken was because the weapons had not been collected in Harare. If, as Maseltha claimed, the South African Government had wanted to teach the meddling Westerners a lesson, there was no incentive to move against Simon until he physically had his hands on the guns.

Whatever the answer the entire plan revolved around one man: not Nick, not Simon – but Abu. Nick had thought he'd been dealing with a Katangese rebel leader: but there was a sting in the tail.

'There's something you need to know,' I told Carla. 'Before we met Masetlha, Nick's wife told me that just after Nick was arrested, Abu telephoned her, trying to reach Nick. He said he could supply an alibi.'

She had put Abu in touch with a lawyer from the South African Special Forces League, who brokered a meeting between Abu and one of the Scorpions' top investigators, Piet van der Merwe. The following day Abu went in to see van der Merwe – who was running the Mark Thatcher investigation – in his office in Pretoria.

'So what happened to his testimony?' Carla asked.

'Well, it seems that, far from providing an alibi, Abu's entire story was – and this is according to the Scorpions – "bullshit".'

In one sense at least, Simon's lawyer in Zimbabwe had been correct that Nick's deal in Katanga had been the cause of everyone's downfall. The moment at which Abu and his rebels became the lynchpin on which the operation turned was the moment that the coup was doomed to fail. The Kolwezi operation, and therefore the *entire* project, could never have succeeded. There were no rebels. The secretive Congolese, the Scorpions insisted, were working closely with the National Intelligence Agency.

After fleeing the Congo for South Africa, Abu, it turned out, had become an informer.

18
THE END

Before I headed home, I gave Nick's wife a hastily handwritten letter to take to Nick for me. I penned it minutes before I left for my flight back to Europe. I was glad I had no time to dwell on it: words did not come easily. Nick was going on trial for his life; I was going to an awards ceremony in Amsterdam for the Liberia film I made with Tim and Jonathan. It was an uncomfortable position. None of the questions I wanted to ask could be written down; and even if I'd tried to write them, there would not have been – could not have been – a response. I wished him luck, and promised that, one day, we'd have another adventure together: there were, I told him, two roast chickens in the Petit Bateau hotel with our names on.

It had been agreed that Nick's wife and Carla would make their way to Equatorial Guinea for the resumption of Nick's trial without me. Almost everyone I asked specifically warned me not to travel to Malabo. In the end, it was Frank's advice from US Intelligence that sealed it. Eighteen months earlier he'd urged me not to cross the bridge in Monrovia; he'd informed me of the death warrant issued against Tim and me – and now, on the phone in Pretoria, he told me, point-blank, that I should expect immediate arrest if I travelled to see Nick.

'Those guys know who you are,' he said.

* * *

Three weeks later on 26 November, at five forty-five in the afternoon, I called Nick's wife in Equatorial Guinea from the lobby of my hotel in Amsterdam. The trial was over. Nick had been sentenced. He had avoided immediate execution, but instead had been given what Amnesty International described as 'a slow death sentence': thirty-four years in Black Beach prison.

'I'm so sorry. I am really, really sorry,' I whispered.

Nick's wife was already crying. Her voice came in fits and starts as she tried to stop it from cracking.

'How can they keep him here for thirty-four years? I need to get through this and I don't know how.' Thick sobs echoed down the line as she recounted the scene. 'I wish you could have seen Nick's face when he came out of court.'

As Nick had been led away, shackled hand and foot, he had been allowed to pause next to her just long enough for them to embrace. She told him that she loved him, and then he had been bundled into a black police car and driven to his cell.

I was completely unprepared for Nick's life sentence. I had been clinging onto a misguided sense of optimism: white men, even mercenaries, were not shot by official firing squads in Africa, nor were they jailed for decades. Either they died trying, or they got away with it – *somehow*. Perhaps that's what Nick and Simon had thought, too – but they hadn't calculated how fast Africa had moved on politically after their excursion into Sierra Leone.

'I know . . .' Now tears welled up in my eyes. 'Okay, you just have to be really, really strong, that's all, and you'll get through it.'

In the months that passed from Nick's sentence being handed down to my film being broadcast, the story of the coup slowly dropped out of the press. The antics of a group of European freebooters had taken up quite enough column inches and other, bigger stories screamed for attention.

The last hurrah in the media was raised over Mark Thatcher's eventual punishment: a $450,000 fine and a five-year suspended sentence. He pleaded guilty to helping finance a helicopter he thought might be used for mercenary activity. Evidently, not everyone close to Thatcher had believed he would get away so lightly: the head of a London-based security firm confirmed to me that his company had been approached by a private source close to Lady Thatcher to get Mark out of South Africa after his arrest and before his trial – and bring him home to Mummy. The plan – which may never have been known about by, or discussed with, Lady Thatcher herself – was considered, role-played and then dropped for what were described as 'ethical reasons'. Extracting Mark Thatcher from South Africa was illegal, and carried massive risk. The director of the security firm asked a contact at the Foreign Office what the 'official' position would be if the rescue went ahead. The verdict was straightforward: it would be 'business suicide' – the Government didn't want to play ball, and the plan was scrapped.

Simon was widely expected to be released after four years of his seven-year sentence, but in the meantime a wall of silence had descended around him. His lawyer, Jonathan Samukange, first told me that I should expect a reply to my letter soon – and then that Simon had decided not to reply after all. Dries Coetzee withdrew Simon's letters from sale – they had, he informed me, been subpoenaed by the Scorpions – and the trickle of leaks that had enlivened early press coverage of the foiled coup dried up.

Other players in the saga fared rather better. In March 2005, Johann Smit – the freelance spook and erstwhile business partner of Nigel Morgan who had compiled the first damning intelligence report on Nick and Simon's operation – was clearly one of

Obiang's favourite people. Smit was named by the Government of Equatorial Guinea as 'Johann Smit, Hero of the Nation' at an official ceremony in the capital, Malabo.

For Obiang, business was booming. So lucrative were the concessions that he sold off to foreign oil majors that he had saved up enough money to deposit half a billion dollars – in cash – into the family bank in Washington. It was a percentage of this money that Simon et al. were probably trying to siphon off with the second 'Captain F' contract. Unfortunately for Obiang, the bank in question – Riggs – fell foul of a US Senate investigation. Following the money led to some interesting discoveries: it turned out that Obiang's lucre was in good company. Not only had the Saudi royal family, twenty US presidents and the Chilean dictator Augusto Pinochet been loyal customers – so was the CIA. In fact, several bank officials apparently had Agency security clearances. Riggs was fined a total of $41 million for breaking US secrecy and money-laundering laws, and effectively collapsed under the scandal.

According to the US Justice Department – investigating Riggs and the source of Obiang's wealth – American oil companies were suspected of paying large bribes to the Equatorial Guinea regime, which was described as corrupt and regardless of human rights. Investigators found that Riggs failed to engage in 'even the most cursory due diligence review of accounts' held by Obiang's government and that members of the ruling family regularly turned up at the bank in person with suitcases stuffed with $100 bills on a strict no-questions-asked basis. Marathon Oil, the second-largest American investor in the Equatoguinean oil industry after the Exxon Mobil Corporation, gave back half a dozen of its concessions. Obiang had no need to worry, though: the Chinese Government was falling over itself to befriend him, and within a year he would be photographed shaking hands with the then US Secretary of State Condoleezza Rice, who welcomed the president as a 'good friend' after all.

Britain had certainly not been a good friend to Obiang. On 1 December 2004, Foreign Secretary Jack Straw retracted his earlier denials that the British Government had no foreknowledge of the coup. He admitted that 'On 29 January this year the Foreign Office received an intelligence report of preparations for a possible coup in Equatorial Guinea . . . It was passed by another government to us on the normal condition that it not be passed on.' Despite adding that 'the Foreign and Commonwealth Office was firmly opposed to any unconstitutional action such as coups d'état', the British Government had singularly failed to notify another sovereign nation (with whom it enjoyed normal diplomatic relations) of an imminent threat to its national security. Straw's statement came forty-eight hours after Peter Mandelson, the former Labour cabinet minister and then European Union Trade Commissioner, denied being involved in discussions over the coup plot with Ely Calil – an acquaintance of his from whom he had rented a flat in London five years earlier.

Mandelson had been put on the spot after one of Nigel Morgan's commercial intelligence reports – drawn up for an oil company, and quoted widely in the British press – claimed that Calil himself had told Nigel that he'd 'recently met with Mandelson about the EG/Moto/Mann issue', and that 'Calil says that Mandelson assured him that he would get no problems from the British government side', and invited Calil to come and see him again 'if you need something done'. Calil refuted the claims; Mandelson repeatedly and vehemently denied having any such meeting of that nature, and no evidence of his alleged sympathies was forthcoming.

The vexatious question of who may or may not have supported the coup appeared to have been partly answered in December 2004, when the missing page of Simon's jail confession surfaced, finally completing the full signed transcript. Simon said that 'the Spanish Prime Minister has met Severo Moto three times. He has, I am told, informed Severo Moto that as soon as he is established in Equatorial Guinea, he will send 3000 Guardia Civile. I have been respectfully told that the Spanish government will support the return of Severo Moto immediately and strongly.' He continued: 'They will however deny that they were aware of any operation of this sort.'

The office of the Spanish prime minister, José María Aznar, did deny the connection to Moto, but it was revealed locally in court that the Spanish Intelligence services had shadowed Moto on every step of his journey to the Canary Islands – and that nothing had been done to prevent his departure. The deployment of Spanish military assets was real enough, too. In January, the Spanish sent two warships carrying Marines into the Bight of Benin, which demanded to dock in Malabo – just in time, of course, for the first coup attempt on 19 February. They were refused. Undeterred, they requested permission to stage a military exercise in Equatorial Guinea's waters. Again, they were denied access – in a move that Obiang called 'provocative'.

In January 2005, the Spanish question was further illuminated by one of the plotters who lived in London. Greg Wales, an old acquaintance of Simon's from the Executive Outcomes days, had been the plotters' political adviser. During both coup attempts, he'd been in the Canary Islands with Severo Moto, preparing with mercenary pilot Crause Steyl to fly into Malabo with their man-who-would-be-king once Simon and Nick had done their job. Greg and I met in the subterranean bar of Fino's Wine Cellar in Mayfair's Mount Street. I found him seated at a table buried at the back of the bar. It was packed full of lunchtime drinkers, suffused with the pungent vapours of uncorked wine.

'Good to see you,' he murmured in the noisy cavern. 'I expect you've been quite busy. Any news about Nick? I always thought his treatment was one of the more despicable aspects of this whole affair.'

He was middle-aged, smartly dressed in chinos and an expensive-looking burgundy sweater. I told him what I knew – which wasn't a great deal. Black Beach was as unyielding as a bank vault.

Our conversation turned slowly to Spain. He maintained that 'Moto had a large contingent and was always accompanied by one or two representatives from Aznar's party, who were there with him in Gran Canaria' in March. Although the Americans and the British knew about the operation, it was (he maintained) mostly a Spanish affair. He believed Simon was wrong to assume that Calil was the main backer. It was most likely that Spain was providing the funding through Calil. It was a hunch, though; he said he had no evidence to prove it. Greg thought that either Calil was using the money himself, and passing the remainder on to Simon, or that the Spanish were only giving Calil the cash in dribs and drabs – which, in turn, forced Simon, as he put it, 'to go begging'. Although Greg's hypothesis appeared substantially to corroborate the content of Simon's letter from jail that Dries had shown me in the lawyer's office in Pretoria, both Calil and the Spanish Government categorically denied involvement.

Furthermore, Greg did not think it was within Calil's power to grant Simon any contractual concessions in Equatorial Guinea. The 'Captain F' documents (which he said he hadn't seen personally) were, he believed, a wish-list concocted by Simon, and without agreement from Moto himself. As far as Greg was concerned, Simon was never 'the main game'. His role was to escort Moto home, as a bodyguard – full stop; any action in Equatorial Guinea would have been the result of a local uprising. It was possible, he thought, that Simon had begun to run his own show, a show for which the script was allegedly neither known nor approved by either Greg or Calil.

Greg also confirmed that one aspect of his role had been to assiduously lobby the United States Government, to garner their approval for regime change. This, in some form, he believed he had won. It wasn't that the US backed them; he thought it was more a case of 'We'll hold your jacket while you hit them.'

He also ruminated on the logistical problems that Simon had getting the Boeing 727 out of America and over to South Africa so quickly. Simon had called on Greg to assist; in turn, Greg had called on an old acquaintance of his, a CIA contract pilot from Maryland. This pilot, who had started flying for the CIA in Air America over Laos at the tender age of nineteen, cleared the 727's paperwork on the basis that the operation was sanctioned by the US. Had he not thought that, Greg maintained, he would not have participated. He then flew the Boeing on to South Africa ('because he's that kind of guy'), and then returned to the States. He was, it turned out, going to fly to Zimbabwe as well – but Simon's South African pilot turned up in the nick of time. Greg flashed me a wry smile over his half-moon spectacles.

'Yes,' he chuckled, 'it was very fortunate he didn't fly to Harare.'

Robert Mugabe would have had a field day.

Greg and I said goodbye, promising to catch up again soon. He was a mischievous man – fond of riddles and of throwing diversions in the path of the legion of hacks who trampled into his underground liquid lounge – but his 'CIA' story intrigued me, and a couple of weeks later I called Ivan Pienaar, an aviation logistics expert whom Simon had engaged to help provide the aeroplanes used in both coup attempts.

It was Pienaar who arranged the DC-3s for the Kolwezi debacle, and Pienaar who helped organise the 727 for the March attempt. The DC-3s were physically provided by the South African company based at Wonderboom Airport – Dodson International Parts SA Limited – a subsidiary of Dodson Aviation in the United

States, from whom Simon then purchased the 727 on 3 March. It was an amazing deal: Dodson supplied the Boeing 727-100 (or 2 CCB, to give it its US military designation) for $400,000, on a promise to buy it back after six months if the engines were undamaged. Simon had got himself a high-specification ex-US military jet airliner for less than the price of a new Bentley.

Dodson Aviation had a long history of brokering aircraft deals with the US Government. Dodson International Parts SA Limited in South Africa, in its possible earlier incarnation as Dodson Aviation Maintenance and Spare Parts (the former company opened as the latter closed down), was owned by one Colonel Fred Rindel – a former South African Intelligence officer and military attaché to the USA. Among other things, Rindel was busy training Charles Taylor's Anti-Terrorist Unit in Liberia between 1998 and 2000, two years before Nick and I arrived to film with the rebels. Rindel and Dodson Aviation Maintenance and Spare Parts were both fingered by the United Nations Security Council Panel of Experts' report on Sierra Leone in December 2000 for breaking international sanctions against Liberia – not least because Rindel was also helping Taylor to train the RUF. The acting manager of Dodson International denied that the two companies were ever connected: the similarity in names was purely a coincidence.

Pienaar confirmed that an American crew had flown the plane from the US to South Africa – and that the pilots had been provided by a 'ferry company' and not Dodson Aviation. My own research verified that the 727 originated in Mena in Arkansas, leaving on 3 or 4 March after having been re-painted in brilliant white and its registration number, N4610, picked out in black lettering. It then, apparently, reappeared in Grantley Adams International Airport in Barbados at just after midnight on 6 March. After re-fuelling, it flew on to Sal in Cape Verde at half past six in the morning, and then continued to São Tomé –

finally reaching Polokwane Airport in South Africa at twenty to one in the morning on 7 March. Later that day the plane continued to Lanseria and then made the short hop to Wonderboom on that same disastrous Sunday, before leaving again at five minutes to seven in the evening, bound for Harare.

In the detail of the flight plans was a curious anomaly. Air traffic control at Grantley Adams airport in Barbados recorded the flight's immediate origin as Hope Air Force Base, North Carolina, USA. There is no Hope Air Force Base in North Carolina. There is, however, a Pope Air Force Base in North Carolina – connected to the United States military complex at Fort Bragg. Pope is, however, no ordinary air force base. It is the operational headquarters for the 427th Special Operations Squadron – which 'provides Short Takeoff/Landing and tactically qualified crews to support training requirements for the US Army Special Operations Forces community' – specifically the kind of flight operations that Simon's specially modified Boeing was designed for. They also provide American Special Forces operators 'the opportunity to train on various types of aircraft for infiltration and exfiltration that they may encounter in the lesser developed countries in which they provide training'. The very helpful woman in public affairs at Pope Air Force Base confirmed that the airport was strictly closed to civilian air traffic; the only civilian aircraft granted landing rights were those operating under military contract.

Pope Air Force Base doesn't just house the 427th, either. Along with Fort Bragg, it's the home of Delta Force, America's equivalent of the Special Air Service. According to one military expert, Delta's mandate involves conducting surgical, rapid-response missions while 'maintaining the lowest possible profile of U.S. involvement': in other words, they facilitate or undertake operations that can't be traced back to the US Government.

Simon would have been familiar with Delta's operational procedures. He had an old colleague called Bernie McCabe from his days working with Sandline International who, before becoming Sandline's US representative, had served in Delta Force for nineteen years. Between 1994 and 1996 McCabe was the unit's commanding officer. Simon had remarked in a postscript in his emails to Ely Calil in May 2003 that McCabe was then the head of global security for US oil company Marathon. Coincidentally, on the eve of the coup attempt employees from several US oil companies were said to have been confined to their quarters in Malabo.

Other, independent, sources had also named the pilot Greg Wales described – and suggested possible US military assistance. The United States Government denied any involvement, or foreknowledge, but did admit that an official from the Pentagon, Deputy Assistant Secretary of Defence for Foreign Affairs Theresa Whelan, had met Greg Wales on 19 November 2003 at a conference on private military companies. They confirmed that Whelan and Wales had met again at the Pentagon in mid February 2004, the eve of the first coup attempt. The Pentagon said that their conversation ranged over many African issues, but that Wales's hints were so general (he had 'mentioned in passing that there might be some trouble brewing in Equatorial Guinea') that they did not call for any action to be taken. It's possible that Whelan simply didn't understand what Wales – a master of circumlocution – was trying to tell her.

From the same back-room office in my flat where I had called Nick in the aftermath of the arrests, I called Colonel Frank once more for some advice. His opinion was straightforward.

'James, Pope is the centre of US Special Forces activity – Delta, 82nd Airborne, the Rangers, the Green Berets . . . you name it, they're there. That's where those Green Berets you met in Guinea were based, and it's where our friends Christians In Action operate out of, too. Anything that you wanted deniability for would run out of Pope. Delta has run specialised operations all over West Africa.'

As far as Frank was concerned, if you could nail flight N4610 to Pope Air Force Base, you could pin US Government involvement onto the coup. He should have known: he had operated out of Pope and Fort Bragg himself.

'Pope is your smoking gun, but you will never be able to prove it. On the very remote off-chance that Christians In Action were in some way involved with this, they will have launched a major ass-covering operation.'

Where N4610 went between leaving Mena on 3 or 4 March and arriving in Barbados on 6 March would be practically impossible to verify independently, he cautioned.

'Okay, I understand that, but is there any way this can be chased down?'

Amid all the smoke and mirrors of the coup, this above all was just too tantalising to let go of without a fight.

'James, I know this is hard for you as a reporter, but there are some questions you don't want to ask. You don't want to know the answer.' Frank assured me that the best advice he could offer was to forget it. 'You're chasing shadows, James. It'll always be the "what if?" It's over. Concentrate on Nick and the other guys in jail.'

'Okay,' I agreed, 'but after everything, are you still saying that the first moment you knew about the coup was when Simon was arrested?'

'Yes. We just didn't know. The CIA, the DIA, and agencies that you don't even know exist – we talk to each other. I didn't know.'

'Fuck it, Frank, I don't even really know who *you* work for. Nothing? Absolutely nothing? For God's sake, even *I* knew!'

On the one hand, Frank was adamant he knew nothing; on the other, he was advising me not to chase this down. I felt like banging my head against the wall.

'Nothing. But we did know about the Congo job, and that Nick was trying to get helicopters. We knew that.'

It was infuriating. Exactly what he knew, and how he'd gathered that information, he wouldn't say – but clearly the US Intelligence services in Africa had not been quite as surprised as they were pretending.

For me personally, the consequences of Nick's *African Adventure* continued to be far-reaching. At the Channel 4 documentary's eventual premiere in Soho in March 2005 – shown while Nick spent another interminable night shackled in his cell – I met my future wife.

At the party afterwards, everyone toasted my 'escape', and, one way or another, asked a version of the same question: how could I reconcile my own beliefs to those of my friend the mercenary?

I struggled to answer then, as I had done when the film was first commissioned. Nick certainly lived by taking risks, steeped in a profession deemed immoral by many, and not without reason. Yet I could not find it within myself to condemn, or even judge, him. With his help, in Liberia I had seen a version of the person I wanted to become. Surviving the privations of jungle warfare together tested that person to the moral and physical limit; and it confirmed in me an enduring desire to make my profession one that told the stories of people living in conflict. Nick was my friend when we limped out of the war in Liberia, and he was my friend still. The unpalatable truth is that adversity breeds friendships that transcend moral judgements.

The film itself had fallen out of favour at Channel 4. After having been signed off for transmission, it was recalled at the last minute without my knowledge, and re-cut. It was deemed that I was too sympathetic to Nick. There was no appetite for the shades of grey that coloured my relationship with him: my voice as narrator was removed from the film, and replaced by that of an actor. The first time I saw the programme was on the night it was broadcast at the screening in Soho.

In the months that passed afterwards, what I promised myself would never happen came to pass: I moved on.

I went to war again, and again – in the Congo, Iraq, Afghanistan, and a score of other, forgotten conflicts besides; I made dozens of films and started a family.

During my long absences from home, my daughter would point to the framed photograph of me and Nick on the sideboard and say, 'Daddy!' And then, pointing at Nick, she would turn to her mother and ask, 'Who's that?' I hoped one day she would find out: I didn't just owe my own life to Nick, but hers, too.

In the years after my film about Nick had been screened, the cast of characters continued to act out their parts in the charade with varying degrees of authenticity and accomplishment. Three years after Kathi and I split up, movie company Paramount Pictures acquired her life rights. *Variety*, the Hollywood trade magazine, ran the piece: '. . . intelligence operative Kathi Lynn Austin, whose adventures in arms trafficking and terrorism will inspire an action thriller vehicle for Angelina Jolie . . . The drama will focus on a fictional arms dealer inspired by [her investigations of] Victor Bout, the shadowy Russian who is considered one of the world's most prolific dealers in illegal munitions.' An intelligence operative for whom, exactly, wasn't divulged.

Simon had been extradited to Equatorial Guinea, 'kicking and screaming', in 2008: bundled into the back of a police truck in secret one night in January 2008, he was unceremoniously and illegally extradited to Malabo. Prior to his trial he gave an interview to *Channel 4 News*. Though his lawyers – and his wife – tried to stop it being broadcast, he insisted the piece be aired. It was eventually shown on 11 March 2008 – Nick's fifty-second birthday.

Simon confirmed that his lengthy signed statement drawn up in Zimbabwe, although obtained under duress, was nevertheless true. In chains, and wearing long hair and a grey prison uniform, he accused Ely Calil of being the 'main man', the architect of the whole 'swash-buckling fuck-up'. 'I was, if you like, the manager', he claimed, of an operation whose 'primary motivation was to help, as I saw it, the people of Equatorial Guinea, who were in a lot of trouble.' Sticking to his line of mercenary-as-liberator, the fact that he stood to preside over a mountain of wonga was of only secondary importance. He also stuck to his guns about the role of South Africa, too. Morgan, he said, had tipped off the Government in Pretoria.

'We were in a desperate situation,' he said. 'I knew that he'd basically blown the whistle. And we went ahead because the other indications I was getting – i.e. from the Spanish Government and from the South African Government, and in this case most especially, the South African Government – were that "We want you to go, so go."' The British and the Americans, he maintained, had never given him a 'nod and a wink'.

Whatever 'other indications' Simon thought he was getting were, ultimately, false – despite the fact that in early 2007 charges brought in South Africa against eight of the men freed from Zimbabwe (including Nick's brother-in-law Errol) were dropped after a short trial. Under cross-examination, the director-general of the South African Secret Service, Hilton 'Tim' Dennis, made it clear that there had been contact between the South African Government and Severo Moto prior to the coup attempt. The nature and purpose of the contact were not revealed, though the defendants claimed that they could 'prove' they'd been given the 'green light' for the operation. The judge threw the case out.

'I blame myself most,' Simon concluded, echoing what any casual observer would have made of the apparently absurd decision to press on in early March, 'for simply not saying "cut" two months before we were arrested. That's what I should have done and there, you know, I was bloody stupid.'

Mark Thatcher he implicated more deeply than the ex-prime minister's son's plea bargain had allowed for: his role was not unwitting, but, he alleged, central. As Simon saw it, Thatcher was part of the team. Mark Thatcher said that his old friend Simon 'must be frightened and acutely distressed'. He repeated his 'utmost sympathy' for him, and confirmed that he had nothing to add to the statements that he gave to the 'relevant authorities' in 2004.

At the time, Calil accused Channel 4 of allowing itself to be used 'as a propaganda tool for the government of Equatorial Guinea'. He, too, expressed sympathy for Simon, a man who 'has made many contradictory statements'. 'I confirm', a rare statement he released said, 'that I had no involvement in or responsibility for the alleged coup.'

In return for giving a star turn as a loquacious canary in court, Obiang did not seek the death penalty. After a trial every bit as outrageously flawed as Nick's had been, Simon got thirty years. Just before the trial Obiang triumphed, as predicted, in another absurd presidential election. He won ninety-nine of the hundred seats.

Then, in July 2008, Calil decided to talk in more detail about the coup plot. It was definitely Simon, he maintained, who was to blame. 'It was his lack of professionalism, his lack of discretion, his lack of judgement that caused this situation,' he insisted. Calil also stressed that he personally knew nothing of the details of the planned operation. 'But yes,' he accepted, 'I financed Severo Moto's political activities, and yes, I introduced Simon Mann to him because of his background in security.' He also accepted that he had financed plans by Moto to return to his country. Calil stressed that he had supported regime change in Equatorial Guinea – but only ever by 'democratic change'.

Calil also maintained that 'there was no coup plot'. Simon's version of events was 'pure fantasy'. There was, though, he said, a scheme agreed between Simon and Severo Moto to fly Moto back to Equatorial Guinea, 'and to protect him while he was in the country. Simon and his mercenaries were engaged to provide military assistance to Moto.' Calil mused: 'Severo's belief was that if he was protected in his home town, and could remain alive for a few days, a political storm would occur that would sweep away the present regime.'

Calil went on to outline a preposterous scenario in which Simon was supposed to land in the neighbouring country of Gabon with his mercenary-laden Boeing 727, meet up with Moto, and then cross overland into the continental part of Equatorial Guinea to Moto's village, where his people would 'start screaming and demonstrating' – despite the fact that such a plan could have precipitated a civil war, and that Moto's village is hundreds of miles away from Bioko, the island part of the country which houses the capital, Malabo, and, of course, President Obiang. Quite why Calil broke cover to posit such an awkward hypothesis is, frankly, mysterious – though anyone able to gainsay his theory with any authority, myself included, was either keeping quiet, or in jail.

What Ely Calil did verify was that it was he (and Mark Thatcher – who, he also insisted, had nothing to do with any coup plot) whom Simon referred to in his jail correspondence: 'I accept as regards the letter that I am Smelly and he is Scratcher,' Calil said, 'but it's not that he is implicating us, rather asking friends for help.'

* * *

The more time passed, the less people wanted to talk. Everyone wanted to move on, no one wanted to look back – no one except Simon, perhaps, who gave another raft of interviews from jail, this time to the BBC. In the filmed conversations at Black Beach prison, he admitted that the original plan to overthrow Obiang had been 'to sail a ship round and pick up a merry bunch of men off the Liberian coast and arrive here'. He had also considered assassinating the president.

Corroborating what Greg Wales had told me in London, Simon maintained that the Americans were sympathetic to the operation.

'America wants no part in a coup,' he said, but claimed that he'd been left with the impression that 'if there is an orderly and legal regime change, even if it is assisted, if it leads into a free and fair election, provided our assets are left intact, we don't have a problem'.

Above all, he maintained that the 'South Africans' had endorsed his plan: 'In fact,' he said, describing their involvement, 'I was told to get on with it.'

From his home buried in the rolling hills of KwaZulu-Natal, Nigel Morgan eventually agreed to talk, by telephone, about his role in his old friend Simon's downfall. He said that he had been approached by the South African Secret Service in May 2003 to help them investigate Simon's activities: they thought his renewed acquaintance with Nick and his trips to Conakry were suspicious, and wanted Morgan to find out what Simon was up to. When Johann Smit's intelligence report confirmed, seven months later, that Nick was recruiting ex-Special Forces operators and deploying them to Equatorial Guinea, Morgan claimed he confronted Simon – who replied that he was only doing legitimate business in Malabo.

'And that's really when we decided,' Morgan told me. 'We set up an operation – or an operation was set up – deliberately to get them. You know, it is not a nice game, but mercenaries are, on the whole, not particularly nice people. They go around killing other people, and they do it for a living like hired assassins, but on a slightly larger scale.'

It looked as though Harry Carlse had been right: Morgan had sold them out. Winning Simon's confidence by posing as a willing conspirator, he said he placed his own man, James Kershaw, in pole position as Simon's personal assistant and unwitting inside man. Morgan also admitted that he had accepted $10,000 from Simon – with which he agreed to travel to Nigeria and lobby oil interests on behalf of Simon and Calil. Of course, he said, he had no intention of making the trip. Given that Simon knew how closely Morgan was connected to the South African Intelligence services, it was easy to see how Simon could have concluded the plot had their tacit support.

In fact, there were so many informers planted in the operation that it was beginning to look like the tail might have started to wag the dog. Morgan confirmed what Billy Maseltha had told me, that other agents and assets penetrated the plot, root and branch – including, Morgan suggested, Harry Carlse and Lourens 'Louwtjie' Horn – an accusation that both men deny. Everything Morgan unearthed was fed back to the South African Secret Service. Even so, Morgan believed that the operation had nearly succeeded in February: apparently, no one in SASS had seen Kolwezi coming. 'We were bloody incompetent,' he admitted. 'We thought we had them properly infiltrated at every level, and then we missed the fucking trick. After that they were dead men.'

I asked Morgan if he was not sad to have been responsible for the arrest of his erstwhile friend. Emotion, he said, had no part to play.

'If the guy's a cunt, he's a cunt,' he said, emphatically. 'If the guy's a crook, he's a crook. And the trouble with Simon was he'd gone crooked.'

Also, on the phone from Pretoria, I asked Piet van der Merwe, the Scorpion's senior special investigator who had run the case against Thatcher and interviewed Abu Baker, if it was plausible that the NIA had placed people inside the operation – enlisted as foot-soldiers – from the beginning.

'Well,' he replied, after re-confirming that Abu had become an informer for the NIA, 'I mean, it depends on what names you were given.'

I suggested that many people, including Nigel Morgan and, obliquely, Billy Masetlha, had posited Horn and Carlse as agents. Van der Merwe dismissed the accusations against Carlse, but not against his friend.

'I would go with a name of Louwtjie Horn,' he said. 'Taking Louwtjie's background . . . being an ex-policeman . . . I would have said Louwtjie Horn was an NIA agent.'

Horn was arrested with Simon and Harry Carlse in Harare as the three men inspected the weapons purchased from ZDI. Van der Merwe was keen to point out, though, that whatever Horn's connection to the NIA might have been, he'd seen nothing to suggest that Horn had actually compromised the operation. It was Nigel Morgan and SASS who had commanded centre stage.

'They played a major role in this. They knew exactly from day one.' Van der Merwe went on to recount the extraordinary testimony given by Tim Dennis, the former director-general of SASS, at the trial of the eight men, including Nick's brother-in-law, in 2007. Van der Merwe claimed that SASS had been in touch with Severo Moto in exile in Spain 'to basically pave the relationship for South Africa if he does get into power', because South Africa needed Equatorial Guinea's 'black gold'. According to van der Merwe, it appeared that SASS had played both sides, before deciding which way to jump. Despite denials from Masetlha, Morgan and Dennis, it could possibly have been the case that the first, Kolwezi, operation got off the ground owing to official indecision, not a failure of intelligence.

On the other side, I also pressed van der Merwe about allegations of CIA involvement.

'That's a fact,' he declared emphatically. 'That's a given. There was a CIA agent that escorted the plane to South Africa, stayed behind, then was booked in at the Lake Hotel in Centurion.'

According to van der Merwe, it was Ivan Pienaar who had met the CIA agent off the plane, arranged his accommodation and put him onto a flight home the following day. Pienaar had given a sworn statement to the Scorpions, confirming the exact details.

'That's a fact,' van der Merwe repeated, 'that's a given.'

No one interviewed Nick; the few that tried, he sent away disappointed. Direct contact with his wife and South African diplomats slowed down, and then ended abruptly. News only filtered back erratically: he had malnutrition; he was stricken by cerebral malaria; he was close to death. And then there was nothing at all. The letters that had trickled out stopped, and even the rumours about his condition dried up. Worn with guilt, I found that by degrees I was letting him go; I had nothing to hold onto but the recollection of those days in Tubmanburg when he'd dragged me clear of the shrapnel and steered me through the charnel house.

Sometimes at night my daughter calls for me. Her cries of 'Daddy' rise in the short time it takes me to reach her bedroom. Her way of asking for me is half-statement – as if by saying my name I must appear; and half-question – the slight lift in her voice at the end questioning when, if, I will come at all.

Her room is a warm, rich funk of milk and biscuits; my hand on her tangled hair guides her back to bed, collecting a film of sweat shed over her night-terrors. Sometimes I think of Rocket, and the other children we saw laid to waste, and of how fragile our assumptions of safety are. I decided months ago that I would not tell her about the war; about what happens in war; about what happened to me in that war and everything that came out of it – until she knows that nothing can shake the walls around us; until she is no longer a child.

Once, when she was barely two years old, she found me crying in our living room as I struggled to swallow the stone that rises up sometimes and catches me when I least expect it. She stopped playing and put her hand on my knee.

'It's okay, Daddy. Everything's okay,' she told me, her eyes searching out the reason for my tears. I knew then why my grandfather, Don, had drip-fed his war to me in careful, deliberate doses. He never mentioned the screams – his screams – that tore through his sleep. He never demanded that I share the burden of his memories, not even at the end.

Bella is asleep again before the door closes. Outside I listen and wait for the wet *click-click-click* of her dummy to stop. Her jaw slackens into silence, and I am left alone on the landing. During nights like this I have found myself standing in the unlit bathroom next door, chasing my reflection among the confusion of shadows thrown by the trees outside. I think of the afternoon when I undressed in front of the cracked hotel mirror in Conakry and saw for the first time the damage my body had absorbed after two months in the jungle with Nick.

I ask who I am, who I was, and what change I might be owed from the cost of all the hubris and bloodletting that became my career. Out of the darkness I try to conjure the dreams that will not come, and face the memories that will not go. Nick in his cell, me in my sanctuary.

And I ask this, too: who is the mercenary?

EPILOGUE

ILLUMINATION ROUNDS

On 3 November 2009, Nick was officially pardoned. He had been incarcerated in Black Beach prison for five years and eight months. His wife was the first to call. The news had just broken on the wires. I was at home in London.

The Equatoguinean attorney-general confirmed that Nick, Simon, and the other South African prisoners would be freed that day. Nick was given twenty-four hours to leave the country. His release was timed exactly to coincide with the state visit to Equatorial Guinea by South African president Jacob Zuma.

Simon Mann flew home smiling on a private jet. Before being whisked away to his family, and his country house in Hampshire, he made a short statement to the press.

'As far as I'm concerned,' he declared in his posh half-lisp, 'I am very anxious that Calil, Thatcher, and one or two of the others should face justice.'

He was very happy, he said, to appear in court in the UK 'as a witness for the prosecution'. Grey and gaunt, he was almost unrecognisable as the man I had met in Paris more than six and a half years earlier.

It took three days for Nick to get home. The South African Government eventually flew him to Johannesburg and debriefed him. That evening, I spoke to him on the phone.

'Mr Brabazon, how are you?'

It was as if the room filled with his voice. Six years dissolved immediately.

'It's so great to hear your voice. It's amazing. I can't quite believe it.' It was a conversation impossible to prepare for. I had no idea where to start. 'How do you feel in yourself?' I asked.

'Ag, not so bad. Physically, I'm underweight. I'm going for a medical test. But on the mental side, mentally, I don't feel disturbed.' He was laughing now.

'That's your story, mate! I'd let other people be the judge of that.' I was laughing, too. 'What about the release? How much warning did they give you? We were all bloody surprised here.'

'It was very casual, as if it was something that they did every day,' he told me. 'They came into my cell and said, "Just sign these papers." I asked what they were and the attorney-general said, "Oh, you've been pardoned."'

He sounded as if he still couldn't quite believe his luck.

'I'm getting on a plane tomorrow,' I told him. 'Is that okay?'

'Ja, man, one hundred per cent. That will be great.'

Despite intense media interest, Nick had decided not to talk to the press. Only close family and the men he was in jail with even knew where he was. As Nick said, it was back to cloak and dagger again.

I was in Pretoria for two days before Nick and I were able to start talking properly. Nick had spent his first forty-eight hours of freedom alone with his wife. I waited at their new home with the rest of the family – his sons, daughters and his future son-in-law – tending the braai, blowing up balloons and stringing out bright, plastic 'Welcome Home' bunting.

Then the slatted side-gate opened, and Nick came home. Head down, he followed his wife, said hello to the son-in-law he'd never met, and moved indoors at a stoop. In an instant he stepped out again from the shade of the house and I saw him clearly. His eyes were dark, and sank back into his head. He was a shadow of the man I said goodbye to in Paris, his arms were skin and bone, his head massive on wasted, narrow shoulders. He was wearing long blue shorts and a blue checked shirt – in his top pocket were tucked a notepad and pen. I was sweating.

'It's great to see you, James.'

We shook hands, and then hugged each other. The muscles that had dragged us through the jungle were gone. He looked and felt like what he was: a prison-camp survivor.

'I feel quite normal. We'll have to see.' He looked around him. 'It's great, just great.'

He was smiling. We stood and chatted slightly apart from the others, and then we went inside so I could give him a bottle of malt whisky I'd been saving for a special occasion since university. I realised I was nervous. The harder I tried, the more difficult it was to be casual and relaxed. His eyes lit up at the sight of the scotch, and he thanked me.

'We'll have to save this for when you have grandchildren,' he laughed, and tucked it away in the cupboard.

I asked him how 'it' had been.

'Well, it was a very interesting five-year bush trip,' he joked with me, trying to put me at ease, 'but those trips are over now. There'll be no more bush trips, no more adventures in Africa.'

His smile faded, and he cut to the chase without pausing.

'What we did, what we tried to do, was wrong.' And then he smiled again and looked at his daughter. 'Marzaan says she's going to take away my passport.'

He was evidently still in shock at the speed of his release. His daughter, now seventeen, watched him intently. So did her new boyfriend. It was hard not to feel sympathy for the boyfriend.

'I mean, of all the fathers to pop up when you were least expecting it . . .' I turned to the slightly stunned teenager on Marzaan's arm. 'Man, you aren't going to know what's hit you.'

Marzaan and Nick had spoken, by phone, for the first time since his arrest only as recently as September 2009. Eleven years old the last time she'd seen him, she now re-encountered him as if for the first time.

'It's strange to come back to a grown-up family. Now I have to get to know them all again from the start.' And then, smiling again, he said to the boyfriend: 'But remember, she's still my daughter!' They blushed.

In between mouthfuls of steak and gulps of beer, Nick joined in with the family banter around him. Incredibly well informed about apparently all aspects of international current affairs, he wanted to talk about the Hubble Telescope and exploding stars; global warming and the drought in Kenya; and the trials and tribulations of the Government in Britain. I asked him how come he seemed to know more about what was happening in London than I did. In fact, he said, he'd managed to get hold of a shortwave radio, which he rigged up to a wire that ran off the light in his cell. For years he had survived by listening to the World Service and reading the Bible. Peppered with references to mercy and repentance, his speech was not just that of a news-junkie and a survivor, but of a convert. He said he'd seen both the error of his ways, and the Light.

'Now I have God in my life,' he said, 'nothing is impossible. Not even being released from Black Beach.'

Before long Nick was reminiscing about the men he served with in the army, and recounted again the time he'd visited the house in Liberia where Deku had been killed – his brains blasted all over the walls, the hastily dug grave out the back. I told him about the films I'd made in Africa – about filming under fire with South African United Nations peacekeepers in Congo, and the expedition I had undertaken deep into the forests of eastern India to film with Maoist guerrillas.

'Tell me,' he asked finally, putting his half-empty beer bottle to one side, 'we never did finish that story about your grandfather. What happened in the end?'

In the days that followed, Nick and I accumulated a catalogue of firsts: the first meal he'd cooked since being arrested (breakfast for me, the following day); the longest walk he'd had for six years (a mile down to the local shops together); the first cup of coffee he'd bought in a café (at the local shops, tired from the walk).

'It's funny walking next to you,' he said, as we strode out to the shops again a day later, this time cloaked in drizzle. 'It's just like in Liberia. Your legs haven't got any shorter, either.'

I slowed my pace, and we ambled to a covered table at the café. We ordered cheese and bacon quiche, milky coffees and sweet biscuits.

There was so much that I wanted to ask Nick – so many gaps in my knowledge – that it was hard to know where to begin. I wanted to find out what had really happened in Kolwezi; if he had tried to back out at the last moment; and why he had gone ahead at all. For six years, I had wondered what it had really been like in jail for him.

I began by asking him how the plot was supposed to have unfolded.

'My job', he explained, 'was to seize control of Malabo Airport – by taking over the air traffic control tower. The two guards would have been immobilised, not killed.'

There was no need for violence yet. Far away from the other airport buildings, where a small contingent of drunken soldiers dozed, the alarm would not have been raised until it was too late. At two o'clock in the morning on 8 March 2004, Nick was to have changed the tower's radio frequency to that of the incoming mercenary flight. Once it had landed, the airport would have been secured; the four-by-four vehicles that Nick would have driven there serving as transport for the newly arrived Fire Force. Nick's role thereafter was to provide intelligence support. He'd told Simon that he didn't want to be openly identified as an attacker in case that undermined later business deals in the new republic.

Under Harry Carlse's command, the mercenaries would have gone into action immediately. Two or three five-man teams would have been dispatched to the presidential palace, another to the police station; the main force would have cut and defended the central arterial route that ran between the army barracks and the palace. The radio station would have been commandeered as soon as possible. Simon was to have remained at the airport, waiting for Greg Wales, David Tremain, Karim Fallaha and Severo Moto – all of whom were due to be flown in from the Canary Islands via Bamako in Mali by former Executive Outcomes pilot Crause Steyl.

We continued our conversation back at Nick's home, gradually slipping back into old habits. It reminded me of the weeks we'd spent on that balcony in Tubmanburg – but instead of the stench of dead bodies, our conversation was now wrapped in the scent of freshly cut grass that wafted through the open windows. On the first day alone we talked for over fifteen hours. It felt as if we had a lifetime to recap: photos of children, details of escapades, and a careful autopsy of the coup plot to complete.

'In the beginning,' he said, 'it was Simon who approached me' – in May 2003. They'd renewed their acquaintance in January that year, over an unrelated aircraft purchase. Despite the fact that Nick was sure the idea was not Simon's own – that he'd been approached by a third party – Simon funded the operation personally, out of his own pocket. 'At first it was quite cheap,' Nick remembered.

Then Nick produced his own copies of the emails between Simon and Ely Calil that I'd found years previously in his office – the correspondence that referred to 'Fisheries Protection' and Simon's forthcoming meeting with Calil on Sunday 18 May. These copies had been stamped and certified by the National Prosecuting Authority

'At this meeting,' Nick continued, pointing to the text on the page, 'if it went ahead, the coup plans must have been finalised. I met Simon two weeks later. That's when he told me about the plan.'

He also said that Simon had told him there was an outside, foreign backer in the Lebanon. Ely Calil's name was not mentioned until the following year – and then only his first name. The first time Nick saw his surname was when he was shown Simon's statement in jail in Malabo. To him, Calil's role (or professed lack thereof) was irrelevant. 'It didn't matter to me where the money came from,' he concluded.

Severo Moto, Nick said, was initially referred to as 'the exiled guy' – he heard his name for the first time at the end of 2003. Mark Thatcher he claimed to have met only once, just before Nick and I had met in Paris in July 2003. As well as discussing helicopters for a project that Thatcher was considering in the Sudan, they also discussed the purchase of an Alouette helicopter to act as emergency medical evacuation transport for the operation, and double up as a gunship. It was clear to Thatcher, Nick believed, that the Alouette would be used in connection with military activity, although Equatorial Guinea was not mentioned in their meeting. Thatcher admitted to financing the charter of a helicopter – to be used in mercenary activity in Equatorial Guinea – but maintained he believed it was an air ambulance, not a gunship.

In May, plans were laid quickly to launch the operation from Guinea Conakry with Liberian rebel support. Nick and Simon travelled there to meet Sekou Conneh, the national chairman of the LURD rebels. Simon, Nick said, gave Sekou a down-payment of around $30,000 in cash to secure his co-operation in their project. Further money was promised if the plan went ahead. It must have been a godsend for Conneh, whose organisation was gearing up for their final assault on the Liberian capital, Monrovia. In return for the money, Conneh was to lend logistical support, as well as men and weapons, if these could not be sourced elsewhere. With Conneh's blessing, Nick and Simon took a boat trip to the islands off shore from Conakry, scouting a good location for a ship to dock. From these islands the ship would be loaded with men and weapons – and a helicopter gunship, if that deal came through – and then set sail for Equatorial Guinea.

'It was a good plan, but it had problems. I was never convinced of it,' Nick explained. 'There were always different possibilities. The main source of weapons had preferably always been Uganda or Zimbabwe. Getting them to Conakry by airdrop or ship would have been tricky and expensive.' The coup in São Tomé killed the idea. Nick and Simon had already been discussing using aeroplanes instead. 'I liked the air option,' he said. It was closer to his experience in Special Forces. 'It's much quicker, with a faster turnaround.'

So plans went ahead to set up front-businesses in fisheries, agriculture and aviation in Equatorial Guinea itself. Although these were originally set up as a cover for the coup, Nick said he became genuinely motivated to help the people of Equatorial Guinea, and claimed he'd persuaded Simon, who was reluctant at first, to fund them properly. It was a bid, he said, to win the good will of the people.

'I knew it was misguided, but I didn't see myself as this forceful colonial master continuing the current state of corruption and oppression just for my own benefit. I saw what happened in South Africa and I really wanted to work with the people. The fisheries idea was my starting point because everybody was raping the country, but nothing came back to the people. Not even fish. In Africa, food supply is the most important economic activity.'

Nick, though, had never seen the vision of Equatorial Guinea the plotters had sketched out on paper. Colonial masters raping the country of its resources were exactly what they had intended to become.

Sitting back on the sofa, Nick conceded that setting up shop with the president's brother and head of security, Armengol Nguema, was a risky move, but plans proceeded. In order to finalise a contract that would grant Nick's company a licence to operate as an overseas flight company operator, Simon suggested they build a bribe of six Toyota Land Cruisers into the proposal for the president's entourage. They would be fitted with tracking devices, which may have come in useful when the attack was launched.

As 2003 wore on, though, Nick began to feel uneasy about the operation.

'I told Simon *many* times that we were being watched by South African Intelligence.'

He sighed and shifted his weight on the couch. An old back injury from a parachute jump made it uncomfortable for him to sit still for long periods of time.

'In October, Henri showed me an intelligence intercept that one of his contacts had come across. It showed clearly that me and Simon were planning this coup.'

'What was Henri's advice?' I asked.

'He told me to leave the operation – that we would get our fingers burned.'

By December, Nick was convinced that the South African Secret Service knew the details of the plot.

'How?' I wanted to know. 'How, apart from the intercepts you saw, did you think they knew that?'

Nick drew his knees up. There was nothing of him.

'Nigel Morgan,' he replied. 'Nigel, and then later James Kershaw. Everyone knew Nigel worked for SASS, and that Kershaw was his man. Kershaw saw everything that Simon did. But Simon insisted it wasn't a problem.'

Nigel Morgan had already himself admitted that it had indeed been a very big problem for Simon.

'People have said that you tried to back out in January, that there was a meeting on January the fifth where you tried to walk away. Is that true?'

'I told Simon we weren't ready, that there were too many security breaks. Equatorial Guinea was changing rapidly. It wasn't the right time. The capital was covered with building sites and new work being done. It was essential to capture the president, if the coup was to succeed, but I told Simon I didn't know where he was. If he escaped, it wouldn't have worked. We just didn't have enough information to be certain we could capture him.'

'And what was Simon's response?'

'He said we had to go ahead because of the Spanish elections. He told me not to worry about the security issue – the Government in South Africa was supposed to support us. He told everyone they had given us the go-ahead.'

Nick was left with the strong impression that the Spanish would support Moto's regime 'for sure' – and that Simon feared a new (left-wing) Spanish government may exile Moto. Nick wasn't aware that any of the funding of the coup was alleged to be coming from Spain, nor that they planned to deploy ships and troops after the operation – and was not reassured. More to the point, he also wasn't aware of any planned local uprising – despite what Greg Wales, Simon Mann and Ely Calil may have said afterwards.

The idea had never rung true to me, either: the whole point of my involvement had been to film the black mercenaries from 32 Battalion to make them look *as if they were* local troops. Nick agreed it sounded like a ploy to lend the plotters a political legitimacy they didn't have.

'No, it was a straight takeover – at least, that's what I was told. I don't know anything about a local uprising. Simon never mentioned anything about it and I didn't discuss it with Harry. If they were planning that – vok! It would have been a disaster.' He looked at me in disbelief. 'Can you imagine? There we are at the airport and a bunch of local guys in uniform turn up that we don't know anything about? It would have been a massacre. They'd have been taken out before they even got close.'

In mid-January 2004, Nick admitted that he had faced Simon down at home in Pretoria.

'You know me, James. I'm not scared of anyone. No one can threaten me. I told Simon that we must not carry on, that it was completely compromised. Simon said that the backers were powerful people, and that they would not let us walk away. I suppose, yes, I was concerned for my family, but I didn't take it that seriously. The main thing was that Simon was sure, sure as sure, that we had the authorisation to proceed.'

In any case, their front-businesses were working out so well that it was barely necessary to mount an attack. Nick thought it might have been possible to get oil deals with Obiang through legitimate channels. Simon wasn't interested. The backers, he maintained, would not agree to that.

So Nick pressed on against his better judgement, concluding the arms deal in Zimbabwe in reasonable confidence that Colonel Dube of the Zimbabwe Defence Industries would not land them in it: he was interested in the cash, full stop. Nick rubbished the idea that ZDI would have been hesitant to supply rebels in Congo's Katanga province.

'I had the impression they were already supplying other rebels, anyway,' he said. 'It was a day's work for them. Easy money.'

As D-Day approached, Nick confirmed he had asked Henri to seek authorisation for the mission from the Scorpions. Nick's logic was simple: Simon had said the South African Government knew. If that was true, then there could be no harm in alerting the investigative arm of the National Prosecuting Authority, too, given that it would be they, the Scorpions, that would have prosecuted them in South Africa. Nick said he decided that their response would determine whether he went ahead or not.

'I didn't speak to the Scorpions myself. Henri did. He told me he'd had a conversation with a woman called Ayanda, who worked for the intelligence services.'

Henri had spoken to Ayanda Dlodlo, now one of President Jacob Zuma's key advisers. At the time, she was a deputy director in charge of strategy at the Scorpions. Nick claimed that Henri had told him that she'd said the plotters should go ahead because the Scorpions wanted to catch the people financing the coup – but Dlodlo denied she had given Henri the green light. On the contrary, she claimed to have referred him to her boss, Bulelani Ngcuka, then the chief of the National Prosecuting Authority, saying that she did not handle informers at all. On 18 February, Henri maintained in a statement he later gave to the Scorpions (that I'd read in 2004) that he and Ngcuka had discussed the plot, and decided to investigate the backers. Ngcuka accepts that that meeting took place, but denies that the coup was discussed. Nick said he had no idea at all that Henri had even met Ngcuka.

'Henri left me with the impression that while the Government here weren't officially going to recognise the coup, we would get some kind of support.'

Whatever the intricacies of who told whom, what, when and where, the outcome was clear: Nick thought – incorrectly – that he'd been given approval to proceed.

'Did you know', I said, 'that Billy Masetlha claimed that the plot had been infiltrated by Government agents? I mean, not just by Nigel Morgan, but that spies were in among the men who were recruited? He said that there were people working for the Government in jail in Zimbabwe.'

Nigel Morgan had also agreed that was the case – that the information from informers had been vital.

'Yes, that's true. Lorenzo, he was an informer. I told Sérgio to be careful. There was another guy in Zimbabwe, too. Lorenzo. He was in 5 Recce. I realised six weeks after he was recruited that he worked for Intelligence. We couldn't get rid of him, so we tried to bring him in instead. He was definitely an informant.'

Other men on the operation had also named Civi Lorenzo and another man from 5 Recce, Bernardo De Sousa Neto. It was said these alleged informers were in fear of their lives in South Africa and had fled to Angola and Mozambique respectively, even though no hard evidence could be produced against them.

To stop intelligence leaks, Nick said he'd urged Simon to get the men out of South Africa as soon as they were recruited. His request was denied and his fears downplayed – and Harry Carlse installed the men in the Hotel 224. The primary reason for the reluctance to move them abroad was lack of funds.

'How much did the guys who were recruited here actually know?' I wondered.

Many of the men arrested had claimed, with varying degrees of plausibility, that they were entirely ignorant of the intended destination.

'The white guys knew. And Neves Tomas, who did the recruiting in Pomfret – he had to know some detail so he could find the right guys for the job. No one on board thought it was a legitimate job, especially not after the first attempt, though most of them thought it was a guard-force job in the Congo.'

'You know', I pressed on, 'that it's also been suggested that Harry Carlse and Louwtjie Horn worked for National Intelligence. Is that true?'

'No.' Nick was emphatic. 'Harry's okay. I brought him in, and Harry brought Louwtjie in. It's impossible.'

'You're absolutely sure? There were widespread rumours at the time. People have pointed to the fact that he and Louwtjie were acquitted without sentence in Zim.'

'Harry? It's not possible. He couldn't have been convicted of immigration offences like the other men on the Boeing because he entered Zimbabwe separately from the main group. He made a plea bargain here, but he wasn't an agent. I really had to persuade him and Louwtjie to join us. They weren't interested at first because their business in Iraq was making good money. Ag, you know, it wouldn't surprise me if someone claimed that I was working for National Intelligence, as well! It seems now everyone who was recruited in this operation was a spy. The Scorpions, Intelligence . . . they spread rumours to try and get us fighting among ourselves. Divide and rule.'

The idea that Harry Carlse and Louwtjie Horn had definitely been informers had never seemed quite right to me, either. Carlse was the only person involved in the coup (apart from the three other men who'd remained locked up with him in Equatorial Guinea) that Nick was in touch with. His evidence was said to have played a significant role in the decision to drop the case against the other men tried in South Africa – even though he was called as a witness for the state. Horn and Carlse were now in business with some of the other mercenaries – which, along with the fact that they'd been prosecuted in South Africa and bankrupted in the process, was another compelling reason to believe that Nick was right.

Given that, by his own admission, Nick knew the inner workings of the plot were exposed, I was at a loss to comprehend why he decided to proceed – 'green light' from the Scorpions or not.

'Ja, it was stupid.' He cocked his head to one side. 'It was stupid to trust Simon.' He paused and gathered his thoughts. 'And Henri. They said we were covered. I thought they were only interested in catching the backers. When we were released from Black Beach, I said to Simon, "Why did you tell Nigel Morgan everything?" He said he had because the South African Government was on board. We had an hour to talk, me and Simon, as we waited together after our release. He told me he has papers that prove the guilt of the backers and the involvement of the South African Government.'

'What kind of documents?'

'I don't know. He just said he kept copies of everything, and that they were in a safe place. He said one of the documents proved the South African Government had authorised the operation.' We considered for a moment in joint silence how profoundly improbable the truth of that statement really was.

'I thought Simon knew what he was doing, but he doesn't have any operational experience—'

'But you do!' I cut across him.

'Ja, James, you might say I do have operational experience, so why trust all those people who don't?' He laughed at the absurdity of his own position.

'But why? Why – and this is something I really don't understand – why, even if you had gone ahead, didn't you run when Simon was arrested? You had hours, and aircraft – and a boat!'

I could feel myself becoming exasperated with him all over again. He leaned forward and opened his palms.

'I thought we'd be okay. We had no guns, no military equipment, no paperwork or plans. If we'd run, it would have looked like an admission of guilt . . .' He toyed with the empty cup on the coffee table in front of him. 'It was greed. Just greed. Losing all of that, the businesses we'd built up.' He gave a half-smile, and shrugged his shoulders.

'In the hour you had with Simon,' I asked, 'what else did you talk to him about?'

I would have loved to have been a fly on the wall for that particular conversation.

'I asked him about Nigel Morgan, like I said, and about Tim Roman.'

Roman was the American aviation and logistics expert that Simon had gone to see (with Carlse and Horn) in Kinshasa, the capital of the Congo, immediately before flying to Harare to marry up the weapons and the men on the Boeing 727.

'What about Roman?'

'I asked him why he went to see him when everyone knows he works for the Americans.'

'Knows or thinks?'

It seemed to me that almost all Americans who lived in the Congo – especially those with a pilot's licence – was suspected of working for US Intelligence at one time or another. Roman was an extravagant character, for sure – a close personal friend of Congolese leader Joseph Kabila (for whom he worked as the presidential pilot). He was also implicated by the United Nations in a series of gun-running and sanctions-busting flights across sub-Saharan Africa.

'Everyone in the region knows he works for the Americans. I don't know why Simon went to see him. I didn't know he was going there.'

Nick seemed convinced of Roman's affiliation. I had no way of knowing whether he was right or wrong. I explained the curious transatlantic flight of N4610 – the Boeing 727 that Simon had purchased at the last possible moment. Did he think that the CIA was involved in the operation?

'I don't know, but ja, it wouldn't surprise me. The details of that flight and Roman being involved somehow – that proves it for me. You'll never get to the bottom of it, though. Most probably only Simon knows those things.'

If Nick didn't know, I suspected my chances of ever finding out were close to zero. Chasing down the exact itinerary of the 727 remained fruitless.

'According to Simon's statement, he went to see Tim Roman to get a back-up plane for the operation – in case there was a problem with the 727,' I reminded him.

'Ja, Simon told me he was struggling to get the aircraft for the coup, but that it was sorted in America. It must have been delayed, because it was only ready for the March operation. I was expecting it in February.'

I didn't quite understand what Nick was telling me. I'd thought the Boeing 727 had been brought in *because* the February attempt had failed. Simon, I had assumed, hadn't wanted to trust the goose-stricken Antonov again, and had made other arrangements instead.

'The DC-3s were Simon's plan. I didn't know anything about it. The Antonov was supposed to collect the weapons and take them to Kolwezi.'

'And in Kolwezi the men and weapons would have all transferred to the 727?'

'Ja, that's correct. I was expecting a 727, not DC-3s, though the Antonov could have taken them. It has a fourteen-ton load capacity. They would have flown on to Malabo, directly.'

The whole Kolwezi connection still didn't make sense to me. It was a hard subject to broach with Nick. I suspected that whatever happened there had watered the seeds of the operation's destruction. I took a deep breath, and ploughed on.

'What exactly happened in Kolwezi, Nick? I find it incredibly confusing. Can we go through this step by step?'

'Ja, sure.'

He stood up and edged around the coffee table, heading into the small, open-plan kitchen.

'Simon told me that the runway in Kolwezi was long enough for a 727,' he said, leaning against the counter, 'but I wasn't sure. I asked Gerhard Merz, who said it was too short.'

True to his Special Forces training, Nick did what any Recce commander would have done – he sent a reconnaissance team to check it out. For this crucial mission, Nick sent two of his best men: Simon Witherspoon (a former Special Forces operator who served first with 1 Recce and then Nick's 5 Recce, before working as a mercenary for Executive Outcomes and then another military contractor on behalf of the US Government in West Africa); and Kashama Mazanga (a former 5 Recce operator and ex-EO soldier who understood the local Congolese language spoken in Kolwezi). They were joined by a third man: the mysterious Abu Baker.

'They got to the airport, but did not physically measure the runway. Simon, Mazanga and Abu asked the people working at the airport if it was suitable for the Boeing.'

Nick stayed in contact with his team by satellite phone. Witherspoon and Mazanga both concluded that the runway was too short for a 727, and confirmed this to Nick.

'So they were trying to establish whether the runway was long enough for a plane that wasn't in fact going to be used?'

'Ja, that's right. There was a bit of miscommunication there.'

'But Kolwezi was chosen specifically because of Abu?'

'Ja, right again,' he smiled. It was like trying to find the corners of a vast jigsaw puzzle. 'We went there because of Abu, but the strip was chosen by Simon.'

'Okay, but even if it was too short for a 727, it would have been okay for the DC-3s and the Antonov?'

'Most probably, but I didn't know anything about the DC-3s.'

'Right.'

'And the second order of ammunition from ZDI, that was meant for Abu's men – the PDD – at Kolwezi? They were supposed to hold the airport?'

'Ja, that was what was supposed to happen,' Nick confirmed. 'The people who were supposed to take over the airport security didn't take over. It was going to be a peaceful operation – Abu had assured us that everyone was on-side. I don't know if they even showed up or not. Mazanga knew that something was not right at the airport.'

The 'hundreds' of rebel fighters that Abu had promised had been nowhere to be seen. In the end, Witherspoon met only ten lightly armed men. Mazanga negotiated with them, and threatened to cancel the operation if the airport was not secured. Abu's men retaliated by placing the unarmed Mazanga and Witherspoon under house arrest. Witherspoon, who wanted to withdraw immediately, called Nick and briefed him in Afrikaans.

'I told them to leave,' Nick concluded, 'and they took the gap.'

Leaving, it turned out, was not that straightforward. With no transport of their own, Witherspoon and Mazanga eventually managed to give their captors the slip and persuaded a taxi to drive them back to safety in Zambia – a long overnight journey that involved negotiating several roadblocks.

I wanted to know who exactly the PDD were: it had never been possible to track them down anywhere other than in Nick's filing cabinet. I told Nick that I'd seen Abu's PDD contract for mining concessions and military assistance. Somehow Obiang's prosecuting lawyer had managed to get hold of a copy, too.

'It's a made-up name. When I signed that contract with him, I said, "You've got to have a name or something for your organisation," and he chose that. It was to make it sound more official.'

The PDD did not exist.

'Who, exactly,' I asked, 'is Abu?'

According to Nick, Abu was a Congolese citizen who lived in Durban, the capital of KwaZulu-Natal province in South Africa. His sister worked in the Congo embassy in Pretoria and organised their visas. Abu, Nick said, had made himself out to be a senior figure in western and central Congolese rebel groups who sought independence for Katanga province in southern Congo; he had also claimed to know a lot about mining – to be on good terms with Joseph Kabila, the Congolese president. It was a seemingly irreconcilable conflict of interest. None of the details made sense. In all likelihood, the ten men that Witherspoon met were planning to re-sell the ammunition promised by Nick to a third party.

'Abu said that in Kolwezi there were stashes of gold that had been hoarded in different locations around the town. I agreed with him that I would fly it out, and take twenty per cent of the value as a commission. It was a bonus, really. Equatorial Guinea was the main thing. Kolwezi was secondary.'

The gold had allegedly been mined as the by-product of illegal uranium extraction – which, Abu claimed (plausibly), was being conducted there by North Koreans. It had been on this basis that Nick had gone to see the US defence attaché Colonel Clarence D. Smith in Pretoria. That could have been how Frank knew about the Congo operation. Abu was briefed about the Equatorial Guinea plot, too.

'You know, the Scorpions claimed that Abu was deeply implicated in work for the National Intelligence Agency?'

Nick could not bring himself to accept that Abu, although probably a fabulist, was also an informer.

'No, that's not true. It doesn't sound true. He met me openly, he never tried to hide. I don't believe that's true.'

Whatever the truth of Abu's motivations – which were, I suspected, entirely self-serving – the consequences of his involvement remained clear: his participation meant that the first coup attempt on 19 February 2004 would inevitably fail. The only conceivable second chance the plot could have had was if Nick's men had been billeted out of South Africa immediately. This might have stemmed the flood of intelligence leaks (which now became a roaring torrent) and damaged South Africa's ability, finally, to move against them on Saturday 6 March. But there were no second chances. In the wake of the disaster at Kolwezi, the subsequent return to the Hotel 224 and the departure by 727 to Harare meant that Nigel Morgan and the other informants could not help but be successful in foiling the operation. Nick didn't want to grasp the enormity of the cock-up in Katanga. It no longer mattered to him; he'd spent interminable months playing 'what if?', and his appetite for even more self-censure was understandably limited.

'Why,' I pressed him, 'why didn't you quit after Kolwezi?' Nick sighed, and then smiled at me.

'It's easy to blame me with hindsight. On-the-spot decisions are much more difficult. I tried to delay the whole process as long as possible. Simon wanted a follow-up after the first attempt within a week, but I specifically told him that we should wait at least three months before a retry. He wouldn't hear of it – maybe because he was under pressure from his financiers. I wanted to step out of it then, but the business prospects were getting better and he convinced me we had the support and approval of South Africa, the UK Government, the Spanish and the Americans.' He shrugged his shoulders. 'I put that together with Henri's feedback and decided to continue. James, the South African Government didn't do anything after the first attempt. They already knew everything,' he paused for a moment, and then echoed Simon's own conclusion from jail. 'I saw it as a signal that they really wanted us to go ahead.'

There was one, personal, question that I did need Nick to answer, though. In the weeks and months that passed after his arrest, I had, in one respect, felt a growing anger towards him. As the full scope of the disastrous operation became clearer, I resented at times the idea that he had ever wanted to involve me at all.

'Honestly,' I asked him, 'after the operation moved from Conakry to South Africa, was it genuinely your intention that I should film the coup, as we discussed?'

'Yes.' He paused for a moment, unfocused, looking back in time. 'Yes. Originally, it was planned for you to come in with the main force, but as things progressed I also thought it might be better to fly you in with the new guy. But the initial plan, definitely, was for you to join the attack force so you were there right from the beginning.'

It was unnerving to hear this alternative version of my fate resurrected from the depths of Black Beach.

'I discussed it with Simon in South Africa, and then arranged for you to meet him in Paris. Simon thought it was a great idea, and that we must make sure you were kept up to date with the whole plan.'

'But when I called you and asked for Simon's number – you remember I lost it? – you told me you didn't have it. Why did you do that?'

'I didn't want you to be in contact with him. James, the operation was not being planned properly. If it had been a proper operation, properly planned, then yes, sure, that would have been different. But it wasn't. It shouldn't have gone ahead. I did that to protect you.'

I wasn't sure whether to be flattered or appalled that he'd sought to protect me above the life of his brother-in-law.

'I've always thought that it was my grandfather who, well, who saved me, really. Is that true? If he hadn't died, would I have ended up in jail?'

Nick answered with a smile at first.

'I look after my friends,' he said. 'Sometimes I'm not that big a cunt.'

We sat and looked at each other, wrapped in the warm air of the tiny house. Whatever plans he'd had for me, and however they may have gone wrong, I didn't think he was a cunt at all. I'd made up my mind to take a risk. My anger, if that's what it was, stemmed more, I suspected, from embarrassment than upset: I had long since accepted that I was jealous I had not been arrested, too.

'Now then, Mr Brabazon,' he piped up, separately emphasising the three syllables of my surname, 'the ladies have left us some bacon and . . .' – he opened the fridge door and rooted around – '. . . some eggs . . . and, ah, great man, some wors.'

'Okay, brilliant. I'll make some more tea and coffee. And . . .' – I fished in my bag for the things I had brought him that day – '. . . I got you some cashews.' I held up a bag of his favourite snack. 'We can eat them while we watch this.'

I handed him a copy of our first Liberia film, *A Journey Without Maps*, which Nick had never seen.

I've lost count of the number of times I have watched Deku shoot the prisoner, or Kali Katigo from Kenema eviscerate the corpse of the man his comrades have just tortured to death. It was only the second time, seven and a half years later, that Nick had seen them in action. Thirty minutes of fighting interspersed with interviews and murder lit up the screen on the mezzanine landing upstairs. Marzaan joined us. I winced at the clumsy storytelling and rudimentary construction. Technically speaking, it is the worst film I've ever made. It is still the film of which I am most proud.

Watching it then, with Nick, had a strange effect. It was as if I'd been holding my breath for nearly six years. Liberia had moved on: the corrupt Transitional Government had been replaced by Ellen Johnson Sirleaf's premiership. She was a truly democratically elected leader – and Africa's first female president to boot. Although a deeply flawed Truth and Reconciliation Commission fudged an imperfect resolution of historical enmities, Charles Taylor, captured on the run in Nigeria, was at least facing trial for war crimes in The Hague. In post-conflict Liberia, LURD's campaign against Taylor was mainly dismissed as being either murderous or, at best, merely self-serving – a verdict that denied the key role it played in ending Taylor's dictatorship. Without men like Cobra, Deku, Dragon Master, and the rebels they commanded, there would have been no election for Sirleaf to contest.

Others had gone on trial, too. I stood as an expert witness for the prosecution for war crimes of Guus van Kouwenhoven – a Dutch citizen accused of smuggling arms to Taylor in exchange for logging rights. He was convicted in 2006 for violating the UN arms embargoes that my reporting with Nick had helped to provide the evidence for implementing – before being released on appeal in 2008.

Good as it was to watch Liberia move on, and participate in the application of international law, I'd never really let go of the story. All the while Nick was locked away, part of that experience was locked away with him, stuck in the past. Now that he was free, so – in a way I had not anticipated – was I.

'That's what your dad and I were up to all those years ago,' I said to Marzaan as the credits rolled. 'You were only nine years old then.'

'It looked awful,' she said. 'I'm not letting my dad go away again.'

'Ja, well. That was great.' Nick spread his massive hands out across his skinny knees. 'It was great to see it after all these years. Have you got any more?'

I handed Nick a stack of films I'd made since he'd been in jail. He shuffled the discs like oversized playing cards, examining their titles.

'You know, when you were arrested, that was all I could think of.' I nodded to the television, and the torture it had just revealed. 'I couldn't believe they'd bring you to trial. I thought they'd shoot you, all of you, out of hand.'

Marzaan looked down, her hand on her father's arm.

'What actually happened when you were arrested?'

'Antonio Javier came to the house where we stayed at eight o'clock in the morning the day after Simon was arrested – the eighth.'

Javier was the government minister Nick was in business with. He took all the men's passports for a 'routine check', and then sat and watched the rugby with the South Africans. An hour later, he took Nick to the police station – where he was arrested. There he met another one of his men, George Alerson. Nick urged Alerson to stick to their agreed stories, and then questioning began. Handcuffs were put on so tight that Nick said his hands swelled like balloons; he was slapped across the face and told that Simon had been arrested. Cardoso and Boonzaier were tortured together: hog-tied and suspended from a pole, they had guns to their heads and were electrocuted and beaten with rifle butts. Nick said that, after they confessed what they knew, he made his television appearance, incorporating details in his confession prompted by his captors.

'On the ninth, they took us to Black Beach. That's when they put the leg-cuffs on. They didn't have any proper shackles, so they used handcuffs. You know, they're too small to go around the ankle, so they got a hammer and hammered them shut about two-thirds of the way down the shin.'

Nick ran a thumb over the spot on his leg where the skin had split down to the bone. He was heavily scarred.

'We were kept separately. I was put on death row, in solitary confinement in a pitch-black cell. Man, it was horrible. There was no light at all – no windows, just a small hole in the ceiling for air, covered by another roof.'

Only the cell door opening and closing let in any light at all. There was nothing to see, anyway: Nick slept on the bare stone floor of a five-by-seven cell. For the first five days they were not fed. Then they were force-fed by the guards. Eventually, food was left on the floor unseen in the darkness, where it was eaten and urinated on by the rats that ran freely around his cell. Typhoid outbreaks were common. Nick defecated where he lay, his hands cuffed behind his back, his legs joined at the ankle. He was unable to stand. Water was left in a plastic bottle with the lid screwed on. He opened it by gripping it with his teeth and thrashing around until it became loose.

The pain in his hands incapacitated him. His toenail was stamped off during daily bouts of questioning; his thumbnails split and fell off; he was kicked, punched and whipped; the wounds turned septic and his eyes were sealed shut by pus. At night the rats would try and feed from his wounds, and bit lumps out of the other prisoners.

'They physically had to tear the shit out of my eyes,' he remembered.

Eventually, he was scrubbed down, naked, in public. After two and a half weeks, he was given a dirty mattress to sleep on – though the guards couldn't see the point. 'You're on death row,' they told him.

Marzaan got up quietly to make tea.

'Why didn't they shoot you?' I asked him.

'It was a political decision,' he thought. 'It was only South African interest that saved us. I was very scared about being put in front of a firing squad.'

He was matter-of-fact about it, but the image of Nick blindfolded before a ragged line of soldiers had nearly been a reality. When Gerhard Merz died, Nick was told that the guards just shrugged their shoulders and laid his body out in the communal cell where the others were held. The threat of sudden death didn't fade. Every week, for six weeks, he was subjected to mock executions.

'Sometimes the guy was so drunk he would drop his pistol. Other guards had to hold him up. It could last for forty minutes. I just had to be calm, and polite. One mistake, and . . .' He trailed off. 'Ja. They kept me in that cell for eight weeks. My hands were tied behind my back for three or four months – until the trial. When they removed the handcuffs from my legs, they had to hammer them off with a chisel. The bones of my wrist were exposed from the chafing and the lock had rusted shut with blood and pus.'

He was interrogated almost every day until the trial began – the Zimbabwean Central Intelligence Organisation were brought in to get a statement from him, too, which they then altered to fit Simon's confession. Halfway through his trial, Nick's defence lawyer was killed.

'One day he was with us in perfect health, urging us to refute the charges – the next day we were told he'd "died of malaria".'

They were on their own. Although they didn't receive the death penalty, most of the prisoners came close to death.

'We all had malaria, cerebral malaria. I had it six times. In the new jail, in March 2008, I went into a coma for five days.'

It reminded me of my other grandfather, Martin, the jungle fighter and would-be mercenary, who had the last rites read over him in Burma after a severe bout of malaria.

'They came in to bring my body out,' Nick shrugged, 'but I was still alive. I don't know how, but I came round and then they said, "Vok it, this guy needs medicine," so they allowed me to have a course of drugs given by the South African consulate. Ja, that was close.'

It was getting late. We had been talking for hours. Downstairs, I could hear Nick's daughter pottering in the kitchen. The years in jail, the torture, the near-death from malaria, these were only the physical parts of his punishment. The legacy of the coup would be felt most sharply here at home. Nick had been in jail or away plotting in Equatorial Guinea for more than a third of his daughter's life; his relationship with his wife was damaged – possibly beyond repair; and he would certainly remain notorious in South Africa until the day he died – a fact that, amongst many things, rendered him almost unemployable. Nick would serve a life sentence, come what may.

In October 2006, Nick and the other men were transferred from the Spanish colonial cells where they were originally held to a newly built wing of the prison. Although he now had a trickle of cold running water and a toilet in his cell (along with an infrared security camera that recorded his every limited move), he remained in solitary confinement for more than four years of his five-year, eight-month sentence. He read the Bible, and began to feel increasingly drawn to the promise of salvation it offered.

'After the trial, when I knew it was not death but a long sentence, I realised that I was changing, that slowly I was developing a true, deep faith in God. We would read verses of the Bible to each other through the cell doors when the guards weren't listening. That's how we supported each other, how our faith grew.'

Apart from that, and his military training, there was precious little else to hang onto.

'If you've been through selection, like I had to for the Recces, you're conditioned to survive. In my mind I was strong. I thank Special Forces for that.'

For three and a half years he was chained hand and foot. For the last twenty months of his incarceration the leg irons were removed in the cell. He remained almost permanently handcuffed until two weeks before his release. His diet did not improve.

'At first, we were fed like dogs. Then they brought us these disgusting stews. James, it made the rice and slop we were eating in Liberia look like a really fancy restaurant.'

Nick and the other three South African prisoners lived mostly on rice, dry bread and the occasional bit of fish, chicken gristle or pig's tail. Three years into his sentence, Nick stopped eating the rice.

'It wasn't like rice as we know it. It was all broken up and mixed with grit and small stones. I'd just had enough. I said, "I can't eat this shit any more",' and that was it.' He lost thirty-seven kilograms, nearly 40 per cent of his body weight.

Over time, eleven of the other men arrested with Nick had been released – owing to bad health or political expediency. Clemency for him and the remaining men had seemed remote in the extreme.

'Then the attorney-general said in March that a possible release was being discussed with the South African Government. We were really waiting for Zuma to come to power here. Obiang and Mbeki didn't get along at all. Even so, we never thought we'd get a pardon. I was hoping at most that we'd be extradited and serve out our sentences in South Africa. If it wasn't for Zuma, we would never have been released. Without him, most probably Simon wouldn't have got out, either.'

We stood up and walked down the short flight of stairs to the kitchen-diner below. Marzaan had made redbush tea and strong instant coffee – a souvenir that Nick had brought back from Malabo.

'You know,' I told him, 'Simon said that in jail he felt more like a guest than a prisoner. It seems like you had an entirely different experience from him.'

'Of course,' Nick smiled, sipping his coffee. 'He's rich. He had a treadmill in his cell, and drank wine with his meals. I don't know what it was like for him in Zimbabwe, though. Not all that great, I think. Ag, you know, it could have been worse for all of us. There are other jails in the world where we would not have survived.'

It was an amazingly generous assessment. I wondered if Nick held a grudge against anyone.

'Everyone assumes you're going to want revenge, to get something out of Simon,' I told him. 'At least, that's what they're saying in the press.'

He smiled.

'No, I'm not bitter about Simon. I wish him well. We were both professionals. It just didn't turn out right. It's one of those things. It was better that way, better it didn't.'

'Nick, this is a strange question . . .' I gathered my thoughts. 'But are you glad you served six years? That you went to jail?'

His answer was immediate.

'Yes. Obviously, it was not ideal. But if I hadn't, then I wouldn't have changed and would have carried on in the same way. And if I had done that, then most likely I would be dead by now.'

He sipped the hot coffee. Already I could not remember what Nick had looked like before he was arrested. It was as if he'd always been this way. Like a schoolboy in his first uniform, his clothes looked too new and didn't quite fit. But he had been a healthy, well-trained soldier in his forties at the time of the coup – ready to fight his way to the presidential palace if necessary.

'Thank God we didn't kill or injure anyone,' he said, considering the military operation he had planned. 'It wasn't right, what we tried to do. It wasn't right at all. It was just greed and vanity.'

'It's a very good thing that plane didn't land in Malabo,' I said.

'Yes. Most likely it would have been successful. They weren't prepared for anything like that, even if they knew.' He looked up at me. 'We had some serious firepower. Seventy guys – that's a Fire Force who's not afraid of anything. A lot of people would have been killed.'

He paused, lost in thought for a moment.

'But that's all in the past now. I just want to move on, and put it behind me. I've made peace with my brother-in-law, and with the guys I was locked up with in EG. Simon has to rebuild his life, too. We all do.'

There was, though, he thought, one positive thing that had come out of the plot to steal Obiang's millions. Before the coup, most people in the West outside of the oil industry didn't even realise that Equatorial Guinea existed: what the plotters achieved, by accident, was to expose the regime to the glare of the international media's uncompromising spotlight. Obiang's horror show was dragged reluctantly into the light of day.

'Things have started to get better,' Nick said, draining his coffee, 'but there is still a long way to go before there is democracy and free-and-fair elections. We had no right to meddle in God's plans for the country, but perhaps what we did will make it better for the people who live there after all. You have to do it politically, but if you want to make Africa a better place, you have to get rid of the dictators.'

Storm clouds were piling up in the night sky outside. Summer nights in Pretoria promised a spectacular sound-and-light show. It was time for me to head back to my hotel. We'd made all sorts of plans for the weeks ahead: there were cars to fix, a job to find, and the wedding of his stepdaughter to celebrate – the mundane and the wonderful trappings of a future rescued from a slow death in jail. We shook hands, and I said goodnight to my friend the mercenary.

'You know,' he said, 'that should be my friend the ex-mercenary.'

ACKNOWLEDGEMENTS

Writing *My Friend the Mercenary* was possible only with the help, support and encouragement of family, friends and colleagues, to whom I am deeply grateful. Errors of fact or interpretation are mine alone.

John Nimly Brownell, President of the European Federation of Liberian Associations (EFLA) guided me on how to reproduce Liberian–English dialogue. Where absolute clarity to the unaccustomed ear was essential, I have made changes to his rendition of Liberian speech.

Cobus Claassens provided many insights and clarifications about the Executive Outcomes deployment in Sierra Leone. Frank employed his keen eye for detail with humour and precision.

Without Tim Hetherington's professional expertise, his loyalty and his friendship, it would not have been possible to successfully film the attack on Monrovia, nor personally assimilate its aftermath. His help with this project, including access to personal notebooks, diaries and his photographic archive, was crucial.

Carla Garapedian gave important insights into the craft of writing this memoir, and told me to 'stop thinking about it, and start writing it'. Access to her notebooks and diaries from the time of our investigations together in 2004–2005 was essential.

I am indebted to Chris Yates, Aviation Analyst at IHS Janes and Principal of Yates Consulting, for his detailed and illuminating work on flight N4610; Kevin A. O'Brien, Fellow of the Department of War Studies, King's College London, for his interesting analysis of the role of Special Forces within the SADF; Khadija Magardie, for spending many hours of her time giving valuable criticism of this manuscript; and Julian Rademeyer of Media 24 in South Africa, for answering a barrage of questions, as well as for his professional integrity and understanding.

Sam Kiley gave characteristically forthright and illuminating comments and clarifications. I am also grateful for his role in having the documentary film *My Friend the Mercenary* commissioned in the first place.

Jonathan Kaplan gave me much needed assistance with this book, and with the original magazine article that spawned it. I am most especially thankful for his brilliantly apposite explanation of the concept of Bad Intelligence, a phenomenon not uncommon in this book.

Andrew Mueller gave helpful advice at every turn and provided endless hours of encouragement – largely focused around discussions of the central, pressing question of *what could possibly go wrong?*

Aidan Hartley, a companion on many of the trips that followed the events in this book, gave advice about how best to approach the world of publishing.

Mat Smith, formerly of *Arena* magazine, commissioned the original magazine article that led to this book. Piers Hernu commissioned me to travel to Sierra Leone at the outset. I would also like to thank Peter Oborne for his encouragement to write about my journey in Liberia in the first place, and I sincerely appreciate the efforts that Dominic Prince made to begin the process of having this project commissioned.

I am grateful to Tim Butcher – who is very familiar with the contradictions of working in Liberia.

I would also like to thank Patrick Smith, Adam Roberts, Anne-Marie Dias Borges, Nicholas Walton and Patrick Wells.

Mei-Ling McNamara was the best researcher I could have hoped for. I was frequently amazed by her patience, impressed by her diligence and deeply thankful for her hard work.

At Channel 4 and Quicksilver Media, I would like to thank Eamonn Matthews, Siobhan Sinnerton, Evan Williams, Ed Watts, Ed Braman and Kevin Sutcliffe for their help and friendship. I would like to thank Tina Carr and the Rory Peck Trust for their unfailing support.

This book relies heavily on the wealth of information generated by the original filming trips made in 2002–2005. I am grateful to everyone – producers, commissioners, cameraman and technicians – who made those programmes possible.

I am also grateful to David Henshaw at Hardcash; Will Thorne; Jacques Pauw; Jonathan Stack; RYP; Karen O'Connor; and Flora Gregory.

To the many people who contributed in-depth interviews for this book – both on and off the record – I am very grateful. I would also like to thank J, A, C, and R – all formerly of 22 SAS – and the personnel at Subsahara Solutions LLC. While writing this book I was in contact with sources close to both Simon Mann and Ely Calil. I was told that they both might be in contact; ultimately, neither man decided to be.

The helping hands extended by June and Will Simpson, Patrick Leigh Fermor, Barry Dunnage, Philippe Wibrotte, Roy Simmons, Lizzie Shirreff and Michael Birt have been invaluable.

At Curtis Brown I have been lucky enough to have two agents – Camilla Hornby and Karolina Sutton – both of whom did painstaking work on this manuscript. Their professional candour, enthusiasm and care have been invaluable.

All the staff at Canongate championed this project, and guided me through the twists and turns of writing this book. I am particularly grateful to Nick Davies, my editor, for his extraordinary diligence and increasingly flexible definition of the word 'deadline'.

My mother, Christine, encouraged and supported me unconditionally. My father, Michael, first whetted my appetite for travel on the sodden roads of Connemara. My grandmother Joy provided a helping hand and peace of mind whenever it was most needed. My grandfathers, Don and Martin, gave me everything they had, and, more than that, a chance to grasp something they never could. My children, Max and Bella, were the inspiration to tell this story and to tell it straight. My wife, Jess, is many wonderful things – not least, I discovered, a patient editor. She passed uncounted hours helping me craft this manuscript. Without her love, dedication and vision, writing this book would not have been possible.

I remain indebted to the people in Liberia who opened their lives to the scrutiny of my lens; who supported me – at times literally – when I thought that I could not carry on. Almost everyone I met while filming was either killed or forced to flee their home. Anything I managed to achieve there in the months of marching and filming pales into insignificance in comparison to the daily struggle for survival that characterised their life in the war.

When I first started to write, there was no prospect of Nick du Toit's release. He began helping me with this memoir within hours of his return to South Africa. Some people have asked – knowing what I know now – if I would still have gone in the first place. I would, as long as Nick was with me. On first reading the book, he wrote this by return:

'James, I read the draft. Not too bad. You never shared your inner feelings and doubts with me, but it's good you do bring it out in the book. It makes me look like an asshole at times, but the

Epilogue does put things a little back into perspective. Thanks also for your loyalty to me. In the end what matters is our friendship, which nobody can take away from us, and I'm sure that you trust me enough to go with me again. Not that I'm planning anything like that.'